TEST CASE

TEST CASE

Italy, Ethiopia, and the League of Nations

George W. Baer

HOOVER INSTITUTION PRESS
Stanford University   Stanford, California   1976

The Hoover Institution on War, Revolution and Peace, founded at Stanford University in 1919 by the late President Hoover, is a center for advanced study and research on public and international affairs in the twentieth century. The views expressed in its publications are entirely those of the authors and do not necessarily reflect the views of the staff, officers, or Board of Overseers of the Hoover Institution.

Hoover Institution Publication 159

To my children

Susan, Charles, Carolyn

CONTENTS

Couriers

They were offered the choice between becoming kings or the couriers of kings. The way children would, they all wanted to be couriers. Therefore there are only couriers who hurry about the world, shouting to each other—since there are no kings—messages that have become meaningless. They would like to put an end to this miserable life of theirs but they dare not because of their oaths of service.

FRANZ KAFKA

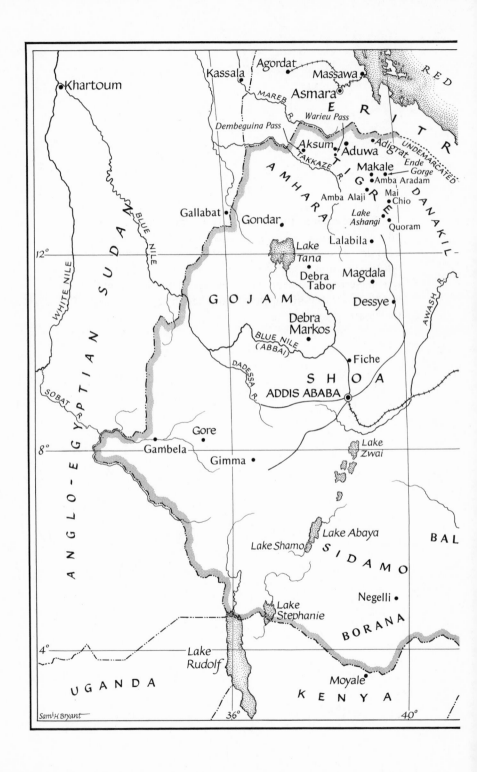

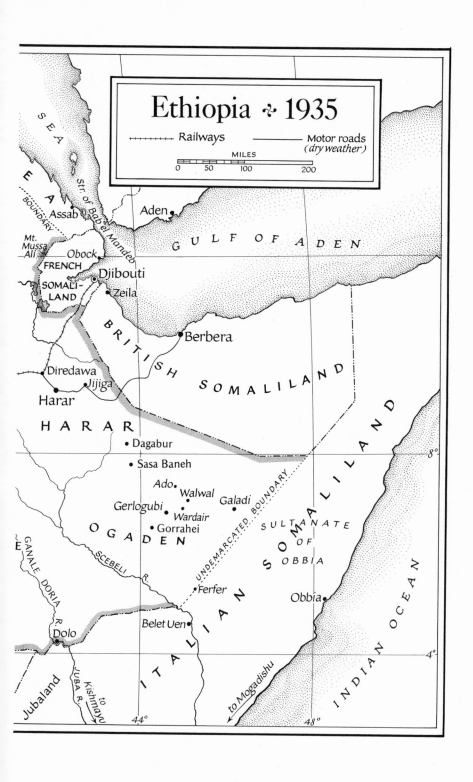

Ethiopia ❧ 1935

Railways ⊢⊢⊢⊢⊢⊢⊢ Motor roads
(dry weather)

MILES

| 0 | 50 | 100 | 200 |

RED SEA

BOUNDARY

Assab

Aden

GULF OF ADEN

Str. of Bab el Mandeb

Mt. Mussa Ali

Obock

FRENCH SOMALI-LAND

Djibouti

Zeila

Berbera

BRITISH SOMALILAND

Diredawa

Jijiga

Harar

HARAR

Dagabur

8°

Sasa Baneh

Ado

Walwal

Galadi

Gerlogubi

Wardair

Gorrahei

OGADEN

UNDEMARCATED BOUNDARY

SULTANATE OF OBBIA

ITALIAN SOMALILAND

SCEBELI R.

GANALE DORIA R.

Ferfer

Obbia

INDIAN OCEAN

Dolo

Belet Uen

4°

Jubaland

JUBA R.

to Kishmayu

to Mogadishu

44°

48°

PREFACE

This book shows how Mussolini's African imperialism became the "test case" of the collective security provisions of the League of Nations. Mussolini thought neither Britain or France would stop an Italian conquest of Ethiopia. Neither had a vital interest in maintaining Ethiopia's independence. Both wanted good relations with Italy. Mussolini tried, half-heartedly, to get them to treat the war as a colonial affair, separate from European considerations. This was impossible, because the invasion violated the terms of international order prescribed in the Covenant of the League of Nations and because it was not a simple colonial campaign but rather a war of modern means and European magnitude against a backward people for whom there was much popular sympathy. Not that Mussolini cared about the League. But there it was, established precisely to prevent the success of aggression against its members, of which Ethiopia, to the regret of many officials, was one. That fact could not easily be ignored, and Ethiopian diplomats made sure it was not. A contract was a contract.

The European policies of Britain and France, such as they were, assumed the continued existence of the League. Mussolini knew limited economic and financial sanctions were inevitable, and he prepared to absorb them. What surprised him was the vigor with which the British government responded in support of the Covenant, impelled by domestic political considerations and, Mussolini thought, a hostile dog-in-the-manger attitude toward Italy's imperial ambition. Britain's opposition encouraged other states. Sanctions against Italy became a "test case" and threatened to go beyond the limited measures applied.

Mussolini did know that the governments of Britain and France were determined to avoid war in Europe. So he threatened war if sanctions were extended to include oil. This was shrewd. Increasingly at odds with each other, both governments took Mussolini at his word and backed off. In order to save the League's prestige and keep Italy from breaking its presumed cooperation with the western democracies in maintaining the existing order in Central Europe, the governments of Britain and France sought to end the Ethiopian conflict quickly. They contrived a policy combining limited sanctions with conciliation, and the anxious membership of the

League was carried along. They stood ready to appease Mussolini if he would negotiate a settlement of the war.

The double policy did not stop the invasion. Everyone expected a long war, of two or three years. Limited sanctions were supposed to work gradually. Their cumulative pressure on the Italian economy was meant to make Mussolini amenable to settlement. In fact, the Italian army won the war in seven months. Sanctions did not save Ethiopia, which ceased to exist as a state. At the end of the war the League's system of collective security was in shambles. So were relations between the two great western powers. Almost estranged themselves, the British and French put nothing in the League's place to protect the states of Europe who feared becoming someday the "Ethiopia of someone."

Conciliation discredited the League without satisfying Mussolini. His outlook was more radical than the desperately hopeful western powers imagined. They wanted Mussolini to be moderate and cooperative. He held them in contempt, rejecting their liberalism, their contractual literalism, and the irresolute and reactive courses they followed. Mussolini manipulated their fears. Aggression paid. That was the lesson Mussolini and Hitler drew from the Ethiopian war.

Winning in Africa, winning against the League, Mussolini also won at home. Sanctions and world disapproval were used to make the war popular in Italy. Mussolini's proclamation of a new Roman empire was a great moment for Italians. It was also the high point of Mussolini's career. He turned his back scornfully on the western democracies. He sought a policy of independence for Italy, and then he tied Italy to the growing strength and determination of Hitler's Germany.

For the governments of Britain and France the double policy did serve. Appeasement kept Britain and France out of a war with Italy. The lesson these governments drew from the Ethiopian war was that, as an alternative to a policy of constraint for which they were not prepared, appeasement worked.

I received financial assistance from three sources as I worked on this book. Faculty Research Funds granted by the University of California, Santa Cruz, and a Younger Scholar Fellowship from the National Endowment for the Humanities gave me time for research and preliminary drafting. I did the writing as a Peace Fellow of the National Fellows Program at the Hoover Institution on War, Revolution, and Peace at Stanford. I am grateful for this sustaining aid.

Another support was the encouragement of friends, in particular Peter Kenez, Floyd Estess, and Gerald Piaget. Martha Nagle Baer held the home front together while I wrote—that was the biggest help of all. And it is a pleasure to write the dedication of this book.

1 TEST CASE

An Instrumentalist League

Mussolini did not intend the invasion of Ethiopia in October 1935 to be the test case for collective security in Europe. From the earliest planning, the assumption in Rome was that a necessary condition for the war that aimed at the "destruction of the Ethiopian armed forces and the total conquest of Ethiopia" was the assurance that Britain and France would not put forward serious opposition.[1] This was already clear in November 1932, in the original exposition of the enterprise contrived in the ministry of colonies. Its author, Minister Emilio De Bono, "presupposed" a "precise understanding," a "policy of precautionary agreement" with both states and an "absolutely tranquil situation" in Europe. When Mussolini took direct command of the preparations for war in December 1934, he emphasized the necessity of telling Britain and France that their interests would be recognized. That done, he expected no difficulties in Europe if the Italian army could rapidly deliver a fait accompli.[2]

No precise political understanding was reached between Italy and Britain and France, however, and by October 1935 the invasion, important to Italy as an imperial issue, was also a major problem in European affairs.

In 1934 Mussolini prepared the Ethiopian war for a time when he foresaw quiet on the European scene. Italian troops sent toward the Brenner Pass during the Austrian crisis of 1934 had caused the Nazis to back off. His low opinion of Hitler made Mussolini confident that Germany would make no trouble in Central Europe for awhile. As for the rest, Italian diplomacy could make the war seem a simple, legitimate, and worthwhile colonial action, not a new departure for Italian policy, not a challenge to existing empires, not a threat to continental settlements in Africa or Europe.

Mussolini did not think it would be difficult to bring the British and the French around. There was a long tradition of diplomatic agreement over the one remaining African state not under Western domination, a tradition entirely favorable to Italy. In the tripartite treaty of 1906, which defined respective interests, the British had not insisted on mentioning Italy's earlier treaty recognition of Ethiopia's independence. An exchange of notes in 1925 had indicated no British objection to Italian economic expansion as long as the

Blue Nile flowed freely from Lake Tana into the Sudan. In January 1935, having resolved on military conquest and political control, Mussolini reopened his dealings with the two limetrophe powers.

The French prime minister, Pierre Laval, expressed France's economic disinterest. Visiting Rome in January 1935, Laval interpreted Italian ambition in terms of an analogy to Morocco, where peaceful penetration had led to eventual hegemony while a useful façade of independence was maintained. Not that Laval cared much about a military show in Ethiopia. As far as he was concerned it was purely an African matter. Better the Italians occupied in Africa than stirring up a commotion across the Adriatic. As long as French interest in the railroad from Djibouti to Addis Ababa was secure, the future of Ethiopia need be of little consequence to anyone in Europe except the Italians. The rapprochement Laval established with Italy was much valued in Paris, ending rivalry (indeed, foreshadowing military cooperation) in Central Europe and freeing seventeen divisions from the Alps for removal to the lightly protected north above the Maginot Line. With the newly won favor of the French, the assurance, he thought, of a free hand, Mussolini believed he could surmount any diplomatic troubles attendant to the campaign. French goodwill was the sine qua non of Italian diplomatic preparation.[3]

Mussolini turned next to London with an overture on 29 January 1935 to discuss subjects of mutual interest in Ethiopia. He received no response, although the military nature of Italian imperialist planning was evident. Sending troops to the Brenner Pass had given Mussolini considerable credit in the West. Why call him down on a yet undeveloped colonial issue in which British interest was not clear? Mussolini, however, assumed that silence gave consent and thus that conquest of Ethiopia would not disturb the European calm.

There was the League of Nations, of course, but Mussolini cared little for the feeble antirevisionism of its main members. He anticipated some protest, for so dramatic a violation of the League's Covenant could hardly be ignored, but with the colonial powers reassured, protests from Geneva could be ridden out. Once before, over Corfu, Mussolini had gotten away with affronting the League. Eric Drummond, the secretary-general who had patched up the bad feelings over that affair, was now the susceptible British ambassador in Rome. Furthermore, no member wanted Italy to leave the League.

As a Fascist, Mussolini had no respect for the democratic predicates of the Covenant. As an assertive nationalist, he disliked the collectivist, pacifist mentality that predominated at Geneva. As a revisionist, he opposed the conservatism of the League, its reinforcement of the status quo. But it was precisely these features that by October 1935 appealed to those who hoped an association could do what individual states could not—provide security in Europe.

On 3 October 1935 Italian troops advanced over the Ethiopian frontier, but by then the European situation was dominated by the fact that in March Hitler had denounced the disarmament clauses of the Treaty of Versailles. This broke the tranquil period Mussolini had envisioned lasting until 1937. German rearmament set European states to reevaluating the terms of their security. Possibilities for collective action were reconsidered, leading to revived interest in the League of Nations.

In January 1935 the British foreign secretary, John Simon, had wanted no fuss over Ethiopia. No cabinet policy was determined. Simon told Minister Sidney Barton in Addis Ababa in February: "It is becoming increasingly important that the Emperor should appreciate the necessity in his own interest of doing everything to conclude an agreement with Italy at the earliest possible date. . . . His Majesty should face facts in a spirit of realism."[4] Simon, maneuvering in Berlin, wanted no trouble with Italy.

Did Britain have interests in Ethiopia incompatible with an Italian conquest? To find out, the Foreign Office established an interdepartmental committee under Sir John Maffey, former governor-general of the Sudan. Its conclusion was to form the basis of a reply to the Italians, but the committee was not established until six weeks after the démarche, did not report until June, and did not send its conclusions to the cabinet until the end of August, by which time the affair was seen in new terms. The machinery of foreign policy worked poorly in foreseeing and preparing for the coming crisis.[5]

The cabinet thought the matter was not urgent enough for a policy decision before the Stresa conference in April 1935, to which Mussolini went expecting some word of warning. Receiving none confirmed his opinion of British noninterference.

Meanwhile, stimulated by Italy's obvious aggressive intentions, a private group called the League of Nations Union circulated a "National Declaration on the League of Nations and Armaments." For this Peace Ballot, as it was called, 38 percent of the electorate was canvassed, showing strikingly large majorities in favor of strong collective measures against aggressor states. The government could not ignore this sentiment. On receiving the results of the Peace Ballot in July, Prime Minister Stanley Baldwin proclaimed that the League was the "sheet-anchor of British policy."[6] Young Anthony Eden, making his reputation championing the League, became a political asset to the government, which soon had to go to the country in a general election. A cabinet shuffle in June 1935 had sent Simon to the Home Office. Eden was not, as he had hoped, made foreign secretary. This office went to a determined, if physically run-down, Samuel Hoare. Eden got a bright new post, with cabinet status, as minister without portfolio for League of Nations affairs, the subject of Italian press attack and the symbol at home of the government's concordance with popular opinion.

The Maffey committee, which finally reported in June, concluded that there were "no such vital interests in and around Ethiopia as would make it essential for His Majesty's Government to resist an Italian conquest."[7] By the late summer of 1935, however, public opinion was aroused to the point where a pro-League policy of some strength was necessary. "It was not her colonial aspirations, but her proposal to achieve them by war, that we objected to," Neville Chamberlain wrote in his diary in July.[8] With Mussolini bent on aggression, with widespread rhetorical proclamations that this was the testing time of collective security, with Eden's apparent determination replacing Simon's indifference, what once might have been a manageable issue of imperial rivalry became a challenge to the European settlement, a major European crisis. This the British government had not anticipated nor stopped in time, and the anti-Italian stance that emerged from cabinet discussions meant "an unwitting change of emphasis" in Britain's policy.[9]

One can understand that Italians found it difficult to accept repeated British assurances, such as that delivered to Mussolini in June, that opposition to their aims was based on considerations "neither egoist nor African, but European."[10] Though the Maffey report, soon enough in their hands, found no local interests incompatible with an Italian conquest, this was recognized as less than the whole picture. On a copy purloined from the embassy's safe by the Italian secret service, someone (in Mussolini's manner, it seems to me) underlined a portion of the covering Foreign Office letter stating that the report did not deal with the wider imperial or international questions or with the effect of a war on internal political matters at home or within states abroad, meaning, presumably, in France, Germany, and Italy.[11]

The Maffey committee in fact eschewed consideration of "factors intrinsically more important than any British interest in Ethiopia—the general situation in Europe and the role which it is desired that Italy should play on the European stage, the question of how far His Majesty's Government are prepared to support the League of Nations at the risk of losing Italian friendship, and the like." The report deliberately took "no account of the wider moral issues involved," to say nothing of the political, and ventured no opinion "on the fundamental question of whether, from a wider standpoint, His Majesty's Government should acquiesce in an action by Italy which would involve a clear breach of obligations undertaken in at least three international agreements, of which both His Majesty's Government and the Italian Government are signatories—the Tripartite Agreement of 1906, the Covenant of the League of Nations and the Kellogg Pact."[12]

Even putting these considerations aside, no Italians believed that the British could be unconcerned about the possible rise of a power athwart the routes of imperial communication through the central and eastern Mediterranean, about the prospect of a rival empire that, with Libya, hemmed Egypt and the Sudan. But to Italian eyes these were "African" considerations. "European" considerations suggested isolating, not generalizing, the Ethiopian affair so that Italy could return more swiftly to a position of anti-German cooperation. Thus British opposition could be explained only by the "egoist" factor: domestic political pressure, false ideology, and selfish interests.

These suspicions seemed confirmed in September 1935 when the Admiralty sent major units of the Home Fleet to Gibraltar and moved the Mediterranean Fleet eastward from exposed Malta to Alexandria, covering the canal. To the rest of the world this looked like an expression of support for the League, for it came at the same time as a revivalist appeal, delivered to the Assembly by Hoare, that seemed to commit the British irrevocably to supporting the Covenant. To Italians it looked like a unilateral threat meant to contain their legitimate expansion, to keep Italy a lesser, dependent state.

Mussolini proceeded to talk in favor of war in the Mediterranean. He was dissuaded by his military chiefs, however, who warned that war against Britain would be national suicide; it would reduce Italy to the status of a Balkan state. The British carefully emphasized that their naval action was not in support of any international system, but was merely a prudential reaction to bellicose fulminations in the Italian press. The Admiralty, in August, had hoped the movement of the ships would be "comparatively unobstructive" and cause "no undue concern."[13] Though the crisis passed, the ships stayed, and the shadow of war in the Mediterranean henceforth hung over the Ethiopian affair.

In the early stage of planning in March 1934, the chief of the army general staff, Alberto Bonzani, had ignored Britain, surmising that France, in control of Djibouti and the railroad, would reinforce Ethiopia's emperor and become the cause of Italy's troubles.[14] Now the major source of opposition lay in London. Mussolini discounted the danger of action by the League. He did not think Ethiopia was important enough for serious opposition. What stakes did European powers have in it that could not be squared? what vital interests? He counted on the restraining power of French diplomacy, for Bonzani's early fears came to nothing. During the entire war the French refused to transport arms to Ethiopia over the railroad.

But there remained the British, pressed to opposition by anxieties about empire, by domestic opinion, by an ambiguous foreign policy. Different causes, similar effects. But would they go as far as war? Emilio Canevari would later regard Dino Grandi, ambassador in London, one of the two real heroes of the conquest of Ethiopia (along with Federico Baistrocchi, who organized supply) because Grandi convinced Mussolini that the British had not the will nor the strength to take on Italy.[15] This conclusion permitted Mussolini to raise the specter of war ever thereafter, and, bluff on his part or not, this frightened the British, who were kept moderate at critical moments by the French.

Still, Italy went to war in blatant violation of the Covenant to which it subscribed. Here was the stickler. There was no desire on the part of any government to humiliate Mussolini, to weaken his domestic position. It is doubtful whether even the Soviet government, in 1935, wished for socialism on the peninsula, fear of which governed the European right. The British told Mussolini time and again how they favored a strong, stable government for Italy, such as Fascism implicitly offered. But respect for treaty contract, the cast of opinion in the Dominions and at home, and concern to find a European policy all militated for a response through Geneva. Arrangements that aimed at territorial security in Europe, existing or potential, if they were to avoid the old alliance system, depended on a sense of cooperation typified by the Covenant. The diplomatic connection of conservative states was the League.

On 10 September 1935 Hoare told Laval that support for the Covenant was the "central body of opinion" in Britain. The League was the "main bridge" between the island and the Continent. "The question whether or not such a policy was possible did not very much matter. The public would insist on it being tried, even though it might be found to fail." At hand was a "test case."[16]

The cabinet feared that if the government let down the League the British people would turn, disillusioned, to isolationism, just when active public interest in foreign policy was needed to support rearmament. At a meeting in late September 1935 the cabinet concluded that it was "necessary" to support the League. Any other course, Hoare said, "would be impossible to explain to the country." If successful, the practice of collective action would be affirmed, to be called upon for later use. If action through the League failed, then "the sooner we know the better."[17]

On 7 October the delegates of the League Council unanimously declared Italy in violation of article 12 of the Covenant, which called for disputes to be submitted to arbitration, judicial process, or Council decision before members entered into war. The cabinet was impressed by this unanimity and on the ninth agreed to play the Geneva hand to the full.[18]

These were great days at Geneva. At a plenary meeting of the Assembly, the delegates of fifty-one states went on record in agreement with the conclusion of the Council; fifty states agreed to the establishment of a Coordination

Committee to formulate terms of action against Italy. "Fulfillment of their duties under Article 16 is required from Members of the League by the express terms of the Covenant," the president of the Council, Enrique Ruiz Guiñazú of the Argentine republic, quoted from an Assembly resolution of 1921, "and they cannot neglect them without a breach in their treaty obligations." It was a triumph for League procedure, the first (and, as it turned out, the only) application of article 16 in the history of the association. An "astonishing and admirable display of unity," wrote Eric Drummond, perhaps wistfully. "Total isolation," the chief Italian delegate confided to his diary.[19]

Members of the League were sovereign states. Nothing stated in the Covenant, nothing that might be resolved at Geneva, no treaty obligation, abridged their freedom by one whit. Collective action was neither automatic nor enforceable. The most that could be done, by an agency of the League or a conference of delegated members, was to make recommendations to the governments of the individual states. Decisions for action remained with each of them alone.

The terms of article 16 were clear. Paragraph 1 called for the complete and immediate severance of commercial and financial arrangements with citizens of Covenant-breaking states. Paragraph 2 stated the duty of the Council to recommend what armed force might be needed to support these prohibitions. Paragraph 3 referred to an intention to provide mutual support to minimize the loss and inconvenience among participating states resulting from such actions.

Paragraph 4 might have been invoked to expel Italy from the League, but with Germany's withdrawal taking place in these very days (on 21 October) no one wanted Italy cut adrift. No state broke or suspended diplomatic relations. None thought twice, hardly even once, about a condition of paragraph 1 declaring that a state that violated the Covenant was deemed at war with all other members of the League. In 1921 the Assembly had resolved that this condition would not be automatically or collectively applied, leaving it to individual states to decide whether to accept belligerent status.

Sanctions were not imposed to punish the Italian people, destroy Fascism, or topple Mussolini. Nor could a government legitimately claim support from the Covenant for such ends. The purpose of sanctions, technically, was not to fulfill a moral purpose—they were not the arm of righteousness. They were to imply no judgment beyond that of a treaty violation by a sovereign state. The popular interpretation might be that Italy was guilty of a crime and sanctions were punishment, and we will see at the end exasperated governments tending toward such inference. But in the strict construction of the diplomats, article 16 was to be applied for a limited and specific purpose: to bring to conclusion a war entered into in violation of treaty obligation. Collective action might, by example, have a cautionary effect on potential aggressors, but its main purpose (or so most diplomats then would claim) was to "support, *sancire,* the qualified prohibition of a resort to war . . . by the prevention in any particular case of the success of the action prohibited."[20]

Of course, article 16 was not applied in 1935 in a vacuum. The workings of the League, seen not as a tribunal but as an association of states, are susceptible to descriptions appropriate to international relations in general. Power and personality, hopes and fears, political and economic pressure—these and more caused governments to operate with an eye partly to the treaty text but even more to what they thought were the realities of the domestic and international scene.

This Covenant, this League, did have certain characteristics to which member states subscribed. These are suggested in the "reconciliationist" model applied to international affairs by Ernst Haas. This model assumes values that are liberal, democratic, pluralistic, secular. Reconciliation, not conflict, is the goal. Ambitions are limited, amenable to negotiation. States are rarely totalistic, comprehensive. Decisions, to quote Haas, "are always based on a kind of bargaining which implies that all antagonists remain in the game and continue to adhere to its rules *even though* no single actor ever wins a complete victory." The model supposes the prevalence of a commonly held set of dispassionate, "instrumental" values. Involved is a "constant calculation of the adjustment of the proper means to achieve limited ends, and a willingness to settle for an approximation of one's beliefs."[21] Thus, since the League had not satisfied the "totalistic" demands of Japan and Germany, both had withdrawn from the "game."

The question was whether Mussolini's imperialism was susceptible to instrumentalist bargaining, without betraying the valued norms of the Covenant. In October governments of member states interpreted their obligations within a reconciliationist framework. The application of article 16 was unavoidable, but sanctions could be limited, applied gradually, work over time. Since the goal was to get Italy to stop fighting without abandoning Geneva and, emphatically, without broadening the conflict to Europe, sanctions could be made congruent with yet another way to end the war—negotiated settlement.

Those with salvationist expectations did not much understand this instrumentalist interpretation. Insofar as politicians echoed or failed to disabuse high hopes, they opened the way to eventual disillusionment when diplomacy, pragmatic and flexible and conducted in secret, was exposed and seen to stand in apparent opposition to the "consummatory" assumptions of

League partisans, when it was revealed that, after all, the attachment of the governments of Britain and France to the League was more from calculation than from conviction and (or so it seemed) all the talk of Geneva had changed very little the workings of international relations.[22]

Even the calculation was based on a fundamental uncertainty. Would an instrumentalist approach work? Negotiation, secular and dispassionate, was the optimal solution for British and French diplomats, but not necessarily for Mussolini. No one was sure whether he might not reject the very prospect of settlement, the very idea of conciliation. Pushed by sanctions, his, and Italians', stake in the war could become more comprehensive, less amenable to reconciliation with the predicates of the League. Italy, like other dissatisfied states, might simply pick up and leave Geneva. Increased pressure might bring Mussolini to the table, or it might alienate him, even to the point of war.

In October, however, the governments in Paris and London held out the hope that a double policy of sanctions and negotiation might, in time, halt the invasion without antagonizing Italy and without breaking the fragile connections of the League. The rationale was that a curve of economic pressure would intersect an opposing curve of Italian domestic dislocation, at which time Mussolini would decide that he stood to lose less by giving up in Africa than by letting discontent mount on the peninsula. The degree of stress would have to be carefully gauged—sanctions strong enough to vindicate expectations of the Covenant yet never beyond the limit of Italian toleration.

Critics have attacked the dual policy as "not merely inconsistent but mutually destructive."[23] As things turned out, there is a good deal to this criticism. But for officials in the British and French governments it was the best (and cheapest) way to avoid humiliation on the one hand and war on the other. Furthermore, from the beginning to the end, strongly and often decisively influenced by the hints and threats from Rome, they convinced themselves that there was some chance for success or, at any rate, that there was no alternative.

There seemed, initially, enough time. Foreign policy deals in futures. The war, everyone thought, would be long and costly. Almost all military opinion, including Italian, assumed it would take at least two years, two campaign seasons, to defeat the Ethiopian forces and several more years to take control of the countryside, putting down resistance and brigandage. The first campaign season would last only half a year, from the dry season of October to April. Then would come the five or six months of the big rains when the army, traveling on dirt tracks, would become mired in the mud. During this time the Ethiopians, having avoided pitched battle, could renew their strength. Moreover, thought the British and French, this would allow time for sanctions to do their work.

Such an estimate influenced diplomacy until at least the middle of January 1936. It was reinforced in Britain by the high ratings given to the determination of Ethiopian fighting men, with proportional skepticism about the ability of Italian troops to overcome the guerrilla strategy proclaimed by the emperor at the outbreak of hostilities. It was bolstered by memories of the outpouring of patriotism at Aduwa, where Italy suffered the worst defeat of a European state in Africa's colonial history. Predictions were made about the difficulties of using modern equipment on the high plateaus, about the undoubted logistical problems with moving men, water, and supplies in a remote land without roads. There was in London a generalized prejudicial view (shared partly by Mussolini) that Italians were lazy and inefficient, unable to stay the course. This contributed to the sense that there was time for a moderate policy, a notion reinforced by the singularly unimpressive initial advance in the first three months of the war.

Decisions north of the Alps were based on limited knowledge. Mussolini kept the British and French guessing to the end. Intercepted outgoing messages told them only what they already knew—what Ambassadors Dino Grandi and Vittorio Cerruti thought. Incoming instructions were few and general, mainly stressing the danger of war. No one could read what counted—Mussolini's mind—and the resulting ignorance and unpredictability, serving the Italians well, was the source of gravest anxiety elsewhere. For the most part, the governments in London and Paris worked with dispatches from their embassies, and the authors of those dispatches, Eric Drummond and Charles de Chambrun, were never loath to heighten the color of the crisis painted to them by Italians.

The Italians had the best secret service in Europe, reading seventy or eighty codes, into every embassy in Rome except that of the Soviet Union, intercepting up to 16,000 messages a year.[24] The foreign ministry indeed provided facilities for transmitting dispatches from the Ethiopian minister to Addis Ababa. Concerning reaction to the Ethiopian war, they saw almost every diplomatic hand before it was played. This notably influenced Italian tactics, but the absence of diplomatic secrecy need not be overrated. There were, to be sure, surprises during the time of our story: the Anglo-German naval agreement, Eden's Zeila offer in June, the Rhineland coup. And there were disputes that a full record of the talks could resolve. Did Laval give Mussolini a free hand? Did he and Hoare rule out war absolutely when they met in September? But, by and large, once a decision was taken it circulated soon to other governments, officially or unofficially, and when dispatches were sent out a measure of interception was assumed. Certainly the British-French policy of moderation was laid out to all, however misinterpreted or conditional it seemed. Mussolini was the only person who found conceal-ment of great value. Diplomatic guessing was concentrated mostly on what might occur in cases where governments had not yet come to a decision.

In this period, valuable espionage and subversion was done by the political section of the Italian secret service in Ethiopia, providing the army with reliable political advice, making contacts and arrangements with restless chiefs, passing bribes. Every official radio message the Ethiopians sent dur-ing the war was immediately intercepted and decoded.[25] The Italians knew Ethiopia as the British did not. Eden acted on information, for example, that put the start of the big rains a month early, proportionately favoring his sanctionist arguments. Nor was much reliable information available about the state of Italian domestic or military preparations. The British, after all, had not thought of Italy as a potential enemy or of Ethiopia as a potential trouble spot.

The French knew little more. With the January 1935 accords, which opened the prospect of cooperation between Paris and Rome, the two Latin sisters had put a stop to gathering military intelligence about each other. The Italian secret service was anti-German. After the Stresa conference of April 1935 it opened a connection with the Deuxiéme Bureau and considered forming a joint anti-German undertaking with Yugoslav intelligence. Such good relations stopped with sanctions. By February 1936 the Italian minister of war was hypothesizing war against a French-Yugoslav combination, and in the course of that year the secret service opened contact with its German counterpart.[26]

It is hard to overemphasize the reinforcement of caution offered by the dispatches of ambassadors, full of evidence and opinion on the need to go slow. Ambassador Chambrun, for example, told Laval that Mussolini had said he wanted a moment of military glory for Fascism, a war for war's sake. Laval took up this idea, embroidered it, and used it on Hoare in September 1935 as an argument that the conflict could be contained. Mussolini would be satisfied once Aduwa was avenged, once he had, if he could get it, a vic-tory or two. Then he would be willing to negotiate. Mussolini vehemently denied this. Such an interpretation, after all, would only bolster the Leaguers and undermine Italy's legitimizing claim to be carrying out a civilizing mis-sion.[27] On the other hand, the idea did exist in Rome. On 11 September for example, while Laval met with Hoare, Dino Alfieri, undersecretary in the ministery of press and propaganda, wrote to his minister, Galeazzo Ciano: "Personally I hope that after a great action in the grand style in East Africa, in which our armies have notable successes, negotiations can begin which will give to Fascist Italy the satisfaction and objectives the Duce wants."[28] The idea persisted in Laval's mind. It was so consoling. It fit the schemes of early Italian planning. It added strength to the arguments for a gradualist approach to sanctions, for keeping the door open for compromise.

It conceded too much to Mussolini, however, to assume that he had self-limiting ambitions. Early thinking in the colonial ministry had run in terms of decisive pitched battles, of limited advances, with the nature and extent of eventual control left uncertain. This changed when, in December 1934, Mussolini stated the objective: complete conquest, as soon as possible. It is true that the fortunes of war can put all in play, and the slow progress of the invading armies in the early months hardly encouraged Mussolini. The initial expectations of prior agreement with Britain and France were not fulfilled. Europe was not calm. Stalemate in the field or serious interference from Europe would certainly alter Italian plans. But Mussolini was determined. The conquest of Ethiopia had become, by October 1935, the most important undertaking of his regime.

Mussolini's War

Plans for an invasion of Ethiopia were conceived in the ministry of colonies. Written up by Minister De Bono in November 1932, what was envisioned was the traditional mode of penetration: a limited force moving gradually southward from Eritrea, establishing bases of strength, and advancing from these against increasingly weakened and disorganized opponents. The invasion would be easy, cheap, safe—and slow. Ethiopians, despite their pose in Europe and at Geneva—so De Bono wrote to Mussolini in March 1932 —were semibarbarous, responding only to force.[29] They were warriors, not soldiers. If they were engaged and defeated in set battle, the chiefs would lose authority, the men would melt back into the countryside, and progressive political disintegration would overtake the land. Without such combat the same would occur as the men got bored, morale collapsed, and the levies headed for home. To win, one had only to stand firm.

This was the traditionalist "Eritrean" mentality of the officials of the colonial ministry, and De Bono shared it. His pet project was not much more than an expanded police action. Continued pressure from strongholds or successful crushing of counterattacks—either was enough to wear down native spirits, cause the collapse of local opposition, undermine the regional authority of the emperor. This done, the Italians could consolidate gains, bring chiefs over to their side, and advance a step further.[30]

The prospect of military action brought the army into the planning, however. In the course of the next two years the army staff, disregarding the colonialists, outlined a very different sort of war. Whereas De Bono and his ministry conceived of localized, almost static operations, the army planned in terms of a major offensive war, an African conflict on a European scale, a massive campaign involving five or six times the number of troops De Bono envisioned. Instead of provoking response from a secure position, the army, counting on the systematic offensive use of artillery and air power, foresaw a constant, crushing advance toward a decisive victory in battle.[31]

In 1934 Mussolini pulled together these as yet uncoordinated projections, decided to go ahead, and, fusing the colonialists' idea of an African campaign with the military's idea of a full-scale war, turned the whole to a nationalist purpose. His government would do what liberal governments had not: avenge Aduwa, found an empire for development and emigration, make Italy an African and Mediterranean power of consequence, and, in the process, impart the virtues of obedience, sacrifice, and therewith pride to the Italian people. By October 1935 a force of over 200,000 Italians, along with some 200 Italian journalists, was present in Eritrea and Somalia, ready for war.

De Bono, now high commissioner of the two colonies, viewed this vast expansion of the scope and nature of the enterprise with some bewilderment. Sixty-nine years old, he had foreseen the war as a "swan song," a personal success with which to cap his somewhat frustrated career.[32] Now, instead of a manageable, leisurely colonial action, De Bono was in charge of something like a national crusade. Moreover, he was in constant rivalry with Pietro Badoglio, chief of the general staff, and Alessandro Lessona, undersecretary of colonies, both harping continually that he was inadequate to the task. Politically and technically, the operation was now extended so far beyond his early dreams as to be, perhaps, beyond his capacity. His cautious and worrisome nature is evident from his diary; in the month before the invasion he recorded crises of nerves caused by his dismay at the "complete political disorientation," the seemingly careless disregard of cost and future with which Mussolini threw troops and supplies in his direction. "You ask for 3 Divisions by the end of October" said Mussolini. "I mean to send you 10, I say ten: five Divisions of the regular army; five of volunteer formations of Blackshirts, who will be carefully selected and trained. These Divisions of Blackshirts will be the guarantee that the undertaking will obtain the popular approbation."[33] Where would the money come to pay for all of this, De Bono wondered. And how could he use it? "I am alone. Rome has no idea of our difficulty." As the international scene darkened he wrote that Mussolini had led them all into a blind alley, but "Courage, Emilio."[34]

It was now Mussolini's war. In October 1935 Mussolini was prime minister and head of the government, leader of Italy's only political party, chief of the Fascist militia, and, since 1933, simultaneously minister of war, navy, air, colonies, and foreign affairs. The Council of Ministers, the Grand Council of

Fascism, the Chamber of Deputies, and the Senate gave ceremonial approval to whatever he wished. There was little room in the final decisions of government for collective judgment or general responsibility, and systematic coordination between departments disappeared. What remained was personal ambition and nest-feathering. What counted was loyalty to Mussolini.

To each armed service, in return for stability and affirmations of loyalty to the regime, Mussolini permitted jealously guarded operational autonomy. The result was twenty years of happy marriage between the services and the government. The services went their separate ways, with little coordination for national defense. Badoglio, chief of the general staff from 1925 to 1940, expressly eschewed a Jovian overview. He was safe in his position as long as he remained without determination and without power. Badoglio never made his office the focus for coordination of the needs and plans of Italy's armed forces. Mussolini, keeping himself as mediator and final authority, removing collaborators at his will, kept the initiative and thus preeminence.[35]

Because he did not assert the centrality of his office to the task of coordination, Badoglio's role was peripheral. His comments on the early Ethiopian planning were mainly words of caution. In May 1934 he asked De Bono if "the game was worth the candle." A few days later he wrote to Mussolini supporting the campaign, but arguing for postponement (beyond October 1935) to give time for additional preparation, and speaking against De Bono as commander. De Bono, he said, was not part of the regular army, was too old, and was a poor organizer.[36]

That all grace flowed from Mussolini is the concept for understanding what organization there was to the central authority structure of the Italian government. On 13 October 1935, Undersecretary for War Federico Baistrocchi wrote in alarm to Mussolini, pleading, in the name of efficiency, for one well-articulated high command for east Africa. The confusion of responsibility was unresolved even as the army took to the field. The colonial ministry claimed political authority, the army the military responsibility. Yet in a colonial war the two could not be divorced. Who was to make the final decisions?[37]

Command structure, disorganization, and the advantages for those who held a line to Mussolini are illustrated in the case of Somalia. In the first stage of planning it was not clear what role the southern front would play, beyond the protection of the distant, dry, largely unknown colony. Eritrea was the center of attention. It was Italy's first colony; officers served time there; what few colonists and modest investors the African holdings inspired settled there. Massawa was a far better port than totally undeveloped Mogadishu. Eritrea was familiar to Rome, nearer to Italy by half than Somalia; it was not the barren Somalia plain, but the high plateau where working, settling, or fighting was imaginable. Above all, from Eritrea could come the resolution of what De Bono called the "broadly psychological aspect" of the Ethiopian question: reclamation of Tigre, revenge for the old defeats at Amba Alaji, Makale, and Aduwa.[38]

In his initial formulation in a memorandum of 29 November 1932, the only objective beyond defense that De Bono ascribed to the Somalian command was the "intermediate" goal of taking Harar so as to stand next to the railroad. Any attack on the line itself would embroil Italy with France, an unacceptable proposition. Given the distance and differing strategic conception, De Bono presumed the Somalian command could function largely independently from the carefully guarded primary field of action and honor that he held in his hands in the north. As the serious planning got under way, Badoglio wanted the matter made more definite. The Somalian front should be unequivocally detailed as secondary. The great battles were to be fought in the north, he wrote Mussolini on 6 March 1935—perhaps with an eye on his own prospects—and the military situation of the south should be proclaimed "exclusively defensive."[39]

Such sentiments infuriated the southern commander, who landed at Mogadishu the day after Badoglio wrote his opinion. Rodolfo Graziani, "pacifier" of Libya, there for thirteen years (1921–34), ambitious, aggressive, Italy's most illustrious colonial general, was no man to accept the second fiddle passively. Originally considered by Mussolini as the logical choice to command the native Eritrean forces in the north, Graziani, good Fascist and dutiful colonialist, was, due to the army general staff, removed south, victim of the rivalries and jealousies of the ministries of Rome.[40] To whom could he appeal? Badoglio, coveting the succession to De Bono's command in the north and urging the argument of age against De Bono, was not the man to help Graziani improve his lot, particularly since Graziani, at fifty-three, angled for the same command by arguing the advantages of his youth against Badoglio, who was sixty-three.[41]

On 8 March 1935 Mussolini asked why Ethiopia should not be penetrated as readily from Somalia as from the north, why Graziani should not take the offensive as well. Badoglio was emphatic in reply—Somalia could not become an equivalent theater. Mogadishu was an unimproved port; ships had to unload standing out to open sea, subject to two monsoons a year. Reinforcements and supplies took another week at sea beyond Massawa. There were no supplies or naval stores on hand. Native forces were inadequate for support. Offensive action would require five times more troops than planned for the colony.[42]

There was a point to this argument. Unless Somalia was reinforced beyond all expectation, a major offensive could not be mounted. The Ethiopian attacks of December and January had shown that the north itself was barely prepared. Port facilities were poor in both major colonial harbors, but Massawa was the better equipped. In his memoirs Graziani claimed that 1,219 tons of goods a day were being unloaded in Mogadishu by October

1935, but a report from the port authority dated 22 October states different-ly. Goods were barged in satisfactorily from outlying ships—getting them ashore was the problem. Only three cranes stood on the docks, and two of them were idle at night. With a target of 2,000 tons a day for October, the first three weeks of that month averaged only 874. Three hundred to four hundred more Italian workers were needed, the report concluded, or soldiers would have to do the unloading.[43]

In his favor, Graziani had the unresolved ambiguity of Somalia's role. Badoglio's insistence that the south stay on the defensive was not conclusive-ly accepted or rejected by Mussolini. Badoglio, head of the general staff though he was, had little direct authority over the planning of the campaign and none at all over Graziani, whose appointment as governor of Somalia came from the minister of colonies. When in the spring of 1935 De Bono was named high commissioner in east Africa he accepted the situation of virtual-ly autonomous commands, recognized Graziani's experience and compe-tence, and left him "full liberty of action."[44] De Bono and Graziani had this in common: above duty to king, army, or state institution, they were loyal to Fascism and to Mussolini.[45] More than once De Bono helped Graziani, sending him troops from Eritrea or urging Rome to send more supplies to Somalia.

Graziani's greatest strength was the rapport he established with Mussoli-ni, through and around the normal chains of ministerial command. On 25 March Mussolini told him that he must, above all, prepare and maintain the defensive. Italy must show no weakness, suffer no defeats. "Only" after the defensive position was secure was he to prepare an offensive action, toward Harar. This was encouraging to Graziani. The condition of security once met, offensive planning could begin. Harar was an important objective. It was not Addis Ababa, to be sure, but it was the capital of the emperor's favorite province and controlled the access routes from the coasts of British and French Somaliland. The route from Berbera via Jijiga went through Harar, and nearby Diredawa sat astride the vital Djibouti railroad. With this message from Mussolini, Graziani claimed henceforth that Harar "consti-tuted the principal and essential objective" of his command and that offen-sive preparations were "according to the orders of the Duce."[46]

Within weeks (in April 1935) Badoglio launched his complaint that Graziani was asking for supplies far in excess of defensive needs. Would Mussolini make absolutely clear the respective roles of the two commands? Mussolini refused to be drawn, replying that a "systematic defense" was needed, one capable of being turned into a counterattack when the occasion arose.[47]

Mussolini never resolved this uncertainty about priorities on the fronts, and it bedeviled the war ministry and held hope for Graziani. By the summer of 1935 Graziani was bypassing titularly responsible channels and appealing directly to Mussolini for supplies. This is an example of the personal alliances that Mussolini encouraged and that were breaking down the traditional command structure of the Italian army. Beginning with the Ethiopian war, wrote Giorgio Rochat, a progressive collapse of conventional authority and institutional allegiance led to "profound moral and political confusion" in the army's high command and eventually to its passive subservience to Mussolini.[48]

Rivalry was the order of the day. Undersecretary of Colonies Lessona, eager to assert his own authority, wanted all communications from east Africa, even those addressed to the war ministry, to go through the colonial office first. Baistrocchi, undersecretary for war, implored Mussolini to let his ministry take sole military responsibility. On the issue of command Baistrocchi was blunt. Interference with military questions he would not tolerate. In December 1935 he wrote to Graziani: as governor of the colony "you depend on Lessona, but for operations, supplies and personnel, on the ministry of war." Mussolini's papers are full of gamy records of dependence and resentment among his followers. When it was reported in August 1935 that Lessona and Baistrocchi were making up their differences, Mussolini wrote: Buffoons! But such shiftings were a reflection of the way he ran his government.[49]

For conduct of the war in east Africa, the question of supply was central. Seek as he might to make the most of ambiguous orders, Graziani depended entirely on Rome for supplies, without which nothing could come of the most vaulting ambition. Graziani's great need was motorized transport. In June, specifically envisioning an offensive against Harar, he asked Mussolini directly for trucks and tractors. Mussolini ordered a shipment, but it contained fewer than Graziani wanted. In November he declared to Lessona and Badoglio that he needed to double the amount then on hand (some 3,000 vehicles) to drive toward Harar.[50] Supplies were easier requested than received, and Mussolini's intervention could not be counted on to support every step.

The war ministry greeted as bluff an appeal in June for more troops, ostensibly for defensive use. Graziani had enough for defense. In light of his ambiguous mission, so Baistrocchi and his assistant Alberto Pariani concluded, the ministry could ignore his hopes for offensive action. Free to think big, the southern commander was at the mercy of the army's supply officers. "Not Alexander the Great, nor Hannibal, nor Napoleon, nor Caesar," he lamented in June, could guarantee success so "paralyzed by lack of means of locomotion."[51]

When Graziani complained of short supply on the eve of the war, Baistrocchi, on 3 October, admonished him to take account of "the many military and matériel demands that must be satisfied" and, on the twelfth, urged him to be calm and have faith in the war ministry. "A monument of filibuster and impotence," Graziani wrote in the margin, and again trucks and tractors were ordered, from America, only after the personal intervention of Mussolini.[52]

The allocation of resources was clearly one of "special delicateness," as Baistrocchi phrased it. Somalia never got more than a quarter of what was sent abroad. During the Ethiopian war Eritrea received about 64 percent of the motor vehicles, compared with 23 percent sent to Somalia and 13 percent to Libya. Of the overall supply of men and equipment sent from Italy by the War Ministry between January 1935 and the end of the war in May 1936, the shares were: to Eritrea 68 percent, to Somalia 18 percent, to Libya 13 percent, to Aegean bases 1 percent.[53]

The Italian invasion began at dawn on 3 October 1935. Mussolini, who once planned to be on hand, was absent.[54] The northern campaign, developed by General Giuseppe Malladra, of long colonial experience, called for a limited advance to a line running from Adigrat to Enticcio to Aduwa.[55] It was a first step, in agreement with the "Eritrean" conception of De Bono and conducted according to the cautions of the colonial ministry, although the commander now had at his disposal 127,500 metropolitan and 83,000 Eritrean troops, had an order for the swift and complete conquest of Ethiopia, and had the eyes of the world (and perhaps the fate of his government) upon him.

This first step included the demanded symbolic victory—revenge for what ardent nationalists regarded as Italy's shame, what De Bono delicately called "the unfortunate events of 1896."[56] Aduwa was quickly enough avenged. It was occupied without resistance, and the theatrical and unnecessary bombing of the city and its civilian population by Mussolini's son-in-law introduced a new era of air warfare—to the horror of most of transalpine Europe. A directive of 4 October from the ministry of press and propaganda forbade publication of dispatches about the bombing runs of Ciano and the two Mussolini boys Vittorio and Bruno, even though Ciano was the agency's minister.[57]

Vittorio Ruggero, enterprising head of political intelligence in Ethiopia, was reportedly furious when he saw his arrangements for peaceful entry destroyed by Ciano's arbitrary action.[58] Expressions of anger and dismay grew abroad. Ciano "costs Italy dear," noted Pompeo Aloisi, the secretary-general of the Italian foreign office and chief delegate at Geneva.[59] But the occupation of Aduwa was a great day for Italians, and Aloisi, the delegation, and Italian journalists at Geneva celebrated the event with champagne.

Within two weeks the northern front was established as planned, concluding the first phase of the advance. There was no resistance, for the Ethiopian troops withdrew unengaged at the emperor's command. De Bono set about preparing logistical support from the rear and consolidating a defensive position in case of an Ethiopian counterattack. Mussolini sent a telegram to Gabriele D'Annunzio, who had publicized the notion of the shame of Aduwa: "Fascist Italy has freed itself of its sackcloth." Meanwhile, the League gathered at Geneva. Mussolini was preoccupied with what this might bode. The orders he sent to De Bono stated, "Halt on the line conquered and await events on the international plane."[60]

2 THE INTERNATIONAL PLANE

Sanctions

League members were under obligation by treaty to apply article 16, but qualifications and reservations over the years and the absence of penalty for nonfulfillment meant they could act as they wished subject only to conventional diplomatic pressure. None of course cared to apply the article literally; none wanted to act without the others. Some instrumentality of agreement was needed, and on 10 October 1935 a Coordination Committee was established to facilitate measures taken by those states who intended to apply sanctions. This standing conference of League members was a voluntary grouping of forty-nine states, not an organ of either the Assembly or the Council. It was guided in its work by a subcommittee of delegates from leading states, the Committee of Eighteen, in which the dominant influence was wielded by the representatives of Britain and France.

The latter governments, however, feared that strong leadership would appear in Rome as specifically anti-Italian and that the collective action their leadership would ensure might provoke Mussolini to war in the Mediterranean. That Italy would be defeated in such a war was never in doubt, but no government wanted Italian bombers over its homeland or ships, and the French government doubted that its country would support a war against Italy in such a case. The service chiefs in London warned that Britain's capacity for imperial defense would be crippled while Japan was showing aggressive intentions in the Far East, construction on the Singapore defenses was unfinished, and, due to economic and political restrictions, the prospect for replacement of any ships lost in a war with Italy was uncertain.

The inescapable involvement at Geneva was therefore to be subsumed entirely under the aegis and instrumentalities of League action as a whole. The League was to test itself, as it were, spontaneously. Foreign Secretary Hoare called it a question of "virility," of the vigor and resolution of the lesser members.[1] Other states were expected to take the initiative, decisions were to be collective, and Britain and France would respond cooperatively to what all members were asked to do—no more. No leadership, no separate responsibility.

This passivity, this resistance to constructive collaboration in strengthening a system of collective security, reflected the serious deterioration of

British-French relations, beset now by mutual suspicion, resentment, and distrust. Immediately at issue was what would happen if sanctions provoked a Mediterranean war. This was mainly a British worry. The French were determined it would never occur. But what if it did? Would Britain have the support of France? The question was raised in London by the service chiefs on the eve of the invasion.[2] Would France play the principal naval role in the western Mediterranean (excepting Gibraltar), freeing units of the Home Fleet stationed at the Rock for support of the Mediterranean Fleet at Alexandria? Would the French offer port accommodation in the western basin to British ships? Would French airfields be available for attacks against targets in northern Italy?

The French were hesitant to give any assurances. October ushered in a period of intense strain between the two governments, resulting in a British decision to act with great caution toward Italy. Unless and until the French gave explicit and unreserved assurance of support, the cabinet concluded at the time of the first meeting of the Coordination Committee, it was "not desirable to press sanctions too actively at Geneva."[3]

To Eden, already in Geneva, this call for caution came too late. When his meetings began on 11 October he acted on a personal letter sent to him by Hoare on the ninth, reflecting the earlier, more affirmative tone of the cabinet conclusion of 2 October "that in the matter of economic and financial sanctions the Government's policy should be to advocate at Geneva the imposition of the maximum of economic sanctions on which agreement could be secured." Strong measures at the outset, it was argued, would have a chastening effect on Italy, benefit the League, and, finally, save face.[4] The cabinet, Hoare wrote, was impressed by the recent unanimity of the League Council. The type of sanction approved—refusal to accept Italian exports—was strong, but also within the bounds of caution, "the only effective way to apply pressure without raising questions of belligerent rights." And, Hoare concluded, the cabinet was "definitely not in a critical mood." "By collective action," he added, "we do not, of course, mean that every country must necessarily take exactly the same action."[5]

Eden's position gave considerable latitude for his own judgment. Not that he was much of an innovator or a strong personality. But as minister for League of Nations affairs he held cabinet status, had his own assistants, and was at a real, though never well-defined, remove from the commands of the Foreign Office. His Majesty's principal secretary of state for foreign affairs sent him a private letter, not a directive.

Eden was more responsive to optimism than most of his colleagues in London. In Geneva he recognized that the League was at a turning point, that any delay in implementing article 16 would cause fatal demoralization. He saw also—despite the French-induced second thoughts of the cabinet, the insistence on *collective* action, and the hints about conciliatory settlement —that ever since Hoare's revivalist appeal to the Assembly three weeks before (a bluff that worked all too well), the overwhelming popular and official expectation reflected at Geneva was that British resolve was firm and that British support, meaning leadership, could be counted on. In this dispute, whether London liked it or not, Britain's predominance in the Mediterranean, in northeastern Africa, along the Red Sea, and, above all, over the Suez Canal, made it the determining power. As Britain went, others, including France, would follow.

The Nordic states, for example, were in deep distress over the Anglo-German naval treaty of June 1935 and were apprehensive about future British assistance in the Baltic. They were growing increasingly skeptical about generalized collective arrangements that, in the face of Germany's rearming, might involve them in wars that endangered rather than enhanced their security. These states were beginning to think of the value of falling back on their own resources. For them, as for others, the Italian invasion was a true test case. While reserving their position on military measures, the Nordic states made British participation their first and foremost condition for taking part in economic sanctions.[6]

Too much reserve, Eden saw, would undermine this hopeful confidence, vitiating the very will to participate that his government sought to elicit. Eden never proposed measures stronger than the cabinet allowed, but he acted according to the encouragement in Hoare's letter rather than the subsequent cautions of the cabinet. In the meetings of the Coordination Committee, of the Committee of Eighteen, and of the technical subcommittees between 11 and 19 October, Eden consistently argued for swift action and sought decisions where others, above all the French delegate Robert Coulondre, sought delay. With such encouragement the Coordination Committee moved "farther and faster than its warmest supporters dared to hope."[7] It appeared that the British would do their share. Morale at Geneva, the sense of cooperation and common concern, rose as high as it ever reached in the history of the League.

When press reports represented the British delegation not only as "the protagonist but as the sole active influence and initiator at Geneva," Hoare checked with Eden. Such a representation, he said, seemed at the Foreign Office "not only unfair, or even dangerous, to this country, but also unhealthy and dangerous for the League."[8] To Hoare's anxiety, if not implicit criticism, Eden replied:

> As to the attitude of nations here it would not be fair to say we are bearing the whole burden.... [There is] universal recognition that we [are] working under article 16 and a general disposition to take decisions to fulfill obligations as rapidly as possible. The attitudes of Holland, Belgium, the Little Entente, the

Balkan Entente, the Soviet Union, Scandinavian states, and the Dominions were unequivocal in this sense. This indeed had a marked effect on French representatives.[9]

Eden was correct. A Swedish diplomat recalled the time in his memoirs: "Enthusiasm for the League of Nations had increased tenfold. . . . If Britain now gave a real lead and Italy was forced to retreat, one could foresee a complete change in the European atmosphere. . . . All countries, but particularly the small ones, felt they had a tremendous stake in this."[10]

By 19 October 1935 the Coordination Committee had adopted five proposals, four for sanctions and one concerning mutual support, and had transmitted them to member governments "with a view to facilitating the execution of their obligations under article 12," as the preface to each read. Proposal 1 (of 11 October) recommended an embargo on arms to Italy and the annulment of a patently prejudicial embargo on arms to Ethiopia imposed in previous months by several states as a futile conciliatory gesture to Italy. All member states promptly complied with the new embargo. But Ethiopia gained little. The French kept their arms market closed and refused weapons shipments on the Djibouti railroad. The British left Berbera open to arms traffic, and during the war 14.5 million rounds for small arms, 14,000 rifles, and 8 antiaircraft guns with 20,000 rounds of amunition came through this port in British Somaliland.[11] But the British government blocked arms sales at home, and Haile Selassie was able (mostly before the war began) to order more weapons from and through German sources than from those two states whose governments were his apparent defenders.

Proposal 2, recommended by the Coordination Committee on 14 October, was a financial measure prohibiting all loans to Italy and was readily accepted. Italy was without great financial resources and growing deeper in debt in commitment to a war. Important American capital sources, the Export-Import Bank, for example, froze credit after the invasion. It seemed safe—and reasonable—to refuse funds that might help prolong the war. By the end of October most states were agreed on imposing this sanction.

Economic embargoes, however, raised more complex issues, larger losses for states with Italian trade, and the fear of economic or political retaliation.

Proposal 3, adopted on the nineteenth on Eden's initiative, called for an embargo on imports. Each member government could follow this course without reference to what non-League states might do. In Britain's estimation, this measure, applied by members alone, would at least halve Italy's export trade, drastically limiting the indebted country's capacity to purchase abroad.

Proposal 4, also adopted on the nineteenth, recommended that member states of the Coordination Committee impose export embargoes on certain

materials essential to Italy's war effort. This was a measure with grave
political and economic significance. It seemed simple. To stop a war, cut off
war supplies. It was a direct, nonbelligerent method, in line with the instrumentalist expectations. But could it be kept nonprovocative? And would
it be effective? The Italians had been stockpiling, or so it was said, and Rome
claimed there would be no immediate shortages. Even with this embargo essential supplies might be obtained from nonmember states. Was there a purpose, beyond honor, to imposing a measure that might be futile and certainly
would be costly in terms of lost sales and alienated markets?

The British cabinet on 9 October had before it an expert conclusion that
such an embargo "would produce serious irritation, while its deterrent effect
would be doubtful, and in any case long deferred." Only a blockade with the
exercise of belligerent rights would make an export embargo effective. Yet,
at stake seemed the future of collective security in Europe. The cabinet,
therefore, provisionally concluded that it would join in an embargo of coal
and oil if other member producer-states, such as Romania, participated. It
would agree to an "essential materials" embargo only "at the request of
other member States," and the imposition of sanctions on coal and oil would
"be subject in appropriate cases to the attitude of non-member States."[12]

This, roughly, is what the Coordination Committee recommended on 19
October. Against a French stand of reluctant support with expressed hopes
for delay, moderation, and eventual pacific settlement, Eden stressed the
urgency of action. His leadership was procedural, within the substantive
terms set down in London. He did, at one point, raise the idea of a sanction
on transport. League members controlled 60 percent of the world's ports,
and a prohibition on the sale or charter of ships could cripple Italian trade.
But Eden's suggestion was not pursued. In London the Admiralty and the
Board of Trade were against it, and the cabinet feared a shipping sanction as
too provocative. Still, Eden's having before him a study from which to cite
figures, which showed that some official had examined the issue in advance,
was taken in Italy as further proof of long-prepared British hostility.

In the end it was decided that exports would be embargoed by degrees,
with direct action taken at once on items for which League members were
Italy's main suppliers. Thus, proposal 4 called for an embargo on horses,
rubber, tin, and some ores, while a decision on coal, oil, iron, and steel was
postponed until the intentions of nonparticipating states, especially America,
were clarified.

These four proposals constituted the first round of sanctions against Italy.
There was no military or political action. No one suggested, for example,
withdrawing diplomatic representation from Rome. No date was set for the
implementation of proposals 3 and 4. They were sent to member governments for consideration, and the governments were to report back to the

Coordination Committee, which would meet at the end of October to establish the date for the two economic sanctions to be put into effect simultaneously by each state.

On 15 October the Italian government asked its representatives in all sanctionist countries except Britain to declare that participation in sanctions
would raise serious problems in future relations with Italy. On the twenty-
third these diplomats were told to try to get the governments to delay their
responses to the Coordination Committee for as long as possible.[13] This
maneuver had little effect, however. On 18 November 1935, some six weeks
after the invasion began, the economic sanctions of proposals 3 and 4 went
into force against Italy.

The decision to go ahead, however, raised the question of mutual support.
Sanctions could be costly. Two states, Austria and Hungary, refused to
associate with the Assembly conclusion that Italy was in violation of the
Covenant. They, and Albania, declined to participate in sanctions. Austria
needed Italian goodwill as a counterweight to German advances.[14] Hungary
wanted to keep its commercial and political ties with Italy, hoping for support in its territorial claims. Albania, wholly dependent on Italy for trade
and the conduct of external affairs, feared isolation. Albanian ports were at
the mercy of Italian guns; an Italian fleet had steamed unannounced into
Durres the month before. This reasoning, at least that of Austria and
Albania, was understood and generally accepted at Geneva.[15]

The Swiss failed to act on proposal 3 arguing that the cost to their economy of refusing to accept Italian imports would be 10,000 unemployed and
that the cost to their polity would be resentment and discontent in Italian-
speaking cantons. The reservations put forward by the federal councillor and
foreign affairs spokesman, Giuseppe Motta, (himself Italian-Swiss) were less
convincing for their stress on traditional neutrality than for the argument
from geopolitical and economic intimacy.[16]

In some remote cases deviation from a collective stand was dealt with
firmly. When the delegate from Venezuela balked at sanctions, Robert Vansittart, permanent undersecretary of the Foreign Office, noted: "We shall
have to pillory Venezuela if she joins Austria and Hungary. We really do not
want or need her in the League in such conditions." And when Eden showed
concern that Argentina, under Italian pressure and harboring a million
Italians, might contract out of economic sanctions, the sobering point was
made in Buenos Aires that the future of the League was as much in the hands
of the Argentine government as of the British.[17]

Mutual support was enjoined by the Covenant for those cooperating states
to whom sanctions brought economic loss and inconvenience. Yugoslavia
and Romania, partners in the Little Entente, were (or at least their foreign
ministers were) convinced supporters of the Covenant, and stood firm

behind sanctions. Yet 20 percent of Yugoslavia's foreign trade was with Italy, and Romanians worried that Austria and Hungary would try to maintain the advantages of League participation without paying the cost. In addition to direct trade losses, Romania eventually would find itself at a competitive disadvantage toward Italy. What Romanians disliked, Foreign Minister Nicolas Titulescu said, "was not loss but injustice." Romania would support sanctions, but Titulescu wanted the Coordination Committee to assert that sanctionist states had an obligation to buy, from the countries suffering excessive losses, sufficient quantities of goods to balance out trade at some average level. In Romania's case this would mean being able to sell elsewhere the oil, timber, livestock, and cereals then consigned to the Italian market.

The committee went part way. Proposal 5 presented a formula of mutual economic assistance by which sanctionist states, in fulfilling their obligations under paragraph 3 of article 16, would favor purchases from and financial dealings with other sanctionist states incurring losses and would correspondingly reduce their purchases from member states not participating in sanctions. Here was a type of pressure against the Central European holdouts, and it honored the pride, if not yet the pockets, of those who stood by the Covenant.[18]

A French Assurance

With the five proposals to implement the terms of article 16, it seemed to partisans of the League that by 19 October "the conception of world-wide resistance to an unlawful act of aggression had been proved to be no mere theory."[19] Insofar as the British hoped for an affirmation of collective action, they now saw it realized. Eden's procedural leadership and the display of force in the Mediterranean were seen in Europe as earnests for the future, for it was understood that the first four proposals were only the beginning of the increasing pressures to be applied to Italy.

Far from gratified, the British government at mid-October was filled with anxiety. Support for Geneva was an experiment, a holding action to keep public opinion firm until a more realistic European policy was contrived and Britain armed to sustain it. Fundamentally uncommitted to the League, the cabinet did not see what transpired as creating an advantage to press home. Far from fulfilling its hopes, the great days at Geneva only made the government more worried about what troubles it might expect from Italy—and France. From France the British awaited word of military support if sanctions provoked Italy to an act of war. No one wanted war, of course, and fulminations claiming this as policy were wrong.

On 2 October the cabinet decided that military sanctions were "out of the question" because of the noncooperative attitude of the French government.[20] On the basis of a talk with Hoare on 10 September, Prime Minister

Laval had been assuring the Italians for the previous three weeks that military measures would not be taken.[21] It is impossible to imagine military sanctions being proposed when French support was lacking and it seemed that financial and economic sanctions by themselves might do the job of rallying the League and ending the invasion. Economic measures were recommended precisely because they did not involve any question of belligerent rights since, strictly speaking, they were noninterfering action involving only individual states.

Still, there was always the unpredictable. Moderate measures could grow to sterner means. How would Mussolini respond then? Gloomy reports from Rome offered no reassurance. Ambassadors Chambrun and Drummond were antisanctionists; both spoke with similar pessimism. If the internal situation got out of hand due to sanctions, and Mussolini fell or went leftwards the ensuing chaos, in Chambrun's words, would be "an incalculable evil for Europe as a whole."[22] Drummond's speculative and apocalyptic reports, in a like vein, imparted an ambiguous but profound sense of imminent serious danger.

In October, as the Committee of Eighteen prepared the sanction proposals and the invasion ground to a stop on the two Ethiopian fronts, Mussolini expressed his somber views to foreign visitors. He had expected moral and financial sanctions, he said, but an economic boycott was another matter. The latter, eventually and logically, would come to constitute a state of siege. Sanctions were meant to be progressive. They would give way to blockade and possibly to the closure of the Suez Canal. These would be military sanctions and would mean war.

Since sanctions, in London's perspective, were absolutely not intended to lead to such a crisis point, Mussolini's logic could be rejected. So his talk of war was either bluff or paranoia, which, if it advanced too far, might lead him to a "mad dog act" (as the possibility of a strike against the British came to be called in the Foreign Office). This was the concern at the time of the invasion. But there was, Drummond asserted in a dispatch of 10 October,

> no element of bluff. Suicidal his policy may very well be; immoral and hateful it most certainly is; but the unpleasant fact remains that, if it is to receive a real check in the near future, only military measures will prove effective —and military measures mean a European war. . . . in the event of a speedy collapse being certain, Signor Mussolini, foreseeing the inevitable end, might well prefer to force matters and perish gloriously by attacking the country whom he now regards as his principal adversary—Great Britain—and inflicting on her as much damage as he possibly can.[23]

To offset this danger the British wanted a clear statement from the French of full military and naval assistance: docking facilities, use of airfields, and management of the western Mediterranean. This would not be cooperation for some military sanction but collaboration that would become operative only in the event of an Italian attack consequent upon British participation in collective action as prescribed by the mutual support provisions of article 16. Not only would the promise of collaboration have to be made, went the British request, but it would have to be displayed at Geneva—a warning in advance. What was considered calculated obstructionism on the part of France would have to stop. Britain was now in danger because of its support of the Covenant—the French had to fall in, not to go further with sanctions but to help protect the most exposed members of the collective enterprise. Until French assurances arrived, the cabinet decided on 16 October, extreme caution was necessary. Britain should hold back at Geneva.

It was in this context that criticism of Eden's apparent forwardness had arisen within the Foreign Office. When Maurice Peterson, head of the Abyssinian desk, suggested that Eden be congratulated for his sponsorship of a declaration on mutual economic support in the Committee of Eighteen, Vansittart retorted on 15 October:

> Such a turn of events is not what I, nor as I believe, the Cabinet expected or desired or had stipulated. For my part I expected that we would not proceed at *all* with sanctions, until we got a declaration of solidarity in all respects, not just economic. If such a declaration were so difficult of obtainment we should have been warned at the time of the original Cabinet instructions and before we reached our present exposed position.[24]

In a private letter of 16 October, noting the "great perturbation" of the cabinet, Hoare wrote to Eden, "The important point is that we should not remain in the dangerous position of making initiatives whilst we are still running the risk of being stabbed in the back."[25] The next day Vansittart drafted a telegram to Eden reading, "In view of the still unsatisfactory and evasive reply of France . . . you should now cease active pressure for sanctions at Geneva." Hoare struck out this last clause, substituting, "It is most important that you should go as slow as possible at Geneva and avoid for the time being both active pressure for specific sanctions and taking the initiative in discussions." The message went on: "How do you think this could be best achieved, while yet keeping the various ministers in line? Would the most useful expedient be recourse to a technical committee? While we should take no further initiative until we are sure of French loyalty, we naturally do not wish to allow other loyalties to lapse or cool off."[26]

"As it happened," wrote Eden, "the warning to me to go slow was a little late." That very day he had introduced a draft resolution of what was to become proposal 3, the first of the economic sanctions.[27]

It was just at this time, on 18 October, that the mutual suspicion embittering British-French relations abated. In a note of that date the French government gave what was asked: categorical assurance of support in the case of an Italian attack resulting from Britain's "collaboration in international action taken by the League of Nations and pursued in concert with France."[28]

"Concert" implied a potential French veto, and the note gave clear indication that no pressure would progress beyond measures economic and financial. This did not disturb the British. The determination to go no further than the French, Vansittart wrote, was "a limitation which made valour safe."[29] Yet during these critical days of the first session of the Coordination Committee, the combination of British caution and French delay might have paralyzed impending decisions on sanctions, with consequent disastrous demoralization within the League. The leadership of Eden, who was running, as we saw, ahead of his government on matters of procedure, prevented this. In pressing the opportunity to consolidate a common front, Eden forced the hand of both his own and the French government. This probably did as much to bring Laval around as did the shock tactics of the Foreign Office, for ultimately France wanted to keep in step with the British, if for no other reason than to rein them in.

French suspicions of the British remained strong. Their hope was to win increased British involvement on the Continent. Surely London must see that secure European frontiers were of greater importance than a colonial squabble in Africa. But one could not be sure. Was British interest in this affair in fact based on Nilotic and imperial concerns? Was the League a stalking-horse for the British empire? Alternatively, how permanent was this new British enthusiasm for collective security? Was it contrived only in response to public opinion at home? The truth in this last seemed confirmed when Baldwin, as the Coordination Committee finished its work on 19 October, announced that a general election would be held within a month. Was this another khaki election, to be won from Geneva? What thereafter? Given the consummatory assumptions of pro-League enthusiasts, the limited purpose of sanctions and the reconciliationist nature of British policy would hardly be stressed in the campaign. What indeed was the government's long-term plan? What objectives had it beyond the almost experimental curiosity about whether other League members, without particular encouragement or clear reward, would respond by sacrifice in a matter of no vital, immediate national interest?

For the certainty of future British support, French participation in sanctions against Italy was worth the risk. But how certain was this support? Already in 1935 the British went behind France's back in matters of great importance. The June Anglo-German naval treaty, Eden's June visit to Rome,

the August dispatch of battleships to the western Mediterranean—all were
done without consultation. As a quid pro quo for support against an Italian
attack, the French tried in September to get some statement of intent from
London should the German government find in Italian involvement overseas
an occasion to move against Austria. This request was turned aside without
answer.

With Britain unreliable, Laval was already exploring new directions in
European policy, and in these the Italian entente of January played a central
role. Laval, too, worked within important limitations. French society was
dominated by pacifism. The Left opposed rearmament; the Right felt sympathy for Italy in the Ethiopian case. Everyone in France was antiwar. The
armed forces had adopted an exclusively defensive posture, with the clear implication that guarantees of support to the old European allies were at an
end. That was the main reason for the Italian connection—to win Italy's help
in stabilizing Central Europe. Laval, no doubt unrealistically, contemplated
a series of nonaggression pacts that, far from isolating Russia and Germany,
would include them. France would play arbitrator rather than guarantor, a
stance congenial to Laval's skill at negotiation and appropriate to France's
military weakness. Was he to throw all this up by alienating Italy to save—
Ethiopia? Not with the British connection so uncertain.

Laval could not ignore the League, support for which (but to the point of
war?) was demanded from the Left. But hostility toward Britain and maintenance of the Italian connection was called for from the Right. Laval was tied
to the Center. In his coalition cabinet sat the president of the Radical party,
Édouard Herriot, on whom his parliamentary majority depended, and he
had to take into account Herriot's fervent pro-League and pro-British sentiments. Further, Laval was preoccupied with the danger of civil conflict
fomented by the rightwing paramilitary *ligues,* by demands for their control,
and by an economic crisis that threatened the stability of the franc.

In this circumstance, eager as he was to play for time and moderation,
he realized that suspicion and hostility toward France had reached crisis
proportions in London because of the apparent delay over some assurance of
mutual support. Anxiety in Whitehall was aggravated by a snobbish, quasi-
aesthetic personal distaste for Laval. Pierre-Étienne Flandin as a later
foreign minister was no different in his demands on Britain, but he looked as
if he had just stepped from an English manor house—tall, fair, tweed-coated,
and pipe-smoking—and that stood in his favor. Laval, on the other hand,
was short, dark, lower class, and once a Socialist. Joseph Avenol, no friend
of Laval's, told Eden that he was a "real calamity," that he was inconsistent
because of a gypsy strain.[30] The prejudice of Foreign Office officials is

indicated by Ralph Wigram's description of him as "the arch trickster of French politics." But Orme Sargent noted in reply that Herriot, although a most determined anglophile, would, if prime minister, be less able than Laval to bring intractable French opinion over to Britain.[31]

In the matter of mutual support Laval claimed that his initial reservations had been misinterpreted. He had his own concerns, and as prime minister of France he would not be pushed too fast. He would not, he told his officials, have France treated like Britain's dutiful client Portugal.[32] Ambassador George Clerk chided that Laval's postponement in responding to the British request need not be taken as proof of perverseness or insincerity. Delay might have been caused by Laval's preoccupation with the complicated domestic crisis, by his slow recognition of how seriously the matter was regarded in London or how swiftly virulent anglophobia was whipped up in France, and by his absence from Paris in Geneva, for Laval served as his own foreign minister. At the start of 1935 a Foreign Office review of leading personalities in France noted, "Laval has always shown himself extremely well disposed towards Great Britain."[33]

In the event, the Foreign Office took to shock tactics to frighten Laval, as Avenol suggested to Eden on 13 October, warning that Laval might lose Britain without having won Italy. London demanded a clear and explicit statement of support. If he won't "face facts," Vansittart warned on 15 October, "public opinion here may turn as anti-French as French opinion is anti-British. That will probably mean the end of our collaboration. . . . It is worth making one more effort to avert this otherwise inevitable catastrophe." "If there were a better hole I'd go to it," Vansittart said, "but there isn't."[34] Eden's leadership at Geneva and the rally of smaller nations there had their influence, and on 18 October 1935 came the French note assuring support.

It gave the British what they wanted and pointed out some telling and unpleasant truths in the process. The threatened British fleet, for which support was asked, cruised about the Mediterranean on imperial business, and it had been sent unilaterally, for a purpose divorced from the collective enterprise now claimed as the basis for demanding assurances of support. The note called the public concealment of the moderate intentions of the British government a bluff, a dishonest practice that contributed to the general anxiety about war. "France," Laval said, "never felt any difficulty in letting the limits of its conclusions be known."[35]

Vansittart shrugged off the sharp tone. "We have had to get it out of the French with forceps and biceps. . . . But we've got it, and we mustn't wonder—or mind—if the client burbles a bit. . . . [This may be] the end of a chapter (But what a chapter!)."[36]

Threat of European War

Two weeks had passed since the invasion. The northern army established defensive positions as planned, without a great battle. Only one Italian soldier died in avenging Aduwa. After no opposition the "first stride" stopped. De Bono insisted on holding fast, on defending his rear and organizing supply.

Criticism arose in Rome that De Bono's vision was too narrowly colonial and military, that he took no account of the fateful political consequences the war was calling forth in Europe. That a modern army, inspired by Fascist principles, did not go further and faster in the absence of resistance made it easier to argue at Geneva that sanctions could work, that Italians might have to compromise. Mussolini's bargaining hand was weak as long as his troops were only two dozen miles beyond the frontier and the Ethiopian forces remained intact.

On 7 October, with the invasion barely begun, he sent the colonial undersecretary, Alessandro Lessona, and the chief of the general staff, Pietro Badoglio, to survey and report on the northern front. Their ostensible purpose was to examine the possibility of an invasion into the Sudan "in the case of a conflict with a European power." The obvious real reason was to check up on De Bono, to report on his strategic assumptions, the work accomplished, and the personal capability of the commander himself, of whom both ambitious men were highly critical.

Lessona, a good Fascist, opposed the slow, deliberate pace, the rhythm of thrust and counterthrust, the time spent for local political arrangements. He argued that Italy would escape the "seriously compromised" diplomatic situation only through rapid military victory. De Bono's plan for a war of two or three years ignored Italy's international situation. Sanctions, given time, could "render victory impossible," while there was equipment available now to "chase the enemy to Addis Ababa."[37]

Badoglio agreed. Although in December, when the Ethiopians counterattacked in Tigre, he learned the need for secure positions, the logic in drawing the foe toward a strategic engagement in decisive battle, in October, he was as ready as Lessona to paint De Bono incompetent.[38] From a strictly military standpoint, he reported, De Bono failed to use the artillery and air resources at hand. De Bono's waiting game dangerously prolonged the conflict. The circumstances were no longer those of 1933 when the plan was hatched. "Either Italy wins the war in a few months or it is lost," Lessona announced when he arrived in Eritrea.[39]

De Bono, of course, viewed their visit with utter dismay. His editor refused to print the diary comments he made on Lessona. De Bono called the pretext of the Sudan study "infantile."[40] That was a matter he could have determined on his own. But his bitter complaint to Mussolini about the visit, about the affront to his dignity, was rejected. His diary records his apprehension, but stay calm, he told himself. His enemies in Rome misrepresented and underrated his position. "They understand nothing in Italy." His retrenchment was to protect the future—that is what they failed to see or to credit.[41]

De Bono was not without political awareness. On 14 October, with an eye to European opinion, to discrediting the emperor, and to the pose as leader of a civilizing mission, he ordered the suppression of slavery in Tigre. The clear European direction of this dramatic proclamation was revealed by Ruggero, the chief of secret service in the field, who said it slowed his work of undermining resistance. It made many chiefs, who were not necessarily inclined to support the emperor, argue that an Italian occupation would cost them the ancient privileges of their position.[42]

De Bono consoled himself that at least he had something else to show upon the arrival of Lessona and Badoglio. On 11 October, Haile Selassie Gugsa, well-plied with bribes and promises and attended by 1,200 men (only one-tenth of his force, however,) had come over to the Italian side. This was an important defection. Gugsa, son-in-law of the emperor, commanded the troops in the center. The emperor said later that his generals estimated that the defection gave two months' advantage to the Italians. Certainly it lowered morale—perhaps in the emperor's camp above all, where Haile Selassie had not taken seriously what he called the "bribery without corruption" of his chiefs.[43]

Gugsa was made puppet civil governor of Tigre. Hoping to protect his share of local spoils, he urged a march on Makale, sixty miles to the south, into his ancestral lands. De Bono agreed on 12 October, and Mussolini concurred for "general political reasons." But De Bono was then dissuaded by his general officers. Such a rush would be a risky overextension. The defensive positions, the lines of support, first had to be secured. His chief of staff, Melchiade Gabba, estimated that it would be at least eight weeks, into mid-December, before a march on Makale could be undertaken. Lessona and Badoglio were in on this discussion, and when General Ruggero Santini told them that in fact the army could move in a month, they used this episode to exemplify the "passive resistance," the "Eritrean psychology," of the high command, that lack of vision that made De Bono incompetent to command this war.[44]

Mussolini, although impatient, agreed to wait. A setback, in the face of the field commanders opposition, would at this juncture be far worse, far more demoralizing, than staying with their cautious strategy. On 17 October he wired De Bono: "I agree you ought not to march on Makale before organizing your rear and before receiving my orders. Intensify the defensive system on the Adigrat-Aksum-Aduwa lines. . . . My orders will reach you when the European situation clears up in respect to sanctions and, above all, in respect to British-Italian relations, which are now in a state of extreme tension with the prospect of war not far off."[45]

Not that Mussolini wanted war in Europe. Far from it. When in September he had contemplated attacking the British fleet, his military leaders had told him Italy would be reduced to the strength of a Balkan state. That specific crisis was now past, and the British repeated that they had no wish to humiliate Italy or lower the prestige of his regime. Drummond even got Mussolini to agree that he would have taken a similar prudential measure in the face of belligerent statements in a foreign press. As for Geneva, Drummond stated explicitly on 23 September that Hoare had never used the word *sanctions* in his speeches and that "such matters as the closing of the Suez Canal or military sanctions had not even been discussed." Britain, he said, thought that the postwar system of collective security was at stake, and this consideration was its sole inspiration.[46]

With these disavowals Mussolini toned down the "ink campaign" and scouted the possibility of "demobilizing" the Mediterranean, withdrawing the two divisions he had sent to Libya in return for Britain's decreasing the fleet strength. Overtures were under way as the invasion began, but that, as Hoare said, "banged the door in our face."[47] The dispute was now generalized.

In the second week of October fear of war resurfaced. Eden's stand at Geneva was stronger and appeared more hostile than Mussolini had anticipated. It seemed, Aloisi noted on 11 October, that the prestige of the two countries was at stake and that the British were determined to push to the end, even if it meant Mussolini's fall. On the twelfth he told Mussolini that British policy was directed against Fascists by men set to carry it through. "Laval is our only safeguard," Aloisi said. The mediation that Laval wanted must be tried. All right, agreed Mussolini, adding that, even so, war with Britain was inevitable.[48]

On 16 October Mussolini told Chambrun that he did not see how war could be avoided. On the seventeenth he wrote to De Bono that it was not far off. On the eighteenth he repeated his arguments to Drummond, blaming the troubles on Britain. The Italian navy sailed under orders that the casus belli would be any sanctions that closed the canal or interfered with the transport of troops or supplies.[49]

Hopes for Settlement

A month earlier Badoglio had said that he counted on Mussolini's diplomatic skill to keep Italy out of war. This Mussolini did, easily, it turned out, against the irresolute opposition of the British. Talk of war encouraged talk of conciliation—the carrot after the stick. Laval is our only safeguard, Aloisi said, and Laval kept the British with him. Laval's position was simple: it was all a question of tact, of "the reconciliation of prudence with principles."[50]

By 19 October principle was asserted. The League seemed vindicated. Proposals for economic sanctions were with member governments for approval, and would, in four weeks or so, go into effect. A détente established by assurance of support on 18 October meant that Britain and France were in a mood for collaboration. The war front was quiet. No Italian advance seemed likely in the near future. There was a predictable month's lull in the crisis, time to try to reduce the tension in the Mediterranean, to alleviate Mussolini's anxiety about war, and to scout once again the possibility of a negotiated settlement.

It was nothing new to try for conciliation. Taking at face value Italian propaganda about the civilizing mission—the need to suppress slavery, to stabilize an anarchical state, to put down border raids, and to encourage economic enterprise—the British and French in August and the League's Committee of Five in September presented Mussolini with plans aimed at satisfying Italy on these lines while retaining the territorial integrity of Ethiopia and the emperor's independent sovereignty. Mussolini rejected both plans, objecting that the Italian role in Ethiopia, however generously allotted and however promising for the future, would remain subordinate to the final authority of the League of Nations. By September, and even more once the invasion was under way, Mussolini would settle for nothing less than substantial territorial annexation in order to fulfill the nationalist expectations raised in his own mind and disseminated among the Italian people.

At the outbreak of war the French and British were engaged in revising the plan of the Committee of Five. With the invasion, however, the British decided to defer conciliation until the League had had its innings. They therefore dampened Laval's enthusiasm for opening negotiations at once.

Military success, a victorious battle or two, continued to elude the Italians. Pessimistic as Haile Selassie was, his forces were still intact. The emperor was subject to the militant patriotism of his chiefs, and this strong xenophobia made it difficult to imagine that he would accept any unfavorable settlement. Difficult to imagine in London, that is, where the sympathetic reports of Minister Sidney Barton made this point. The sterner dispatches of Minister Albert Bodard encouraged the Quai d'Orsay to think the opposite: the emperor would bow to whatever the British and French might jointly demand. For Haile Selassie the British were *his* only safeguard, and his dependence was almost total. The more the British supported sanctions, the firmer the emperor's resolve, and proportionately, the more difficult for them to budge him toward compromise. The opening unprovoked air attack on unarmed cities further discouraged diplomatic thinking. Were such acts to be reward-

ed with concession? On 9 October the cabinet agreed that any Italian "overtures for a negotiated settlement outside the League of Nations should be
received very coolly at the present time."[51]

The door to negotiation was shut, not locked. When some Dominion delegations suggested that diplomatic relations with Italy be suspended, Hoare
replied that that would "only make conciliation more difficult." "We are
bound to consider," he continued, "that the prospects of conciliation will be
improved by pressure now to be applied."[52] What was needed was some sign
from Mussolini that conciliation was worth pursuing.

The diplomatic corps in Rome included more than the masters of the
French and British embassies. Concerned with the fate of Italy, excited by
the dramatic situation, eager to be in on the action, representatives of Japan,
Chile, and Argentina rushed about with plans and proposals that they hoped
would lead to the opening of settlement talks. These efforts were discounted
in London and Paris. Even if the schemes were inspired or encouraged by
Mussolini's office at the Palazzo Venezia or the foreign ministry at the Palazzo Chigi, they seemed too indirectly presented, the intermediaries too unreliable, to be taken seriously even as trial balloons. Irritation was added to
skepticism. Matters of high European significance were too important to be
meddled with by persons of dubious merit from marginal states.

But negotiation must begin somewhere, and the Italians refused to make
their wishes directly known. The most conspicuous of the plans floating
around was one touted (probably on Italian official inspiration) by the busy
Japanese ambassador, Yotaro Sigamura. His plan, floated on the eve of the
invasion, proposed extending the proposals of the Committee of Five in
Italy's favor by enlarging the area to be placed under "mandate" and speci-
fying Italy in the mandatory role. No state was so named in the original design of the committee.

These ideas were turned down in London. "The League," said Hoare on 4
October, would be "laying up for itself a heritage of woe by fathering such a
plan." Any territorial adjustments in Italy's favor had "far better be outright, otherwise Italy would have to report to the League in the guise of a
mandatory but really as an annexationist." The League would have to
swallow these reports, "which would make it look ridiculous." Besides, there
were endless problems of detail and definition (what constituted *non-Amharic* provinces?), and no Ethiopian ruler could agree to put the bulk of his
country under foreign domination, especially at a time like this.[53] The only
imaginable course in London was some outright cession to Italy of certain
areas, in return for which Ethiopia would receive appropriate compensation.

As much as anyone, the dignitaries of the Vatican feared Mussolini's fall,
or his coming to think he might fall. A leader taking Italy to the left, a

radicalized fascism, a collapsed regime and the onset of bolshevism—what, in any of these circumstances, would happen to the Lateran agreements, to church privilege and holdings? Dominated by this local perspective, almost seeing themselves as an interested party, the goal of the churchmen was to end the conflict swiftly by agreement or, in any case, to contain its troublesome European complications. It was first necessary, however, to learn Mussolini's mind and impress on him the need for caution.

Their overtures influenced Mussolini not at all. He used Vatican representation for his own ends. At the beginning of October the nuncio in Rome, Francesco Borgongini Duca, saw the head of government on behalf of the pope. He urged moderation and came away discouraged. Another line was open through Pietro Tacchi Venturi, S.J., who, since acting as intermediary in the Lateran negotiations, had been Mussolini's most regular unofficial ecclesiastical visitor. Mussolini was once asked what significance should be placed on the visits of Tacchi Venturi. This prelate had no special duties, Mussolini replied, but "I need lots of information and have many ways."[54] Accommodation was thus sought in uncertain, roundabout fashion during these first two weeks of October. The Vatican's efforts were as tentative as those of Sigamura or his Argentinian counterpart, Ruiz Vicuña. And, like the latter, they ran up against British skepticism, dislike of minor state interference, and insistence on procedure.

In October came a particularly inept try evidently organized by the none too competent acting secretary of state, Giuseppe Pizzardo, sitting for the vacationing cardinal secretary, Eugenio Pacelli. Earlier, in July, the pope had tried to send a personal letter concerning the coming Ethiopian war to the king of England by way of the archbishop of Westminster. The archbishop, Arthur Hinsley, was refused an audience. The Foreign Office denied him permission to bypass customary channels. According to the act of settlement of 1701 the king could not carry on a clandestine correspondence with a foreign monarch or conduct foreign affairs outside his ministry. The Vatican would not agree to relay a private letter through the Foreign Office, even when it was explained that in constitutional practice it would eventually have to go there anyway. As the Ethiopian crisis grew, the Foreign Office saw this as an opportunity missed and decided to permit one sealed letter from the pope (not to represent a precedent), if transmitted through the legation at the Holy See. On 4 October there arrived at the legation a letter to the king, but it was signed, not by the pope, but by Cardinal Pacelli. This was too much. An exception might be made for the pontiff, but not for a mere official. The letter was declined, and with this second rebuff the Vatican tried no more to reach the king.

It was an awkward set of incidents, reflecting British unwillingness to be drawn into indirect negotiations in these opening and uncertain days of the

war. It also reflected an increasing suspicion of Vatican intentions. The Holy
See has "not behaved well," noted E. H. Carr in the Foreign Office. On 23
October the pope, through Pizzardo, asked to speak to Ambassador Drummond. Permission, judged to be inopportune and subject to misconstruction,
was refused.[55] By this time negotiations with the French were in train—a
double set seemed superfluous, even dangerous. A month later, in a message
to British representatives in twenty-eight countries, Hoare complained that
the "voice of the Vatican has come to be scarcely distinguishable from that
of the Italian Government" and asked for information of "to what extent, if
at all, the Vatican has, through their own machinery, endeavoured to sway
world opinion against League action and in favour of Italy."[56]

In the first two weeks of October, then, the British refused to be drawn
into discussions of terms through intermediary agents. On the fourth Eden
had been instructed to discourage at Geneva any initiatives from Italians or
from Laval along the lines of the Sigamura plan. If Laval sponsored such a
course just at the outbreak of war, Hoare said, it was foredoomed to failure,
and "the atmosphere of heated rejection which he would create would not
fail to prejudice prospects of our own far more reasoned and moderate
ideas" of straightforward territorial rectification instead of mandate. "I do
not want bad currency to drive out good," Hoare continued, nor to be
associated with any enterprise that would "make us seem disloyal."[57]

Ambassador Chambrun pursued the search for settlement more insistently
than anyone else. Despite his talk of Italian moderation after dramatic
battles, talk which influenced Laval's thinking, Chambrun himself worried
that a succession of military victories, far from appeasing ambition, might
lead Mussolini to stiffen his resolve. Worse, sanctions would lead to rising
prices, weakening an already inflated economy. Popular discontent in Italy
and a stiff-necked government might cause Mussolini's fall or send him
careening to the left. The French ambassador in Moscow reported that the
Soviet government was set to exploit unrest. No good for France could come
from an alienated or enfeebled Italy. There was no time to lose in the search
for a conciliatory settlement, League or no League. It was vital, Chambrun
told Drummond on 8 October, to do everything possible to stop the war
before the Italians were so committed that they could not draw back.

The Italians were no help. Fulvio Suvich, undersecretary in the foreign
ministry, told Chambrun Italy would not take the initiative in the face of
British intransigence. Chambrun worked from what was roughly the Sigamura plan, but no more than Drummond could he answer questions posed
by the Italians: What would be their opportunities for colonial settlement,
the terms for exploitation of natural resources, the assurances for the security of Italian interests?[58]

Chambrun's role as intermediary was not accepted in London. The mandate solution was rejected, as was Chambrun's fitness for "serious business." He was, Maurice Peterson commented, a "menace." The fear was that Chambrun, exaggerating conciliatory possiblities, might reach an agreement with the Italians, only making matters worse when he could not "deliver the goods."[59]

To end the standoff, Laval took the initiative. On 14 October, as the Coordination Committee sat at work, he asked the Italian ambassador, Cerruti, to "ascertain as soon as possible the conditions which Mussolini would consider offered the possibility of a friendly settlement." Financial sanctions were recommended at Geneva, and he felt very strongly, he told Ambassador Clerk, that "before proceeding to more severe [economic] sanctions" it was "important to exhaust every possibility of conciliation" and to "bring the Italian Government into the open and oblige it to say whether it would or would not reject a friendly settlement of the conflict." Laval asked expressly for Mussolini's minimum terms, which he said he would first consider along with what the League and the Ethiopian government might accept and would then submit to London.

His own preference was for an Italian mandate over the "non-Amharic colonies" and a League mandate over the rest of the country. These were easy hopes, and Laval was at this stage largely, one might say carelessly, ignorant of the complexity of the matter and of the strong British reservations. The British thought the Ethiopian government would never accept League oversight of the core land or any diminution of sovereignty and independence. Hence British opposition to the various mandate plans and their preference for a compensatory territorial exchange. Nor was the League likely to reward Italy so generously "for the act which the unanimous vote of the Council and the opinion of fifty-three nations had condemned."[60] To the British, eager to generalize opposition, there were three parties to the dispute, each of which would have to be independently satisfied. Laval tended to think in terms of two, against one of which—Ethiopia—Anglo-French pressure could be successfully applied. The League would then accommodate to a fait accompli.

Where to carve the empire would depend in large part on how much of the territory was already conquered. Suvich and Aloisi, for example, used this argument ("in view of the proposed mediation") in advising Mussolini on 12 October to override De Bono's caution and order him to press on to Makale. Hence Mussolini's order of the thirteenth recommending advance for "general political reasons," an order which De Bono, as we saw, refused, on military grounds, to follow.[61]

On 16 October Mussolini presented his terms to Chambrun. Visitors reported Mussolini in a pessimistic mood. To the Chilean ambassador he spoke of the probable loss of Somalia, Eritrea, and the Dodecanese Islands in a European war. To Chambrun he painted a despairing picture of the results of such a war: France faced with 80 million Germans; Austria without an Italian counterweight, absorbed in the Reich; German influence extended to the Bosporous.[62]

Mussolini, expecting rejection of his terms, was probably not feigning depression. He took article 16 more literally than those about to apply it. Britain and France promised to avoid military sanctions, he told De Bono on 20 October, but "I have little faith in the one or the other." Logically, sanctions must intensify. It was just a matter of time. And with the arms embargo toward Ethiopia lifted, weapons would soon be arriving there "in great quantities." Time, he said, "works against us," and he urged De Bono to move forward to occupy as much territory as possible in the shortest possible time.[63]

De Bono, the day before this message arrived, had optimistically noted that a spirit of détente existed in Europe. It most probably would give rise to a comprehensive settlement, and he resolved, he had told his diary, to "wait with patience."[64] Now, against his judgment, he was pushed again to move up his advance on Makale from the planned six or seven or even eight weeks to a fortnight: between 1 and 5 November, Mussolini instructed. The European situation was in fact no better, Mussolini insisted; the lessening of tension was only a matter of form. In the end Mussolini's determination prevailed. Italian troops advanced on 3 November and took Makale on the eighth. The thrust overextended the front and exposed the flank. Badoglio, who had concurred in the local judgment that 10 November was the earliest possible date for advance, would later use this example of endangering interference to demand, and win, independence for himself from Mussolini's and Lessona's military command when he took De Bono's place as the northern army leader.[65]

Meanwhile, in the latter half of October, Mussolini, subject to unexpectedly strong international condemnation, felt himself cornered. British hostility had not yet turned into the asset it later became as the cause for a patriotic rally of the Italians to the government. So Mussolini was edgy, and he floated the idea of negotiation as a way to win time and take off some of the heat. He expected his terms to be rejected.[66] But as a diplomatic maneuver the prospect of conciliation had worked well in the past and, given Laval's eagerness, might work well again, well enough, at any rate, to allow the troops time to advance at least as far as the point from which Italians were expelled in 1896.

On 16 October, therefore, Mussolini had stated to Chambrun his minimum terms for ending the war. They were stiff: direct Italian administration of the (ill-defined) non-Amharic territories; Italian participation in a League assistance program (along the lines proposed by the Committee of Five) for the remaining territories; pure and simple annexation of conquered land in the north; boundary changes in Italy's favor in the south. In return, permission would be given to use the port of Assab in Eritrea on a basis analogous to Ethiopia's present use of Djibouti and Berbera—that is, the port and access remaining under Italian control.[67]

These terms opened a new chapter of negotiation. Here was the word, straight from Mussolini, something direct and concrete to work with at last. The Italians had at least made a move in the right direction, Vansittart said, "a distinct step in advance."[68] Indication of the terms came at the same time from the Vatican, and there the British made an initial response: they would use their influence only as a member of the League; the definitions of territory were too vague and probably unacceptable both at Geneva and Addis Ababa, and no formal mandate seemed possible, although the question of Italian participation in economic development seemed soluble in practice.[69] Since the Vatican démarche, however, was too secondhand, that connection was not taken up further, superceded by the direct line opened through France. Two sets of negotiation were impossible, and, as we saw, on 23 October Drummond was refused permission to discuss the matter with the pope.

Mussolini requested that the terms of any negotiation bear the stamp of French initiative. This would keep him off the hook and facilitate coordination with the British. "What we need now is a result," noted Assistant Undersecretary Lancelot Oliphant in the Foreign Office. It was not important to "stand on ceremony" over how this was obtained.[70] The détente established by the French note of 18 October made it easier to take up Laval's recommendation to determine a common policy forthwith. On the twenty-second, at a meeting attended by Hoare, Vansittart, Oliphant, and Peterson, it was decided that Peterson would go at once to Paris to begin conversations with the French. It was important to act quickly, in the spirit of the recent détente and before further hostilities in Ethiopia complicated matters any more.[71] This was the first step of the bilateral negotiations that emerged two months later as the Hoare-Laval proposals for settlement.

The next day, the cabinet announced that any settlement must take place within the framework of the League. This marked the doom of a plan, hatched by the Argentine and Chilean ambassadors in Rome and endorsed, if not inspired, by the Palazzo Chigi, to ask the Council to suspend preparations for economic sanctions and to delegate authority to find a settlement outside the League to the three most involved European powers.[72] It was accepted in Rome that Haile Selassie would accede to whatever the British and French put to him. The idea, to which Laval would no doubt subscribe, was to remove the threat to the Italians, during negotiations, of impending sanctions. On 28 October, the date for putting sanctions in force was to be set at Geneva. The British rejected a tactic of postponement. To defer action, said Eden on 23 October 1935, "would be quite fatal to the sanctionist effort."[73]

3   DOUBLE POLICIES

Britain

Postponement of sanctions, at least in the liberal states, would be difficult to justify beyond the walls of ministries. The Italian-Ethiopian affair caught the interest of people throughout the world more than any international matter since the Great War. There was a partly escapist fascination with exotic Ethiopians. They might be painted in Italy as savages to be controlled and civilized, but to the sympathetic, reacting against the clanking arrogance of Italian aggression, they were innocent defenders of their homeland, and Christians to boot. For supporters of internationalism this test case aroused all the old Wilsonian hopes; for its opponents, all the old reservations.

There was spectacle on the grand scale. Horror, and fascination too, greeted the reappearance of modern warfare. Jules Romains, walking in Paris, was plunged into dread and uncertainty for Europe as he saw headlines announcing the bombing of Aduwa. Such sorties and the eventual bombing of noncombatant missionary stations and Red Cross units—to say nothing of the use of poison gases reported from the first days of the war (the *Times,* 15 October)—turned much sentiment against the Italians. Graziani understood this, and on 17 October defined strictly military operations for his air force. Action beyond such targets would dangerously stir up the foreign press, causing more trouble than any corresponding local benefit.[1]

In the popular eye, juxtaposed against the almost melodramatic application of modern weaponry was the equally well-described state of the opponent: barefoot, poorly organized, carrying spears and bulletless rifles, and led by chiefs in lionskins riding on donkeys. The Ethiopian cause benefited greatly, then as later, from the grave and dignified demeanor of the emperor. His calls to morality, his righteousness, and the sanctity of treaty struck tender nerves north of the Alps. Italian propaganda describing the Ethiopians as vicious, uncivilized, multiraced barbarians never supplanted the post-imperialist, liberal-romantic sentiment that saw them as free and noble people, most of them Christians, with a notable Jewish population as well, now brutally assaulted by "the Machine Age" as *Time* magazine expressed it in naming Haile Selassie its 1935 Man of the Year. For many, the issue was more than just a test of collective security. Policy became an affair of national honor, of action on behalf of the League and its predicates and also, in a depression-ridden world, on behalf of the oppressed.

Politically, morally, and dramatically, it was a great affair. Some 180 correspondents were accredited in Addis Ababa, many of them youthful, naïve, sympathetic to the underdog. Herbert Matthews wrote that "journalism, on the whole, failed its public in the African campaign" with inflated reporting.[2] The American chargé complained after three months that "75 per cent of the newspaper reports which have gone out from here regarding military events have been pure guesswork and padding."[3] Such conclusions are not without exception. Matthews himself, for the *New York Times*, attached to the invading forces, gave ample coverage and sympathetic judgment to the Italian advance. He also wrote a superb account of one of the greatest Ethiopian strikes, the ambush at Ende Gorge, an ambush that would have been an annihilation had not the Ethiopian force withdrawn instead of pressing its overwhelming advantage.[4]

On the Italian side, 200 correspondents filed stories, poems, and panegyrics of emotional nationalism, more in the form of propaganda than news. "News" was left to the terse war bulletins, terse, indeed laconic, in the early months, because after Aduwa and apart from Makale there was little to report.[5]

Badoglio put a brake on reportage in late November by restricting the movement of foreign journalists, but by then the tremendous volume flowing from their pens had made a lasting impression in their homelands. In Italy the domestic press was controlled and foreign papers suppressed, and it was forbidden to tune in foreign radio stations in public places.

All media were involved now. The war gave the Fascist regime "its first full-scale opportunity to use the radio for a systematic propaganda campaign," to which it devoted 30 percent of broadcasting time.[6] Newsreels came into their own. Movietone built ten special cameras, designed field laboratories, and sent armorized trucks and motorcycles equipped with sidecars. Paramount placed camera teams on both sides and established bases in Libya, Somalia, Khartoum, Djibouti, and Addis Ababa.[7] Some cinema coverage, certainly all released in Italy, contained political messages. The first production on the Ethiopian campaign by British Paramount News (released 7 October 1935) ran fake action footage and a cautionary commentary that "war is abroad over the land. War means mass murder and the massacre of millions."[8]

Such coverage reflected, and stimulated, a dramatic upturn in popular interest in international affairs. Three studies by Ithiel de Sola Pool, through content analyses of editorial positions of "prestige papers" in the major European powers around this time, show a growing preoccupation with the increase of nationalism and militarism in the world.[9] Increased interest in foreign affairs did not set a common position toward the Ethiopian war, however. *Le Temps* consistently supported accommodation, but the *Times* "was a house divided against itself."[10] Editor Geoffrey Dawson was closer to British public opinion than to the Foreign Office in his dislike of Italy's African pretensions, but while anti-Italian in this case (as a British imperialist) he was also antisanctionist, ultimately sharing the confusion of the government as to the best course to follow.[11]

Ethiopia was headline news for weeks on end. The problem of dealing with the war brought forth great debate in the *Times's* correspondence columns, enlarged for the occasion to provide a public forum in which arguments on the merits of the League, Italy's case, and Britain's role ranged wide and were carried on in discourse of high quality. Ordinary people wrote directly to the secretary-general in anxious hope that the League could stay war. There are several linear feet of telegrams and letters in the archive in Geneva, most in English and many from America.[12] It was a time for manifestos and countermanifestos. Liberal assumptions were put to test. For many it seemed that the future of Western civilization was at stake—to be destroyed either in a European war (the appeasers) or by a failure to live up to its ideals (the pro-Leaguers).

The problem for the British government was that it planned one way but was understood in another. Committed to a dual policy of sanctions and negotiation, it was seen by its public and the Italians as standing foursquare behind enforcement of the Covenant, as the leader of the sanctionist states. The contradiction is illuminated by the distinction mentioned earlier between values dichotomized as consummatory or instrumental. "Consummatory values," wrote Ernst Haas, "imply a devotion to the integral realization of strongly held beliefs; instrumental values involve a constant calculation of the adjustment of the proper means to achieve limited ends, and a willingness to settle for an approximation to one's beliefs."[13] Pro-League opinion, and anti-League sentiment in Italy, carried consummatory value. Moralistic qualities were attributed to the League. Questions of honor, of the validity of the liberal assumptions, of credibility, were involved.

The Fascist perspective, while critical, also took a consummatory stance. The League, when not viewed as a convenient cover for the conservation of the status quo or a stalking-horse for British imperialism, was seen in Italy as doctrinal liberalism run amok, part of an evangelical, anti-Fascist, laic mysticism associated with Jews, plutocrats, Masons, and Bolsheviks, "the extreme incarnation of the enlightenment filtered through one and a half centuries of democratic romanticism."[14]

Opposed to seeing the League through the consummatory lens was the instrumentalist position described earlier, one held by professional diplomats —officials used to assessing national interest on the basis of official information, making secret deliberations, reaching secret conclusions, and coming up with secret resolutions of international problems. These officials paid small heed, except as part of a domestic political problem, to partisans of Wilsonian diplomacy. They realized, in Britain for example, that the popular enthusiasm for collective security was vital to rearmament and a more active continental policy, but they continued to regard public support for the League with suspicion, as ill-informed or misguided. Public support was not systematically developed or encouraged for defensive or internationalist purposes. For instance, one argument advanced in London was that a diplomatic settlement would help the League because it would defer, not force, its testing time, thereby avoiding the strain of sanctions on the association and on the British-French entente, a strain, it was thought, that neither would survive. Whatever the merit of this argument, the public knew very little about it, and the results of a partial enforcement policy were not at all what popular opinion or many smaller governments had been led to expect.

For the governments of Britain and France, sanctions were established within the limiting framework of reconciliationist perspective, in which coercion was kept to a minimum and accommodation was the primary goal. Conciliation was deemed appropriate; reports from Rome made it seem possible; and officials in both capitals had no doubt that it was desirable. So a double policy made sense—sanctions to exert pressure and rally the League, negotiation to settle the war after the pressure made the Italians seek a way out, and all without broadening the conflict.

What the professionals did not see was that reconciliationist assumptions undermined the longer range strategic and political goals behind a collective security policy. The best that can be said for the dual policy is that it was a short-run expedient to deal with an immediately vexing situation without making it worse. A Foreign Office minute of 2 December concerning the Hoare-Laval plan reads: "Our object is to overcome the immediate dangerous crisis, not to solve the Abyssinian question, which will be with us for years. But if we can stop the war, passions will cool and there will be more chance than at present of reducing all these rather general and perhaps slightly theoretical proposals [for a negotiated settlement] to shape."[15] What the long-run implications of either enforcement or conciliation might be was not thought through. Appeasement by itself was not developed as a substitute for a League policy, but that was all that remained if enforcement failed.

Thus British actions seemed formalistic, "evasion by technique," in the words of League official Emile Giraud.[16] As long as the British government failed to communicate or seemed to dissemble its vision of national security, it was unreliable as an ally or as a leader. When the government insisted, for example, that British interests in the present conflict were only contingent, it exposed its lack of real support for collective security, as no national interest seemed involved.

The failure to foster public understanding of the complexity of the policy in train was due to more than neglect. The double line was formulated late in the day, for want of something better. In the meantime, improvisations served as policy, permitting if not encouraging exaggerated expectations. Strong words of support fanned such "leagueomania" that the government had to respond to its own rhetoric. Hoare professed amazement at the immensely favorable reaction to his speech of 11 September 1935 before the Assembly, although the speech was contrived (with the help of Neville Chamberlain and Robert Vansittart) to elicit such a response.

What was applauded and remembered was Hoare's peroration: "In conformity with its precise and explicit obligations, the League stands, and my country stands with it, for the collective maintenance of the Covenant in its entirety and particularly for steady and collective resistance to all acts of unprovoked aggression." His careful qualifications were not noticed, for it seemed silly that a great power like Britain would let smaller states determine its course of action. "If risks for peace are to be run, they must be run by all. The security of the many cannot be ensured solely by the efforts of a few, however powerful they may be." But even this hedging was followed by an apparently clear expression of support: "On behalf of His Majesty's Government in the United Kingdom, I can say that, in spite of these difficulties, that Government will be second to none in its intention to fulfill, within the measure of its capacity."[17]

The speech created a sensation and received, as Hoare called it, "universal acclamation." There was a sense of something new and forceful, of Britain's asserting leadership in foreign affairs once more. The king sent his congratulations. Reflecting general opinion Wickham Steed wrote to Hoare that the speech was "taken as laying down a very definite policy on the part of His Majesty's Government in support of the League" and, as such, said Steed, was "welcomed unanimously in this country and did more to win respect and confidence for British policy than anything that has been said or done for a long time."[18]

Yet the speech was a bluff. The government had neither a plan nor much desire for capitalizing on the pro-League sentiment it aroused. Still, the months of poorly coordinated improvisation, of department actions without much regard for political consequences, had gotten officials in this fix, and they were, like it or not, bound to a significant degree by the pro-League support now generated. By October 1935 the government was assuming an apparently anti-Italian posture with which its members were most uncomfortable. To keep the Mediterranean order became the aim of the cabinet. As in the Foreign Office, the main concern was with Germany and France, so the current Italian problem simply had to be ridden through without a radical departure in policy.

The men of the cabinet and Foreign Office were self-assured and complacent. Undemanding of one another, unbothered by outside calls for a policy of principle, "realistists"—minimalists, really, concerned with minimizing costs and losses—secure in the House of Commons with a majority of 492, they were confident in the exercise of power.

The cabinet included, in addition to the incumbent Hoare, two previous foreign secretaries, Ramsay MacDonald and John Simon. Neville Chamberlain, chancellor of the exchechquer, was increasingly sure of and influential with his opinions on foreign affairs. At this stage he backed Eden on matters of collective security, for he did not see appeasement of Italy as a necessary part of the general approach to Germany until later. Eden, despite his outside reputation for independence, was, within 10 Downing Street in October 1935, an aspiring new member who deferred as often as he persisted in a point.[19] Baldwin's heart was not in foreign affairs. His contribution was to urge caution. Hoare's way around the dilemmas of the Ethiopian war was, as we saw, the dual policy.

To the cabinet members the merits of the double approach of sanctions and conciliation seemed self-evident. It was a sensible, safe, and presumably viable course. Beyond what appeared to them to be honest and sufficient statements of the policy, they saw no need to go further, to correct—if indeed these were recognized—the misapprehensions of the public. What the world came to see as contradictory they saw as complementary. Not until the uproar over the Paris plan of December and the subsequent plunge in the government's credibility did they admit how far official actions had strayed from the spirit of support called up by Hoare in September. Meanwhile, what was important was to avoid European war, to get through the affair with as few bad effects as possible.

At the first of October the Labour Party Conference carried by a representative vote of 2,168,000 to 102,000 a resolution that read in part: "The Conference calls upon the British Government, in cooperation with other nations represented at the Council and the Assembly of the League, to use all the necessary measures provided by the Covenant to prevent Italy's unjust and rapacious attack. . . . The Conference pledges its firm support of any action consistent with the principles and statutes of the League to restrain the Italian Government and to uphold the authority of the League in enforcing peace." This resolution, following what the chairman called "possibly the biggest and most important discussion that the conference ever had to deal with," was also adopted shortly before by a meeting of the Trades Union Congress by approximately the same majority.[20]

This strong sentiment overcame the pacifist tradition, unseated George Lansbury as leader of the parliamentary Labour party, and sidelined his deputy, Stafford Cripps. Cripps opposed both the war and the League as manifestations of capitalist imperialism. He argued against handing Baldwin the opportunity for victory in a general election through Labour's pro-League support, for the cost would be the downgrading of social and economic issues. The new parliamentary leader was Clement Attlee, ready to go along with the government's League policy. "Where there is Government there is force behind it," Attlee told a party meeting. "We are in favour of the proper use of force for ensuring the rule of law."[21]

The government, in fact, was receiving an almost embarrassing number of affirmations of its apparently firm and determined stand. The Liberal party on 10 October gave "its unswerving support." The archbishop of Canterbury declared of the League of Nations: "The use of military force in the last resort cannot be excluded. If no attempt were made by the State to restrain—if need be by force—those who deny the law anarchy would follow. . . . if there existed any community of nations surely the same considerations would apply."[22]

On 17 October Robert Cecil, leader of the League of Nations Union, wrote to his nephew, Eden's deputy, Lord Cranborne. Blocking the Suez Canal, said Cecil, "would be far the best plan." Minor sanctions were worrisome because they would "merely cause irritation without being definitely effective. Never fire over the heads of rioters!!"[23] When the same suggestion was put to Simon (why not just an accident, a sunken ship would do the job?) his answer told the story: "We couldn't do that: it would mean that Mussolini would fall!"[24]

On 19 October—with public support in hand, with Mussolini's terms for a settlement as transmitted to the French on the sixteenth opening the most promising possibility yet for a negotiated settlement, with the adjournment of the Coordination Committee that had set the League's sanctionist course, and with the French note of the eighteenth laying to rest the disturbing issue of support in case of war—Stanley Baldwin (as Cripps feared) called for a general election, set shortly for 14 November.

It was a well-chosen time. "Our party is united, Labour is torn with dissensions, Liberals have no distinctive policy, L.G. [Lloyd George] has ceased to interest. The issue has been diverted from our weakest point, unemployment and distressed areas." So said Neville Chamberlain on 19 October. He hoped rearmament would be the main issue. "I intend to stress support of the League as an instrument of peace, a new defence programme to enable us to perform our task of peace-preserver, the benefit of this programme to employment. . . ."[25]

Baldwin, however, was "frightened of making defence the *prime* issue."[26] The mood of the electorate he thought, like his own, was directed mainly toward keeping the peace. The day after the Italian invasion Baldwin spoke to a Conservative party gathering and stressed above all the need to avoid war in Europe. As to his other points, Thomas Jones puts it well: he "reconciled the Party to the League by supporting rearmament, and reconciled the pacifists to rearmament by supporting the Covenant." The *Times*'s correspondent wrote that "it was the general feeling that, though strictly speaking the occasion was a party gathering, Mr. Baldwin was speaking as a representative of the whole nation at the most critical moment since the Great War."[27] The government seemed to know what it was doing. The limitations of its policy in the Ethiopian affair were not yet obvious, in Whitehall or in the country. It seemed consistent, as far as it went, and no one intimated it would go as far as war. Start with some rearmament, stick with the League, try to end the African war without betraying the League, and avoid war with Italy. The beauty for Baldwin was that this could be promoted in generalities.

Against this strategy the Labour party, disunited and led by the colorless Attlee, posed little challenge. Parliament sat from 22 October to its prorogation on 25 October with the Treasury bench preempting the Labour opposition's argument for collective security. Hoare asserted a policy of national unity: "I can claim that not only is [the government's policy] the policy of this House but it is also the policy of the great majority of men and women in the country as a whole." Baldwin expanded on this the next day, 23 October. "The policy which has been pursued by His Majesty's Government not only has general support in the country, but it is the policy of the whole British Empire, which is of itself a fact of remarkable importance."[28] No one could deny it. All parties stood behind the Covenant. All renounced any course to war.

Arthur Marwick wrote an article in which he discussed a "very large ground work of social and political 'agreement' . . . [from which] arose the ideological structure which took Britain safely through the forties and brought her to rest in the fifties."[29] The positions Marwick discussed were espoused by forward-looking, center-holding progressives of both parties and included acceptance of a mixed economy, rejection of strict state planning, continuity of economic policy, a form of the welfare state, and opposition both to militant fascism and to communism. Harold Macmillan was a man of such thought.

Another characteristic Marwick saw illustrates that central body of opinion Hoare referred to. This was "the profound conviction as to the utter wrong-headedness of the international politics which had led to World War

I." The League of Nations Union was born of this sentiment, as was support of the Covenant against Italy. Marwick makes a harsh judgement: "One of the most important and most tragically ironic themes in British history in the interwar years is the way in which the "peace movement" in all its aspects grew in force, 'till in the thirties it is an important magnet for men whose entire mental and moral make-up unfitted them for a genuine grasp of its fundamental principles."[30]

Attlee never questioned the policy written into the National party's manifesto, of which Chamberlain was chief draftsman, and, as written, it is hard to see that he might.

> We shall take no action in isolation, but we shall be prepared faithfully to take our part in any collective action decided upon by the League and shared in by its Members. We shall endeavour to further any discussions which may offer the hope of a just and fair settlement, provided that it be within the framework of the League and acceptable to the three parties of the dispute—Italy, Abyssinia, and the League itself.[31]

The best Attlee could do was to challenge the earnestness of the government's intentions. His criticism was rambling and too vague to strike home. Labour's program was "socialism and peace." As for the League, if its members "honestly and whole-heartedly apply economic sanctions, this war can be brought to an end."[32] Attlee's attacks on rearmament and on Chamberlain as warmonger did him little credit.

Meanwhile, the government held out to Italy the opportunity for conciliation. On 19 October Baldwin defined the objective of the League as "peace, and not war," adding, "We are always ready to avail ourselves of any opportunity that may present itself for conciliation." The next day Mussolini wrote to De Bono: "There will be no complications in Europe before the English elections." On the twenty-second Maurice Peterson, head of the recently constituted Abyssinian department in the Foreign Office, was sent to Paris to discuss Mussolini's overture with the French. These talks continued during most of the election campaign, encouraging an open stance toward Italy. In an address of 22 October—"A Statesman's Speech," the *Times* called it—Hoare stressed peace and lack of hostility to Italy and, in the light of Mussolini's threat of reprisal by war if military measures were imposed, discounted the ability of the League (defined by "collective agreement") to go beyond economic sanctions. "I was the first public man . . . outside Italy who admitted [in his speech of 11 September] the Italian case for expansion and economic development," Hoare said. In a cable from Addis Ababa Barton spoke of the depression caused there by Hoare's words, which were seen as weakening the attachment to the Covenant and encouraging a negotiated settlement. When the parliamentary debate was over, Aloisi concluded that war with Britain would be avoided.[33]

The election of 14 November 1935 proved a solid victory for the government. Over half the total vote went to National candidates. The government returned with an overall Commons majority of 242. Baldwin had made no mistakes, summed up Thomas Jones:

> The election is a personal triumph. He timed it correctly in his Party's interest. . . . He has only very slowly and with obvious reluctance proclaimed the need for more armaments. . . . He has strictly confined the extent to which he was prepared to move against Italy and distinguished Mussolini from the Italian people. Labour Pacifists, on the other hand, have clamoured for closing the Suez Canal and other bellicose sanctions. . . . Overall he has thrown that halo of faith and hope, free from meretricious ornament, which inspires confidence.[34]

Baldwin cannot be faulted for choosing the time he did for an election, for stealing the opposition's thunder, for capitalizing on prevailing sentiment, although Eden warned him that "previous khaki elections have a nasty record and I would rather our majority was less striking than that the country should feel any resentment at the way in which we gained it." In the event, Baldwin might have listened more closely to the warning. The public had not, after all, understood the double policy. After the elections secret negotiations took place in an attempt to satisfy Italy. When they were revealed, the public took them to be a betrayal of the League, of Ethiopia, and of the cause the government had most stood for in November: fidelity to the Covenant. In the wake of the Hoare-Laval plan of December 1935 Neville Chamberlain wrote: "If we had to fight the election over again we should probably be beaten."[35]

France

With the popular mandate in its favor, Baldwin's National government stood secure. In contrast, Pierre Laval's ministry of National Union faced an uncertain future. It maintained itself in office by an increasingly unstable parliamentary coalition. Laval, in the first months of the Ethiopian war, faced two exceedingly serious domestic crises: the defense of the franc and the civil strife attendant to the rise of the *ligues*.

The Chamber of Deputies elected in 1932 had returned a large Left majority. In February 1934 came the political-financial scandal of the Stavisky affair. The Right, with much unscrupulous exaggeration, fastened responsibility for this and the subsequent public violence (the worst since the Commune) on the government, and rightist organizations took to the streets to discredit the Radical leadership who, stunned, withdrew from the public scene. To govern France there followed a number of coalition ministries representing the parties of the Right up to and including about half the centrist Radicals.

Laval became premier in June 1935 and served also as foreign minister, a post he had held in the three preceding ministries. Laval, holding the confidence of the governors of the Bank of France, took power to arrest the deteriorating financial situation. His parliamentary mandate was to save the overvalued franc. During the summer and autumn of 1935 his major preoccupation was thus domestic finance, not Italy or Ethiopia. Given exceptional power to govern by decree-law through the end of October, Laval issued hundreds upon hundreds of decrees to halt speculation and the flight of gold and, by the deflationary policies of maintaining a rigid economy and balanced budgets, to restore public confidence. Reviving the economy was a difficult job, likened to energetically blowing air into a leaky tire.[36]

The *ligues* posed the other major internal crisis. By November bands dominated by the Croix de Feu and the Jeunesse patriotes swelled on the militant Right. Opposed to these antirepublicans stood the League for the Rights of Man and, from the Left, the loosely organized but very numerous "self-defense" organizations that rallied to the emerging Popular Front. The Right raised the demand for law and order and the specter of bolshevik revolution. The Left responded with charges of profascism and anticonstitutionalism. Demands to dissolve paramilitary organizations and forbid armed and uniformed groups were taken up by the government, but outbreaks of violence (such as a riot at Limoges in mid-November 1935) raised serious questions about the government's willingness or ability to lessen public tension and further alienated the Left from any cabinet of "national union."

The Left had recovered from the shock of February 1934. Radicals in the Chamber were increasingly unwilling to be joined at the vote with the clerical and nationalist Right. They were convinced that the country was moving leftward. The leadership of the Croix de Feu, capable of brawling, lacked a positive program for government and never became the political force many had foreseen. The royalist Action française stood fast in simple negativism. The Left, meantime, reemerged stronger than ever with the growth of Popular Front sentiment. There was a rapprochement between Socialists and Communists—made possible by a growing awareness of the menace Hitler posed and by the turnabout in Russian policy following Laval's initiatives toward a Franco-Soviet pact. A general election was due in May 1936. The Radicals had overthrown two governments with impunity and without explosion from the rightist *ligues* and were increasingly reluctant to support the government through an unrepresentative majority. Socialists and Communists, while unwilling to take office in a coalition bourgeois government, were spoiling for a fight.

This does not mean that in November 1935 the Radicals wanted to bring Laval down. The party itself was in confusion. The ministries responsible for managing the *ligues* and the economic crisis were both headed by Radicals. The Radicals, who by and large supported Laval's deflationary policy, knew that if they took over the government before spring they would simply inherit the intractable economic difficulties. If the Bank of France withdrew its support they would be held responsible for any panic and devaluation. The months ahead, they hoped, would show the weakness of the National Union government, discrediting it by the time of the elections. On the other hand, to avoid alienating the Left and certainly out of righteous indignation (the target of one of the most virulent attacks from the Right was Herriot), the Radicals insisted on a firm policy of control toward the *ligues.* When the parliament reassembled after recess on 28 November there was before the government fourteen interpellations on financial and economic policy, twenty-one on the *ligues* and the recent acts of violence, and only one on foreign affairs—on the then current negotiations with Italy and Britain concerning Ethiopia.

Laval called for votes of confidence on both finance and the *ligues.* About half the Radical delegates supported his policy of deflation. Herriot, the key to victory, feared a run on gold and devaluation in the event of a Popular Front ministry. The vote on 29 November went 324 to 247. Debate on the *ligues* began on 3 December and concluded on the sixth. A spokesman for the Croix de Feu dramatically proposed disarming all *ligues,* leftist and rightist. This was accepted by Socialist leader Léon Blum who, with the concurrence of Communist leader Maurice Thorez, agreed to dissolve the leftist paramilitary organizations if the Right (which then concurred) did likewise. Laval thereupon tabled three bills that proposed dissolving such groups, making it illegal to carry arms at public meetings, and tightening press laws to suppress incitement to murder. He took the vote of confidence on 6 December by 351 to 219. The Radicals split about in half, Socialists and Communists voting against. "It is impossible for us to consider M. Laval the symbol of national reconciliation," Blum said.[37] The votes, and the laws duly passed and promulgated, relieved the urgency of domestic crisis. "Let's go and eat a dozen oysters," Laval said on 6 December after the vote of confidence. "Tomorrow I have to work for peace; I am meeting Sir Samuel Hoare."[38]

During the summer and early autumn of 1935, foreign affairs had taken third place in public attention. The increasingly serious implications for France of Britain's emphasis on collective security forced official concern, however, and, as the significance of Italian imperialism became better known, argument in the country over France's policy became intense.

Communists followed Moscow's support for collective security as enunciated at Geneva by the Soviet Union's foreign minister, Maxim Litvinov. Socialists, denouncing imperialism, attacked Laval's "personal policy" of compromise. Léon Blum, for one, called for military sanctions and accepted the risk of war as probably necessary to stop the aggression.[39] With the internationalist antifascist Left taking an interventionist stance, the nationalist Right turned against involvement. "Not a man, not a penny," for a war with Italy, declared Pierre Taittinger a rightist deputy and leader of the Young Patriots.[40] The Right, much of the Center, and, it was said, the Russian ambassador Vladimir Potemkin, held the opinion that war would end in the sovietization of Europe.[41] The corollary: if Mussolini fell Italy would go communist. If he was even seriously threatened he might take Italy, and Fascism, radically leftwards. Denouncing Blum as a warmonger, seeing loss and danger for France in sanctions, indeed, fearful for Western civilization, the Right demanded a policy of disengagement from Geneva, good relations with Italy, and acceptance of that government's claim to colonies. The villain of the piece was found, not south of the Alps, but north of the Channel.

September saw an anti-British campaign in the French press unrivaled in its hostility since the Fashoda crisis of 1898. The motives of the British government were impugned. The old charge of hypocrisy came out—the British were hiding behind the League to protect the empire. Because of some strange masonic-liberal hatred of Mussolini, Britain was trying to separate the Latin sisters and drag France into its war. On 11 October Henri Béraud editorialized in *Gringoire:* "I hate England in my own name and in the name of my ancestors. I hate her by instinct and by tradition. I say, and I repeat, that England must be reduced to slavery. . . . Concord between the continental nations alone can save Europe and the world."

There was cold fury in Whitehall over this article. Exasperation and suspicion toward France rose to new heights. Would not Laval control his press better than that? The tension became almost unbearable as the British felt themselves exposed and endangered, unable to count on France. All this was welcome to Mussolini. A month earlier, two weeks before the invasion, he had sent a million lire to each of his ambassadors in Paris and Brussels, instructing them to promote the anti-British and antisanctionist press campaign.[42]

The Left's antifascism and antiimperialism were reinforced by the Italian invasion, but traditional pacificism conflicted with support of possibly military sanctions. No more than the government was the Left ready for France to go to war for Ethiopia. The day after his call for military sanctions Blum published an article in *Le Populaire* (9 October 1935), "Sanctions and Disarmament," in which he argued that collective security would have to be founded on a general renunciation of arms. This was fantasy and no help to the government.

Commentators have noted that the Ethiopian crisis was a "line of demarcation" between Right and Left. "This fissure that opened in 1935 is what
divided France after the defeat" of 1940, wrote Max Gallo.[43] Issues even
broader than the security of France seemed at stake. On the morrow of the
invasion 64 intellectuals, including 12 members of the French Academy and
claiming the adherence of 850 other signatories, published in *Le Temps* a
manifesto calling "for the defense of the west and peace in Europe." The
terms of the conflict, they said, were misconceived. The "dangerous fiction
of the absolute equality of nations" and the "false juridical universalism that
equates superior and inferior, civilized and barbaric," put obstacles in the
way of the mission of civilization. Accepting the Italian contention that sanctions meant war, they argued that such a conflict, "coalescing all anarchies,
all disorders," would spread chaos (read: bolshevism) over Europe and in the
process destroy the superior spiritual, social, and cultural achievements of
Western civilization.

Le Populaire (5 October) called the manifesto "fascist and royalist"
propaganda. On the same day Jules Romains published a counterattack endorsed by fifty other writers and by members of the Committee of Vigilance
of Anti-Fascist Intellectuals. This protested allegations of the inequality of
races and the assumption of an anti-Italian bias among pro-Leaguers and exhorted support from "all governments who fight for peace and for respect
for international law."[44]

Conflict left the papers. A target for rightist attack throughout the war
was the law professor Gaston Jèze. Jèze, whom Eugen Weber described as
"if anything, a man of the right," had early in the conflict lent his expertise to
the Ethiopian ministry in Paris.[45] Here Jèze carried on the tradition of
brilliant, logically compelling diplomacy that made Ethiopia's case before
the world and forced the League into action. This was a product, above all,
of the emperor's skilled and devoted foreign advisers, the Swede Eric Virgin,
the Swiss Jacques Auberson, and the Americans Everett Colson and John
Spencer. The job of the Paris mission was to represent Ethiopia at Geneva
and keep the legal and moral issues alive there. Indeed, Jèze occasionally
took initiatives that went further than Addis Ababa had allowed.

In November 1935, attacking his presumed anti-Italian position, student
demonstrators forced Jèze to suspend his lectures in the Sorbonne. This was
a scandal, and one that worsened the following January and February as
Jèze attempted to resume his teaching under police guard. Hostile rioters
caused the law faculty to request permission to close its doors. Police went to
eject students who had staged a sit-in. The dean of the faculty was struck by
the police and resigned. The rector (in touch with the minister of education)
insisted that the faculty remain open—under police guard—and counter-
demonstrations, protest strikes against the rioters, followed. In March Jèze's

courses were moved elsewhere in Paris, apparently a rightist success, and this further inflamed politics.[46]

Through all this the most lively sentiment among politically influential Frenchmen remained the determination to avoid war with Italy. At a conference of the center-right Democratic Alliance on 16 November, Laval's centrist minister of war, Jean Fabry, drew the picture of a future war: "For every city, for every village, for every family, for every individual, at all times and for weeks and months and perhaps years, restrictions, hard and cruel fatigue, sickness. There would be short supplies, rationed bread, hearths without coal, painful work without joy."[47]

The next day (the day prior to the imposition of sanctions) Pierre-Étienne Flandin, president of the Alliance, a former premier, and soon to be foreign minister during the crucial early months of 1936, spoke to the same conference:

> None of good sense is ignorant that a new war would be, for France, the ruin of its institutions, the irredeemable decadence of its civilization. . . . If other nations think themselves able to accept the risks of war, that is their affair. But in no case will France find itself dragged in in spite of itself. Collective security is a far off ideal. . . . We would be impious to deliver the future security of our children, the children of those who died for the country and for peace, to the hazard of hopes that will be one tragic day deceived.[48]

Fabry's speech on the horrors of war recalls Baldwin's address to the Conservatives on 4 October. With the "march of science," Baldwin had said, the danger of an air war now faced Britain, and if the island perished, the empire would perish with it.[49] Baldwin exaggerated the current danger. The Italian air commander, Giuseppe Valle, was at the moment describing his air force as in a state of crisis, with the majority of the force composed of older units, worthless after several days of hard use. Badoglio used Valle's description to warn Mussolini in September that a war with Britain would be a "true catastrophe."[50] When Baldwin let rise the fear of England "perishing" under an air attack he was projecting a widespread but not universal anxiety. (In April 1936, in the crisis following German remilitarization of the Rhineland, the French air minister, Marcel Deat, spoke against a tendency "of certain persons" to exaggerate the air threat. "It is not true that a city like Paris could be destroyed in a night," he said.[51] German air strength at this time was only half that of France.)

Laval's critics charged that he used and perpetuated the war scare for his own purposes, and they attacked him for panicking public opinion by announcing that Italy wanted war in Europe.[52] There is validity in these charges. It is true that the Italian ambassador was constantly whispering war to him and that Chambrun sent the same warning from Rome, but the French government was less susceptible to the "mad dog" theory than the

British. Although Laval, and after him Flandin, worked hard and successfully to make war unlikely, they did little to set to rest the overcharged atmosphere of public anxiety. Both used the alarm to serve their policies of moderation and appeasement. The fear of war that he sensed in Paris influenced Samuel Hoare when he made his ill-fated visit in December.

What of the Radical party? The Chamber votes on finance and the political *ligues* showed the party divided almost in half and tangled in parliamentary intrigue. The balloting gave votes of confidence to Laval. He was secure as long as he kept Herriot's support, and Herriot endorsed Laval's financial policies. On the other hand, Herriot opposed Laval's foreign policy, especially over Ethiopia. Here he stood almost alone among the Radicals. Still, president of the party and dominating the swing bloc on the left end of the government's supporters, he was capable of bringing down the ministry by stepping out or by engineering a defeat in the Chamber. His position was important to Laval because of this, not because he reflected any general agreement on Ethiopia within the Radical party, for no such agreement existed.

The situation was summed up by Peter Larmour. "Some deputies were anti-Italian; others were not so sure." Some on the conservative side supported Laval's hesitations over the League. Laval, c'est la paix.

> Even among the Radicals who supported the League, the arguments were blunt and unidealistic. . . . The standard sanctionist argument had nothing to do with international law and morality. The British, the argument ran, were forced by their imperial commitments to oppose Italy's justifiable need for expansion. Since France needed the British alliance more than the Italian for defense against Germany, France had to support the League of Nations. Most Radicals showed no concern for the Ethiopians as such. . . . Virtually all Radicals were fully convinced that Italy had a real need, and a right, to expand because of her exploding population.[53]

Where Herriot differed from his rival Édouard Daladier and from most party regulars was in his emphasis on the need for ready application of measures of collective security. Always a staunch proponent of close relations with Britain as essential to France, he now insisted on the unnegotiable quality of France's agreements under the Covenant. "Are we for or are we against the League?" he asked the party congress in late October, in a speech that brought him a letter of appreciation from Alexis Léger at the Quai d'Orsay. Herriot wanted automatic application of sanctions, including the imposition of an oil embargo. At the University of Reading to receive an honorary degree on 1 December, he told Austen Chamberlain that Laval and Paris did not represent the opinion of France at large and that, the firmer the British government, the more support they would get.[54]

Herriot, since August, had been a delegate to the League Assembly, with the assurance that he could act on his convictions. But with Laval, premier and foreign minister, in attendance at most sessions and sitting also on the Council, it was Laval or his deputy who spoke for France. Torn between supporting the government on the vital issue of finance and opposing the drift of foreign policy, Herriot, in Larmour's words, was "reduced to almost abject incoherence." Unwilling to bring the government down, his only strength in the threat of resignation, he stayed on until mid-January 1936, increasingly unhappy with his equivocal position and wounded by venomous attacks for his pro-League stand.[55]

The rest of the Council of Ministers and the chiefs of the armed forces did not share Herriot's strict constructionism. Support for the Covenant could not be denied—too long had popular hopes been associated with France's championship at Geneva. The League, once the present troubles were past, might hold future benefits that it would be foolish to reject in advance. The foreign ministry's ranking permanent officials, eyes on Britain, shared some of Herriot's stress on fulfillment of obligations. But to Laval's mind, the immediate cost of sanctions was too great and not offset by assured gain. France was in no state to play policeman for Europe. The British, for all their fine phrases, equivocated over questions about the specifics of mutual support against possible *German* moves.

Domestic considerations likewise argued caution. Laval justified his innumerable decrees with the hope that by encouraging public confidence business would be inspired and that economic growth would calm social unrest. The Ethiopian crisis jarred this hope. In mid-September the news that the British (without consulting France) were sending the Home Fleet to Gibraltar and reinforcing the Mediterranean Fleet brought home the seriousness of the situation and caused a sharp and severe drop in the prices of bonds and issues. Since Laval's decree laws these had risen steadily; now they collapsed below predecree levels. A growing excess of savings deposits turned almost overnight to an excess of withdrawals. In the six weeks between the invasion of Ethiopia and the advent of sanctions on 18 November, the net withdrawal of gold amounted to 1.5 billion francs.[56]

In Laval's view France could not, and Frenchmen would not, stand the strain and unsettlement of a war with Italy—not, at any rate, without far more clear and definite assurances of British support for France's future European position. He would stand or fall on that. In testimony before the foreign affairs committee of the Chamber on 23 October 1935 he said: "It will be another ministry than mine that would propose military sanctions."[57]

In both France and Britain, once it was determined to avoid a war the governments acted to make war less likely. Speeches stressed the horror of war, and shows of public determination, far from being encouraged or used, were ignored or discounted. On 27 November, a week after the first stage of sanctions went into force, Laval told the nation in a radio address, "I have had and will have only one thought, to protect the peace of your homes."[58]

The policy of caution was endorsed by chiefs of the armed forces. German rearmament created a new situation for France to the east. Rearmament was not in itself surprising, but the level and the pace were greater than anticipated. The French military budget of June 1935 contained appropriations sufficient to the need, but corresponding production was beyond the existing capacity of industry. Now the tension with Italy and the sanctionist stance of France obliged the government to increase these estimates of needs even more, and modernization of equipment, already long overdue, became an ever more acute requirement. Field maneuvers in September (to which Badoglio came as an observer) were the first in two years and, in the words of the war minister, "overabundantly demonstrated the poverty in quality and quantity of our equipment—particularly tanks, the total lack of coordination between air and ground troops, the inability of all concerned to use material in any way defective."[59]

French security seemed to rest all the more on diplomatic skill. For example, the good relations with Italy established by the January accords had permitted the army to plan for the withdrawal of seventeen divisions from southeast France and from north Africa and for repositioning them in the lightly defended northeast above the Maginot Line. In the event, as France found itself constrained to stand alongside Britain and so became ranged against Italy, this benefit of the Italian connection was removed. Of the seventeen divisions, only three were spared to go north to stand against Germany.[60]

Until the complications of the Ethiopian war, Laval had been in the midst of developing a policy by which to reduce French commitments in central Europe. His design was grand, sometimes only half-formulated, and probably misconceived. He yearned for nothing less than a general pacification of Europe, associating as many states as possible in a series of mutual agreements and proclamations, in regional pacts both east and west, largely outside the existing alliance or League frameworks. It was a heady vision, unrealized in the event, but sustaining enough to give him, during the course of 1935, a sense of infallibility.[61] Little, however, worked out. The Franco-Soviet pact was not completed, reflecting Laval's own ambiguity toward it. Nor did anything come of the attempt to insure German favor as his Italian connection—the keystone to his plans—weakened. During the third week of November, as sanctions were about to be imposed, Laval, out of the blue and with nothing concrete to advance, asked Hitler for a public declaration of good neighborliness and mutual trust. So stated, a rapprochement would be a "preamble" for future talks, aimed ultimately at a non-aggression pact. But all this was so vague, the value and purpose of it so uncertain to Berlin, that the request was turned down out of hand.[62]

Laval's planning complemented the defensive attitude dominating French military thinking and embodied in that "army of concrete," the Maginot Line. In March 1935 the minister of war and national defense, Joseph Maurin, said, "Would we not be mad to go, beyond that barrier, to I know not what adventure." The Center deputy Paul Reynaud, whose speech prompted that outburst, commented that "this was public and cynical notice that France was not going to honor the engagements which she had taken toward her allies." In late November 1935, at a meeting in Belgrade of the general staffs of the Little Entente states (Romania, Czechoslovakia, and Yugoslavia), the Yugoslav delegate argued that the three countries could no longer count on effective military assistance from France. In December Laval told the German ambassador that "public opinion was increasingly coming to realize that the French army should only be used in defense of French soil, and in no circumstances beyond France's own frontiers."[63] To be sure, these remarks were made in particular circumstances. Maurin was responding to Reynaud's argument for the establishment of a permanent offensively oriented mobile armored corps such as Charles de Gaulle proposed. Laval was trying to answer German complaints that an alliance with Russia might drag France into an anti-German adventure. Nevertheless, there is no denying that these words reflected strategic thinking in 1935.

The Franco-Soviet pact was a device to put onto other shoulders responsibility for protecting the friendly states of Central Europe. Perhaps (even primarily, suggests Pierre Renouvin) it was meant to disquiet Hitler enough to make him amenable to negotiation.[64] (As it turned out, talks with the Soviets merely permitted French Communists to join the Popular Front opposition to Laval, and Hitler used the Soviet pact as a pretext for remilitarizing the Rhineland.) Good relations with Italy were played to a similar end—making a well-connected France seem more attractive in Berlin. Then too, friendly relations with Italy would keep the dictators apart and reduce friction along the Danube and the Adriatic. France might facilitate a rapprochement between Italy and Yugoslavia, and the job of protecting Austria would be shared.

Ethiopia, therefore, posed a great dilemma for Laval. He favored independently negotiated bilateral or multilateral pacts, not the general prescriptions of Geneva. Yet just when his own skepticism about the value of the Covenant was at its height, there arrived the chance to test its worth. Many states whom Laval courted regionally rallied to the League. France could not stand aloof, especially since the Italian connection and Italy's future involvement in Europe now became uncertain. What of dreams of cooperation when the states of the Little Entente now ranged themselves so emphatically and so precisely against Italy? Should Laval press on to revive the tradition of mutual arrangements when the very states he hoped to bring to accommodation were unexpectedly set against each other? Or should he work for a new order based on the still untried, but at last seemingly promising, fulfillment of collective security through the Covenant?

The problem might not have been so serious. Mussolini recognized that the liberal states could not desert the League. He distinguished between economic sanctions (expected and accommodated to) and military sanctions (which he said meant war) because he knew the former could not be denied if the League was to continue to exist. Mussolini, at least initially, did not want or expect the Ethiopian affair to overturn the European settlement.

The complication was the strong stand taken by the British. As they threateningly moved their ships, as they sent demands for French support in the case of war (demands that were intercepted by the Italians and added fuel to their suspicions), as the British—deny it though they might—took on, or were seen as taking on, championship of the League, Laval found he was less free to play a moderating hand at Geneva or to keep up good relations in Rome.[65]

The closer Laval felt compelled to stand to Britain, the greater his efforts to avoid appearing the opponent to Mussolini. The more he hesitated, the more insistent the British became, determining, meanwhile, to withhold from France guarantees equivalent to what they themselves demanded. So sourness and suspicion grew on both sides of the Channel. After all, said the French, the British moved their ships and inflamed the Mediterranean situation, not as a consequence of article 16, but in their own interests. If this action threatened Italy it was not France's responsibility. Support in time of war would come only from collective action under the Covenant, over which the French had influence, if not veto power.

Yet the tie with Britain could not be dropped. The liberal states had too much in common. There was no better hole for the French, either. "For us Italy is important; England is essential," wrote the chief of the army staff and vice-chairman of the defense council.[66] So at least a semblance of good relations was necessary, even if the tremendous, sometimes psychological, obstacles to anything approaching alliance cooperation could not be overcome.

The day after Béraud's ferocious attack of 11 October in *Gringoire*, Laval privately (not publicly, for his own election to a senate seat was only a week off) told the British ambassador of his dismay. To stem the anti-British propaganda he called four other papers, asking them to show disapproval of such tirades and to publish an appreciation of British friendship.[67] The sustained public rancor of these years, the vehemence of personal attacks, the level of vitriolic hatred appearing in the press, is difficult to imagine in our day. And Laval's power was not complete. His first impulse was to seize *Gringoire.* Instead he asked the proprietor to moderate his tone because of its embarrassing the foreign ministry. The owner replied that, to oppose the government's pro-British policy, he was ready to flood Paris with cheap editions condemning the sanctionist course.[68] But Laval had showed the British his concern and this ended the issue.

On 18 October came the French note of immediate assurance in case of war, thus ending that "grave and distasteful" chapter of contention. London denied French allegations of indirect and perhaps unwitting interference in French internal politics, pressures supposedly aimed at strengthening Herriot and opposing Laval (some said in Paris that the British secret service worked to overthrow the ministry).[69] Indeed, as we saw, sentiment in the Foreign Office was that Herriot might only bring fresh trouble, as he could not carry the Right. Leftist governments, Wigram noted, were likely to be "inefficient and inept." The Right, including the general staff and industry and finance, had to approve a pro-League, pro-British policy for it to work. So better they in power than Herriot, who might further unsettle France, run the risk of riot, bear the tag of an English hireling, and be unable to carry the country. Better, because more stable, said Wigram, a rightist government carrying out what appeared to be a leftist policy of cooperation with the League, in the genuine interests of an attachment with Britain.[70]

These matters settled, Laval in mid-October could turn his attention to the League, fulfill the obligations asked from Geneva (economic and financial sanctions), avoid all suggestion of military or provocative measures, formally give the British what they wanted, and turn, in clear conscience, toward what he thought would be the most sensible way of settling the whole affair—negotiation.

He asked the British, in the note of 18 October, to join in a public declaration that military sanctions were excluded. This would end misunderstandings and reduce suspicion, hostility, and tension in Italy. The British government, about to embark on the election campaign, refused and ignored Laval's contention—formally incorrect, for Hoare's statements were provisional—that he and Hoare had, a month before, "agreed to exclude, in any contingency, measures other than economic or financial arrangements." The French, more open about their intentions, were annoyed that the British would not speak their minds. Four days before, at a meeting of the Committee of Imperial Defence, Ramsay MacDonald had urged that the question of military sanctions not even be brought up; it was "essential that ministers be in a position to say that no discussion on the subject had taken place."[71]

4   GETTING SET

Sanctions Established

The Coordination Committee adjourned on 19 October 1935 after recommending to participating governments four measures against Italy: an embargo on arms and ammunition, prohibition of loans and credits, refusal to accept Italian exports (except books, newspapers, maps, and printed music), and an embargo on certain war-related materials the major part of which customarily went to Italy from members of the League. In addition, a declaration of mutual support was urged, by which economic losses incurred by states supporting article 16 would be offset by other sanctionist countries.

These recommendations were distributed on the twenty-first. By the time the Coordination Committee reconvened on 31 October, some fifty states had indicated adherence. In the ten-day interim—a somewhat anxious time in Geneva, for the replies of Britain and France did not come for a week—news of each acceptance was relayed immediately, to encourage the others, by the League's Radio-Nations. One of the surprises of the time, an observer noted, "was to learn how complete the world's wireless equipment has become," adding hopefully, "and how easily the League can organize it in an emergency."[1]

On 2 November the committee fixed 18 November as the date when each participating state would implement these sanctions. Alexander Loveday of the financial and economic section of the Secretariat served as secretary to the committee. A committee of experts headed by Karl Westerman of Sweden was established to verify and keep in accord the measures of application undertaken by the various governments. Liaison was established with the International Labor Organization by Hugh MacKinnon Wood of the Secretariat's legal staff.

A few states (Austria, Albania, and Hungary) did not participate. Switzerland and Venezuela reserved full cooperation. Other states presented reasonable technical questions. Did aluminum and aluminum oxide in proposal 4 apply only to raw aluminum or also to semifinished products? The answer: "It depends on the individual governments applying sanctions in giving detailed instructions to their customs authorities, to decide to which items of their customs nomenclature the embargo should apply." Romania wondered about the recovery of 10 million dollars (all figures in 1935 values) of credit outstanding to Italy. What was its claim to this credit now? Chileans customarily sent copper and nitrates to Italy between July and November; payment was made between December and April. Shipments for 1935 were complete and some 5 million dollars was due. Did their claims hold? An airplane was sent from Belgium to Italy for repairs in April. Could Belgians now import the newly installed Italian parts? In March France contracted with an Italian agency to lay a telephone cable the short distance from Modane to the Italian frontier. Could they import replacements of material found defective?

On outstanding claims, the Coordination Committee decided, debts payable by Italy remained valid and collectible. The Committee of Eighteen decided that if sums due for a contract engaged were paid prior to 19 November, as in the Belgian and French cases, exception could be made for importing Italian parts. A number of like cases were submitted, and each was judged on its merits. A special subcommittee gave its opinion on specific exceptions to general policy. Altogether the exceptions granted, all entirely reasonable, represented an insignificant value of less than 2 percent of total Italian exports for 1934.[2]

On the whole, the participating states, accounting for some two-thirds of Italy's export market (1933 base), entered into sanctions on 18 November with good grace and apparent determination. Nonetheless, the press of sanctions was unequal and so, eventually, was the degree of application. Australia, remote and with minute trade, argued the need for successful precedents and adopted strong penalties for breach of sanctions by its nationals—an unlimited fine or three years' imprisonment. Romania, immediately affected, noted that 36 million dollars of profit from normal trade was now "sacrificed on the altar of the League" in exchange for "a piece of paper promising compensations."[3] No help was immediately forthcoming, but Romania stood by loyally. Mutual economic assistance was a matter of greatest importance. For states closely involved with Italy, success depended on how well the burdens shouldered by participating states were shared and offset among themselves.

The five proposals of the Coordination Committee were also sent, on 21 October, to states that were not members of the League with the comment that the committee "would welcome any communication." Egypt agreed to cooperate in sanctions; Brazil refused; Japan made no reply. But most attention was directed toward Germany and the United States. Here the League's démarche was caution itself. The governments there were given an opportunity to declare neutrality, while they were privately informed that it would help the League if exports to Italy could be kept to the average of the two preceding years. Great care was taken to avoid the appearance of in any way exerting pressure or interfering with precious independence.

Considerable sacrifice, political and economic, was asked of participating members. Trust and a sense of common purpose alone were to prevent one country from benefiting at the expense of another. Local authorities had to determine whether Italy was the point of origin or the ultimate destination of products crossing a border, regardless of the address on the label. Indirect supply, through colonial possessions, for example, or direct supply by false bills of lading had to be prevented if the system was to hold together, and this depended largely upon trust.

But what of the great outsiders? No one wanted the vacated markets to be immediately filled from a nonparticipating state. If Canada gave up nickel shipments, how disheartening if Americans (who processed Canadian nickel) seized the trade. This concern was expressed by the editor of *Le Temps,* Jacques Chastenet, who said on 19 November, "The financial and capitalist powers outside the League are free to mock it and pursue their search of gain in a disordered world. . . . France alone pays the cost of an insensate policy."[4] If Germany and the United States held their trade in embargoed products to a prewar level, they would at least not neutralize League action or make the sacrifices seem in vain.

The fourth proposal, for a direct export embargo, enumerated only certain goods, raw materials over which League members exercised control: raw rubber, iron ore, bauxite, tin, aluminum, and some other minerals. Left aside was a second group of materials, oil, cotton, coal, and coke, and, at least subject to being so interpreted, processed goods made from the materials listed in proposal 4, including iron and steel.

On 19 October, as the Committee of Eighteen considered the nature of the export embargo, Spain's Salvador de Madariaga protested the illogicality of excluding finished iron products and urged that they be included in proposal 4. Eden and the French delegate, Robert Coulondre, answered that the major suppliers of iron products stood outside the League and the intent of the proposal was for more certain control. This reasoning bothered the Canadian representative, Walter Riddell, concerned that Laval was playing Mussolini's game. What Italy wanted, he said, was in fact the finished products—tin cans, not tin ore. Sanctions must be comprehensive. Riddell's argument, unsupported by Britain or France, was turned aside, and proposal 4 was not extended to finished products.[5]

When the Committee of Eighteen met on 2 November to consider the date of entry for the proposals, the Spanish delegate (this time R. R. Cantos y Saiz de Carlos) again raised the issue of "logic and principle" in the matter of finished iron products. These, he argued with unassailable reasoning, were more useful to Italy's war effort than the raw materials from which they are made and should have been at the head of the list: "The object of every measure taken at Geneva must be to bring real pressure to bear on the Italian Government in order to prevent it from continuing the war. But the embargo on iron ore would bring no pressure to bear, because the Italian Government would have all the iron and steel it wanted." Coulondre responded. The recommendation, "though logical, was not practical." Further, the cost to Italy of buying steel was greater than that of buying ore, and the aim of sanctions was to diminish Italy's purchasing power. Augusto de Vasconcellos, the Portugese delegate, said that, while the Committee of Eighteen could not modify the list of the Coordination Committee (he was chairman of both), it could add iron and pig iron "as the Canadian delegate proposed." This was the setting for the resolution that Riddell then made that oil, coal, iron, and steel be added to the embargo list "in principle" and that this extension be brought into operation as soon as its acceptance appeared to be sufficiently general to ensure its efficacy, with the Committee of Eighteen to propose a date for bringing this extension into operation.[6]

Riddell's proposal, however, went beyond the restraints of caution and control on which proposal 4 was based and opened the problem of action by nonmember states. Riddell himself was shortly thereafter disavowed by Ottawa and removed from the Committee of Eighteen, victim of the fear of involvement and of the risk implied by this expansion of sanctions. The new (as of 23 October) prime minister, Mackenzie King, even wanted him dismissed from the diplomatic service. Eden, in his memoirs, discounted Riddell's responsibility, recalling the "business-like" meetings in which the committee "worked as a team." Of the inclusion of oil Eden wrote, "Though supplies of oil were regarded as important, they were not then considered as outstanding or decisive as they later became."[7]

The opening of the oil question developed from the objections of and was part of a response to the Spanish delegation's position on the matter of iron goods. In the *Official Journal* Riddell's resolution comes under the heading of an issue raised by Spain, and when the proposal was presented to the Subcommittee on Economic Measures on 4 November, the chairman introduced it simply as "closely connected with the Spanish motion concerning the embargo on iron ore."[8]

This is not to discount the importance of Riddell's initiative and the independence of his stand. His concern with comprehensiveness and his suspicions of the French made him a likely author of this step. Unable to get instructions from Ottawa in time, Riddell acted largely on his own. It is now apparent that he misinterpreted the Canadian government's position toward sanctions, which was one not of genuine support but of grudging acquiescence. Riddell recognized the significance of his move. His list would "do more to defeat Italy than all the other sanctions together."[9]

Riddell's list was not to be imposed at once. Outside the League, warned Coulondre, "there were countries—one in particular—with a considerable production of oil." Riddell's resolution asked only for a decision on principle, and "was not to come into force pending the accession of the nonparticipating countries whose cooperation was required for the effectiveness of the measure proposed."[10] This was the general understanding. The final wording, drafted by a favorably disposed subcommittee composed of the delegates of Canada, Spain, Poland, and the Soviet Union and accepted by the Committee of Eighteen as proposal 4-A, was complete and definite as to the measures to be sanctioned and was qualified as to the terms of implementation. The embargo would cover the full range of products made derived from oil, iron, and coal. It would be proposed upon realization of "the conditions necessary to render this extension effective."

On 7 November this proposal was accepted in principle as a second round of sanctions and was formally submitted to member governments. It was left to the Committee of Eighteen, if warranted by the replies "and the information at its disposal," to propose a date for the extension to go into force.[11] Thus the sanctions listed under 4-A, while disassociated from those going into effect on 18 November, were a progressive and potentially very serious intensification of pressure on Italy. The question of nonmember action was clearly drawn—all the more important became the position of the governments in Washington and Berlin.

Not Quite Neutral

When De Bono's armies crossed the Mareb River on 3 October 1935, President Franklin Roosevelt was off the California coast beginning a fishing and relaxation cruise, not to return to Washington until 24 October. Earlier, Secretary of State Cordell Hull had prepared a series of proclamations that, when he heard of the invasion, Roosevelt ordered released at once.

Policy, and the nature of the proclamations, was determined by the neutrality act of 31 August 1935 and by the administration's anxiety to avoid stirring up isolationist opinion in Congress. The act, a joint resolution in effect until the end of February 1936, was designed to constrain Roosevelt over the congressional recess, during which time Congress expected the Italian crisis to erupt. The United States was to stay uninvolved in the conflict or in any troubles arising from the imposition of sanctions. Roosevelt was to proclaim "upon the outbreak or during the process of war" an embargo on the shipment of "arms, ammunition, or the implements of war" to all belligerent countries.

The president could decide when to apply this embargo. He could, in theory, wait until the last hour of the conflict before declaring the existence of a state of war. This was an important consideration if he wanted to see whether the British were drawn in. But, sympathetic to Ethiopia's plight and annoyed at Mussolini's aggressive violence, Roosevelt on 4 October ordered Hull to issue the declarations. Hull delayed until the night of the fifth. From Geneva the minister to Switzerland, Hugh Wilson, advised delay. Wait, he said, to see which way "the states over here are going to jump." An immediate proclamation "might influence the decision of the Council and involve us in responsibility for the course of action which they adopt. Other states might use a declaration of neutrality by America to declare their own, dealing a death blow to collective action by the League."[12]

But it was precisely because the administration wanted to preserve its independence, not because it was motivated by idealism or an internationalist wish to influence the League, that Hull acted promptly. There were two days of continuous debate within the Department of State on the timing of the announcement. With Hull, determined to preserve the image of American independence and to avoid any implication of cooperation with the League, stood R. Walton Moore, his close friend and fellow ex-congressman, and Joseph Green, chief of the Office of Arms and Munitions Control. Arguing for delay until the League formulated its own position stood Undersecretary William Phillips; head of the Near Eastern Division, Wallace Murray; economic adviser Herbert Feis; legal adviser Green Hackworth; and chief of the Western European Division, James Dunn. All agreed that in any case, whether it came sooner or later, an American announcement would have to precede any statement of position from Geneva. As Hull said, it was necessary to "state an attitude about trade with the belligerent countries before a formal request is made to us about sanctions." The joint resolution insisted on an arms embargo; the League would surely make this one of its initial sanctions. By acting first the administration hoped to avoid any suggestion of cooperation, to avoid, in Hull's words, giving "deadly ammunition" to isolationist critics. Roosevelt later observed that "by checking the dates you will see that, as a matter of fact, we have preceded Great Britain and the League in every move made."[13]

Aboard the U.S.S. *Houston* with the president on the morrow of the invasion, Interior Secretary Harold Ickes recorded that "sympathies of everyone were with Ethiopia." This was true in the country at large. The Ethiopian war "caused Americans to turn against Mussolini."[14] This did not mean that the citizenry was ready to embrace the League. Yet there was a quickening of interest in Geneva, a turning away from the neglect of the early postwar years when communications from the League had been ignored and correspondence unanswered.

The Department of State in the early 1930s realized the inconvenience in the lack of liaison. Existing informal arrangements, such as relying for information on Arthur Sweetser of the Secretariat, were inadequate. In 1930 Prentiss Gilbert had been made consul in Geneva. Gilbert maintained a "school for ambassadors" and sat at the Council table during the Manchurian crisis. He was of the consular, not the diplomatic service, however, and this handicapped his ability to negotiate. In 1932 Hugh Wilson, minister in Berne, had established himself in Geneva as well, but Gilbert and Wilson were not matched. Personally they got along poorly; professionally they and their staffs were rivals. Gilbert became increasingly bitter and heartbroken with the neglect and isolation he and his people received from the foreign service officers, and he with a staff four times the size of the legation's.[15]

In 1933 the department considered a plan to send to the League a permanent representative with the rank of ambassador. In December 1934 Roosevelt agreed, as an opening move toward American entrance. The next month, however, Congress rejected a bid for American adherence to the Permanent Court of International Justice. This made plans for formal connections with international organizations seem premature, and the idea of an ambassador to the League was dropped.[16] On 9 October 1935 Hull instructed Wilson to discourage any invitation to participate in any way with sanctions. The country, following its "own policies and limitations," would maintain an independent course in the light of developing circumstances.[17]

It was to be an independent course, but not one calculated to stand in the way of sanctions. The timing was considered in view of its impact abroad. Prior to Roosevelt's proclamations on 5 October, Hull had canvassed the British to see if they had any objection to an immediate presidential statement. No, Hoare replied, "the sooner the better." The proclamations were influential at Geneva, and appreciated. Mussolini had deliberately refrained from a declaration of war.[18] The president's assertion that a state of war existed was the first official acknowledgment of this fact and helped to gather support for activating article 16. There was no room left for Laval's suggestion that the Council might draw a distinction between "recourse to war" (which led to action under the Covenant) and simple "hostilities." When the Committee of Eighteen met to draw up its proposal for an arms embargo, it followed Eden's suggestion and adopted, "for practical purposes, and not for any political reason," exactly and entirely the prohibition list proclaimed by Roosevelt.[19] The political dimension was not absent. When the Board of Trade and the Air Ministry in London objected to the inclusion of civil aircraft, Hoare was adamant: "We most certainly cannot afford even to appear to lag behind the Americans."[20]

On 5 October, in addition to the arms embargo, Roosevelt declared that all Americans doing business with either belligerent did so at their own risk. The next day, against the advice of Hull, who thought Italians would take it as a "gratuitious affront" and "in the nature of a sanction," the president withdrew government protection from travelers on vessels of the belligerent nations. These measures, technically neutral, of course, affected maritime, solvent Italy rather than landlocked, shipless, creditless Ethiopia. So Roosevelt intended, and he wanted to go further.[21] On 10 October, imagining discretion to interpret "munitions of war," he asked Hull to consider adding to the embargo list such materials as processed copper and steel and making public the names of persons trading even in nonprohibited materials. While the United States "cannot and will not join other nations in sanctions," Roosevelt said, it should be made clear at Geneva that the government would "go as far as laws allow to avoid giving material assistance to belligerents to further their conducting" war.[22]

Hull opposed publicizing the names of exporters. It was too early to say whether the administration had their support, and they could take refuge in dummy fronts. Hull recommended staying in "cooperative method with our public at the moment." Herbert Feis saw two other objections to the publicity Roosevelt suggested. It was the responsibility of the government, not the public, to decide what was to be allowed. Furthermore, the value of publicity rested on a sense of wrongdoing in trade, something Feis thought many Americans, sympathetic though they might be to Ethiopians, did not feel.[23]

Seeing them as fettering executive prerogative in foreign policy, the Department of State regretfully conceded the mandatory provisions of the joint resolution. It remained for the administration to define implements of war. This had been done in September by the National Munitions Control Board, headed by Hull and including the secretaries of the Treasury and Commerce Departments and the service chiefs. For convenience Hull limited the list to obviously military articles. This list was what made up the embargo proclaimed on 5 October as sanction proposal 1.

This narrow list was apparently regarded at first as provisional. Hull indicated as much to the cabinet, and Roosevelt, we saw, thought of adding to it.[24] When it was published in September, officials in the department indicated that the administration could, and might, extend the list to cover "borderline" raw materials. The secretary of commerce echoed Hull in talking about commodities that might be added "in light of future developments." When the American ambassador, Robert Bingham, consulted Hoare on 8 October, he said Roosevelt was ready to "consider a wider definition if and when the League adopted an embargo of wide scope."[25] The next day Hoare reported this news to the cabinet, adding the ambassador's assurance. Hoare speculated that a wider embargo might even include cotton—surely an important concession of the Americans. Two days earlier, however, the chief of the Office of Arms and Munitions Control had told French officials that while the president could proclaim additions, "an extension of the list to include raw materials would involve stretching the terms 'arms, ammunition and implements of war' beyond its recognized meaning." He pointed out that the joint resolution avoided the term *munitions,* which had a "general meaning and which could easily be understood to involve various raw materials."[26]

On 10 October an unambiguous opinion from the State Department's influential legal advisor, R. Walton Moore, ended the hope of keeping as free a hand as possible, of holding a threat of further embargo, of flexible response to League actions. Moore, eager not to offend the isolationists on Capitol Hill who were already planning new neutrality legislation for February, pointed out that the intent of Congress was clearly narrow construction. Senate debate had been conducted with reference to an arms traffic convention wherein armaments were strictly defined as those directly contrived for use in combat. Wheat, corn, and cotton were excluded in the same debate. The intent was so clear, Moore said, that the courts would uphold it against any attempt to broaden the enumeration to include raw materials or other finished goods. This settled the matter. The department concluded that redefinition was impossible without action by Congress.[27]

Roosevelt accepted this. A *New York Times* editorial on 24 October urged embargo extension to "food, copper, chemicals, oil and cotton." In a private letter the president gave his response. Under normal circumstances these are not "implements of war. The letter of the law does not say so and the trouble is this spirit of the law, as shown by the debates during its passage, does not allow me to stretch it that far out—no matter how worthy the cause." This conclusion was not made public, permitting speculation and perhaps also enjoining caution abroad. Within the administration, except for some specialists on the Far East with an eye to teaching Japan a lesson, few counseled bold leadership. Feis entitled two lectures on this period "The Great Agony of Indecision" and "The Vacuum beyond the Neutrality Proclamations."[28]

If extension of the embargo was judged impossible, how was the administration to make good its wish not to thwart the League? The answer was the moral embargo, an appeal to private restraint. Hull expected more from this than he got. The appeals had too little bite. Henry Stimson, Hull's predecessor as secretary of state, urged strong leadership. Instead of simply regarding both belligerents alike, Stimson said, a more significant distinction should be drawn between Italy's violation of international agreements and the efforts of the League to uphold them, and policy should follow accordingly.[29] Neither Hull nor Roosevelt cared to go that far, so they were limited to appeals to Americans for a spirit of neutrality and reflections on the wish to localize and shorten the conflict.

Signaling abroad, Roosevelt and Hull did time their most forceful statements with a major occasion of the League. Government policy, Hull said on 30 October just before the second session of the Coordination Committee, was to "discourage dealings" with the belligerents, and Roosevelt spoke against accepting "tempting trade opportunities" that might prolong the war.[30] On 15 November, on the eve of sanctions, Hull said, and note a veiled form of the publicity threat:

> The American people are entitled to know that there are certain commodities such as oil, copper, trucks, tractors, scrap iron, and scrap steel which are essential war materials, although not actually "arms, ammunition and implements of war" and that, according to recent Government trade reports, a considerably increased amount of these is being exported for war purposes. This class of trade is directly contrary to the policy of this Government . . . as it is also contrary to the general spirit of the recent Neutrality act.[31]

A much stronger statement was prepared for delivery by Roosevelt. Two days before, Hull had submitted a text to the president listing the same materials, followed by an "appeal to our citizens to enter into no new transactions to furnish the materials above named to the belligerents." This, said Hull, would carry the government "one step further," proposing a "ban" on these products.[32] The statement was never made, and Hull could not make so strong an appeal on his own.

A *Fortune* magazine poll of public opinion taken in late 1935 indicated that a plurality (47.9 to 40.8 percent) favored economic pressure in cooperation with other states to preserve international peace and that Americans were not fearful of provoking a war. Nevertheless, the moral embargo failed to arrest increases over prewar levels. Trade with Italy in war-related goods in the last quarter of 1935 was almost 20 percent above the comparable period in 1934. The administration, Brice Harris notes, had hoped that "an outraged public would force recalcitrant companies to reform or would demand more effective legislation from Congress."[33]

During October and November the government had moved cautiously in an internationalist direction and showed signs of good wishes toward the League. The next move was for Geneva. The proposed second round of sanctions included oil, but by the end of November no action had been taken by oil-exporting League countries that was as strong as the (admittedly minor) pressures exerted on American firms by the United States government. While the American Shipping Board Bureau prevented the sale of a ship to Italy and held up the transport of oil on a vessel to which it held the mortgage, Iran continued as the third largest supplier of Italy's oil and the second of its gasoline, and in the Anglo-Iranian Oil Company the British government held over half the ordinary shares, the controlling interest.[34] On the matter of petroleum the American government was ahead of the British. Hull's speech of 15 November mentioned oil, which was more than any sanction did.

Schadenfreude

No state drew more advantage from the Ethiopian war than Germany. Out of the League since 21 October 1935—a "proud day in Germany history," Minister of the Interior Wilhelm Frick called it—the Germans were free agents and watched, satisfied, as systems meant to contain them twisted in the strain. *Schadenfreude,* pleasure in others' misfortune, was the dominant sentiment in the government, tempered by caution. There seemed little to lose and perhaps much to gain from a quarrel in which Germany was not involved.

There was no reason to be overtly pro-Italian. Indeed, the initial impression in Berlin was that the war had emerged from an anti-German posture on the part of the Italians. The Ethiopian enterprise was launched when relations with Germany were sour, in the wake of Mussolini's strong stand in 1934 against the attempted Nazi coup d'etat in Vienna, when Mussolini sent troops toward the Brenner Pass. There followed an abusive press campaign against German ambitions and the entente with France in January 1935 —clearly anti-German. The Ethiopian undertaking, in its first stages in early 1935, was construed in Berlin as reflecting Italy's new confidence. The tie with France and the assurance of French collaboration showed the small value Italians put upon improving relations with Germany. The old fears of isolation rose. If war came between Italy and Britain, some officials contemplated, Germany might assume an openly pro-British position and perhaps even return to the League as a means of winning approval in London.[35]

By summer 1935, however, after this period of suspicion and animosity, German officials saw that the increasingly complicated affair held dangers as well as benefits for them.[36] As international opposition grew and French support was shown to be weak, it appeared that it would be Italy who faced isolation. This meant a weakening of the Stresa front. That was to the good. On the other hand, play toward Britain was not bringing in much. There was the naval agreement of June, useful, but not of pro-German inspiration. No loans or concessions or much abatement of suspicion came forth. As Britain took on a pro-League role other problems arose. League action against Italy was regarded, and not the least by the Russian Litvinov, as a test case. If Italy were stopped, Germany might be stopped later. For what else was it a "test"?

In the summer of 1935 the German foreign office decided on strict neutrality. Neutrality permitted watching without commitment. Time would show what benefits to draw, what moves to make. The Italians, looking then for all the help they could get, complained that efforts to improve relations led to no "practical cooperation." Foreign Minister Konstantin von Neurath replied in June to Ambassador Ulrich von Hassell in Rome: Why should Germany help Italians impose hegemony in the Balkans? Aid to Italy in leaving the League would only blacken Germany's name in London. "We have no occasion to hasten to extricate the Italians from this predicament. Perhaps one day a situation will arise therefrom which will enable us to discuss and settle the Austrian problem with Italy."[37] An Italy preoccupied in Africa was an Italy less involved in the Alps and the Adriatic. Let Abyssinia replace Austria as the center of attention. Italian imperialism also revived the German colonies question, which was being raised with the British.[38] Lastly, an ostentatiously neutral stance gave credibility to Hitler's image as a pacific statesman. Prudently avoiding the appearance of being pro-Italian, the Germans thereby avoided European reaction.[39]

The German government, of course, did not want Mussolini to fall or turn left. No more than the pope or John Simon did Hitler want to see bolshevism on the peninsula. Almost as bad, worried Hassell, would be Italy's sinking, in case of defeat, "into complete vassalage to France."[40] Little support, then, but also little opposition, was Germany's course. "If I had taken a stand against Italy then," Hitler reflected in 1943, "it would have collapsed immediately."[41] But a standing Fascist Italy was a monument to dictatorship. A strong Italy that looked southward was a constant distracting pressure on British spheres of influence. The task before the Germans, as long as Fascism was not seriously threatened, was to prolong the Ethiopian war, to fish in the troubled waters and react to events they saw no ready need to influence.

Some secret hope was given to Ethiopia. Repeated assertions were made to Rome in April, May, and June 1935 that the German government was in no way helping the emperor.[42] In July, in the face of these denials and on the personal order of Hitler, Neurath authorized sending to Ethiopia, as a gift, some 10,000 rifles, 10 million cartridges, and additional arms, worth 350,000 marks (drawn from secret funds). Some shipments through German ports were arranged for arms bought elsewhere, primarily in Czechoslovakia. A consignment (via Norway and Belgium) of a large shipment of weapons, worth 1.2 million marks, came shortly after the outbreak of the war.[43] Such material aid, the emperor acidly pointed out later, was more than any other country gave for Ethiopia's defense. But beyond this the Germans did not go. The government turned down requests from Ethiopian representatives for credit, for permission to purchase through German subsidies abroad, and for aircraft.[44]

Limited help to Ethiopia—but limited help to Italy, too. Mussolini's later claim that the Axis was born in the autumn of 1935 was sheer rhetoric. Massimo Magistrati, who was sent to Germany in August with the new ambassador, Bernardo Attolico, to warm up relations kept cool by the preceding envoy, Vittorio Cerruti, said, "We certainly did not see this [an emerging Axis] in Berlin at the time."[45] German officials that autumn thought sanctionist pressure and British opposition, or Italian military incapacity, would keep victory distant.[46] So, far from open support, Germans behaved with much restraint. An Axis could not have been built from German policy as it stood in the early months of the war. Further inspiration was necessary to forge a conjunction of the dictators, and this came later in reaction to Blum's Popular Front government in Paris, from Italian fears of close British-German relations, from Hitler's false assurances about Austria, as well as from Italy's eventual victory in Ethiopia and over the League and the success of Hitler's dramatic remilitarization of the Rhineland. During the Ethiopian conflict, relations between the two countries were not "inspired by mutual pursuit of friendship and aid."[47]

Italy did not ask much help, and the German government, lacking political need, was not ready to subsidize aid. A decision was made in October not to sell 500,000 rifles to Italy because the price offered did not cover the cost of production. Thereafter, public policy forbade sale of arms to both belligerents. The arms traffic to Italy during the conflict, in the words of Manfred Funke, was "absolutely insignificant."[48]

Restraint and prudence characterized commercial dealings. On 18 October the government, fearing devaluation of the lira, advised German industrialists to take payment in gold. On the twenty-fifth the press was told that sanctions were an economic question at the moment. On 6 November export controls were imposed on many goods. On 1 December Italians were informed that gold alone was acceptable for coal purchases. This was viewed in Rome as an unfriendly act and was modified in agreements made in Munich on 20 December: two-thirds in clearing credit was allowed. German economic interest came first.[49] A note relating to the Munich agreements stated that authorities would determine "before granting the export permit, whether Germany's internal economic supply position allows of the export being effected or no." Hitler told the Polish ambassador Józef Lipski on 18 December that he thought in terms of the economic situation of German mines, where "each ton of exported coal contributes to the reduction of unemployment."[50]

As it turned out, by careful purchasing, stockpiling, and keeping existing sources open, Italy did not need much from Germany beyond coke and coal. This meliorated the impact of the close, nationalist restrictions of the German market. Italy's dropping her western connections and turning toward

Germany was a good threat with which to belabor the French and British, and eventually it came to pass. But distrust on both sides remained strong throughout the Ethiopian war. Mussolini concluded that there was little favor to be had from Germany and that it was Hitler who restricted either open or covert commercial relations during the war. Hitler, Italians remembered, was born an Austrian.[51]

On 21 October the president of the Coordination Committee asked non-member states for their views regarding the sanction proposals adopted on the nineteenth. Albert Speer recalled Hitler's views: "This was the moment, Hitler remarked, when he had to decide whether he should ally himself with the English or the Italians. The decision must be taken in terms of the long view, he said. He spoke of his readiness to guarantee England's empire in return for a global arrangement, a favorite idea of his. . . . But circumstances left him no choice. They forced him to decide in favor of Mussolini." The decision was a tip toward Italy, and Hitler was gratified when the sanctions imposed were so mild. According to Speer, Hitler concluded that both Britain and France were "loath to take any risks and anxious to avoid any danger."[52]

In practice, all this meant at the moment was that, British urgings to the contrary, Germany would stay neutral. "Participation by Germany [in sanctions] is out of the question," Foreign Minister Neurath had established. But while staying aloof from sanctions gratified Italians, little was done to help them. On 21 October came Hitler's view that the coal trade (the principal export item to the peninsula) must remain below the "optimum attained up to the coming into force of economic sanctions against Italy." On 9 November, after seeing how the United States proposed to act, the German government, likewise stressing its independence of Geneva, issued a law (proposed some months earlier, incidentally, with an eye to the domestic response) strictly regulating exports and imports, supplementing the already enforced prohibition of war materials to both belligerents. The reason given was to protect the "home market," to conserve materials and protect the economy from "the indirect effects of sanctions," to end panic purchases and profiteering deals which resulted in important raw materials being drained away from Germany.[53]

Thereafter the Germans waited on events. British irresoluteness perplexed Hitler. Italy could be forced back or brought to favorable terms, and he did not understand why the British failed to do either—unless they were too weak.

German neutrality neither helped nor hindered Italy. The political report on Germany drawn up at the end of 1935 by the Italian foreign ministry concluded that the relations with that state ended the year in an "atmosphere of continued uncertainty."[54] Not until sometime around the end of January

1936 did Hitler decide that Mussolini would win in the field, refuse compromise, and be satisfied only with victory and that no war in Europe would
ensue.[55] It was then that he decided to take advantage of the Ethiopian affair,
to move troops into the Rhineland without, at that particularly delicate moment for Italy in early March, bothering to inform Mussolini.

No Arms for Ethiopia

The Ethiopian government needed more than a well-argued judicial position
and widespread popular sympathy. It needed money and permission to buy
arms. Nothing came from attempts in summer 1935 to secure loans in London and Berlin. Upon the outbreak of war the British were again asked for
credit. The request was refused, with the suggestion that Ethiopia try the
League.[56]

On 1 November 1935, citing its limited resources, its depleted treasury,
and the difficulties raised by trade embargoes, the Ethiopian government
asked League members for financial assistance. The request was based on a
draft convention, adopted by the Assembly in 1930, which stated the importance of "creating a system of financial assurance in the form of guarantees
for loans to be given in the event of international disputes likely to lead to a
rupture or in case of war." The first article was specific: a member state the
victim of aggression "shall at his request receive the financial assistance provided in the present convention." Article 3 defined this assistance as "ordinary guarantees and special guarantees covering . . . the service of loans
(which term shall include short term credits)" which the government in question would float. The draft convention was not in force but, as the Ethiopian
note pointed out, sanctions themselves were voluntary.

The request went the rounds of the Secretariat. All agreed that the convention was designed to meet a situation such as that Ethiopia faced. But what
about procedure? Ethiopia needed money immediately. Appropriately, the
Council could ask a few financially powerful states to make the necessary
arrangements. The next regular session of the Council, however, was not until January 1936. No official thought it was possible to call a special session.
Frank Walters of the Secretariat, therefore, with Avenol's agreement, concluded on 9 November that, as no treaty obligation was involved, it was unlikely that the Ethiopian request would "lead to any practical result."[57]

No government took up the cause. In London the Treasury argued that
any credit to Ethiopia was a financial risk. In the Foreign Office it was said
that a loan would prolong the war and might end in having "to press not
only Mussolini but the Emperor as well to get peace."[58] The British decision
was to leave the matter with the Council and avoid any initiative. The Ethio-

pian request was thus killed by a pocket veto, by inaction. No Council member, no one in the Secretariat, brought it up again.

George Steer, correspondent for the *Times,* said the emperor spent a million pounds sterling in the course of the conflict, exhausting his own resources. Steer estimated that a loan of another two million pounds would have enabled the emperor to hold on until the rainy season of 1936 (May or June to October), during which time all military operations would stop and the effect of sanctions would tell in Italy.[59]

The emperor obtained no money. Could he get more arms? There were in the country only 50,000 to 60,000 modern rifles, half in the hands of local chiefs. A third of the arms so bravely flourished were good only for show. Worse was the lack of ammunition. At the outbreak of the war the British military attaché estimated that only 20 percent of the men had operational rifles, with 30–40 rounds for each. There were 600–800 machine guns, with ammunition for firing each for perhaps six minutes. Haile Selassie commanded 371 bombs and eleven slow and unarmed airplanes, three of which did not fly and one of which was in service for the Ethiopian Red Cross. He had 20 field guns and three dozen antiaircraft guns, all inadequately supplied with ammunition. Where, and how, was the emperor to get more?

Ethiopia's capacity for self-defense was undermined in spring and summer 1935 when, bowing to Italian pressure, Belgium, Switzerland, and Czechoslovakia stopped arms shipments. In July Britain and France prohibited arms sales to both antagonists, a blow to Ethiopia, not Italy. Then, in October, the first article of sanction proposal 1 (embargoing arms to Italy) instructed League member governments "enforcing at the moment measures to prohibit or restrict exportation, re-exportation or transit of arms, munitions and implements of war to Ethiopia" to "annul these measures immediately." Most of the major European arms-producing or -trading states participating in sanctions complied. They had imposed embargoes to please Italy; they raised them now to please the League. The French and the Swiss, however, maintained their embargoes on arms to both belligerents. France, for example, refused to permit arms traffic on the Djibouti railroad. But elsewhere there was now reopened the possibility of supply from European sources.

The British government, when it raised the embargo on 12 October, had no policy about supplying arms, but there was before it an application from the Soley Armament Company for a license to export 100,000 rifles and 50 million cartridges to Ethiopia. This was a very large amount indeed. If delivered, it would double, if not triple, Ethiopia's store of ammunition and would triple the number of modern rifles, with untold implications for stiffened resistance, for prolonging the war, for wearing down the Italians.

The arms were to be purchased from surplus stock held by the War Office, then resold by Soley. It was a strictly private arrangement—all Soley requested was an export license.

On 28 October Hoare gave his approval. The next day the Board of Trade was told the Foreign Office had no objection. The decision was sent around to Lord Stanhope for final wording. Instead of a draft, Stanhope came up with an issue: if a government mark was stamped on the barrel and Italians captured some rifles, it would appear that the government had sent the arms. The War Office, which had tried to sell these old rifles for years, said it was doubtful whether the marks could be erased. Moreover, the weapons, Lee-Springfields, were easily identified by make as British. On 30 October Lancelot Oliphant minuted: "We must run the risk." But the next day Vansittart considered the case, and his disagreement changed the entire situation. The question of marks altered his view, decided Vansittart. "I do not feel disposed to run such risks. This sort of thing might be the finishing touch if the situation were still as strained and it will probably get more strained. The Abyssinians have not much money. They must devote what they have to buying arms which are not notoriously British government stock. There is all the difference in the world between letting them get arms and appearing to arm them direct." On 2 November word went to the Board of Trade that "on grounds of policy" the application should be refused.[60]

Eden lamented, but did nothing. "I confess," he wrote on 29 November, "that the Abyssinians seem to me to have had a consistently raw deal from us in the matter of arms. For many months we maintained an arms embargo which has no justification in equity, but seriously handicapped the Abyssinians and has, according to the War Office, made it almost impossible for the Abyssinians to win a victory." Vansittart's caution carried the day. "I am strongly in favor of helping the Abyssinians with the trade. This must be possible—and if not, should be *made* possible. But I am sure this is much the safest way, and the right way."[61]

Soley came back with another proposal. They asked for an export license for sixty Hotchkiss machine guns, also in ex-service stocks. These guns could be changed in calibre, the marks erased, and then sent to Ethiopia. Since they were in more general use than the Lee-Springfields, these weapons could be better effaced and their origin would be less obvious. On 21 December Soley received permission to export these sixty guns on the condition of obliteration of all official marks. In the five months prior to this date only two licenses had been given. One was to Vickers-Armstrongs for 2 million cartridges, the other to Wilkinson for 510 swords. Now sixty machine guns. This was hardly *making* trade possible. Of assistance, of clearly determined policy, there was too little and too late.

Mediterranean Détente

Eden, twenty-five years later, concluded that the British failure to supply arms was a "cardinal error of policy," determined "by an optimistic belief that Mussolini might still come to terms, by a reluctance to do anything which might goad the Duce into some rash act, and by an insufficiently clear view of whose side we were on. In fact, wishful thinking and a desire to appease were already doing their insidious work."[62] Appeasement, the relief of a tense situation, was indeed in evidence, but Eden's "insidious" represents a judgment after the fact. The Mediterranean seemed at flash point. Warnings came that Mussolini, in frustration or anger, might strike out. The British tried to separate imperial rivalry from the question of violation of the Covenant. This led to approaches aimed at a Mediterranean détente. Simultaneously, and continuing as long as tension there remained unabated, came strenuous efforts by Britain, France, and several other states with Mediterranean interests to establish terms of mutual support in case war did come to the inland sea.

The immediate cause of the Mediterranean crisis was the dramatic defensive action taken by the British Admiralty in September, following bellicose outpourings of the Italian press. Caring nothing for Ethiopia, the British government responded to a potentially aggressive rival on its imperial route to the East. Anti-British radio messages sent from Bari to foment discontent in Palestine and Egypt, combined with alarm and some exasperation at its military weaknesses when faced, entirely unexpectedly, by this threat, led the British to precautionary measures. The exposed position of Malta meant moving the fleet—to Alexandria, safer from air attack and thereafter directly athwart the canal. Heavy units of the Home Fleet were sent to Gibraltar to draw Italian naval units into the western basin, away from the critical eastern routes. All this took place just as Hoare proclaimed Britain's loyalty to the Covenant in a speech universally interpreted as supporting the League. To these actions Mussolini responded by intensifying anti-British propaganda at home and sending two divisions to the Italian colony of Libya to menace Egypt by land. British anxiety was heightened by a perception of Mussolini as capable of rash and perhaps suicidal action, a view that gave to his melancholy predictions the character of potentially unrestrained desperation.

In dealing with Mussolini, the problem was to determine intention. From Mussolini's own lips came the interpretation that sanctions, once started, would progress inevitably to blockade, to military measures, to war. "To economic sanctions," Mussolini declared in his mobilization speech of 2 October, "we will oppose our discipline, our sobriety, our spirit of sacrifice. To military sanctions we will respond with military measures. To acts of war we will respond with acts of war." Both Chambrun and Drummond were convinced that Mussolini was not bluffing, that he would not back down, that, as he told Drummond, if Italy were faced with the choice between yielding or war, he would definitely choose war, even if that meant "the whole of Europe went up in flames."[63]

Drummond was not above overdramatizing (Hoare once had to remind him, "We must clearly be careful of our language")[64] and Chambrun spared no paint in illustrating the gloominess of the scene. Their words of alarm complemented the policies evolving at home. Realizing this, the Italians intensified a diplomatic offensive organized around the assertion that progressive sanctions meant war. Mussolini's pronouncements were embroidered in the Palazzo Chigi and reiterated by Grandi in London, by Aloisi and Alberto Berio in Geneva, and above all by Cerruti in Paris. Furthermore, the domestic value of the idea of Italy against the world was now evident. As we will see, the government took the threat from Britain, the sanctions, and the fleet movements to make the Ethiopian war popular in Italy. Nationalist responses to sanctions and patriotic anglophobia were encouraged as safety valves for releasing accumulated tension and frustrations and, more positively, were orchestrated into a rally to the regime.[65]

Who knows if Mussolini in 1935 or 1936 might have plunged into a European war. In September, at the time of the fleet movements, he was easily dissuaded by the service chiefs from a surprise preemptive strike against the ships. No further offensive plans were even developed. Commercial shippers were told in October that the merchant marine must avoid any incidents with units of the British navy.[66] The Italian fleet contemplated war in response, not to the oil sanction, but only to a blockade or closure of the canal.[67] As late as February 1936 the navy's commander in chief was in Rome, uninstructed by Mussolini as to strategy or even sector defense, reflecting that, while it would have made some sense to attack the British in the previous summer, now there was nothing to hope from war.[68] Italian air power, feared and overrated abroad, was known at home to be inferior to the British and inadequate to prolonged combat. There was some upgrading of coastal defenses—new antiaircraft batteries at Palermo and at Taranto where the fleet was based, new alarm signals at Spezia and Bari. These were of little importance compared to serious operational problems posed by inadequate training of pilots and officers—here the Italian naval academy was singled out for particular criticism—and by the lack of fighting spirit in both the navy and the air force.[69]

By October the best Mussolini could hope for was to gravely wound the British in a first strike. Likewise the British knew they could win a war with Italy but feared that, with no margin for loss, any injury would cost them the balance east of the Suez. The thought of national suicide might restrain

Mussolini or it might not, but the British did not want to put the question to the test. Instrumentally, military sanctions, blockade, and closure were seen as unnecessary yet, and by the French as absolutely prohibited. Practically, Mussolini was regarded as so unstable that relations with him were the object of extreme care. As far as possible he was to be kept unprovoked, appeased. Bluff or not, Mussolini's threat of war worked.

On receiving Drummond's dispatch of 29 October 1935 recording Mussolini's acceptance of the possibility of setting Europe ablaze, Geoffrey Thompson in the Foreign Office minuted: Britain was dealing with a "mental irresponsible," although events of the previous months showed Mussolini could "live up to his word." His threats, Thompson continued, were not to be taken lightly.[70] In Mussolini's frame of mind war, if not likely, was possible. Here was the idea of a desperate plunge, of the "mad dog act."

Evidence on Mussolini's mental state was not clear. In December 1935, for example, Owen O'Malley, head of the Southern Department, wrote, "We are all agreed the whole Abyssinian question turns very largely on the operation of one man's mind. Surely therefore it is elementary that we should know what the condition of the mind is and its pathology." Did Mussolini have tertiary syphilis, as rumor said? It is possible, O'Malley wrote to the embassy in Rome, "if not treated quite adequately at the right stage," that such a disease "may attack the brain in precisely that way to produce megalomania as well as other 'illusions.'" This idea had struck Alexis Léger, the permanent head of the French foreign ministry, three months earlier when Léger, trained in medicine, had asked the counselor of the French embassy about Mussolini's pupillary reflexes. As it was, no information was gathered about Mussolini's health except for a report that he had duodenal ulcers. Opinion solicited from Harley Street physicians discounted the connection of his actions with a syphilis infection.[71] The "mad dog" expression remained a departmental cliché—a tag for what was not understood—all the more significant with its ominous and pejorative overtones.

Apart from this, as we saw, there was cause for tension in the Mediterranean. Besides generalized resentment, there was the fact that the British, through control of the Suez Canal, directly governed the fate of more than 200,000 Italians in east Africa, the reputation of the Italian government, and perhaps the fate of the Fascist regime. Against this, and with less than war, there was some pressure Mussolini could apply. Anti-British broadcasts to Arabs under British rule was one way; another was direct anti-British propaganda in population centers such as Cairo.[72] Then there was the possibility of naval and air strikes and of threatening Egypt itself from the western frontier, from Libya.

On 15 September, reacting to the fleet movements, Mussolini sent two metropolitan divisions to Libya, expanding the force there from 20,000 to 74,000 men.[73] On 5 October journalists were forbidden admission to the colony. "Silence," declared Lessona, "is fundamental to surprise."[74] A week later a third division was secretly introduced. Italian soldiers now vastly outnumbered the normal Egyptian garrison of 10,000 British and 10,000 Egyptian troops. In case of war one division would advance through the border post of Sollum and west along the coast to Sidi Barrani. Simultaneously with sending the troops, the Italian government ordered 1,000 trucks from the Ford Motor Company for delivery to Libya, asking Ford to keep the destination secret.[75]

The British worried that if war came the navy and air force, occupied elsewhere, could not stop this coastal thrust. Sidi Barrani was 50 miles inside the frontier. The range of the eighty-four Italian bombers in Libya in October 1935 was 250 miles. Alexandria, the position of the Mediterranean Fleet after being removed from even more exposed Malta, was 290 miles from the border. Thus, an air strike from Sidi Barrani against the harbor became possible. And the harbor was virtually unprotected. If its narrow mouth were blocked the warships would be bottled up inside. The fleet had ammunition for only some fifteen minutes continuous fire and antiaircraft protection was almost nonexistent. There were, as late as December 1935, only eighteen slow fighter planes, four antiaircraft guns, and six searchlights to directly defend Alexandria. But most constraining and worrisome was the lack of trained personnel to man them.[76]

The British decided to maintain bases as far westward as possible. A British mobile force went to the border post at Sollum, replacing the Egyptian battalion there. Battle plans called for a counterattack by air against landing fields in Libya. Since British bombing craft had a range of only 200 miles, those forward bases were essential.

To better protect the fleet it had been decided back in August to send it, in the case of a state of emergency, to the anchorage of Navarino (which would be seized if the Greek government did not concede its use). From this base the navy could control the central Mediterranean and cover Malta. Navarino was only 250 miles from Italy and hence (like Alexandria) in the range of the 160 Italian home-based heavy bombers with a range of 480 miles and the flying boats with a range of 375 miles. It was proposed that offensive action by France and Yugoslavia against fields in Italy would relieve this danger.[77] Discussions to secure such support began shortly, and in October an immediate diplomatic effort was made to lessen British-Italian tension and bring about some degree of demobilization in the Mediterranean.

In mid-September the British sent fulsome assurances that naval deployments were not meant to menace Italy. This helped Mussolini over a bad patch of prewar nerves but did not otherwise change the situation. The problem of agreeing on the nature and degree of demobilization remained. This was a matter for negotiation. But the unprovoked attack on Aduwa, Hoare told Grandi, "banged the door in our face." The cabinet on 9 October 1935 decided there was to be "no question of diminishing" the Mediterranean forces, although if Mussolini withdrew the reinforcements sent to Libya, Britain would cancel a dispatch of reinforcements for Egypt—5,000 men for immediate needs. With the delicate state of Anglo-Egyptian relations, however, more might be needed if internal order were threatened.[78]

The Ethiopian war was the occasion, not the cause, of a crisis in Egypt. The Wafd party demanded more representative government, abolition of certain rights reserved to Britain, and Egypt's admission to the League of Nations. The nationalists took advantage of Britain's preoccupation with the Italian-Ethiopian affair to press these constitutional and treaty demands. This was a source of constant concern to the British government until a treaty of alliance was signed in August 1936.

On 19 October 1935 the Italian position was stated as the simultaneous withdrawal of two divisions in Libya and recall to home waters of the two great battle cruisers, *Hood* and *Renown,* then at Gibraltar. Three days later Suvich announced that one division was to be unilaterally withdrawn. This stirred the British to action. Vansittart minuted that the "Italians have gone ahead without bargaining on *half* the bargain we want of them." If a cordial response was not forthcoming, they could put the blame on Britain for continuing the tension.[79]

Hoare took this argument to the cabinet on the following day, 23 October. He reported the recommendation of the Defence Policy and Requirements Subcommittee (of the Committee of Imperial Defence) that no approach be made to Italy until the French gave specific assurances about support in time of war, more specific than the general statements of the note of 18 October. But, Hoare said, matters were moving fast. He asked for and received cabinet approval to begin talks with Italy at once, on the condition that, before agreeing to remove the two ships, the French conceded British use of Toulon and Bizerte in case of Italian attack and accepted responsibility for control of the western basin, excepting Gibraltar itself. Further, the cabinet decided, the question of military détente in the Mediterranean should take precedence over and be preliminary to overtures for a negotiated settlement of the Ethiopian war.[80]

On 23 October, then, the British set out to pin the French down. There were four requests: (1) guaranteed use of the two ports in case of war, (2) assurance of the "readiness of French forces . . . to contain the important naval forces now in the western basin," (3) operational cooperation between the fleets in the event of a hostile act by Italy, and (4) recognition of "the desirability" of some arrangement with Britain "as to the movement of French aircraft to the Italian frontier." Once the first two assurances arrived the British would offer to withdraw the battle cruisers, subject to reduction of the Libyan force by at least two divisions plus a change in attitude of the Italian press toward Britain. The French gave assurances on the first two points on the twenty-sixth, and talks to arrange the third and fourth opened within a week.[81]

The British request, French acceptance, and ensuing naval talks meant closer relations between those states. They opened, for the British, a new opportunity for dealing with Italy. And they renewed the sense of isolation and pessimism among officials in Rome. Italian intelligence agents intercepted Hoare's message of 23 October to Clerk outlining the requests to be put to Laval. It confirmed all suspicions about British double-dealing. To Italians it seemed as if a definitive military alliance was being built against them. The precise conditions seemed meant to set the stage for intensely applied sanctions. Cerruti thought it meant the end of any discussions about détente and paid Laval two agitated visits on 25 October. Mussolini, without mincing words, wrote to Laval that if France continued such a course it would mean the end of the January accords.[82]

Certainly the prospects for a détente had dimmed. In two weeks they faded away altogether. Drummond met Mussolini on 29 October: "He was in a more depressed and bitter frame of mind than I have yet found him, and extremely pessimistic as to the chances of avoiding war in Europe."[83] It was not an easy time in Rome. The day before, at the celebration of the anniversary of the March on Rome, talk among ministers was that Mussolini might find it impossible to continue the war and, after taking Makale, have to suspend military operations.[84]

On 29 October Drummond presented the British conditions: (1) if there was a marked improvement in the tone of the Italian press and Bari radio stopped anti-British propaganda, the battle cruisers would be withdrawn; (2) Italy was to substantially reduce the Libyan force—one division at least, two at best. Nothing was said about Italy's earlier statement that one division would be withdrawn voluntarily. The stiffly presented terms did not salve Italian pride. Indeed, Drummond stated that, regardless of what the Italians did, more men might have to be sent to Egypt yet.

Mussolini replied. He had withdrawn one division without pressure and gotten no credit. And there was no comparison between divisions and ships. Moving troops took much preparation; moving ships was just a matter of sending them off. Thus all Britain offered was a token gesture.

Then Mussolini opened a larger issue and doomed the talks. He would no longer consider the matter piecemeal. He would discuss the British terms only within the context of Mediterranean demobilization as a whole on land and sea. Until a general settlement was reached, Italy would not withdraw one more man from Libya.[85]

Here was an impasse. Laval and Aloisi, hopeful middlemen, tried to encourage Britain to another start, but Mussolini disowned these initiatives. He would not discuss specifics, he told Drummond on 7 November, until a more substantive issue was resolved: What, in the future, was to be the "normal" balance between British and Italian forces in the Mediterranean? As for the Bari broadcasts, why were the British so alarmed? Suvich collected all broadcasts delivered in October and found them, while nationalistic, sometimes favorable to Britain. Suvich was correct. The British had overreacted. Maurice Peterson gathered the fullest collection he could, running from 9 September to 17 October, as grounds for complaint. Its contents are not particularly offensive.[86]

With this the British government stopped its search for a Mediterranean détente. On 11 November it was decided that as soon as the election of the fourteenth was over Laval would be asked for his views on a new effort toward a negotiated settlement of the war itself. Vansittart, in a swipe at the French, noted on 15 November that the only reason for having pushed the matter of détente was that "we were given to understand we might miss our market." Now it was clear that the market did not exist except on unacceptable terms. Furthermore, Owen O'Malley observed, a secret Mediterranean deal eliminating the prospect of war would break the Geneva front.[87]

Despite Vansittart's complaint, the British again asked the French to do a market analysis. On 16 November Ambassador George Clerk went to Laval. With nothing resulting from the détente talks, the British government did not want "to lose any further time in pursuing the longer and more important line of the possibility of the main political settlement." Clerk, opening the new chapter, asked Laval if he had "any further contacts with Italians . . . or . . . any new suggestions to offer."[88]

Mutual Support

Article 16 of the Covenant stated that members should "mutually support one another in resisting any special measures aimed at one of their number by the convenant-breaking State." The French, as the staff talks with the British got under way, were still bothered by the ambiguity of the British position. An Italian strike would fall mainly upon the British in the Mediterranean. But how was one to define the nature of the provocation? It was those ships that threatened the Italians, and the ships were moved without reference to the Covenant, before the invasion, for imperial defense. Yet now, by the end of October, the governance of those ships was closely, inextricably, tied to British sanctionist policy, or so the Italians certainly believed. It had just been proven impossible to separate the question of détente from the problems arising from sanctions, and the British request for French assurances was interpreted in Rome as preparing a definite military alliance against Italy. The French asked if it was any longer possible to draw a line between Britain's imperial interest and its action supporting the League. Could an Italian strike be defined either as against a sanctionist power or as against an imperialist rival? Only in the former case could Frenchmen be legitimately drawn into war. None would fight for the British empire.

The French government asked these questions early. Indeed, they asked if the naval buildup of September did not go beyond any means approved or even contemplated at Geneva. This concern was reviewed in the note of general assurance of 18 October, which precluded military sanctions and limited military support to "the possible attack by Italy upon Great Britain *by reason of the latter's collaboration in the international action undertaken by the League of Nations and pursued in concert with France.*"[89]

When assurance of support was renewed on 26 October, the French government suggested that staff talks include not only naval and air arms but military officials as well. If mutual benefits were to be drawn from this awkward situation, let France get some measure of continental security. So that there was no doubt of French intentions, on 31 October the government reopened a long-standing request for British assurances in case of a violation of the Covenant by force in Europe—meaning by Germany. The British refused to broaden the discussion. "We are talking about Italy and will only talk about Italy," said Vansittart. "Only a little resolution will be necessary to hold to such firm ground."[90] It was in this mood of reluctant cooperation and partial purpose that the first round of talks between naval authorities took place between 30 October and 9 November 1935.

The French had their worries. Italian armed strength represented a more direct threat to the French than to the English. The immediate danger came not from the army. Italy might move against Nice, but the Alps would soon be covered with snow. Rather, what caused pessimism in the service ministries was the estimation that, taking its naval and air forces together, Italy possessed superior offensive strength. The French general staff concluded that nothing prevented the Italians from establishing a defensive posture in the western basin or launching brutal attacks against France. Despite the notorious air exploits in Africa, the bulk of the air force remained on the peninsula, and major French targets were within easy range. Despite a numerical superiority of aircraft, French defensive capacity (warning systems, antiaircraft guns, and interceptor planes) was inadequate to prevent air penetration. The Italian fleet, with modern cruisers, much-vaunted torpedo boats, and a strong complement of submarines, seemed almost the equal of the French. The postwar years of neglect had taken their toll on the French sea arm. The fleet, lacking new construction and modernization, was far from its 1936 goal of readiness for combat in Europe. There was no way of remedying defensive inadequacy without mobilization, and men and equipment were already stretched to the limit. At Toulon and Bizerte the few antiaircraft guns were unmanned, the harbors unobstructed, the ships unprepared for war. As with the British, trained personnel were in pitifully short supply.[91] Laval, sworn to avoid war, refused to proclaim a national crisis, and subject to strong antiwar political pressure, refused to call for mobilization.

This was the state of affairs reported by Rear Admiral Jean Decoux to Admiral Ernle Chatfield, chief of the naval staff, when the two met in London on 30 October 1935 to open naval talks. Decoux readily conceded two points. In case of war arising from sanctions, France would come to the British side. Docking and repair facilities and metropolitan and colonial ports would be at the disposal of the British navy. The French would take responsibility "in principle" for the western basin, the British for the east. But, in case of war, this did not commit France to engage its service arms against Italy. Weeks would elapse before mobilization assured operational levels of readiness. So, the French delegate proposed, in the event of hostilities, while granting the British the use of ports, France would delay a declaration of war until the forces were prepared. Furthermore, depending on troops from north Africa to supplement home forces, France asked British help to bring these men across.[92]

These arrangements, Hoare concluded, were as "good as could be hoped for," given the internal situation of France. "We could not ask them to mobilize while we were not mobilized." First Lord of the Admiralty Bolton Monsell pointed out that the French, early proponents of a Mediterranean détente, now admitted that, far from being much active help, they would need aid even to transport their own troops across the western basin.[93] Leaving the *Hood* and *Renown* at Gibraltar seemed more sensible than ever.

November saw renewed pessimism and suspicion in British-French relations. The French wondered what they were letting themselves in for. In the absence of further concrete planning the British wondered if they could count on the French after all.

Decoux returned to Paris with a disquieting report. First, he was struck by a remark Chatfield had made to the effect that dictators are unpredictable and that no one knew whether Mussolini might not act desperately if Italy were "cut off from Africa." Did this mean Britain contemplated closing the Suez Canal? If so, the French had not been consulted, and such an idea was contrary to Laval's understanding with Hoare to avoid provocation. Second,

Decoux raised the questions of British motive and possible French benefits. What was France getting in return? The British received assurances of support, guarantees of the use of bases. But only France, it seemed, was being approached in this matter of mutual assistance. Decoux concluded that there was a further aim to these maneuvers—to compromise France in Italian eyes and put the French-Italian rapprochement in jeopardy.[94] These reflections gave the French government reason to pause.

Staff talks were not renewed. The delay, running through November, increasingly irritated the British. The French naval staff made some effort to keep channels of information open. One finds references to British officers visiting Bizerte and Toulon in civilian dress. Beyond such limited activity the naval ministry dared not go. Progress depended on policy direction from the foreign ministry, and Chatfield reported the opinion of the navy chief of staff, Durand-Viel, that there would be no help from the Quai d'Orsay in getting the talks resumed. This seemed borne out by a French proposal to reopen talks under the cover of the London Naval Conference set to begin on 9 December. The French representative was not even a member of the naval staff. Both sides were angry. It looked, said Chatfield, as if France "again wished to burke the issue."[95] In France the British were seen, at least by Decoux, as wanting only passive French cooperation, as unwilling to push harder for substantive long-term and broader-range cooperation.[96]

The British government at last took the initiative, prompted by the collapse of the détente talks, with an oil sanction in the offing, and in the face of reports from Rome about renewed dangers of a suicidal act by Mussolini. On 26 November, at a meeting of the Defence Policy and Requirements Subcommittee, Hoare said it was time to get another assurance from Laval. It was time to know whether Britain was to be disowned. "The results might even change our attitude on the whole policy of sanctions." Strong words, and even stronger was Baldwin's pessimism that in the event of war the French would not come in. This view was shared by Monsell, who said there was a strong possibility of Italian aggression and no possibility of French cooperation. Vansittart and Hoare brought out the old formula: demand another clear statement from Laval, relay this to Mussolini, then ask Laval to "implement this affirmation by concrete action," such as manning the southern air defense posts—without which existing assurances of the use of Toulon were worthless. Finally, Laval was to renew the staff talks. Cooperation was on the line. This procedure was to be the "practical test whether the French Government were able—or unable—as has been suspected—to implement their recognized obligations of practical and effective cooperation."[97]

Clerk spoke to Laval the next day, 27 November. Did Mussolini "understand that if he dropped a bomb on a British battleship he would be going to war with the whole of the League, including France?" Mussolini must be disabused of any illusion that France was a "benevolent neutral." Laval "should make clear to Rome that any attack on Great Britain meant an attack on the whole League and thus France." Laval said he would, and told Cerruti—there could be no isolated attack on the British.[98]

To the cabinet on 2 December Hoare reported this as a "categorical affirmative. . . . No assurance could be clearer." The next step was to press for a resumption of the naval talks and extend them to the army and air staffs—limited always to the Italian question. Consultation on the question of mutual support with other Mediterranean states, Greece, Yugoslavia, and Turkey, would be left to the future. Hoare and Vansittart saw Laval in Paris on 7 December and argued that in light of the imminence of the oil sanction and the then critical point in preparations for a negotiated settlement the staff talks should begin at once. Laval agreed, and within two days military and air conversations opened.[99]

In the military conversations of 9 and 10 December, the British chiefs of staff hoped to get assurance of French operations on the frontier meant to paralyze northern Italy's industrial and commercial centers, particularly Milan and Turin. Such assurance the French refused to give. General Maurice Gamelin, head of the army general staff, feared any commitment that, if discovered by the Italians, would prejudice the delicate negotiations for peaceful settlement of the Ethiopian war according to the formula just arrived at in the Hoare-Laval plan. As a result, all these talks accomplished was a promise of the French staff to study prospects for an early-warning observation system for any aircraft headed over France toward Britain, for a possible offensive action from Tunisia against Tripoli, for the possible raising of further local forces in the Levant, and for a joint effort to protect the Somalian possessions of both states and the Djibouti railroad. In its turn, the British staff would study the use of an Iraqui-Syrian route for reinforcements from India and the joint defense projects in Somalia. The British hoped that the French would show their commitment by manning antiaircraft batteries or mounting a "winter exercise" in the Alps, but for the rest, such as calling up reservists or permitting British troops to enter French colonies, political decision was needed, and this was beyond the scope of the talks.[100]

In the simultaneous air talks, the British posed two requests. In case of air attacks on Malta, French bombers would strike airfields in Sicily and southern Italy and later, possibly, permit British use of bases in Tunisia. In case of attack on London, the French would provide immediate aid from the airwatch stations in southeastern France and later the possible use of French airdromes there and on Corsica.[101]

An air raid on London became a dreadful possibility. In an article "L'inghilterra e la difesa aerea" published in 1928 in *Educazione Fascista,* the military theorist Giulio Douhet had noted that, thanks to air power, "the

Mediterranean is no longer an English lake." To use it, the British should pay a price. The Channel was useless now as a protective moat. London, the heart of island and empire, lay exposed. An air attack there, "including the use of offensive chemical weapons," could destroy the city at the start of hostilities. The "discouragement of social life" would bring about "the death of the city." Douhet concluded: "The air defense of London is impossible."[102]

Douhet, with his emphasis on air power as something more than a supplement to the military and naval force, was not, it appears, much read in the Royal Air Force staff college, but British officials arrived at similar conclusions.[103] Hugh Trenchard, long-time RAF chief of staff, argued for an independent and strategic air arm. There was plenty of worry that an aerial bombardment would so demoralize the civilian population that the resulting panic might, in the words of the man responsible for an official report submitted in 1930, "bring about a collapse, certainly of the community of London, if not the whole country."[104]

For Trenchard and Douhet, and for Badoglio, who soon put the theory to the test in Ethiopia, the significance of strategic bombing lay more with the devastation of civilian morale than with the infliction of material damage. The airplane could do better what the long-range cannon did in the Great War—shatter the enemy into demoralization.

London seemed as exposed as Douhet said. "The bomber will always get through," Baldwin said to the Commons in 1932. The "man on the street" should realize that "there is no power on earth that can protect him from being bombed." Baldwin's opinion was the same three years later. Some described Britain as a rich and unprotected orchard garden, open for plunder. London, in Churchill's words, was "the greatest target in the world, a kind of tremendous fat cow, a valuable fat cow, tied up to attract beasts of prey." In the summer air exercises of 1934, night flights "destroyed" the air ministry on the first raid, the Houses of Parliament on the second. Only two of the five bombers were "interrupted."[105] Against an air attack, Britain was defenseless.

The air danger was at the front of Baldwin's thought in his first speech after the outbreak of the Ethiopian war, at a time generally thought, the *Times* wrote, to be Britain's "most critical moment since the Great War." The "destructive abilities" of the "march of science" put at stake the future of Western civilization. The "facilities of modern transport" made the world "infinitely closer." Baldwin warned: "Our frontiers, which a few short years ago were simply defined and easy to guard, are now neither. . . . If this island perish, with all that it stands for, I doubt if the Empire could hold together, and in my view maintenance of the Empire will depend on the maintenance of the position of this heart of the Empire in Europe."[106]

On 14 October the air minister reported that Italy had 120 bombers that could, under favorable conditions, reach Britain and return. Hoare thought this "a very unlikely eventuality." In order not to disquiet the public, no territorial antiaircraft battalions were called up. On 6 December Drummond reported that both his and Chambrun's naval and air attachés agreed it was "most probable that there exists a picked body of between 100–200 volunteer Italian pilots willing to take exceptional risks in air attacks on the British fleet. An air raid on London without expectation of return to Italy is spoken of in several quarters." On the copy of this dispatch purloined from the embassy safe, someone, probably Mussolini, put large exclamation points in the margin next to the reports of a suicide squadron, and we know now that the Italian secret service had a hand in spreading the rumor.[107]

Baldwin's fears were reaffirmed. The Air Ministry thought an attack was possible. In his famous speech of 10 December, defending the government in the wake of the exposé of the Hoare-Laval proposals, Baldwin said in Commons: "My lips are not yet sealed. Were these troubles over I would make a case, and I guarantee that not a man would go into the Lobby against us." He elucidated these mystifying words to Thomas Jones. "I had in mind the menace of war; our fleet would be in real danger from the small craft of the Italians operating in a small sea. Italian bombers could get to London. I had also Germany in mind. Had we gone to war, our anti-aircraft munitions would have been exhausted in a week. We have hardly got any armament firms left."[108]

The fear of war reflected the opinion that the intricate economic, social, and political systems of Britain and France could not absorb such a major shock without devastating disruption. This judgment Baldwin and Neville Chamberlain shared with Laval and Fabry. The British government tried to assess the potential damage. Home Secretary Simon said on 20 December that he was told Italy could make two raids a week to the southern part of the island, each raid with fifty aircraft carrying twenty-five tons of bombs. In the Great War, the casualties per ton of bomb had averaged fifty: seventeen killed and thirty-three wounded. Lord Swinton, the air minister, estimated that Italy's air power was less than Simon had reported. Two squadrons of nine aircraft were available to the Italians, each aircraft carrying ten tons of bombs. Raids depended on good weather and the winter months were now in Britain's favor. Some preliminary preparations were under way against an air raid. In London the Metropolitan Water Board and the principal gas companies made emergency plans. But to minimize public anxiety the Home Office took no steps to consult the chief constables.[109]

During this time, after guns and ammunition had been sent to reinforce Alexandria, Malta, and Aden, less than 10,000 rounds of antiaircraft ammunition remained in the United Kingdom, and trained men were lacking to man existing guns.[110] So shorthanded were British forces that, had war come, "many parts of the air defence system would have been lacking and no part could have functioned with full efficiency." Coastal defenses were "completely out of date;" gun emplacements in the empire had not been modernized for thirty years; there was no gun "not outranged by those of a modern six inch cruiser."[111] In 1934 the British government had abandoned the no-war-for-ten-years rule and named Germany as the principal potential foe. Limited rearmament had begun. But no matter how fast rearmament took place, the armed forces warned the government not to risk national security, not to go beyond the capacity to enforce policy, until it was completed.

Apart from diplomacy, the best defense available for the island, the fleet, Malta, and Egypt was the capacity for retaliatory strikes, to be ready to hit targets in northern Italy.[112] This could be carried out either by the French air arm or by British planes using airstrips in southeastern France. The ministers in November authorized a contingent of aircraft to supplement the French force, and earmarked for this mission the entire thirteen squadrons remaining in the British Isles.

For any of this, of course, French support was essential, the "vital factor." To sound the French was the job of the British delegation when air staff talks opened on the morning of 9 December, talks, as we saw, meant to be a "practical test" of French intentions, of the sincerity of their promise of assistance in time of war.[113]

The arrival of the British staff representatives in Paris, "without warning," Fabry described it, caught the French high command by surprise. On the morning of 9 December they received the two requests: retaliatory strikes or later use of French bases in case of an air attack on Malta; assistance in case of an attack on London in the form of airwatch and airbase use. The three French service ministers and the chiefs of the general staff met that afternoon to fashion a reply. They agreed that unqualified aid to the British was beyond their capacity to determine. The air forces in southern France would not be ready for combat use until April 1936. The scope of envisioned measures was such that it would involve the recall of reserves, a policy matter. To place the air arm on even a partial war footing entailed some degree of mobilization, an uncertain prospect given the state of public opinion, and possibly provocative to Italy. Without reserves, however, the air force was capable only of frontier watch. Then too, the British request came just as the Hoare-Laval plan to end the war was sent to Mussolini.

Léger was called to the meeting. It was not possible for the Italians to reject this plan, he said. Peace would be saved. Italy would appreciate French help and such good will would evaporate if there now came close military collaboration with the British. On the other hand, Laval's policy was to give all possible satisfaction to the British, and staff talks need not bind the government. So, it was concluded, Air Minister Denain could give an affirmative reply to the two requests, while the ministers agreed to take up only those engagements entailing the least risk of war.

At the staff talks Denain therefore dwelt mainly on the reservations of his government. "Active" measures, such as recalling reservists, might provoke retaliation and had to be avoided. The location of France exposed it to "grave and immediate" risks. For distant Britain, such risk was "light." The air ministry preferred that British planes prepare to locate neither on French mainland soil nor on Corsica (the limited size of airdromes was mentioned) but on Tunisian bases instead. Plans for British action should aim at Sicily and the south of Italy. France would cover its southeast and the route to London.[114]

Swinton told the cabinet on 10 December that the initial air discussions "could hardly have been more unsatisfactory." No preparatory action was possible before mobilization; this political move the French were not about to make. There would be no action against Italy from southern France unless France was attacked. Ten days later he said the French air staff thought Italian overflights going to raid Britain would constitute a hostile act for France, but this was not yet government policy.[115]

By the time of the dramatic events of mid-December—the threat of an oil sanction and the proposal, revelation, and reversal of the Hoare-Laval plan—staff talks had produced nothing definite in the way of technical cooperation. There was another round of inconclusive naval talks in January 1936, and, after Hitler's move in the Rhineland, staff talks in the spring. A few reserve specialists in France were called up by postcard for "training." Some officers started thinking more precisely about the needs of war.[116] But almost no detailed cooperative planning took place during this emergency.

Multiple strategic objectives, differing views of primary danger, and non-congruent definitions of national interests sum up the general categories of disagreement. Was the primary danger naval or air? in the Mediterranean or in Europe? What about the Far East? That question was never raised. What about the Near East? a matter barely mentioned. The ambiguity of the British position in the Mediterranean gave the French reason for pause. In return, Englishmen held back from cooperation on the Rhine. So the French were all the more reluctant to lose the Italian connection. And, in early December, the running hope was that the Ethiopian crisis would be shortly resolved by negotiation. Laval was set on conciliation. His Council of Ministers approved.

The British had no wish to widen the talks. Instead, they looked after themselves. Without definite mutual support, League obligation was at odds with imperial defense. On 6 December 1935 the chiefs of staff warned of "the danger which would arise if political agreements on the application of fresh sanctions [meaning oil] outran arrangements for co-operation between the forces of the Powers concerned. . . . it is essential that this country, alone, should not be committed to risks for which other Members of the League are militarily unprepared."[117]

At no time did the British chiefs of staff consider any action against Italy other than full-scale war. There was no planning for blockade, stopping shipping in peacetime, or closure of the canal. Military sanctions meant war, Mussolini had said, and this threat was not disputed. It was against the contingency of some presumably irrational "mad dog act" that the chiefs prepared, and the concern was that an oil sanction would provoke such a response.

There was no fear among the service chiefs that Britain would lose a war with Italy. With or without the French, despite their intense dislike of a foreign policy based upon collective obligation, which confused and dispersed national and imperial defense priorities, the chiefs were confident of victory. The Mediterranean Fleet at Alexandria; the two battle cruisers at Gibraltar with their complements of cruisers and destroyers from the Home Fleet; minesweepers from the Malta reserve; four ships from the East Indies moved to Aden; a division of destroyers from the China station; ships from the West Indies; the Home Fleet in readiness, fully manned, at Portland; merchantmen in service as ammunition carriers; all fleets up to full company with stores for four months; and ships, equipment, and personnel ready at Alexandria and comprising a Naval Base Defence Organization for Port X (Navarino)—all this tremendous capacity was standing by at the first of December. Regardless of Italian preparations for war, regardless of the success of Britain's opening offensive action—a night attack by the fleet air arm against the main naval base in the Taranto harbor—as long as Gibraltar, Alexandria, and Aden lay firmly in British hands, with the readiness to close the Turkish straits as well, the Royal Navy could isolate the armies in Africa and pinch off 75 percent of Italian trade. This, in a short time, would be enough to make the Italians sue for peace.[118]

But it would be too costly a victory. The navy, limited by the naval conference of 1930, constrained by political and economizing sentiment opposing rearmament, measured by an only recently modified ten-year-rule, was hesitant to take losses in the Mediterranean. Admiralty eyes were on the Far East. Supply preparations were for a war with Germany in 1939. War with Japan might come earlier. The year 1936 was, in the opinion of the chiefs of staff, "likely to be a critical one . . . since Japan will have almost completed the modernization of her capital ships and for the most part her air forces, including the Fleet air arm." For this the British force was unprepared. Fortifications at the Singapore garrison were incomplete. The Manchurian affair and Sino-Japanese conflict of 1931–33 revealed the bankruptcy of a Far East policy not backed by secure bases. At the end of 1934 the chiefs had said that every effort had to be made "to avoid incidents which might lead Japan to take precipitate action at a time when she would be in a stronger position" vis-à-vis Britain "than ever before."[119] Weakness itself could be a provocation. The figures of naval strength in the Pacific in the 1930s make sobering reading. In 1935 the Japanese had 9 battlecruisers and battleships there, the British China squadron none; Japan had 102 destroyers, Britain, 10; Japanese submarines numbered 65, British, 15.[120]

So the service chiefs and the defense ministers never argued for caution more successfully than in the days of December 1935, when they warned that the political situation was extending Britain unsafely beyond its military capacities, that the gap between foreign policy and the state defense was "too wide." So urgent did this seem that a statement, almost a political threat, was made in the cabinet that, if losses occurred in a war with Italy and warnings from the defense chiefs became known, public opinion might "not easily forgive the government."[121]

The diplomatic consequence of these worries—renewed search for a negotiated settlement—we will soon discuss. At the time, diplomacy was the main arm of government action. In the meantime, the services continued with their plans in the event of war in the Mediterranean.

On 12 December 1935 the Egyptian garrison was declared strong enough to repel attack from Libya. The garrison was reinforced with a thousand men from Indian barracks. More infantry and tack and mechanized artillery units were sent from England, ending the restraint in fortifying Egypt previously held as a concession to Mussolini in the bargaining over a Mediterranean détente. Antiaircraft guns and ammunition were increased somewhat, but by mid-December, for the direct air defense of Alexandria, there were only eighteen fighter planes, fourteen antiaircraft guns, and six searchlights—staffed by still poorly trained crews.

All available reserves went to the Mediterranean. A report of 16 March 1936 regarding a possible war with Germany declared:

> The dispatch of military reinforcing units to Egypt has resulted in a situation which will prevent us from sending overseas any further formations of any kind without mobilization. . . . We have at present no naval forces in Home waters which could take any effective action to protect our trade routes or to prevent German forces from bombarding our coast. . . . [Anti-aircraft weaponry in the south amounted to] sixteen guns and twenty-five searchlights. . . . from the point of view of immediate readiness for war *today* the R.A.F. could produce no offensive or defensive effort whatever.[122]

It was possible, in the aftermath of the Rhineland occupation, to man only one-third of the positions thought necessary for the protection of London alone.

On 9 December 1935, with the Egyptian garrison secure, a decison was made to keep the fleet at Alexandria in case of war. The plan, held since August, to send the ships to an advanced, temporary anchorage at the Greek port of Navarino was abandoned. Italian long-range bombers now being mass-produced could reach Navarino, and Italians knew of the plan. The decision was further determined by the reluctance of the French to cooperate. The British needed the active support of France to control the central Mediterranean, cut communications between the peninsula and Africa, and stop seaborne trade. If the French would not promise offensive air operations against northern Italy, Italian air power would not be diverted from attacks on Malta, the fleet at sea, and Navarino. If the French navy was not prepared to threaten Italy's western coast and thus tie up the Italian ships in the western basin, Italy could concentrate its fleet in the center against the British. The Navarino plan was therefore dropped. Should French cooperation become more effective, when antiaircraft equipment was in greater supply, when the menace of Italian air power was better determined, then the question of Port X could be reconsidered. In case of war, after all, as Chatfield said, the navy might wish to "advance closer to Italy in order to force things to a conclusion."[123]

Support from France was necessary, cooperation from other states desirable—both for the convenience of the navy and from the viewpoint of British policy, the rationale of which was to establish the degree of commitment to collective security held by League states. In December 1935, upon ending the round of staff conversations with the French, the British government circulated to a number of states a request for information about their intent to fulfill their obligations under article 16 of the Covenant. This note went in the face of the Italian message of 11 November to sanctionist states, protesting sanctions and warning of reprisals. On 11 December Eden told the cabinet that Greece, Turkey, and Yugoslavia had replied with general acceptance of the obligations under article 16, paragraph 3.[124]

5   SEARCH FOR SETTLEMENT

Delay on Oil

When the Coordination Committee closed its session on 6 November 1935, the initial round of sanctions (proposals 1 through 4) were set to go into effect on 18 November. This duly occurred, and the day was denounced by the Grand Council of Fascism as a date of "shame and iniquity" in world history. Orders were given for houses to be draped with the Italian flag for the twenty-four hours of the eighteenth. Stones were set in municipal buildings to stand as records "throughout the centuries" of the "enormous injustice perpetuated against Italy."[1]

The question of enlarging the scope of sanctions to include iron, coal, and above all oil remained. Proposal 4-A, recommending this extension, was accepted by the Committee of Eighteen and on 7 November submitted to participating governments. The committee was to receive replies, consider the probable reaction of nonmember states, and, if all seemed promising, propose a date for its implementation.

Reaction from the American government was encouraging. Irritated at the quickening volume of trade with Italy, on 15 November Hull declared that, since trucks, tractors, iron, and steel, while not formally implements of war, were associated with the war effort, trade in them was "directly contrary" to government policy and against the "general spirit" of the recent neutrality legislation. This warning, on the eve of sanctions, resulted in a widespread assumption in Europe that pressure would follow to restrain exporting firms. On 21 November the American petroleum administrator, Harold Ickes, when asked about oil exports, said that everyone should comply with government efforts to prevent the export of munitions to belligerents. This was interpreted as a call to oil producers to limit their Italian trade. Several companies, Gulf, U.S. Shell, Tidewater, and Standard Oil of New Jersey's Texas affiliate, Humble, announced they would take no more Italian orders.[2] On 23 November Roosevelt instructed Hull to see whether Standard Oil was organizing a Swiss branch to facilitate entry of American oil into Italy and, if this were so, to tell the press.[3]

America, in the first nine months of 1935, provided only 6.3 percent of Italy's oil imports. In the final quarter of the year the percentage rose to 17.8. Still, the year's average was only 10.5 percent, not much more than the 10.4

percent for 1934. The remaining 90 percent of Italy's oil supply came from members of the League. Taking figures from the first three quarters of 1935, the major suppliers were Romania (46.5 percent), USSR (13.1 percent), Iran (13 percent) and the Netherlands West Indies (11.2 percent, refining mainly Venezuelan oil). Export from America did not have to halt completely for an oil sanction to work. If the moral embargo could hold exports at the prewar level, and the League suppliers applied the sanction, Italy's imports would be drastically restricted, the straitened economy would be put under severe pressure, and, it was thought, Mussolini could no longer conduct colonial war without unacceptable domestic strain.

The Netherlands returned a noncommittal reply on 14 November, but its government stated privately that it was ready to cooperate. France, with an insignificant petroleum trade with the peninsula (1.2 percent of the Italian imports in 1935) would, in the circumstances, give its political support. The Soviet and Romanian governments stated their cooperation with proposal 4-A, "provided," as Litvinov's letter of 17 November read, "all the States Members and non-members of the League which export the products in question announce their readiness to apply the same measures."[4] It would take some diplomacy, but if the United States held the level down perhaps that would satisfy the reservations of Romania and the Soviet Union. Of the great powers, Britain, dominating the Anglo-Iranian Oil Company, remained to be heard from.

The Committee of Eighteen had adjourned on 6 November, to reconvene when replies to proposal 4-A were in. The attitude of the United States was encouraging; affirmative responses came from Moscow and Bucharest. On 22 November, after sounding Paris and London and receiving no objections, Chairman Vasconcellos called the meeting for 29 November. Vasconcellos had not sounded deeply enough. This date was sooner than the British, engaged in conciliation, wanted. Further, it conflicted with the scheduled parliamentary debate on Laval's financial policies set in Paris for 28 and 29 November. Laval, foreign minister as well as premier, wanted to attend the Committee of Eighteen in person, not to leave France represented at this crucial time by a civil servant. It was impossible for him to be in Geneva on the twenty-ninth with the fate of his government at stake. On the twenty-fifth, therefore, he asked Vasconcellos to postpone the session. He specified no new date, but it could not be postponed for long if the sanctionist momentum was to be maintained.

Vasconcellos granted Laval's request, for reasons of courtesy to the French government and the wish to have France represented by as authoritative a delegation as possible. But there was malevolent speculation concerning Laval's intentions. The secretary-general of the League called his request a "transparent pretext" to avoid facing the issue.[5] For all this it is extraordinary that the conflict with Laval's parliamentary schedule was not foreseen in Geneva. In hindsight we see a major turning point in this postponement, where the sanctionist powers broke their stride.

There was a sigh of relief in the Foreign Office when Laval asked support for his postponement request. By the end of the month, he said, either he would be confirmed and able to speak the more strongly for France or he would be on his way out of office. The English swiftly assented. A "most reasonable request," wrote Vansittart, "an excellent let out for us." Vansittart urged Hoare and Eden not to proceed with oil sanctions until support from France was clear and British defenses were improved. "We are getting very near the knuckle."[6]

Postponement of the decisive meeting of the Committee of Eighteen, however, jeopardized American cooperation. American support was not a matter of obligation. The moral embargo depended on the expectation that collective action was seriously intended by members of the League. It assumed a League embargo. The American government had responded favorably to the early show of firmness in Geneva. Now, with the postponement of the crucial meeting of the Committee of Eighteen, the mood in the State Department changed to caution and anxiety.

Delay on a decision on proposal 4-A left the American government alone in asserting opposition to oil exports and exposed to isolationist or noninterventionist critics. Those who understood the delicateness of Hull's relationship to the European scene grew worried.[7] On 29 November Hoare received a message from Laval stating that because of a further vital debate in the Chamber, this time on domestic policy and the government's handling of the *ligues*, he could not go to Geneva as planned. All had assumed the Committee of Eighteen would meet at last at the beginning of December. Now it was postponed again, to 12 December. With this further delay some explanation was owed the Americans.

On 29 November Hoare told Ambassador Lindsay to state that Britain wanted to take no action that would embarrass the American government or make its cooperation less easy. It would be a "calamity," Hoare said, if "responsible people in America" inferred that the League was not prepared to make an effort to restrict oil exports when American officials were using their moral influence in that direction. But Mussolini might be driven to some "desperate act," and the British needed time to clarify the matter of mutual security. There was now indication that Mussolini might be ready for a settlement and, said Hoare, it was essential to "test the reality of these reports." So, Hoare concluded, Britain welcomed this breathing space so as to make another "serious attempt" to get negotiations under way. Whether or not it would be thought "wise" to impose the embargo at the meeting on 12 December would depend on the progress of peace talks. Thus, Lindsay was instructed to say, even apart from the immediate delay due to the French government's requests, a further postponement might be necessary due to the "intensive efforts" at conciliation. While regretting the embarrassment to the administration, there was "no other course that could be safely adopted."[8] The same day Avenol asked Washington what effect postponement would have on the American position.

These approaches contained an implicit assumption of a closer, more reciprocal, relationship than Hull was prepared or could politically afford to admit. To Gilbert in Geneva he wrote on 2 December: "Sight is being lost of the entirely separate and independent course and program of policies which this country has openly and avowedly pursued. . . . The very purpose and occasion for our independent course was to avoid any agreements or understandings of a cooperative nature with any other nation or group of nations." To Italy's Ambassador Rosso and to Lindsay, he denied that the American government was "out on a limb." America had its own neutrality program and would go its own way regardless of anyone else's postponements, delays, or peace talks.[9]

This left open the question whether, if the League did impose an oil sanction, the Americans would, or could, keep oil exports at the prewar level as Hull had requested. Further delay certainly would lessen American resolve. Hoare worried about this at a crowded meeting of the cabinet on 2 December 1935. First, after long discussion, it was decided that Britain would adhere to a League embargo. There was really no choice. Oil, said Hoare, was "obviously an effective sanction." To back out of collective action after "having taken the line that we have and fought the election on it . . . would be disastrous and indefensible."[10] But when to begin the sanction? The governor of the Bank of England favored the oil embargo precisely because it would resolve the Italian question quickly. Speed, however, was what the Foreign Office had taught the cabinet to fear. Filled with French and Italian hints and warnings, the diplomats sought, instead, more time. Settlement, appeasement, was an alternative route to peace—and it was safe. Following this line, the cabinet recommended on 2 December 1935 that the oil sanction be pursued in two stages: first, acceptance in principle at Geneva; then establishment of the data for enforcement, to hold over Mussolini's head while negotiators strove, once more, for the terms of an acceptable compromise. But, Hoare worried, such a "breathing space" might embitter the American government, make its effort to control exports impossible, or even break the existing sanctionist front altogether. Until the sanction was imposed, after all, Anglo-Iranian planned to continue its flow of oil to Italy. It was insulting as well as futile to hope for voluntary restraint in America while a firm dominated by the British government shipped freely. Both Anglo-Iranian and British Shell refused to endanger their Italian market by voluntary restraint.[11]

Sir John Cadman, head of Anglo-Iranian, thought that if a League embargo were put in force an informal voluntary embargo by American firms would follow. He volunteered to talk to the chairman of the board of Standard Oil about this. The problem was not only with the giants, however. Herbert Feis, watching the American oil scene for the State Department, concluded that the large established companies tended to accommodate government appeals for restraint. The newer oil dealers, Feis noted, acted solely in the profit interest and took up the business others dropped.[12] Until the League took definite action, future American moves were uncertain. The *Wall Street Journal* favored restraint as a necessary payment "on the altar of war immunity." In general, however, in the business community at large the moral embargo received a chilly reception, as contrary to the principle of unimpeded trade with countries on good terms with America.[13]

Hull was annoyed by the importune questions put to him by Hoare, for one. What would Hull do to prevent last-minute Italian buying in case of further postponement? How could Britain be sure American oil would not nullify a sanctionist effort? Might not American companies capture, "it may be forever," the Italian market given up by League states?[14] These queries, the assumption that America was responsible for the success or failure of collective action by the League, angered Hull. His government went as far as it could, while League members backed and filled. How wrong, he wrote, to use "the fact that the United States government did not have legal authority to impose an oil embargo as an excuse for their not taking action."[15] Why did the League, fifty-two nations assembled in the cause of peace, continue to hesitate? Were they going to "lie down and die" at the first difficulty? He stood amazed that League states should "halt and seek to make the impression that they would not even attempt to go further" without American assurance. The League, he told Lindsay on 7 December, should "sweep right ahead at once." If it then became clear that an outside power was thwarting League action, that state would have responsibility for "crucifying peace."[16]

Italian Diplomacy

Italian diplomats encouraged the fear of war, fed the hope of settlement, and helped postpone the day of reckoning on the oil sanction. The oil problem worried Rome in November and December 1935. League experts estimated at the end of the year that Italy held between 700,000 and 800,000 tons in reserve and that this was the limit of reserve capacity, equivalent to about three months' consumption. Supply from the United States during these months, important as it was, was largely in fulfillment of earlier orders. After Hull's speech of 15 November and Ickes' comment on the twenty-first, Italians thought they could not firmly count on this supply for the future. Mussolini talked of oil from Albania and of promises from Japan to furnish gasoline to the colonies. But this was not certain, and Albanian oil was dismissed by League experts as of poor quality and no quantitative importance.[17]

On 24 November, the day before the meeting of the Committee of Eighteen was postponed and when everyone was expecting League action, Aloisi found Mussolini "extremely nervous." Mussolini said many Fascists of long standing urged an attack on Britain before Italy was weakened. He told Aloisi to say to Russia and Romania—the important suppliers from the east—that Italians would fight with the courage of the hopeless rather than let themselves be strangled.[18] Bluff it may well have been. Mussolini himself probably did not know how he would respond if the oil sanction were imposed. He was a master of the melodramatic gesture. He showed the Japanese ambassador a loaded revolver kept in his desk should he decide, in desperation, on suicide.[19]

Such talk frightened Drummond and Chambrun. On 26 November, anticipating a meeting of the Committee of Eighteen, Drummond wrote of the "catastrophic consequences of a failure to realize the strength of Italian opinion." He believed Mussolini's threat that, if forced to yield to humiliating terms or go down fighting, he would choose war, even if all of Europe went up in flames. The Italian people could be worked up to almost any degree of exultation, "with consequent risk of commission and condonation of almost any act of folly." This dispatch, through the clouds of qualifications, alternative hypotheses, and pros and cons that make Drummond's communications a model of poor diplomatic style, came down solidly on the side of caution, of delay. It was given wide circulation by the Foreign Office, to king, cabinet, and Dominions, and no doubt influenced the cabinet on 2 December. Minuting the dispatch, Geoffrey Thompson wrote:

> It follows that we may have to recommend to the League—lest worse befall—the basis of a settlement which, while not giving Italy all she sought, may yet be more favorable than anything she could have hitherto secured by negotiations. While unfriendly critics might suggest the exchange of Tigre as partial payment for an Ethiopian outlet to the sea would compromise the Covenant, a slight sacrifice of principle is a small price to pay to preclude the possibility of the Ethiopian war spreading to the Mediterranean—and perhaps beyond.[20]

Italian diplomats recalled with pride their work during the war. They had little direction. Mussolini as foreign minister made policy from his office in the Palazzo Venezia with little reference to the ministry staff in the Palazzo Chigi. Raffaele Guariglia, head of the Ethiopian bureau established in April 1935, did not have a single audience with Mussolini during the seven months of the war. Within the ministry no such dominating figure as Vansittart or Léger gave daily supervision to posts abroad. Undersecretary Fulvio Suvich had nothing like the command of the department that Grandi had had prior to his removal in 1932. Lacking influence in determining policy, many of them faced with the conviction that the war was politically if not morally wrong, the diplomats responded to the dangerous isolation of their nation with patriotic fervor. At the moment of sanctions, wrote the ambassador to France, diplomats were conscious as never before of serving, not a regime, but Italy, "only Italy."[21]

All sought to ward off anything that might extend the war to Europe. This goal was approached in several ways. Guariglia saw the opportunity to use sanctions as a "safety valve" through which to vent the frustrations, fears, and anxieties that had accumulated dangerously in the months just prior to the invasion, when depression about the future of what was then an unpopular, unwanted war reached its height. While it was not the task of the foreign service to encourage domestic patriotism, Guariglia saw the possibilities, through formal protests, of leading sanctionist states to think sanctions were not having intended effects and thus slowing down or mediating the application of further measures.[22] Important in this effort were Italian representatives abroad: Giuseppe Bastianini in Warsaw, Ugo Sola in Bucharest, Bernardo Attolico and Massimo Magistrati in Berlin, Carlo Galli in Ankara, Gabriele Preziosi in Brussels, Pelegrino Gighi in Cairo, and above all Augusto Rosso in Washington, Pompeo Aloisi, Renato Bova Scoppa, and Alberto Berio in Geneva, Vittorio Cerruti in Paris, and Dino Grandi in London, at the heart of the enemy coalition.

Others helped. Guglielmo Marconi, honored inventor and member of the Fascist Grand Council, broadcast by air from Rome and, at Mussolini's request and against medical advice, set off on a long trip in October to Brazil, Britain, and France to speak on Italy's behalf.[23] A former diplomat, Daniele Varè, spoke to the Royal Institute of International Affairs in London on 19 November: "No more cruel insult has ever been thrown at a proud and sensitive nation than the assertion . . . that the Abyssinian question was "a test case" for the League. . . . Italy is the rat for vivisection, the guinea pig, on which to try the vaccine of sanctions."[24]

Rosso got nowhere in his complaints about American policy. On 22 November 1935 he charged the government with violating neutrality. This gave rise to an outburst by Hull. It was Italy who was violating international law and on whom rested responsibility for the "awful repercussions" of the war. Roosevelt called Hull's retort a "classic," and Hugh Wilson wrote from

Geneva that Hull's response made him proud of his country.[25] Rosso sent dispatches to Rome optimistically recording evidence of favorable American opinion—rallies by Italian-Americans, for example—but these were self-serving messages that greatly exaggerated the extent of pro-Italian sentiment and Rosso's role in encouraging it. Official and unofficial opinion was overwhelmingly set against Italy in this war.

The diplomatic effort at Geneva, feverish as it was, was not important enough to be the "masterwork" Bova Scoppa claimed. Aloisi, head of the delegation and secretary-general at the foreign ministry, lobbied constantly. Bova Scoppa, secretary to the delegation and permanent delegate to the League, had many contacts. Berio maintained liaison between the delegation and the League Secretariat, where Berio's chief, Massimo Pilotti, was deputy secretary-general. These activities kept the Italians well informed, and Aloisi reported regularly to Mussolini. But important decisions were made, not in Geneva, but by governments in their capital cities. Mussolini played his own cards in his own way. Those initiatives available to the Genevan delegation were usually peripheral to the basic issues at stake. In September 1935, for example, the Palazzo Chigi presented to the Council an elaborate document arranged by Guariglia and meant to establish that Ethiopia was composed of uncontrolled racial factions, that the ostensible government systematically violated treaties and bothered its neighbors, and that barbarous and repellent practices such as slavery, legal amputation, and castration of prisoners put Ethiopia "outside the Covenant." The attempt to impugn the validity of Ethiopia's case failed. No one took it seriously. Overshadowed by the enormity of Italy's own aggressive imperialism, the document, patently insincere and clumsily presented, fell "in a void," Guariglia mournfully recorded. "No one paid attention to us."[26]

The most important hand to play at Geneva was the threat to leave the League. On the day before the invasion Mussolini said that if measures against Italy were pushed too far participation would end.[27] The sanctionist countries emphatically did not want this, for the reconciliationist mode assumes that all players remain in the game. Indeed, at this time it was more imaginable that Mussolini would commit an extreme and desperate act of war in Europe than that he would strike off on a European policy of his own. In 1935 few Italians wanted isolation, or dependence on Germany.

Yet their pride was affronted, and officials in Rome regularly considered the question of leaving the League. On 7 November the delegation at Geneva reported the unanimous sentiment there that Italy would cave in after sanctions. This, they concluded, would force abandonment of the League. The same conclusion was reached by two men who, before Pilotti, had held high positions in the League. Giacomo Paulucci di Calboli Barone, secretary-general at the Palazzo Chigi from 1922 to 1927, then undersecretary-general at Geneva from 1927 to 1932, stated this opinion on 9 November. On the twelfth Bernardo Attolico, undersecretary-general of the League in 1920, wrote from Berlin: "To remain in Geneva after 18 November [the day sanctions were imposed] would mean not only accepting the punishment but recognizing the justice of it." The Stresa front had been weakened by the Franco-Soviet treaty and the Anglo-German naval agreement. Further collaboration with the western countries was possible only for a strong and united Italy, and impossible if Italy were "humiliated and disabled." Leave the League, Attolico argued, to have a free hand for the future.[28] Suvich and Guariglia argued in favor of remaining. The Ethiopian affair might yet end to Italy's favor. Grandi in mid-November was reporting good relations with Vansittart and a British willingness to begin negotiations for a settlement. Mussolini decided to wait. The threat remained, but lessened by the recognition in Italy that departure from the League might leave Italy in an even more exposed position. And the threat of war seemed to be working just fine.[29]

No diplomats took more initiative and worked harder—or claimed more credit—than the Italian ambassadors in Paris and London. Cerruti, an energetic, enthusiastic person, was notorious for his constant representations to Laval. Whenever British ambassador George Clerk met with the premier, Cerruti invariably asked for an interview immediately afterward. Acting largely without instructions from Rome, worried about a collapse of good relations between France and Italy, sustained, as he said, "by a feeling of duty," Cerruti credited himself with the "timely intervention," with "persuasive work of such energy" that the French government "at the last moment" decided against the oil embargo.[30] Baldwin thought Laval was in Italian pay.[31] But it was enough that Cerruti told Laval what he wanted to hear. His repeated warnings against the oil sanction, together with the alarms coming from Chambrun in Rome, gave Laval arguments for mediation as an alternative course.

Cerruti's reports of November 1935 exude optimism. Despite sanctions, important French banks—the Crédit Lyonnais, the Banque de l'Union parisienne, and the Banque pour le Commerce at l'Industrie—announced themselves ready to act in a liberal spirit toward Italy. The Société générale and the Comptoir national d'Escompte would maintain a correct but nonhostile stance. Only the Banque de Paris et des Pay Bas was unfriendly, dominated, the historian Luigi Villari asserted, by Masonic and Jewish influences. A senator told Cerruti the Senate's foreign affairs committee was against sanctions. The problem, concluded Cerruti, lay at the Quai d'Orsay, where Léger and his top assistant René Massigli were under British influence and leftist leaning.[32]

Like other Italian ambassadors, Cerruti loaded his dispatches with exaggerated accounts of pro-Italian sentiment. The Italians in France, he reported, were in a state of "superb discipline, enthusiasm, virile strength, and firmness." A French legion was forming to fight in Ethiopia with the Italians, rallies were held, and so on. It is remarkable that reports of such activity from the various ambassadors were seen of sufficient significance to be included in the annual "political situation" résumés of the foreign ministry, for the events described were not influential in the countries.[33] But, accepted as evidence of support when Italy stood condemned, they gratified officials in the Palazzo Chigi. There was, it seemed, sympathy for Italy's case.

On 26 November, after asking for and receiving postponement of the meeting of the Committee of Eighteen, Laval told his Council of Ministers that he would oppose the oil sanction.[34] The matter, he said, was not urgent. What he had in mind, no doubt, was to use the next few days to complete the last stage of negotiations for settlement terms. The next day, Italians drove home the point of good relations by announcing the cancellation of army leaves and the movement of troop formations. No indication was given of the new location of the troops. It was left to be imagined in France that they were going to the Alpine frontier, and in Britain that they were off to north Africa to put additional pressure on Egypt.[35] Two days later Rome announced that the movements were not to the French frontier.

Laval knew that he probably could not remain apart from a decision of the Committee of Eighteen to apply the embargo, especially once the British decided to adhere, as they did on 2 December. On 30 November Bova Scoppa delivered a verbal warning to a number of states on the committee (other than Britain and France) that application of proposal 4–A would be an "unfriendly act." The same day Laval saw Cerruti to warn him that France could not avoid adherence and to urge upon Italy the importance of using the breathing space of the next few days to conclude the war by a settlement.

Dino Grandi admired the British and in turn was well liked by them. He sought the London post upon being turned out of the Palazzo Chigi in 1932 and continued to maintain the faith in conventional diplomatic practices and the conviction that Italy's future was tied to cooperation with the western countries that sustained him as foreign minister from 1929 to 1932. Mediation, negotiated settlement, was his goal.

The Foreign Office, which cracked the Italian code and read his cables, thought Grandi was not much listened to in Rome. Word had it he was out of favor for failing to convince officials early on that behind British informal warnings against an Ethiopian war lay serious considerations. Mussolini, said an emissary, thought Grandi had earlier failed to warn him of the potentially hostile state of British public opinion.[36]

But how serious, how strong, was British opposition really? Emilio Canevari, as noted earlier, counted Grandi as one of the two men without whom the empire would not have been won. Grandi's contribution, said Canevari, was to correctly assess British intentions in the critical days of September, when the nerves of Italian officials were shaken by the redeployment and reinforcement of the British fleet in the Mediterranean. Grandi had then convinced Mussolini that Britain had neither the capacity nor the will to fight, helping Mussolini to ride out domestic opposition to the continued pursuit of an apparently dangerous colonial war.[37] And this line Grandi continued to assert. Despite all the flapping, Britain would not go to war for Ethiopia.

In late November 1935, while adopting, as instructed, an intransigent attitude in the face of sanctions and with instructions to close the embassy if the oil embargo was imposed, Grandi did not need to fan concern lest a war break out. Of course he, like Cerruti, never left it far from his conversation, but this anxiety was amply developed in London by Drummond, the Admiralty, Vansittart, and half the cabinet. Mussolini was skeptical about British intentions and the value of what London might concede, but he did not discourage the initiatives Grandi took in conversations with Vansittart following the government's success at the polls on 14 November. Grandi claimed that the Hoare-Laval proposal of December should rightly be called by his and Vansittart's names.[38] Grandi's contribution fits well into Bova Scoppa's contention that in the face of Mussolini's "impermeability" it was diplomatic activity that upset League timetables, deflected the oil sanction, and constantly moderated hostile forces.[39]

Grandi's initiatives were important, for British concessions were to be harder won than French. But they should be seen as part of a more widely developed search for terms engaged in after economic and financial sanctions were imposed on 18 November and the question of an embargo on oil and vital raw materials loomed on the horizon. The governments of Britain and France wanted peace too.

Setting Some Terms

By mid-November 1935, after all, far more was involved than merely ridding European affairs of the troublesome matter of colonial claims. The British cabinet on 23 October stated it would accept no settlement outside the "framework of the League." The international organization, the British insisted, was one of the three parties to the dispute, and any plans for settlement had to be acceptable to its members. This spelled the end of the various plans going around Rome to ask for a suspension of sanctions (those of 18 November, which did not include oil or steel) in the hope that the three most involved European powers would find terms of settlement outside the League. It did not mean the end of extra-League initiations of settlement terms. The British and French governments had before them Mussolini's stiff demands as submitted on 16 October. Italy was to administer directly the so-called non-Amharic territories. Italy was to participate fully in any League-sponsored assistance programs. Land conquered in the north was to be directly annexed to Eritrea. Boundary changes in Italy's favor were to take place in the south. In return, Italy would grant permission for Ethiopian use of the port of Assab, with port and access remaining under Italian control.

On 22 October, taking advantage of the renewed good relations with France after Laval's 18 October assurances and eager to act before Italian military victories or further demands for sanctions complicated the hope of settlement, Hoare, Vansittart, Oliphant, and Peterson decided that Peterson should go to Paris. There he was to draft a reply to Mussolini in cooperation with the French—in the person of René Saint-Quentin, head of the African desk at the ministry in the Quai d'Orsay.

Peterson and Saint-Quentin first decided against counterproposing an exchange of territory. This idea, mooted on the eve of the invasion, had been the basis of a final prewar attempt to satisfy Italy by the outright cession of certain parts of southern Ethiopia, notably the region of Bale, in return for an Ethiopian outlet to the sea at Zeila on British donation, or perhaps at Assab as an Italian contribution. Peterson and Saint-Quentin argued that such prewar terms were no longer acceptable. At the end of October, when neither side had sustained a military defeat, such an exchange of territory—which would in practice be Zeila, for Italy would certainly not give up Assab—would be "closely scrutinized by a now thoroughly aroused world public opinion" and, in their judgment, would seem too much like a reward for aggression. Furthermore, in his terms of 16 October Mussolini had demanded parts of the Ogaden and the Danakil as well as "annexation pure and simple" of "conquered territory." To add the more fruitful and habitable Bale province as well would be regarded as a "decisive Italian success." Lastly, implementing an exchange of territory was outside the function of the League.

Instead, so as to keep within sighting distance of the Covenant, Peterson and Saint-Quentin refurbished the plan of assistance recommended by the League's Committee of Five in September. The Italians, in September, had rejected this plan, protesting the subordinate part assigned to Italy in the international, League-sponsored commission to oversee Ethiopia's political and economic development. These objections were, we know, largely formal. The aims of the impending conquest had nothing to do with the catalog of complaints about Ethiopia's underdevelopment, to which the League responded good-naturedly. But the proposal, and the objections, gave Peterson and Saint-Quentin something, and something League-approved, to work from. Furthermore, on 16 October Mussolini returned to the idea in his list of terms with a demand for clearly defined Italian participation in a League supervisory commission for the Amharic regions (defined as Tigre, Amhara, Gojam, and Shoa). Rather than an international writ on the remaining regions, he specified an Italian mandate or its equivalent. Whereas the Committee of Five's proposal left the army intact and under the emperor's control, Mussolini now demanded disarmament of the entire country.

Peterson and Saint-Quentin, excluding the claims for territorial concessions, sought to satisfy these demands. After all, everyone had long conceded to Italy a special place in the economic development of Ethiopia. There would still be a central commission in Addis Ababa under League control. But in the territory south of the eight-degree parallel, the area now defined as the non-Amharic lands (including Kefa, Borana, and Arusi and excluding Harar), the advisory administrators would be exclusively Italian. They would report, not to the entire commission (which under the Committee of Five plan were to have collective responsibility), but to one of the four commissioners—the Italian—who would in turn be responsible only to the senior (and non-Italian) commissioner delegated by the League.

It was a jerry-built plan, but, in Peterson's judgment "nothing could be more disastrous . . . than that His Majesty's Government sponsor a scheme inacceptable at Geneva" and "only by some such means will we satisfy even approximately . . . Italian pretensions."[40] The Peterson–Saint-Quentin draft was submitted on 26 October. It met with a cool reception in the Foreign Office. The League, it was held, would never accept Italian administrative preponderance in the south. A report the previous day from Minister Barton in Addis Ababa had stated that the emperor stood little chance of inducing his chiefs to concede what Italy wanted. Stanhope argued for care, lest the emperor be pushed from his throne. The danger of anarchy arose. If Ethiopia became an impossible neighbor Britain in a few years "might have to join France and Italy to repress it, which would be absurd and anomalous."[41] There was another stumbling block. The Peterson–Saint-Quentin draft mentioned a body of troops in the southern zone to preserve order, probably under Italian officers. This needed clearing up. Any intimation of Italian troops, of a veiled protectorate, would never get by Geneva or the emperor.

Laval was discouraged that the British did not intend to press the proposals. There must be no delay in opening talks with the Italians, even though he described the draft as "an insufficient base for negotiation."[42] In this description he was correct. When the draft was forwarded informally to Rome, it was judged entirely unsatisfactory both to Mussolini's list of demands and to the more moderate expectations of the diplomatic service.[43]

Hoare and Laval had a chance to talk when on 1 November they met in Geneva for the Coordination Committee's meeting to set the date for sanctions to go into effect. The issues were getting so complicated and directed so exclusively to the Italians that, if the talks continued without acknowledgment to the League, France and Britain might be seen as deserting the collective front. The League had to be informed enough to offset anxiety but without letting on to the details. Too much had to be worked out before anything was ready for Geneva, Addis Ababa, or, indeed, for a formal response to Mussolini's terms as presented on 16 October. At a secret meeting on 1 November it was decided that mention of the talks should be made at the closing session of the Coordination Committee the following day.

On 2 November, just before adjournment, Laval rose to say there was yet another "duty" beyond the establishment of sanctions—the search for an "amicable settlement." Hoare rose immediately to second this. Referring to the British-French talks, he said:

> There is nothing mysterious or sinister about these discussions. It is the duty of all to explore the road of peace. . . . If and when these suggestions take a more definite form, we shall take the earliest opportunity to bring them before the Council. . . . Nothing is further from our minds than to make and conclude an agreement behind the back of the League.

Next spoke Van Zeeland of Belgium. The League, he said, "has just given striking proof of its vigor and its moderation." In these circumstances, "does it not seem right that efforts towards conciliation should, from this moment, be placed under the auspices and the framework of the League itself?" Since British and French officials "have already devoted a large part of their time and talents to this task, why should the League not entrust to them the mission of seeking, under its auspices and control and in the spirit of the Covenant, the elements of a solution?"[44]

The delegates knew that Hoare and Laval had coordinated their comments beforehand. Van Zeeland's unsolicited contribution, however, went further than anyone had expected. Frank Walters records that the mood of the meeting went "from one of confidence to one of discomfort."[45] Who knew what it might imply for the collective action hardly yet under way that the two great colonial and Mediterranean powers would take negotiation into their own hands? Would it be possible to keep terms acceptable to Italy within "the spirit of the Covenant?" League-sponsored negotiation raised new opportunities for obstructionism that could compromise or cripple the sanction effort. All this came as a surprise on 2 November. Seven delegates endorsed Van Zeeland's suggestion, which was a personal expression, not a motion, and was never put to a vote. Chairman Vasconcellos enlarged upon his own opinion: "I feel I am speaking for the Committee in saying that . . . this Committee note the hope expressed by [Van Zeeland] and give it their full approval."[46]

Hoare and Laval claimed after the meeting that negotiations were thereafter conducted with the concurrence of the League. Useful to legitimize them, this interpretation strained the fact. Hoare told the House of Commons that the League was "solidly behind" and "almost unanimous" in bestowing its "particular blessing" on the search for settlement. Perhaps —but the delegates had not been polled. The seven endorsements were in large part warnings that any solution must conform to League principles. Walters wrote that Vasconcellos's assertion of full approval was "more courtesy than truth."[47]

It was back to the drawing board for the British. Reluctant to press the Peterson–Saint-Quentin draft, the Foreign Office concluded that a less complicated alternative was to return to the idea of simple exchange of territory. Peterson continued to object that Ethiopia would never cede conquered territory in Tigre and that the cession of Zeila in return for a transfer to Italy of Bale and the lands in the south would have a "devastating effect on the League." It would seem the worst of old imperialist bargainings. He was overruled by Vansittart and Eden, who thought League members would accept a clean cut on a smaller scale rather than take on endless future troubles by giving Italy a thinly veiled protectorate in the south. No solution was possible, said Vansittart, "unless Italy gets a good deal."[48]

No new word came from Mussolini. Laval, happy to accept anything that might work, offered no assistance. The worrying was left to the British. On 11 November the Foreign Office decided that as soon as the general elections of the fourteenth were over a new approach was necessary to get Laval "to show his hand further." The hope of a Mediterranean détente was over; sanctions were to be imposed on the eighteenth; the oil question was coming up for resolution. The British could not do everything by themselves. Since no rapid settlement was likely, the League should now be brought into the projected negotiations, perhaps by reconvoking the Committee of Five to decide in principle which line to pursue: territorial exchange or a plan of assistance with Italy's participation defined therein. A mood of exasperation set in. Vansittart said on 15 November: "The sooner this responsibility becomes general rather than particular the better."[49]

Italian documents state that Laval proposed a halt in the fighting between 14 and 18 November so as to make a new effort toward conciliation, but this was turned down in Rome.[50] When Clerk asked him on the sixteenth and the twentieth if he had any new lines to suggest as a result of his contacts with Rome, he replied he did not. Italian conditions stood as defined by Mussolini a month before, and terms would have to accommodate to that.[51]

Peterson was sent again to Paris, and on 23 November Laval presented to him and Saint-Quentin a new set of Italian conditions conveyed by Cerruti and, according to Aloisi, approved by Mussolini as offering a serious basis for negotiations. The Italian terms rejected the idea of territorial exchange, insisting instead on claiming a right of conquest, which the Foreign Office regarded as the most impossible of all bases for settlement.

Italy was to get all of Tigre, including Makale, conquered on 8 November. If not annexed directly to the colony of Eritrea, Tigre would have to be converted into an autonomous principality under Italian sovereignty. The British had always thought the disposition of Tigre the chief obstacle in the way of settlement. Lying in the north against the Italian frontier, it contained sites neither side would give up: Ethiopia's holy city of Aksum and Italy's newly "reconquered" Aduwa. Suvich compared Italy's claim on Tigre to France's on Alsace and Lorraine. The bulk of Italian forces now stood in Tigre—in the only territory they had, with such fanfare, yet conquered.

Next in the Italian demands conveyed by Laval on 23 November was frontier rectification of the Ogaden and the Danakil, along as yet undemarcated lines. Lastly there was the demand for a special zone in the south (west from the eight-degree parallel to the thirty-seventh meridian, not including Harar), to be under the emperor's sovereignty but with complete freedom for Italians' economic exploitation and colonial settlement. There was to be no League interference in this zone. Italy would renounce participation in League schemes of assistance elsewhere, all the more readily since the war made acceptance of Italian personnel in the central highlands unlikely.

No quid pro quo was volunteered in the proposals Laval submitted on 23 November, but Saint-Quentin claimed Italy was prepared to cede a port and corridor in Eritrea. This would not be Assab but a road of less significance near the frontier of French Somaliland. Zeila could be substituted if desired. The French would accept the establishment of a rival port to Djibouti.[52]

The British rejected these proposals. An unsupervised free hand in the south went against all League-sponsored thinking. It was just too much to demand all of Tigre as a right of conquest.

To keep the conversation going, Peterson suggested some modified terms. "Subject always to the ultimate assent of Addis Ababa and Geneva," he proposed that Ethiopia be induced to exchange part of Tigre (roughly along 1896 lines), the Danakil excluding Aussa, and most of the Ogaden, in return for a port and a corridor. This was less than Laval presented, and it returned to the idea of exchange. It corresponded to a more limited set of demands presented not long before by Suvich, a discrepancy that led Peterson to conclude Laval was doing "the Italians' bargaining for them" and "putting terms higher than they do themselves." To help the talks along, the French suggested a chartered company for the special zone, with non-Italian personnel attached to protect native interests and to represent the League, which would act as final arbitrator in disputes. The British could promise to help secure for Italy the fullest possible facilities for economic development and settlement. Such were the minimum terms, Peterson said, that could ensure continued conversations.[53]

Hoare, Eden, and Vansittart agreed. Fear of European war was running high in the Foreign Office in the last week of November 1935. General Ezio Garibaldi came to London, claiming to speak for Mussolini and warning that, while Mussolini wanted an honorable settlement, he would go to war over oil. On 26 November Drummond sent a dispatch warning of the catastrophic consequences of a failure to realize the strength of Italian opinion against sanctions, asserting that Mussolini was not bluffing and was capable of "almost any act of folly." A "suicidal act" by the Italians was possible. This dispatch was sent to the king, the cabinet, and the Dominions. The heightened anxiety, the renewed "mad dog" fear, pushed toward appeasement and lessened the reluctance to cede parts of Tigre. On 28 November Peterson was told to go ahead on the lines recommended from Paris, "the best we can hope for," said Vansittart. "We should be very happy if the Italians accept."[54]

There were points of procedure to consider. Laval wanted to submit any terms on which the British and French agreed to Rome before presenting them to Geneva. At the very least, any discussion at the League should be postponed until a tentative plan for settlement was worked out. The League, Laval maintained, expected the two powers to come up with something substantial and would be embarrassed at having to deal with a premature plan. Geneva, eager for a settlement, would not balk before reasonable proposals. Moreover, too much talk there would prejudice the room for maneuver needed in negotiations of detail. There was also the danger that any proposal that did not come with firm British and French backing would be scuttled by opposition from, say, the Soviet Union or Turkey.

The Foreign Office conceded these points. Hoare held that the reason Mussolini rejected Eden's Zeila proposal in June and the Committee of Five's proposals in September was that premature press disclosures foreclosed the possibility of negotiated compromise. As for getting in touch with the emperor, that would be held off until there was something concrete to offer from Europe.[55]

Meanwhile, in this last week of November, pressure grew to bring talks to a head. Postponement of the meeting of the Committee of Eighteen beyond

29 November gave breathing space for conciliation, time to allay Italian suspicions, to forestall a violent reaction. From Rome came hints, mainly from
Suvich and Aloisi and spread about by Chambrun, that Mussolini was anxious to reach a settlement at the earliest moment. General Garibaldi's visit,
however, indicated that Mussolini still held firm in his demands. The terms
Garibaldi conveyed were similar to those sent through Laval. The Foreign
Office wondered if their opposition to such a broad concession was understood in Rome. Indeed, cues and messages were garbled. What *was* Italy's
position, and by whom conveyed? Mussolini seemed to pay little attention to
Drummond. As an intermediary Garibaldi was not reliable. Grandi ground
his own axes, and no one knew the extent of his influence with Mussolini.
And the old suspicions of the French were revived. Laval's reliability was in
constant doubt. The value of secondhand dealings through him fell accordingly. Yet Mussolini could not come to London, and it was out of the question for Hoare to go to Rome.[56]

Paris therefore remained the central link, yet Cerruti was suspect too.
Laval was supposed to have assured Cerruti that in case of any Italian attack
in the Mediterranean France would stand with the British. Hoare worried
that Cerruti would not pass on the full dose of this warning of solidarity. Messages, he said, "were apt to be modified or watered down in
transmission" when sent through Grandi and Cerruti, thereby encouraging
Mussolini's intransigence. He asked Laval on 28 November to have Chambrun repeat this message directly to Mussolini. But five days later Drummond reported Chambrun had received no such instruction. The Foreign
Office was in a fury. An official minuted: "The whole of our future action
vis-à-vis the French government is dependent on the *knowledge* that Laval's
promised statement has been sent to Mussolini *direct*."[57] The French
apology was this—the draft telegram was still on Laval's desk. On 5
December Vansittart gave vent to his anger.

> This is another instance where Laval is playing fast and loose with us, and a
> great deal more loose than fast. This is in fact intolerable. He has, of course,
> plenty of time to go through the simple and honest action of initialling the
> draft, and his failure to do so . . . no doubt had a bad effect in Rome in the
> sense that we have missed the boat. This is one of the points on which I think
> we must have it out with him in Paris. . . . [58]

A British visit to Paris had been planned since 26 November, when with
Hoare's approval Vansittart had suggested going to talk directly to Cerruti.
Laval could not be trusted—yet in a week, Vansittart then hoped, the Anglo-
French talks would be advanced enough to open negotiations. But Peterson
made no progress after the twenty-sixth in his talks with Saint-Quentin. So
the Paris talks stood still. When Peterson asked for further instructions he
was informed that Vansittart and Hoare himself would soon arrive on the
scene. Hoare was going in order to prevent Laval from coming to London.

Laval wanted direct talks, but Hoare could not face the flood of public rumor and the possible danger to peace-planning that such a visit would raise. He refused Laval's request to come, and instead accepted an invitation to stop in Paris on his way to an overdue recuperative vacation in Switzerland. He thought, he wrote later, that his "personal intervention was needed to prevent a rupture between the French and ourselves over the oil embargo. . . ."[59]

Peterson was by now in dismay. As of 5 December Saint-Quentin was still without instructions. Their superiors were going over their heads in matters of state and behind their backs in developing terms of settlement. Laval was intensely preoccupied with parliamentary affairs; his government withstood daily attacks on its entire domestic policy. So he reverted to the diplomatic style he liked best—last-minute personal intervention with the hope for the best. Vansittart had opened his own set of direct talks with the Italian ambassador Grandi in London on 29 November, pushing his authority to the limit. Peterson argued later that if he had been given broader instructions and left alone he could have secured French agreement on terms favoring Italy less than the Hoare-Laval terms and without direct involvement of ministerial prestige.[60] This may be true, but it ignores the overriding concern of Vansittart, Hoare, and Laval to smooth overall relations at the highest level in the moments before the decision on an oil sanction—possibly a decision on war—was due.

The large cabinet of 2 December 1935 established the frame of reference for Hoare's Paris visit. The cabinet resolved to support a collectively subscribed oil sanction at the forthcoming meeting of the Committee of Eighteen set for 12 December. "Collective" was a condition here, as was tacit American cooperation. Hoare proposed to use the time before that meeting to pursue terms of settlement, as swiftly as possible. He spoke encouragingly. There was a "regular barrage" of peace feelers from Italy. Grandi was about to return to Rome, and Hoare wanted to give him the British view directly. In Paris he would "press peace talks" with Laval. If their discussion went well, argument could be made at Geneva to postpone the date of application of the oil sanction, expected for just before Christmas. The principle of cooperation once established, enforcement could be delayed if Mussolini, under this threat, began negotiations. To all this the cabinet agreed. There was full knowledge, and no criticism, of the foreign minister's visit to Paris. Any agreement, any plan, would need cabinet approval before being sent to the three contending parties. What was important now was to set out some acceptable terms.[61]

Terms were discussed in three ultrasecret meetings between Vansittart and Grandi on 3, 4, and 5 December. Given his determination to avoid a Mediterranean conflict, the importance everyone attached to the present moment as the last chance for settlement, and his dominant position at the Foreign

Office, Vansittart's talks were more than an exchange of views. They were meant to establish the British position to take to Paris. He told Grandi he kept Baldwin and Hoare informed daily. It must have been agreeable to make a run around the hitherto central French connection. Grandi kept in close touch with Rome, which does not, however, mean that he was constantly directed by Mussolini. On 2 December he received a list of maximum and minimum demands from the foreign ministry. Each night he sent a courier to Mussolini's office.[62] Mussolini sat back and waited.

The Ethiopians were never consulted. This is what Laval wanted. He saw a way off the hook if Italy accepted British-French terms and Ethiopia refused them. Vansittart perhaps agreed. In any case, the sense of urgency facilitated ignoring the Ethiopians. Geoffrey Thompson and Patrick Scrivener summed up the sense of the Foreign Office in a note to Vansittart on 3 December. This may be taken as the text behind the Hoare-Laval plan. "Our object is to overcome the immediate dangerous crisis, not to solve the Abyssinian question, which will be with us for years. But if we can stop the war, passions will cool and there will be more chance than at present of reducing all these rather general and perhaps slightly theoretical proposals to shape."[63]

Grandi said the basis for what became the Hoare-Laval plan was "midway between the proposals Vansittart made to him on 3 December and the concession Vansittart accepted on the fifth."[64] Vansittart conceded a good deal beyond what had been permitted for Peterson. Hoare and Baldwin, if in fact they were informed daily, were either in agreement or napping. The central problem was the disposition of Tigre. Vansittart sought to solve it (for the short run) by admitting, to an unknown, probably negotiable degree—our evidence is slight—that Tigre could become an autonomous state eventually ceded to Italy. Thompson proposed that Tigre first be designated a land of indeterminate status, to be supervised by a League commission charged with ascertaining native sentiment. If Mussolini's claims of popular support proved true, then self-determination would favor Italy. This was a face-saving device. Italy was set on keeping at least northern and eastern Tigre. Self-determination provided, or so it seemed to these diplomats, a way to detach the land from Ethiopia without appearing to reward aggression too directly. Vansittart did also concede a chartered company for exploitation and economic domination of the large development-settlement area in the south. These concessions might save Italian pride and, with concessions elsewhere, be accepted by Haile Selassie if they ended the threat of invasion.[65]

What was Ethiopia to get in return? The French now appeared set against the Zeila transfer, fearing a rival port to Djibouti, particularly if the Ethiopians established a line connection to the Djibouti–Addis Ababa railway. The British indeed wanted to give up Zeila only as a last, and absolutely necessary, resort. The British empire was not to be frittered away. Assab, Italian-held, little-developed, and less accessible, was therefore preferred. The Italians had stated they would grant only economic privileges, not sovereignty, at this port. When on 5 December Saint-Quentin suggested an outlet to the sea at Assab, Peterson ridiculed the idea. Imagine in return for its many concessions, Ethiopia's getting only a swimming hole! He was not aware that on the same day this is what Vansittart agreed to with Grandi.[66]

The Grandi-Vansittart talks, according to Aloisi, made a good impression on Mussolini. On the other hand, simultaneous with Aloisi's report came Drummond's warning from Rome that Mussolini might well be more intransigent than his diplomatic agents had led the British to believe. It was Grandi, Cerruti, Suvich, and Aloisi who were prone to enthusiasm and optimism about the chances for peace. Mussolini continued to withhold comment.[67]

It was decided in London to send some signals to Mussolini, to encourage a conciliatory mood. Hoare spoke to the Commons on 5 December. There was no word about the substantive talks forthcoming with Laval, no word about how far serious talks on terms had already proceeded. Eden, too, was left in the dark, although Hoare was to meet with Laval on 7 December. Before crossing the Channel, Vansittart consulted Reginald Leeper, head of the press bureau in the Foreign Office. How long would it take to change public opinion in favor of removing sanctions if they found settlement terms? Three weeks, Leeper replied. "We have only three days," said Vansittart, and this was to be too little.[68]

To the Commons Hoare stressed the urgent need for peace. A negotiated settlement might be "a hopeless task," but "we intend not only to go on trying but to redouble our efforts during the short period of time that is still open before the Geneva meeting." He made an appeal to Mussolini. "We have no wish to humiliate Italy or to weaken it." Britain wanted "a strong Italy governed by a strong government." "Cannot we lay aside these suspicions and concentrate in the immediate future upon finding a basis of settlement and making it possible for the world to return to normal life?"[69]

An invitation invites a response. Mussolini was scheduled to speak to his Chamber of Deputies on 7 December. A telegram went out to Drummond. "There would seem to be a chance of finding . . . a solution, given reason and goodwill, and it is with the desire of finding it that I am going to meet M. Laval in Paris." It was most important, Drummond was to say to Mussolini, "that he should make some response that will facilitate and not impair the prospect of settlement." A warning was included. Without such encouragement in Mussolini's speech, immediate imposition of an oil embargo was certain.[70]

Mussolini did not oblige. He would never negotiate under threat, he said, and sanctions, once determined, would be applied automatically. In his speech he deftly turned back Hoare's arguments. Italy's proposals had been delivered a month and a half ago. But "instead of concrete conversations there came forth sanctions." Recent days had showed an improvement in the atmosphere, but, he cautioned the deputies, "it is my duty to put you on guard against the premature and excessive optimism." "Good," chorused the Chamber. Hoare talked of wishing to see a strong Italy. That was impossible if colonial needs were not met. As for the League's attempt to kill Italy by "economic suffocation," an attack leveled precisely because Italy was assumed to be poor in raw materials, what was forgotten by the "humanitarians of Geneva" was that the spirit of Italians could transcend these limitations. The "end of this crisis will come only with full recognition of our rights and the safeguarding of our African interests." The speech slammed no doors, said Drummond, but it gave none of the encouragement Hoare sought.[71]

6 THE HOARE-LAVAL PROPOSALS

The Paris Meeting

Enough has been said to show that the meeting of Hoare and Laval in Paris on 7 and 8 December was no chance matter. It had cabinet approval on both sides. Both foreign ministries had worked on the terms for a proposal to end the war. The terms had been clarified in the talks between Vansittart and Grandi and between Laval and Cerruti. It seemed there was one last chance for conciliation before the oil embargo. The Paris proposals were formulated by men who viewed them as merely one more chapter in the diplomatic effort to end the war, which was the objective, also, of sanctions. Neither the talks nor the terms represented any new departure. So ran official thinking. Yet the Paris talks had another quality, often ignored. The Hoare-Laval conversations were meant, primarily in fact, to ease the tension between Britain and France.

On 6 December, the day before Hoare went to Paris, the chiefs of staff warned of the "dangers which would arise if political agreements on the application of fresh sanctions outran arrangements for cooperation between the forces of the Powers concerned." On that same day Vansittart wrote to Hoare that it would be "suicidal" to proceed with oil sanctions "until and unless we come to a full and concrete agreement with the French and other powers militarily concerned." The first question Hoare put to Laval on the seventh concerned France's readiness to support Britain. Laval replied that France would honor its obligations, and he accepted the beginning of air and military talks and the renewal of naval conversations. This partially satisfied Hoare. The talks showed "a real attempt on the part of France to come into line," and Hoare reported to the cabinet that Laval's reply was "more satisfactory and categorical than expected."[1]

But the residue of recent suspicions left the British delegates open to contrary suggestion. Rumors in Paris were full of the talk of war, of strong public sentiment against further sanctions, and of uncertainty whether the government could carry the country in a war against Italy in the cause of defending the British. Laval did nothing to dispel these anxieties. Cerruti and Chambrun had convinced him that Mussolini considered an oil sanction a military measure and would respond "in the spirit of despair." Frenchmen would honor their obligations, said Laval, but would have to feel that everything possible had been done to find a way out of the crisis.[2]

Ambassador George Clerk drew the conclusions from these suggestive words. The discussions, Clerk later wrote, were conditioned by the recognition of British military and naval weakness and by the situation in France. France, and Laval, were determined not to go to war with Italy. "To force France against her will to fight would have meant a definite break of the Anglo-French understanding, and therefore risked the end, not only of the League of Nations, but, far more serious, of European civilisation." The basic fact, Clerk said, was that "no Frenchman was ready to go to war save in defence of his country, and any French government that called upon them to do so [after, for example, an Italian strike against the British fleet] would have been thrown out there and then. This was a feeling which His Majesty's Government could not ignore."[3] Georges Mandel, whom the president of the republic was thinking of as the most likely successor for Laval should the premier fall, told Vansittart that French opinion was changing, in Britain's favor. Vansittart agreed. But it takes time to reeducate opinion. This, in Vansittart's view, gave all the more reason to "avoid any situation in which France found itself called upon for immediate warlike measures," and Vansittart was an influential participant in the Hoare-Laval talks.[4]

Stanley Baldwin, after the terms of the Paris proposals leaked in the press, with the country in an outrage but with Hoare still absent from London and the cabinet not yet fully informed, stood before the Commons on 10 December and said: "I have seldom spoken with greater regret, for my lips are not yet unsealed. Were these troubles over I would make a case, and I guarantee that not a man would go into the Lobby against us. . . ." This sealed-lips expression, the subject of much speculation, ridicule, and embarrassment and, by Baldwin's admission, "the silliest thing" he ever said, was meant to conceal his opinion that Laval was playing Italy's hand and France would not act with Britain in case of war. "If orders were given to mobilize the French army," Baldwin told Lord Beaverbrook, "there would be revolution and rioting in France." To Thomas Jones he said, "I had repeatedly told Sam [Hoare] 'Keep us out of war, we are not ready for it.'" Baldwin explained: "Until we got agreement with the French we would have to go singlehanded fighting Italy for a month or so. French mobilisation would have led to riots. They are not ready in the air without mobilisation. . . . Sam was therefore ready to spring more than he ought to have done, and so was Van[sittart]." As to his remarks to Commons: "I had in mind the menace of war; our fleet would be in real danger from the small craft of the Italians operating in a small sea. Italian bombers could get to London. I had also Germany in mind. Had we gone to war our anti-aircraft munitions would have been exhausted in a week. We have hardly got any armament firms left."[5]

Hoare himself was dissuaded from making a speech of "utmost frankness as to the position M. Laval had taken in the event of sanctions." Alfred Duff Cooper, war minister, insisted that as foreign secretary Hoare was not "entitled to say that no other nation was willing or ready to fight." In fact, he said, "the French army were better prepared" than the British. Lord Zetland noted Hoare's admission that Laval's assurances were better than expected and argued that they had to be accepted.[6]

Duff Cooper's criticism was no doubt correct, given the question of public utterance. And Zetland picked up a statement that confirmed one side of what Hoare saw but deserved more reservation. Better than expected is not the same as fully satisfactory. What, *in the event,* determined Hoare's agreement was the sense that the engagement of which Laval spoke was subject to legal and political qualification, that war might be imminent with the oil embargo, and that unless he seized this chance for one more try at conciliation, as Laval insisted, France might be lost to Britain.

We can also credit Hoare's own defense. He told the Commons that the proposals "were the minimum basis upon which the French Government were prepared to proceed. . . . much as I disliked some features of the scheme, I could not withhold my provisional assent. I felt that the issues were so grave and the dangers of the continuance of the war were so serious that it was worth making an attempt and that it was essential to maintain Anglo-French solidarity." Peterson put the situation to the cabinet thus. Laval, presumably through soundings in Rome, thought the proposals would work. It was possible the French would have accepted terms less favorable to Italy, but such terms would not have much prospect for success.[7]

The question of success related only to approval in Rome. The Ethiopians were not consulted. The Palazzo Chigi was easily reached by telephone; there was no telephone line to Addis Ababa. The emperor, in any case, was out of reach, gone to his field headquarters in the north. The Paris talks lasted only two days. Concurrent communication with the emperor, even if desired, would have been impossible. Nor was he consulted in the preliminary planning of the terms. The British delegation had two concerns for Ethiopia. One was to avoid compromising the emperor too greatly before his chiefs, which would jeopardize his leadership. This was a limitation on concessions to Italy. The other was to encourage him and his leaders to accept a settlement without further resistance. In a poignant admission, Hoare told Commons: "I have been terrified with the thought . . . that we might lead Abyssinia on to think that the League could do more than it can do—that in the end we should find a terrible moment of disillusionment in which it may be that Abyssinia would be destroyed altogether as an independent state." To encourage resistance by government without the means for effective help could mean, Hoare said, "that in the end their fate was worse than it would have been without our sympathy."[8] Hoare seems to have assumed that the Italian advance would continue until the country was totally conquered. The League would be saved from debacle only by immediate termination of the war. Laval, too, was evidently convinced that Ethiopia could continue military opposition no longer than another month.[9]

With this understanding of the atmosphere of Paris, we can turn to the actual terms of the Hoare-Laval proposals. Drawing on the planning that went before, Hoare sought a "judicious mixture" of exchange of territory and economic concession. The trade-offs were weighed on a balance; they had to be acceptable to the League as not rewarding aggression and at the same time be enough to end the war. Laval said Mussolini must have part of Tigre. Hoare agreed, his way paved by Vansittart's concession in the talks with Grandi. But it was not to be all the land under occupation, as Mussolini wanted. Italy could have Aduwa, Adigrat, and Makale—the line was drawn just east of Aksum. Italian troops were to withdraw west of that boundary. In a note to the cabinet urging approval of the proposals, Hoare stated the "practical impossibility of getting negotiations even started" without letting Italy keep part of the conquered land. In return, Hoare insisted on moderation in the rest of the terms and on compensation for Ethiopia.

Compensation took the form of the port of Assab and a corridor, to be ceded by Italy and held by Ethiopia in full sovereign right. Should the emperor prefer, Zeila could be substituted for Assab. This alternative was held in abeyance. In the south and east, since Italy was to get part of Tigre, the land proposed for cession was substantially reduced. Italy would get merely frontier rectification in the Danakil and the Ogaden, not the cession of more salubrious areas such as Bale. This made possible an enlargement of the area determined for Italy's economic monopoly. Here, Hoare thought, so long as it was not a matter of transfer of sovereignty or the institution of a mandate, "the bigger the area the better." In this region, now extended south from the eighth parallel and westward to the thirty-fifth meridian, Italy would enjoy exclusive economic rights. Contrary to Mussolini's demands, however, administration of the area would not be exclusively Italian, but, following the idea recommended by the Committee of Five, would ultimately be the supervisory responsibility of a League-appointed non-Italian adviser sitting in Addis Ababa. An Italian might be his delegate for supervising assistance services in the reserved zone, but sovereignty would remain Ethiopian and the Italian delegate would be responsible to the League. This brought the League back into the forefront of any settlement.[10]

Hoare made concessions on procedure, also. The terms were secret. After governmental approval in London and Paris, they would go to Mussolini before the emperor. If Mussolini agreed, the whole matter would be referred to the Committee of Five (long the League's agency for negotiation in this affair), which would in turn propose a further delay in the meeting of the Committee of Eighteen (set for 12 December, to decide on the oil sanction). During the period of talks, which Laval envisioned continuing from 14 to 18 December, full responsibility for adjournment and for settlement would be with the League, out of British and French hands.[11]

The Paris talks achieved their goal. A common policy was set for these days of crisis. British and French agreement—that was the important thing. Without a common front, neither further sanctions nor diplomatic settlement would follow. Vansittart and Clerk congratulated Hoare on his success. Content with his work, the foreign secretary on 8 December went on his vacation in Switzerland. A communiqué stated that the still secret proposals were formulated "in the spirit of conciliation and inspired by close Franco-British friendship" and that both ministers were "satisfied with the result."[12]

First Reactions

London

The next morning, Monday, 9 December, Peterson went to Eden's house in London carrying a copy of the proposals, initialed by Hoare and Laval. He also had a note from Hoare urging immediate approval of the proposals at the cabinet already called for that day at Hoare's request. The commitment implied by Hoare's initials was reinforced by the communiqué expressing mutual satisfaction and announcing that the belligerent governments and the League would be informed as soon as the British government gave its approval. The government in London saw itself committed to either approving the terms or disowning its foreign secretary and thereby jeopardizing the new common front with France. Halifax said later that Hoare's communiqué, by putting the cabinet on the spot, "was the *fons et origo* of all our troubles, . . . an amazing mistake for him to have made."[13]

The cabinet met on Monday the ninth, ignorant of what, in detail, had gone on in Paris. No message of explication was sent with the proposals; there was only the admonition to keep in line with France. Baldwin did not call Hoare back from Switzerland. So the cabinet did not know what reasoning had dictated Hoare's decisions. Some imagined that a revelation of Laval's unreliability in a crunch had led him to such concessions. A cabinet as close as Baldwin's was not about to disown an absent colleague without a hearing. Baldwin later challenged the members of Commons to think whether they would have acted differently.[14] The cabinet, Eden among them, trusted Hoare. The foreign secretary had a good reputation as a careful and sensible official. To repudiate the proposals Laval claimed were Italy's minimum terms would turn the French against any further conciliation and perhaps lead them to pull out of sanctions altogether. Who knew what effect that would have on Britain's European relations?

To approach Mussolini first was nevertheless considered intolerable. No one knew the thoughts of Haile Selassie. The emperor might well have to reject the terms as a basis for discussion. If Mussolini were permitted to start the dealing, giving provisional, tactical acceptance, responsibility for the collapse of talks might go solely to Ethiopia. The emperor would appear stiff-necked and intractable, Mussolini conciliatory and amenable. This was an unfair advantage the tough-minded realists in Paris were willing to impose. But to Eden and the rest of the cabinet it seemed urgent to avoid any semblance of procedural injustice—that very day the gist of the proposals had appeared in the press.[15]

The emperor, and all others, now saw how much less the new terms favored Ethiopia than had the plan of the Committee of Five on which they were modeled. To many it appeared not only that Britain and France had sold Ethiopia out, but that this was done behind the back of the League by means of discredited secret diplomacy. Eden argued, and the cabinet agreed, that the emperor had to be officially informed of the plans simultaneously with Mussolini. The cabinet did conclude that the emperor should be "strongly pressed" to accept the terms as a basis for discussion, or at least not to reject them out of hand. The cabinet, no less than Hoare and Laval, wanted an argument for postponing the decision on oil. Eden suggested the means. Let the Committee of Eighteen meet as scheduled on 12 December. The British and French representatives would state they were engaged in a peace effort and ask the committee to refer the matter to the Committee of Five. Then, Eden said, the Committee of Eighteen would probably adjourn and the decision on an oil sanction would be put off.

In his memoirs Eden reproached himself for not arguing more emphatically against the terms.[16] He had limited his observations to the comment that "some features were likely to prove very distasteful to some members of the League." Eden was loyal to his senior cabinet colleague. He thought, as did Hoare, that these would be seen as *proposals,* that final terms would be worked over at Geneva until acceptable to all three parties. Nothing too terrible could be ascribed to preliminary suggestions. Eden, minister for League of Nations affairs, knew that it was only subtle bonds of trust that held the sanctionist front together. He, more than the others, believed in the value of these bonds, and his position led him to affirm the Geneva line. But Eden's was not a forceful personality. He was inclined to go along, not to buck the tide. And no argument based on hopes for the Covenant could stand against the immediate anxieties, determined will, and national-interest arguments of Vansittart, Clerk, Drummond, and Hoare. For these men

—realists, they would have called themselves—the sensitivity of small, uninvolved states was hardly considered in the vital pursuit of preventing a Mediterranean war and winning Laval's support should one come.

This, then, the cabinet decided on 9 December: to endorse the Paris proposals; to inform both parties simultaneously, with Minister Barton to try to "induce" the emperor to accept; and to go ahead with the meeting of the Committee of Eighteen on 12 December but deflect oil sanctions by substituting the Committee of Five as peace negotiators.[17]

Paris

For Laval the Paris proposals were a great success. He thought they settled the Ethiopian problem. The terms, he thought, were acceptable to Italy, and British agreement meant they could be forced on the League and Ethiopia. As he took leave of Hoare he said, "Now we are finished with Italy."[18] On 10 December Laval laid the proposals before his Council of Ministers. Only Herriot stood opposed—neither the League nor the emperor would accept them. Perhaps, Laval agreed. What, Herriot asked, would France do if Italy agreed to begin talks but Ethiopia refused? Laval's answer was simple. In that case France would not join in an oil sanction.[19]

That would be a perfect way out of the mess. If the Ethiopians did not cooperate one did not have to go out on a limb on their behalf. Minister Bodard in Addis Ababa thought the emperor would refuse to accept the plan for discussion precisely to bring the oil sanction into play. This trap Laval was determined to avoid. It was because of this that he had argued against informing the emperor of the terms of the proposals until Mussolini's assurance was secure and the League, through the Committee of Five, was locked into the negotiations.

Therefore, when early on the morning of 10 December Vansittart told him of the cabinet decision that Addis Ababa must be informed simultaneously with Rome, Laval agreed to this only with the understanding that if the anticipated refusal materialized there would be no question of taking fresh measures against Italy. Laval insisted this understanding be in the form of a clear advance engagement. The French public, he said, would never accept an oil sanction in such a condition. British air and military experts were in Paris on 9 and 10 December for staff talks. Opinion might view this as part of a Machiavellian design on the part of the British to precipitate a crisis by ensuring a breakdown of the talks on the Ethiopian end, thereby bringing about the dangerous oil sanction before France was ready. Only a definite prior understanding could prevent subsequent embroilment with Britain and the states gathered at Geneva. To Laval's request Vansittart and Clerk gave their strong assent. If such an agreement were not forthcoming, Vansittart warned, a "grave setback" was likely for the negotiations and for Franco-British relations.[20]

The cabinet met on 10 December to formulate a reply to Laval's request. Eden said Laval had good reason to believe the emperor would refuse the offer for discussions. Time was running short for the British government. The Labour opposition was to raise a question of information in Commons that afternoon. The general meeting of the Committee of Eighteen was two days away. The venture into peace negotiations was getting more complicated by the hour as the public clamored in growing opposition and alarmed delegations returned to Geneva full of confusion and fear. The connection with France seemed in as shaky a state as ever before. Swinton reported the air discussions in Paris the previous day "could hardly have been more unsatisfactory." We saw that the French defense ministers, meeting immediately afterward, decided against any engagement that offered the slightest possible risk of war. But the cabinet could not concede Laval's request without destroying the Geneva front. So they tacked, sought a compromise—and destroyed the Geneva front.

The emperor was to be informed of the proposals simultaneously with Mussolini. It was indefensible to submit terms to the aggressor while withholding them from the victim. The British would not state that if the emperor refused to undertake discussion there would be no oil sanction. That decision was up to the League, and the British position would be made "in light of developments." Nor would they ask for a postponement of the meeting of the Committee of Eighteen. But the committee would be asked to refer the question of settlement to the Committee of Five and then adjourn. This would assure postponement of the sanction. These points agreed, Neville Chamberlain carried his colleagues one step further. If one cared to pick a moment when the tide of sanctions was turned, this would be a good choice. Chamberlain proposed, the cabinet agreed, and it was so communicated to Paris, that if Italy accepted and Ethiopia refused to consider the proposals, the British government would neither propose or support the imposition of further sanctions "at once nor before it is clear that no chance remains of settlement by agreements."[21] While not engaging the cabinet to oppose further sanctions at some later time or in new conditions this stopped the momentum, which is what Laval wanted. During what Walters called the "week of misery" of 11-18 December, the sanctionist front lost the moral and political force it had before the Hoare-Laval proposals.

So the proposals were transmitted to the two belligerent governments. In addition, the British and French sent out a supplementary message. If, for either side, the question of an Assab strip stood in the way of settlement, access to a port at Zeila could be substituted. This was quite a concession. The aggressor would keep more while paying less, for Britain would concede territory, a concession hitherto expected exclusively of Italy. The Zeila offer also meant the suppression of the primary legitimizing principle behind the settlement terms, for one could no longer argue the justice and reasonableness of a territorial exchange as being made simply between the belligerents.

A further lien was to be placed against Ethiopia that, when revealed in the White Paper of 14 December, seemed to put in question even more the fairness and good faith of London and Paris and showed yet another concession of the British to the French. The two governments agreed to "obtain" from the Ethiopians "at the appropriate moment an undertaking not to construct from the port which it acquires [Assab or Zeila] any railway communicating with the interior and also an undertaking to conclude with the French Government all necessary arrangements to safeguard the interest of the port of Jibuti and the Franco-Ethiopian railway."[22]

Hoare's absence continued to restrain opposition within the cabinet and public statement without. On Attlee's question in the Commons on 10 December as to whether or not the press reports accurately portrayed the proposals, Baldwin waffled, complaining that such revelations "made a very difficult and delicate matter incomparably more difficult and more delicate." That evening Baldwin spoke again. As to the realities of the case, he said in the famous phrase, "my lips are not yet unsealed." He then progressed, in a mournful speech, to impute frailness to what a few months before he had called "the sheet-anchor" of British policy. "Some people," he said, "speak of the League of Nations as though it were some kind of celestial body which is always right, whereas it is really a human body of fallible nations gathered in council and represented by fallible statesmen trying to do what they can."[23]

To this fallible, and now extremely alarmed association Eden proceeded. A cabinet on 11 December agreed he should use his own discretion about how far to champion the proposals. In the face of mounting opposition at home, in the Dominions, among other members of the League, and from those of liberal spirit throughout the world, their future looked bleak. But they could not be simply jettisoned, in the absence of Hoare, pending replies from Mussolini and the emperor, and with Laval set to modify them even further, if need be, in Italy's favor. The matter of waiting for replies meant, in effect, that the Committee of Eighteen would defer setting a date for the oil sanction. Indeed, Eden went with one clear instruction: avoid fixing a specific time for its application. If the question of oil arose, Eden was to deal with it, in Baldwin's words, as "a business proposition." An investigation should set out to determine its practicality, especially how it might be affected by any American action.²⁴ The oil sanction, in other words, was to be shelved.

Within the Foreign Office Ralph Wigram, noting talk of a French double cross, minuted on 11 December: "I venture to wonder if we shan't in the end be rather thankful that M. Laval in this matter has shown himself not merely a crook but a clever crook." In spite of the great embarrassment Hoare caused the government, there was in many official quarters this sense of relief. At least the British were off the hook on oil for the moment. Eden, when he first saw the proposals, had told Baldwin neither the League nor the emperor would accept them. Baldwin replied: "That lets us out, doesn't it?"²⁵ As Laval foresaw, in one sense it did. Especially if Mussolini accepted the idea of talks, there would be no oil sanction. But it was to be a costly release.

Geneva

Distress was intense in Geneva. Britain and France had, it appeared, breached faith with Ethiopia and the Covenant. The first published reports shocked sanctionist states. No one had imagined Hoare and Laval would go that far. The Mexican delegate to the Committee of Eighteen said he assumed published versions "went far beyond the reality." He spoke on 13 December. That day the proposals were transmitted officially to the Council. They were worse than expected. In the way they were contrived—secretly, apart from the League, in consultation with Italy, not informing Ethiopia or other League members—they were an insult and a threat. They gave to Mussolini more than he had won in battle, more than Italy on any reckoning other than fear might hope to get. Above all, it was clear that they were proposed precisely to avoid extending the collective pressure being mounted. In these few days the authority of the Covenant and the potential for collective security had lost "all the ground thus gained, and much more."²⁶

Frank Walters, then a high official in the Secretariat, speaks of the sense of betrayal.

> It was bad enough to ask Ethiopia to give up twenty times what she could hope to receive, and to call it an exchange. But if it was hypocrisy to speak of an exchange, what was to be said of the zone of Italian settlement? Was not this simply equivalent to the annexation of half the country? The zone, and the new Italian territory in the south-east, would have a common frontier 400 miles long. Could anyone doubt that Italy would find that the safety of her settlers and the free development of her enterprises necessitated the military occupation of the zone? And how long could the central area, surrounded on all sides by Italian territory, retain any semblance of independence? Was the plan anything less than the consecration and reward of aggression, proffered

to Mussolini in the name of the League? How could it be reconciled with the repeated promises of its authors to take no action that should be inconsistent with the Covenant?[27]

There were other worries. The plan went behind the back of the League, went to Mussolini and the emperor before going to the Council. What if Mussolini accepted? Or delayed reply to string out conciliatory hopes? What was to happen to the impending decision on oil, the very decision for which the delegates to the Committee of Eighteen had gathered at Geneva on 12 December?

Up to this point it had been a time of great expectations. Prior to the Hoare-Laval proposals, as members prepared for the meeting, confidence in the British government was at the highest point since the armistice of 1918, and confidence in the League was at a state unmatched since the founding days, when the United States was expected to be the leading member. On 5 December Hoare had told the Commons that the League's machinery was working well, and Eden said: "At this moment international politics are passing through a phase of evolution when far the greater part of the nations of the world are striving to substitute the rule of law for the rule of force in international dealings." "Perhaps," he continued, "on this occasion the attempt is being made on a wider scale and with a greater measure of hope and confidence than ever before."[28] This general confidence impressed Hitler and encouraged the sympathy of the American government. The Committee of Eighteen was preparing a January date for the application of the oil sanction, hoping, among other things, that this show of determination would influence the reconvening U.S. Congress to add oil to the American embargo.[29]

The Committee of Eighteen met on 12 December 1935. The next day it received an experts' report on the sanctions undertaken so far. Some fifty states were acting under article 16. Only four, Albania, Hungary, Austria, and Paraguay, refused to participate. Chairman Vasconcellos hailed "this splendid and noble example of solidarity."[30] And so it was. The report bespoke the League's greatest moment of success. But it came precisely when the vital "hope and confidence" of which Eden spoke the week before was shattered.

The Committee of Eighteen, after all, expected to meet on 12 December to build upon this confidence by extending collective action to oil. On the thirteenth it adjourned without action. There was no choice. Eden and Laval announced their intention of calling the Council, to submit the Paris proposals just sent to the governments of Italy and Ethiopia. The proposals went to Council members on 13 December. "It is Sadowa," Paul-Boncour said to Herriot, referring to the fateful Prussian victory over Austria in 1866 that changed the course of international affairs in Europe. The Covenant, *and what the Covenant stood for,* was betrayed. Vasconcellos told Eden that angry members of the Committee of Eighteen were asking: "Why have our countries been asked to put on sanctions, to suffer loss of trade and other inconvenience, if the only result is that Italy should be offered by Britain and France more, probably, than she would ever have achieved by herself alone, even if sanctions had not been put on?"[31]

But there was nothing the Committee of Eighteen could do but let itself be passed over in favor of the Council. There was a little resistance. On the Committee of Five, which Eden and Laval hoped would settle the negotiation process, the delegates from Turkey and Poland refused to take any responsibility in the matter. The government of Sweden instructed its delegate to remind the committee that conciliation "does not relieve the Members of the League of the duty of continuing to ensure the application of the Covenant." Yet, when on 12 December Ethiopia requested that the Assembly be called for "a full and free public debate" on the "true practical significance of the proposals," the request was turned down as procedurally inappropriate.[32]

The progress of sanctions was arrested by British and French action, as those governments wished. But in the process of lessening the tension, expectations of collective security collapsed. What else could many smaller and dependent states in Europe count on for security, save Britain and France? And how could they count on them save through the League? British participation at Geneva was proclaimed as the bridge for a continental policy. Now whatever worth this had was called into question. Was the future of British policy to ignore supporters, those who at some cost to themselves had stood up against Italian aggression? It was a question of fairness and reliability.

Nicolas Politis of Greece told Eden of the grave anxiety of the Balkan Entente, which Britain only recently had approached about assistance in the event of an Italian attack on British forces in the Mediterranean. While considering these requests, agreement with which would seriously hurt relations with Italy, there came the announcement of the Paris agreement. Was this a change of policy, from opposing aggression to appeasement? Bozhidar Pouritch of Yugoslavia noted that the verdict of the world would be that aggression paid, that a dictator's bluff had intimidated the democracies. What would be Mussolini's next step? Albania? And what then from the League? Holding Britain in contempt, Mussolini would turn to Germany. What then of the small states who saw their security in Britain's support of the Covenant? Could they count, themselves, on not being betrayed?[33] Alfred Nemours of Haiti once warned the Assembly that the risk of not supporting the Covenant was the danger that any of the members might, "one day, become the Ethiopia of someone."[34] That warning took on a new and somber note. It was not only aggression that now was feared—it was also desertion in one's hour of need.

Tension might have been relieved, but so were the developing ties for mutual support. On 12 December the Yugoslav government said it would delay a note to Italy asserting the principle of mutual assistance with Britain, since the Hoare-Laval proposals indicated the prospect of a settlement. In Berlin the representatives of Romania and Czechoslovakia said the Balkan states would withdraw from the League if the Hoare-Laval plan were applied. It would mean there was no security for them in such a League.[35] Prentiss Gilbert, studying the confusion in Geneva, canvassed the delegates of Turkey, Bulgaria, Finland, and Poland and concluded that confidence among the smaller powers was so badly shattered it might never be regained.[36] Vasconcellos, speaking to Eden about Britain's long-time ally Portugal, said the proposals constituted a "terrible precedent." If aggression led to settlement rights, Germany might soon be asking for such privileges in Portuguese colonies.[37] Vasconcellos was certain Lisbon would reject the proposals. Madariaga said he would not help sponsor the proposed terms, which, when laid before the Council on 13 December, confirmed the worst reports in the press. The Soviet judgment was that Britain was anxious in the Mediterranean, Litvinov wrote, and Laval was a "consistent and inveterate enemy of the collective security system."[38] Representatives of the British Dominions, meeting on 10 December, showed their alarm. New Zealand refused to associate with the terms. The government of South Africa registered with the cabinet its "profound dismay" at the "departure" from the earlier stand of strong support and warned that the "unsatisfactory character" of the terms might lead to a loss of that confidence in the League "requisite for its continued existence." Vansittart ridiculed this as "somewhat insolent language from a non-combatant state"—but it was true. From Finland to Turkey came reports of a crushing blow to British prestige. Watching them arrive, Laurence Collier, head of the Northern Department in the Foreign Office, was prompted on 16 December to write what might be the theme for this period: "We have paid a very high price for Franco-British solidarity, if that has indeed been achieved."[39]

For one thing, unless the situation were undone the proposals meant the end of any further American cooperation. On 10 December, the day after the press revealed the plan, Lindsay cabled that if the terms represented the final policy of the British government, such would "effectively nullify any efforts" the American government could make to influence public opinion in support of the League. Cooperation of the government was conditional, based on the frailest of ties, the most important being the confidence that the League was working well on its own. Now, far from encouraging effectiveness, the proposals seemed made precisely to avoid further sanctions and in terms, so Wallace Murray said when he analyzed the matter for Hull, that seemed "almost to place a premium on aggression."[40] The leaders of the League had backed off at the very moment of some success.

Roosevelt thought the plan was an outrage. He told the archbishop of York that it killed whatever favorable opinion of the League there was in America. Ambassador William Dodd wrote that it was "the biggest mistake since the war."[41] The call went up for a return to strict neutrality. Congress was soon to assemble and would redraw the neutrality legislation set to expire at the end of February 1936. There was no chance now that oil would be included in the embargo. Senator Arthur Vandenburg said American interests demanded mandatory neutrality legislation. Senator William Borah urged disassociation from all European entanglements.[42] Roosevelt on 19 December agreed with the call to avoid European politics. "What a commentary on world ethics these past weeks have shown."[43] And, immediately, the exposure of apparent double-dealing weakened the arguments Hull counted on for the moral embargo.

Addis Ababa

The Ethiopians faced a difficult choice. Support specifically for *their* plight was tenuous enough in the chancelleries of London and Paris. If they turned down the proposals as a basis for discussion, and if Mussolini accepted, the British might claim they had done all they could and start to back away, while the French would surely say that in the circumstance they would not support an oil sanction. Yet for Haile Selassie to concede was to risk losing his very legitimacy as patriot-king and to court the extinction of Ethiopian sovereignty.

When the Paris terms were sent to Addis Ababa on 10 December 1935, Minister Sidney Barton was instructed as follows:

> You should use your utmost influence to induce the Emperor to give careful and favourable consideration to these proposals and on no account lightly to reject them. On the contrary, I [the Foreign Office, in Hoare's name] feel sure that he will give further proof of his statesmanship by realizing the advantage of the opportunity of negotiation which they afford, and will avail himself thereof.[44]

This instruction could not be carried out. The French minister Albert Bodard, with similar instructions, carried no particular weight with the emperor, and Barton was never able to exert his own "utmost influence," on which Whitehall counted. The emperor was absent from the capital, at his field headquarters at Dessye, several hundred miles to the north. The Ethiopian northern force was about to launch its December offensive. Communications between Addis Ababa and Dessye were very limited. Barton was never invited north. The two ministers, therefore, had to make their representations to the foreign ministry. They presented the terms on 10 December and pressed the case again on the thirteenth, asking for a reply by the seventeenth. The foreign minister did nothing but forward the messages to Dessye. The members of the Council of Ministers, formally empowered to decide political issues, were bewildered and angry, vacillated, delayed, and, knowing their ultimate incapacity, refused to do anything without the emperor to lead them.

Meanwhile, the Ethiopian representatives in Europe presented their opposition. On the twelfth the Genevan delegation asked the League for a "full and free public debate" at a meeting of the Assembly on "the true practical significance of the proposals . . . and on the general problem of the conditions which were indispensable if a settlement between the victim of a properly established act of aggression and the aggressor Government is not, in practice, to result in destroying the League of Nations." Eduard Beneš, Assembly president, with Avenol's approval, turned the request down on the grounds that the Council—the appropriate organ of the League—was to meet shortly to take account of the proposals.[45]

In Addis Ababa the emperor's loyal and supremely valuable foreign affairs adviser, the American Everett Colson, wearing out his health in service on the high plateau, lost his patience at the shilly-shallying of the Ethiopian Council of Ministers and resolved to fly to Dessye. Colson was extremely alarmed. The Ethiopian government was being treated "worse than dirt." Colson and the emperor saw only one course—to play the League hand to the limit. To accept the Hoare-Laval terms would simply improve conditions under which Italy could, at a later date, attack again. And, once having signed away Ethiopia's claims under the Covenant, the rights to territorial integrity and independence, no further appeal could be made to Europe when the Italians came to try again to absorb the land.[46]

On 16 December Haile Selassie flatly rejected the British-French plan. To accept it even in principle, he said,

> would be not only a cowardice towards our people but a betrayal of the League of Nations and of all the States which have shown that they could have confidence up to now in the system of collective security. These proposals are the negation and the abandonment of the principles upon which the League of Nations is founded. For Ethiopia they would consecrate the amputation of her territory and the disappearance of her independence for the benefit of the State which has attacked her. They imply the definite interdiction for her own people to participate usefully and freely in the economic develop-

ment of about a third of the country, and they confide this development to her enemy, which is now making its second attempt to conquer this people. A settlement on the lines of these proposals would place a premium upon aggression and upon the violation of international engagements.[47]

Formal refusal went shortly thereafter to the League, and to London and Paris. Ending an extended catalog of criticisms of the plan, the Ethiopian statement to the League on 18 December read: "Before producing an opinion on the 'Paris suggestions,' let every Member ask itself whether, if it were the victim of an attack, it would accept 'suggestions' such as those that are today submitted for the approval of the League."[48]

Rome

What of the response from Rome? Leaving for the next chapter comment on the internal life of Italy and the course of the war itself, it is enough to say here that the Italian economy was not much disturbed after three weeks of economic and financial sanctions. Indeed, what with the initial and easy victories in Africa, the systematic nationalist propaganda, and the sense of being unfairly judged and unjustly punished, the government enjoyed a rise in the popularity of the war. On 9 December the Senate declared its "total solidarity" with Mussolini, certain that he would "safeguard the honor and rights of Italy."[49] But by this date popular support was in fact beginning to thin out. The duration or outcome of the war was by no means clear. Badoglio had replaced De Bono at the end of November, promising a more aggressive strategy. But no Italians were yet past Makale, where De Bono had left them, and there was no prospect of imminent advance, although this was a much-felt need. More than ever, Alfieri wrote to Ciano on 9 December, international events were tied to military operations.[50] The pinch of sanctions would soon be coming, and up to the time of the Paris proposals the oil embargo seemed certain. Mussolini was still in deep trouble internationally.

Hoare and Laval timed their proposals to offset the certain favorable decision of the Committee of Eighteen on the oil embargo. This, with the generous terms accorded Italy, was seen as a "complete about-face" for British policy. Conceding to Italy the smallest part of Ethiopian territory denied the claim that Italy had no right to the land. This neutralized the accusation of aggression and treaty violation, undercutting the basis for League action. As such, the Hoare-Laval proposals—so it was argued in the Palazzo Chigi—should be accepted. They embarrassed the League and its champions. The issues were sufficiently complicated to offer "infinite possibilities" for drawing out subsequent negotiations—all the while postponing further sanctions, demoralizing the Geneva front, and buying time for military success.[51]

Many observers, perhaps most, thought Mussolini would see these values in opening negotiations. Laval told his Council of Ministers on 10 December that he was "quasi-certain" Mussolini would accept. Looking back, Drummond said Mussolini would have accepted if the terms had come "as a firm offer." Chambrun, too, believed "without a doubt" that agreement was certain had the plan, as originally scheduled, been delivered secretly to Mussolini.[52]

Certainly there was a disposition to favorable consideration among the moderate Italian officials, men such as Aloisi, Suvich, Pilotti, Berio, Bova Scoppa, and Guariglia. Those directly involved, Grandi and Cerruti, sent active endorsement, Grandi arguing there was no need to discomfort the British and French further.[53] Mussolini later wrote to Laval that he had not contemplated outright refusal. He did not want to accept it, he told Lessona, nor did he want to make a blunt rejection. How to respond was a perplexing problem for him.[54]

Upon receiving the terms officially on 11 December, Mussolini refused to be stampeded to a swift decision. He did not tarry unduly, it is fair to say, but he was not pushed by the urgency felt in London and Paris. The proposals, after all, were the formal response to his presentation of terms on 16 October. It had taken the British and French two months to reply to that. Now he claimed a few days. A meeting of the Grand Council of Fascism was already scheduled for 18 December. He would leave the final decision to this body and deliver his answer the following day. Resting the case with the party's Grand Council would absolve Mussolini of sole responsibility. There was much at stake, advantages and disadvantages in going either way.

Publication of the plan on 9 December had greatly complicated the matter. As Mussolini told Chambrun and Drummond when they formally presented the terms on the eleventh, the press leaks limited liberty of negotiation, and their request for an immediate reply (prior to the meeting of the Committee of Eighteen set for the next day) appeared to put him now in the intolerable position of acting under an ultimatum, under the threat of an oil embargo. There is no doubt the public exposé made things immeasurably more difficult. Premature disclosure was an excuse Mussolini had given for not accepting the Zeila exchange in June 1935 and the Committee of Five's proposals in September. Hoare and Mussolini both claimed later that publicity killed the new scheme as well.[55] In addition, however, there were substantive considerations and new events to take into account before a final decision could be made.

Mussolini raised some initial objections. He took exception to the exclusion of Aksum from Italian holdings. Aksum was occupied; it was a city of considerable symbolic significance and useful to Italian control in the north; and, his argument ran, the clergy and population of the holy city welcomed the invading troops. To hand it back to Ethiopia would subject the citizens to reprisal. There was not too much to this last argument. De Bono wrote that the clergy accepted occupation fatalistically as an act of God and the welcoming applause of the citizenry was manufactured on Italian orders.[56] On 12 December Mussolini warned Badoglio to be alert to hostile uprisings now that it was public knowledge Aksum was excluded from the land offered to Italy. On the sixteenth, to confirm his case, he told Badoglio to get as many clergy as possible to sign a letter requesting Italian sovereignty. Aksum, he said, would not be given up. Further, he protested that Italian settlers in the area for development would be exposed to the mercy of the emperor. More security was needed on their behalf. Lastly, he said the gift of Zeila would offer too great an advantage to Ethiopia. If Ethiopia had to have access to the sea, better Assab, under Italian eyes.[57]

These initial objections were seen in London as "comparatively trifling." According to Aloisi, on 11 December Mussolini was ready to "interrupt" the war, annex the conquered territory more or less as the plan suggested, and wait for an appropriate occasion "to finish the job." Chambrun and Drummond thought the differences could be ironed out at Geneva. The main sticking point, they said, was whether or not there would be an oil embargo. If that could be postponed by adjourning the Committee of Eighteen, then, they cabled on the twelfth, Mussolini would accept in principle the opening of negotiations.[58] In his own name, Laval sent Mussolini a stiff warning on 12 December. He had led the British government to the limit of compromise and he could do no more. Mussolini should be more accommodating. Otherwise it would be Italy who assumed responsibility, by a refusal to talk, of prolonging and aggravating a crisis in which the friendship of France no longer could serve to moderate events.[59]

The Vatican, no longer involved in formulating peace plans, warmly welcomed the Hoare-Laval proposals. The *Osservatore Romano* on 10 December headlined "Confident Expectations of Announced Negotiations," and called for a peace through the League based on "justice and equity" and "mutual generosity." The Vatican, since its mid-October activity as Mussolini's intermediary, had stayed strictly neutral. The pope said nothing publicly on the subject of the war or League action after the opening of hostilities. The *Osservatore Romano* made no criticism of sanctionist states, nor did it say anything about the utterances of some of the Italian episcopate in support of the African war. Not until 16 December did the pope mention the troubles, and then only to say that he would not refer to the conflict for fear his words might be misrepresented or misunderstood. He had done all he "justly and legitimately" could in support of "truth, justice, and charity."[60] It was a defensive comment, and the pope was sad. Sad, because Pius XI had hoped to use this occasion of a consistorial allocution to announce the happy news that Mussolini had accepted negotiations and peace would be at hand. Of the pope's thought there is no doubt. He disapproved of Mussolini's aggressive war. On the other hand, he thought Italians were suffering because the sanctionist states were too rigid, too unsympathetic to the legitimate national needs of his native land. Disliking the strident pro-Fascist patriotism of some of the clergy, he did not oppose it for fear of alienating sympathy for the church. Above all, the dread of bolshevism colored the pope's opinions. His advisers, Cardinal Pacelli, secretary of state, and Father Wladimir Ledochowski, the head of the Jesuits, spoke of the possibility of international revolution. If Mussolini fell or the Fascist regime moved leftward, forces hostile to the church would take control in Italy, depriving the church of its educational and religious privileges, repudiating financial agreements with the government, and possibly even denouncing the Lateran Treaty and the Concordat. Hence his unwillingness to anger Mussolini or encourage foes of the regime.[61]

The most satisfactory solution was, then, a conciliatory compromise. So he thought Mussolini should immediately accept the Paris plan. On 12 December Pius sent his intermediary, Pietro Tacchi Venturi, to Mussolini, urging acceptance without delay. Tacchi Venturi had a special relationship as a *missus dominici* for the pope. Through him private messages bypassed the formal bureaucracy. Cardinals Pizzardo and Ottoviani were inclined to be pro-Fascist, wordy, and too likely to shade messages with their own biases. So too the papal nuncio, Francesco Borgongini Duca. And all were more likely to be received by Suvich than by Mussolini. Cardinal Pacelli stood at one with the pope, but it was hardly appropriate to send him off to the Palazzo Venezia. Bonifacio Pignatti Morano di Custozza, the Italian ambassador, was not to be entrusted with the pope's personal messages and, anyway, he too usually ended up in Suvich's office. The job went to Tacchi Venturi, official historian of the Society of Jesus, frank, free-spoken, familiar with Mussolini, a negotiator and eager protector of the Lateran accord, and one who, at the request of Pius, had seen Mussolini almost weekly since the outbreak of the war.[62] So Tacchi Venturi saw Mussolini on 12 December, stressing that the "honor and interest of Italy demanded acceptance." He returned thinking that Mussolini agreed. But the Duce was as little susceptible to papal counsel as to Laval's pleas.

Everyone at the Vatican thought the fate of the proposals, in light of the public revelations, depended largely upon how swiftly Mussolini acceded to them. The day following Tacchi Venturi's visit the pope told Cardinal Verdier, the bishop of Paris, who was visiting Rome and had been asked by Laval to do what he could to encourage acceptance, that he thought Mussolini would accept. Pacelli was less optimistic. He thought Mussolini would make further reservations, raise more claims, and quibble on various points. Pius had hoped to announce the news of acceptance at his consistory on 16 December. Failing that, he looked to have it at hand when he responded to the Christmas wishes of the cardinals on the twenty-fourth.[63]

The proposals went for consideration to officials of the colonial and foreign ministries, Fulvio Suvich, Pompeo Aloisi, Raffaele Guariglia, and Gino Buti. These men drew up a list of points for elucidation. This list was not so much a set of alternative demands as items on which the Italian view was at variance with the Paris proposals. Why, for example, should the line in Tigre be drawn between Aduwa and Aksum when the latter city was in effective occupation, its chiefs had submitted, and holding it was important to the security of Eritrea? Clarification was needed on the suggested lines of demarcation in the Danakil (was the sultanate of Aussa fairly treated?) and in the southeast (tribes should be better identified, as some had submitted to Italy). There were questions about the governance of the zone of expansion, claims for mineral rights, and whether or not Ethiopia was to be disarmed. Ethiopia could have access to the sea, but not territorial sovereignty on the route thereto. Held back for later bargaining was the claim that there would have to be a territorial connection between the two existing Italian colonies, a long-standing claim conditionally conceded by Britain and France in 1906. Overall, Suvich concluded, "the plan as presented is no good and ought not be accepted." The list was sent to Grandi and Cerruti, to be presented for clarification, without in any way committing Italy to accepting the Paris suggestions as a basis for negotiation—that was a political decision, reserved for Mussolini and the Grand Council.[64]

Grandi took the list around to Vansittart on 16 December, to a cool reception. Vansittart refused to discuss it. The original proposals, he said, were just an outline, deliberately not filled in. The job of working out the details was for the League, for the Council, where responsibility now rested. All questions for supplementary explanation would have to be addressed to Geneva.[65]

Mussolini awaited the Grand Council meeting on 18 December. He could not easily reject the proposals out of hand, but he was not happy with them or with the turn of events. His coworkers found him extremely nervous. In the French embassy Mussolini was likened to a trapped beast.[66]

On the domestic side he did not want to appear to be stopping a much-propagandized war. To be sure, the objectives of the war were never publicly proclaimed, which made the possibility of negotiation easier to contemplate. And what was offered in the proposals could be gussied up to seem like an Italian victory. The battle front was not moving. Indeed, just at this time, on the morning of 15 December, Ras Imru's advance guards crossed the Takkaze River toward the Dembeguina Pass and Aksum, the first move in the Ethiopian counteroffensive that opened the "black days" of the war for

Italy. Pessimism grew in Rome. Yet Mussolini would stand for no compromise. The early successes of the invasion, the rally to the regime in October and November, the sanctions that permitted him to raise the call of
Italy against the world, all these would soon—on 18 December—be capped
by a great Day of Faith, the "wedding-ring day" when the women of Italy
were to donate their wedding bands as precious metal for a state under the
siege of sanctions. Personally, as we saw, Mussolini was most reluctant to
appear publicly to be bending to the threat of the oil blackmail.

On the morning of 18 December—as the Council gathered in Geneva and
the world press was full of news of Ras Imru's advance and the simultaneous
counteroffensives beginning by Ras Kassa and Ras Seyum in Tembien and
by Ras Mulugeta against Makale—Mussolini in a truculent mood, went to
inaugurate the new town of Pontina on the reclaimed marshland near Rome.
He gave a rousing justification of the war and his leadership. "It is a war of
the people," he declared.

> It is a war of the poor, the disinherited, the proletariat. Against us stands the
> front of conservatism, of selfishness, of hypocrisy. . . . A people of 44,000,000
> not only inhabitants but souls [anime] does not permit itself to be throttled
> and still less tricked with impunity. Sure of a unanimous and profound con-
> sent of all the Italian people—men, women, and children, the whole nation
> living in its historic and eternal expression—sure of this consent the regime
> will go straight ahead. . . . it is a trial which is testing the virility of the Italian
> people. . . . Time will be needed, but when a struggle has been engaged in,
> comrades, it is not so much time that counts, but the victory.[67]

It was a strong speech, a harangue, really. The reference to trickery was
Mussolini's first public allusion to the Paris proposals. The speech was widely lamented in the Vatican. But Mussolini's ridicule and rudeness did not, as
Cerruti (and others) claimed, "change the situation completely."[68] The
speech was not a formal diplomatic reply, nor did it turn down negotiation.
It was a mixture of the nationalistic themes common to his propaganda. It
may be that the Pontina speech was a sop to Fascist extremists. Perhaps it
was a piece for the occasion, to relieve Mussolini's own mind as to his
patriotic standing before (in the tense military and diplomatic situation) he
negotiated away some of his hopes for conquest.

Mussolini's formal response was determined by other factors, not the least
of which was his evaluation of Italy's international position. Britain and
France seemed ready to give him half of Ethiopia. The rest could be absorbed in good time. Grandi argued for the chance to alleviate the strain, end
the oil threat and the isolation of Italy, and devastatingly dish the League.
To accept negotiations in principle would result in disarray at Geneva, a
diminution of British prestige in Europe and Africa, and a reopening of
revisionist possibilities on both continents. To snub the opportunity would
result in the oil sanction. Although aware of the swelling opposition to the

proposals in Britain and France, Mussolini never imagined that this would cause the governments to reverse their stated policy of conciliation, the terms of which were formulated by foreign ministers and approved by cabinets. Thus foreign policy considerations bade him accept.

Suvich and Guariglia, on Mussolini's instructions, prepared on the afternoon of 18 December a communiqué to be issued after the Grand Council meeting that night. The communiqué stated Italy's appreciation of the British and French efforts and the council's decision to "consider the proposals as possible bases for discussion, leaving to the Government the necessary reservations to safeguard the rights of the nation."[69] This was what Hoare and Laval wanted—acceptance in principle of negotiated settlement. Nothing was said about terms. The cautious formula followed a suggestion made the previous day in Geneva by Laval. All that Italy had to do was to agree to begin talks. If so, then the Council of the League would never dare go against the wishes of Hoare and himself when it came to arguing details. Guariglia went to bed on the evening of 18 December thinking the matter was all settled. When he awoke the next morning, he opened his newspapers and was astonished to find no sign whatsoever of his communiqué.[70]

By the time Guariglia awoke, the Hoare-Laval plan was dead, killed, but not by reaction to the Pontina speech or by rejection on the part of the Grand Council. That body, meeting on the evening of 18 December, in fact contained a majority in favor of accepting negotiations in the manner suggested by the communiqué, in order to get Italy out of its perilous position. But just as the Grand Council assembled, word arrived in Rome that Samuel Hoare had resigned. With that news, indicating Britain's repudiation of the proposals, Mussolini adjourned discussion. There was no need now for him to make an immediate response. Hoare's resignation took the matter out of his hands.[71]

The Very High Price

Hoare resigned on 18 December 1935, scapegoat for a government faced with a storm of popular criticism and political opposition. The chasm between official thinking and the popular expectations gives this episode its overtones of tragedy. Enough has been said to show that officials in London and Paris were more bedeviled by the troubles League action brought than willing to grasp the opportunities it offered. And then came the revelation of the plan, so secretly prepared, so generous to Mussolini, so contrary to the popular assumptions about what was expected of League members. For Hoare and Laval they were the best terms that could be managed in the circumstance, and they refused to recant, regretting only the absence of time to educate the public in the need, indeed the legitimacy, of compromise. Outside their circle, outside the walls of their ministries, an outcry went up—the terms were a betrayal of trust—and the recent optimism that collective action would defend the Covenant, save Ethiopia, and end the war turned to despair.

"If the man in the street is hypocritical," Robert Barrington-Ward had written earlier, about "a very simple feeling of right and wrong" in the Ethiopian affair, "at least he doesn't know it."[72] The fears of men like Chatfield and Hoare were not shared by the public. Baldwin's government spoke too generally or too obtusely to be understood. So the assumption of simplicity in this matter persisted, on the street and in the palace. The king, fresh from chivying Eden about pursuing too forward a policy at Geneva, now expressed his anger with the peace terms that seemed a betrayal of national honor.

The evening the terms were published (9 December) Barrington-Ward, deputy editor of the *Times,* attended a reunion dinner of his wartime comrades. He wrote in his diary that night: "One and all revolted by the Paris terms . . . now the electorate is sold. . . . I went to bed utterly humiliated and dispirited and ashamed of my country. The first time that a public event ever so worked on me. We have sacrificed honour and interest together."[73] Certainly the plan looked bad on its face. Secret dealing went on (it seemed) behind the League. Mussolini was consulted; the emperor was to be "induced." It looked like a sellout to Mussolini's threats, a sellout of Ethiopia, of the electorate, of all the League stood for. "A cynical manoeuvre," said Clement Attlee, leader of the Opposition.[74]

When it was revealed on 16 December that the Ethiopian government would be asked not to build a railroad in the corridor given in return for the loss of nearly half its territory, Geoffrey Dawson let loose with a damning editorial in the *Times.*

> The Emperor, we are told, was to be informed "at a convenient moment" (presumably when he had recovered from the first shock of dismemberment) that he was forbidden to build a railway along his corridor. It was apparently to remain no more than a strip of scrub, restricted to the sort of traffic that has entered Ethiopia from the days of King Solomon, a corridor for camels. . . . The suggestion seems so incredible, so completely at variance with even the most cynical interpretations of a "civilizing mission," that its origins should be investigated before there is any fresh attempt at peace terms.

The *Times,* soon to become a proponent of appeasement in Europe, vigorously opposed concession to Italy in Africa. Dawson was no friend of sanctions; what he disliked was a threat to British imperial interests. Despite this different perspective he was proud of the way the paper now represented "the average view."[75]

Above all, the government could not ignore the fact of strong reactions within the House of Commons of outrage and bewilderment, with members' indignation increasingly reinforced by awareness of the public outcry. "It is the worst thing that has happened in my experience," said J. H. Thomas, minister of the colonies.[76] A parliamentary observer wrote: "I never saw since Lord R. Churchill's sudden resignation in 1886, such a panic in a Government camp." Neville Chamberlain wrote in his diary on 15 December: "Nothing could be worse than our position. Our whole prestige in foreign affairs at home and abroad has tumbled to pieces like a house of cards. If we had to fight the election over again, we should probably be beaten."[77] In dealing with this general dismay the cabinet faced two questions: what to do about the proposals and what to do about Samuel Hoare.

There was no doubt about the first. The Paris plan had to go. Large sections of the Conservative party and the Tory government's Liberal supporters were in revolt. Abstention of a large number, perhaps led by Austen Chamberlain, was in the offing. They did not want the newly elected government to fall, but its moral and political authority was at stake. National Liberals and the Labour party opposition denounced the plan. With a handful of the cabinet unwilling to go along, the proposals had to be declared dead or the government would break apart. Younger members of the cabinet, whom Neville Chamberlain called "the Boys' Brigade"—William Ormsby-Gore, Alfred Duff Cooper, Oliver Stanley, and Walter Elliot—at once began pressing on the parliamentary correspondent of the *Times* their views against the proposals and for Hoare's resignation.[78] On 16 December a ministerial meeting approved a speech for Eden to use at the League Council on the eighteenth. Eden was to declare that if—as was now evident—the proposals would not win ready acceptance at Geneva, the British government would press them no further. Hoare agreed. This was the death knell of the Paris plan.[79]

The question of Hoare's future remained. Hoare had been, since his return from Switzerland on 16 December, laid up in his house with a broken nose. He had not appeared before the cabinet to defend the plan or his own action. He was unrepentant. He agreed the proposals were finished. He did not agree they were ignoble or unwise. His intention was to defy the clamor and defend his acts. It was time, he thought—and Neville Chamberlain relayed this to the cabinet on 18 December—it was time for plain speaking. He would have to say "with utmost frankness" that other states, most especially France, were not prepared to pursue sanctions or to give help in the event of an Italian attack, that the oil sanction brought Britain into a "danger zone," and that the public must have the brutal facts.

Hoare's determination alarmed the cabinet. Now, in addition to the political arguments for Hoare's resignation (presented to the cabinet by Duff Cooper, Stanley, Ormsby-Gore, and Elliot), there was the danger that blunt words would put Britain's dependent weakness in bold relief, encouraging Mussolini to throw out caution. "Sam must go" was the word around Whitehall. Dawson supported it. He thought Baldwin "was probably more culpable than Sam," but he did not want to see the government fall. Sometimes there was explicit argument for a scapegoat. On the other hand, there was the cabinet tradition of collective responsibility and loyalty and the strong antipathy of Baldwin and Neville Chamberlain to using a scapegoat. Baldwin's last words to Hoare on the seventeenth were, "We all stand together."[80]

The problem was thrashed out at a cabinet on 18 December. Chamberlain reported on the strong speech of defense Hoare had prepared with the help of Lord Beaverbrook.[81] Duff Cooper said Hoare was not entitled to say that another nation was unwilling or unready to fight. This was a formal point—such a conclusion determined the actions of Hoare and his advisers in the Foreign Office and the service ministries. Lord Zetland said that in fact assurances of support were in hand from France, Greece, Turkey, and Yugoslavia. This was true, but, in the eyes of most ministers, of little consequence.

When discussion was done, the cabinet stood against Hoare. Over half its members were prepared to resign if the proposals were not dropped, and Hoare with them. Ormsby-Gore said Hoare had involved the cabinet in a "humiliating crisis," and, Simon noted, if Hoare still thought the proposals were right, and the government rejected them, then he must go. If he remained, said Thomas, especially if he spoke in his defense on the grounds of British weakness, "he would be discredited at Geneva and mistrusted everywhere in Europe, and his policy would always be suspected." As the plan stood, furthermore, it was a betrayal of the principles on which the election had been won. The country, said Thomas, was staggered and demoralized by it. Members who supported the government would go to their constituencies to find themselves "faced with disintegration."

Baldwin could not but agree. The situation in the Commons, he said, was the worst he had ever known. Lord Halifax, on whom Baldwin leaned, spoke strongly for resignation. This clinched the matter for the prime minister and for Neville Chamberlain. Halifax concluded that what was at stake was the "whole moral position of the Government before the world. If the Prime Minister were to lose his personal position, one of our national anchors would have dragged." Halifax's words ended the discussion and carried the day.[82] Chamberlain took word of the cabinet's mood to Hoare at his home, and on the evening of 18 December Hoare resigned. His pride and high ambition were salved by a promise from Baldwin to call him back to the cabinet when the storm had blown over.

The next day Hoare appeared at the House of Commons, speaking from a back bench, with a "personal explanation." He gave a long speech.

Chamberlain and Baldwin had persuaded him to adopt restraint, and, no doubt owing to their hints of an early return, he kept from embarrassing the government. Hoare made the most of the familiar themes. The closest he came to revealing the determining anxieties of the Foreign Office and the urgent cautions of the Admiralty was his declaration that "not a ship, not a machine, not a man has been moved by any other member State." Hoare's was a better speech than Baldwin's following statement. Despite his strain, the speech was spirited compared to the listless and toneless delivery of the prime minister. The proposals, declared Baldwin, were "absolutely and completely dead."[83] Was the government saved?

Austen Chamberlain's biographer claimed that at this time, before the division on a vote of confidence on 19 December, Chamberlain was "clearly the arbiter of ministerial fortunes, for the Back Benches were flocking to him for a lead." The implication is that if Chamberlain had abstained from the vote or voted against it, the government would have been out. This overdraws the case. Back-benchers did express their dismay to Chamberlain. His own criticism of the government's conduct no doubt greased the skids under Hoare. But with Hoare out on the evening of 18 December and the proposals buried, there was no reason for Chamberlain to lead a revolt. Perhaps his biographer relied on Chamberlain's statement: "Had I thought it compatible with the public interest I believe that after S.B.'s miserably inadequate speech and the initial blunder, I could have so reduced his majority as to force his resignation."[84] But this is a self-serving hypothesis. Baldwin told the cabinet on the eighteenth that even with imagined abstentions the government would still have a majority of a hundred votes. On the other hand, Baldwin was naturally apprehensive, since Chamberlain seemed willing, from his backroom conversations, to stage a demonstration of disapproval even if he was unwilling to press it to the extreme. As with Hoare, Baldwin whispered hints of future office in Chamberlain's ear, hints of the Foreign Office after the vote was taken.[85] To a man aged seventy-three, whose greatest ambition was becoming foreign secretary, this meant a lot. The strain on Chamberlain's loyalty was not so great as many thought.

Then, in the course of debate on 19 December, Attlee made the tactical mistake of associating the Paris proposals with "the honour of the Prime Minister." This gave Austen Chamberlain a chance for a face-saving compromise, a chance to renew his fidelity, help the government, and earn his ministry. "The past is past," he rose to say, and Attlee's imputation about Baldwin's honor "made it certain that no supporter of the Government would abstain."[86] Chamberlain's concession meant there was no leader for the remaining dissidents. The House divided on the question of "full support" of the government's foreign policy, with 390 voting for, 165 against. The next day the Commons adjourned until February 1936, and the miserable episode was declared closed in London.

Closed, except for bad feelings, scars, loose ends, and remaining consequences. Chamberlain did not get the Foreign Office. Baldwin told him he was too old and offered him a nondepartmental advisory cabinet position instead, which Chamberlain refused, writing: "I came to the conclusion that what he wanted was not my advice or experience, but the use of my name to help patch up the damaged prestige of his government."[87]

Vansittart had his wings clipped. Neville Chamberlain told the cabinet he thought Hoare "had been greatly misled by his staff," meaning Vansittart. Ormsby-Gore was more blunt. Hoare, he said on the eighteenth, should resign, but if he stayed he would have to "put a 'British' official at the head of the Foreign Office."[88] Vansittart felt the chill of ostracism and ebbing power when he returned from Paris. "The old movement to oust me gathered strength."[89] He was dissuaded from resigning by Beaverbrook, who argued there would be no public service if public servants left over issues of policy.[90] Yet Vansittart had virtually made the disowned policy, through Hoare.

On 22 December, after unpleasant and unnecessary beating about the bush, Baldwin gave Eden the post of foreign secretary, which he assumed on 2 January 1936. The Ministry for League of Nations Affairs was eliminated. Eden, one newspaper said, was Baldwin's Christmas present to the nation. Vansittart's iron grip on dispatches was loosened. He still had his friends in Orme Sargent and Ralph Wigram, who pursued the same courses "by less visible paths."[91] But Eden kept his distance. Hoare had relied on Vansittart without question. Eden brought his own undersecretary, supportive Lord Cranborne.

It seems fairly clear that Baldwin's mistake was in not insisting upon the government's using the Ethiopian affair to consolidate public opinion behind the need for rearmament and a more realistic foreign policy. Since the Great War there had not been any foreign issue around which people of Britain rallied so closely to their government as they did in support of the League. Because Baldwin did not constantly draw out the central value of this popular confidence and show ways to use it beyond short-run political advantage, and because he did not keep a careful, integrating control over foreign affairs and their domestic import, Vansittart and Hoare were able to pull off on their own. The double policy seemed a convenient way through an incongruent situation. The potential for conflict between its two lines was minimized or ignored in the daily workings of government. Political confidence given the government at home and abroad was not tended with even elementary care and eventually was harshly abused. Conciliation as a means of settling the Ethiopian war resulted in the debacle of the Hoare-Laval plan.

Hoare's resignation on the evening of 18 December 1935 came simultaneously with the meeting of the League Council in Geneva and the meeting of the Grand Council of Fascism in Rome.

At the League meeting Eden laid the proposals to rest without actually declaring them dead. Laval tried to dissuade him from the text the cabinet had prepared, arguing that Mussolini had yet to return a reply. But Eden could not alter a statement so carefully written. Laval had to content himself, in his own speech, with projecting hope for a future settlement. The Council deferred comment. The Committee of Thirteen (the Council membership minus Italy) set out "to examine the situation as a whole." Meanwhile, there was no change in sanctions. A month would pass before much more was heard from the League.[92]

The events of 18 December were variously interpreted at Geneva. Ethiopians claimed a victory. Their delegation cabled Addis Ababa (in a message intercepted by Italian intelligence): "Sanctions will continue. We have obtained complete satisfaction. Avoid field engagements and continue guerrilla warfare on all fronts." Aloisi saw the reference to the Committee of Thirteen as something of an accommodation. Things could have gone worse. Other Italians in Geneva were disappointed. Pilotti, Berio, and Bova Scoppa had their hearts set on furthering proposals with such evident negotiating advantages.[93] Delegates from the Little and Balkan ententes determined to insist henceforth on strict application of the Covenant. Proponents of the League, of course, acclaimed the British rejection of the Paris terms. With Eden's appointment they hoped, as Walters observed, that "a new impulse to action would shortly be given from London."[94]

News of Hoare's resignation reached Rome as the Grand Council of Fascism met to decide whether to agree in principle to open negotiations. Disinclined though Mussolini was, a majority of the council and certainly all his diplomatic advisers were in favor. Learning of Hoare's ouster, the Italians took no action. The Grand Council, meeting again two days later, simply noted British "repudiation" and the "manifest disorientation and contradictions" in the behavior of the sanctionist states.[95]

These moves of the Grand Council disappointed the diplomats. Guariglia sent a message to Laval thanking him for his help. There was little more to do but wait. What a shame, lamented Aloisi. "Had we handled things differently," presumably meaning an early acceptance, "the sanctionist states would have been seriously embarrassed." Now that particular opportunity was gone. The international situation, wrote Aloisi on 20 December, is "absolutely uncertain, confused, and without direction." The next day he recorded the mood of the ministry in Rome: "great uncertainty and disquiet."[96]

No one pretended to know what the future held. Eden's appointment only increased apprehension. Visitors to Mussolini noted his spirit of fatalism. He avoided discussions. Instead he preferred to let go in polemics written for the papers. A good example is his article "With Inflexible Determination," which appeared in *Il Popolo d'Italia* on 22 December. Europe, he contended, was old, jealous, exhausted, and hypocritical. Italy had rights to work and life. Votes at Geneva were obtained by pressure, threats, blackmail. And so on.[97] The strain on Mussolini was showing. The articles indicate his readiness for exhortation, simplified denunciations, calls to action. They, like the Pontina speech, are the best glimpse we have of Mussolini's thought at this time, and they indicate disquiet. "My victory, my victory," he called out in front of Chambrun, "when is it going to come?"[98] He was dependent on events, hoping a solution on the battlefield would solve his problems. But these were Italy's darkest days in the African campaign.

It was an unhappy Christmas in Rome, the saddest, said the *Osservatore Romano*, since the Great War. The pope had no dawn of peace to salute in his allocution on Christmas Eve. He said to his cardinals that he had done all "his very limited powers" permitted and had hoped to have good news at Christmas. But all he could offer now was hope "even in the worst contigency." Cardinal Pacelli said Mussolini made an "incontestable error" in not swiftly accepting negotiation. The pope agreed, alarmed that Mussolini was beyond the reach of advice. "It is grave, very grave," he said.[99]

Laval vented his disapproval in a long letter to Mussolini on 22 December. He keenly regretted that Mussolini had not replied with "immediate and spontaneous acceptance." It was a great shock, a disappointment "after the incessant appeals" he had sent. In October Mussolini had declared that the fate of Europe, the peace of Europe, was in the hands of France. Laval now turned the compliment back: future peace was with Italy. Mussolini insisted on an immediate reply, sent off on Christmas Day. It was a conciliatory response, thanking Laval, blaming the British, and leaving the door ajar for future negotiations if favorable terms were found.[100] Meant to flatter Laval, the letter expressed an empty wish.

Mussolini was discouraged and perplexed by the attack on Laval's foreign policy on 27 and 28 December in the French Chamber of Deputies. There would be no more help from France. On the thirtieth, at a meeting of the Italian Council of Ministers, he declared the proposals dead from the time of their publication. The terms, the council also announced, "were far from satisfying the minimum demands of Italy, especially from the point of view of frontier security and the security of Italian subjects." Publication, Mussolini told Hubert Lagardelle, had permitted sanctionist propaganda to take on gigantic proportions and had encouraged the emperor to refuse.[101]

Public outcry against the proposals in France was limited to recognized opponents of Laval. Most Frenchmen supported Laval's prudent course, from which the plan of compromise followed naturally. Laval, more honestly than Baldwin and Hoare, had never raised false expectations. Conciliation

with Italy was his proclaimed intent. Mediation, the prevention of a European conflict, was given a specific purpose—"to protect the peace of your
homes," as he said in a radio speech of 27 November 1935. There was no
peace ballot in France, no ringing affirmations by clergy or government
leaders. Laval never called for support of the Covenant in the way Hoare did
in his bluffing September speech to the League Assembly. Laval did not
claim to base his government on a national consensus, as did Baldwin. His
parliamentary strength did not rest on an electoral victory of which professed support of the League was a major cause. So, while his opponents
charged horse-trading and there were some strong attacks on the overall
orientation of Laval's foreign policy, resentful dismay, the sense of betrayal,
the charge of a secret about-face, did not arise much in France. French
politics were roiled by crosscurrents that diluted both Laval's support and
opposition on this issue. Debate, and vituperation, centered mainly on
domestic concerns: finances, the economy, the *ligues,* and the personalities of
leaders.

Laval's cabinet, the ninety-ninth in the Third Republic, was a coalition of
the Center and the Left. His foreign policy had not been an issue thus far.
The Ethiopian affair had not been discussed in the Chamber of Deputies
after that war began. Laval's determination to avoid war with Italy was
accepted by the Left, endorsed by the Center, and—particularly when
associated with hostility to Britain—enthusiastically approved by the Right.
Britain's imperial problems were not Laval's concern. He was after European peace. His goals were formulated before the African imbroglio, and he
was loath to give them up.

By the end of December 1935 Laval should have seen that many of his expectations no longer could be realized. Germany was far from ready to accommodate his vague requests for generalized declarations of peace by
which the former client states of Central Europe were to be succored, and of
which an understanding with Italy was the now uncertain cornerstone.

The complications of the Ethiopian affair ended Laval's first hope of
"managing" Europe. It put Britain and Italy at odds, and Laval could afford
to alienate neither. Britain was the more important to France, ultimately, but
why antagonize Italy unduly, and who ran Britain anyway—the government
or popular opinion? Laval did not want to close any doors. Simpleminded
and somewhat irresponsible this may have been. Perhaps the time for flex-
ibility was over. France should perhaps have stopped running with the hares
and hunting with the hounds, and declared a clearer, long-term national purpose. But in December 1935 Laval did not think this was yet demanded.

Things were still too uncertain. Events on the war front could still influence Europe. Mussolini might win or be forced to terms. Then the
tightrope act of moderation and reconciliation would bring France through.

Once this vexing matter was concluded, Rome could be approached in the spirit of the January accords. Once again there would be room for maneuver. No Frenchman wanted war with Italy, and this, after all, was what Laval most conspicuously was avoiding.

The Council of Ministers accepted the Hoare-Laval plan at its meeting on 10 December 1935, after the terms had become public knowledge. Minister Bodard, like Minister Barton, was instructed to press the emperor for acceptance. This decision was more definite than the endorsement by the British cabinet the day before. There Hoare was absent; acceptance was made on trust. In Paris, Laval—coauthor, foreign minister, and premier—presented the plan at the table.

Officials at the Quai d'Orsay did not doubt the wisdom of the proposals. The present mess, Massigli, Saint-Quentin, and Coulondre told Hugh Wilson on 13 December, was due to the "deplorable accident" of publication. Given the danger of war from the oil sanction and the assumption that France would never "mobilize nor fight for negroes," or, they added, "for Great Britain," the original conception was an "entirely permissible piece of negotiation."[102]

By the end of January 1936, however, Laval was out of office. Dissatisfaction with his foreign policy, sharpened by criticism of the Paris plan, was a consideration in the desertion of Radical ministers on whom his coalition government depended. Laval's ministry was six weeks in dying. Debates in the Chamber of Deputies tell part of the story. The inner tensions of French politics tell the rest.

Publication of the terms gave the Socialists and leftist Radicals of the newly formed Popular Front a chance to add a foreign policy grievance to their domestic criticisms. On 17 December Laval told the Chamber that the terms were meant to keep the peace and to protect French homes and that, if "without eclat," they at least satisfied his conscience.[103] Léon Blum, leader of the Socialist opposition, insisted on immediate debate on foreign policy. Laval agreed to take up this interpellation, but not until the session of 27 December.

In the sessions of 27 and 28 December, French policy toward the Italian-Ethiopian war (or foreign policy, for that matter) was seriously discussed in the Chamber of Deputies for the first time since the war had begun. This suited Laval's highly personal style of conducting foreign affairs, although it annoyed the Radicals in his cabinet and the Socialists outside of it. Throughout his career Laval was condemned as much for how he did things as for what he did. Within the snobbish British Foreign Office, he suffered also for how he looked.

There were three important speeches on 27 December. Blum, no friend of the connection with Fascist Italy, attacked Laval's personal policy and

France's responsibility in enfeebling the mechanism of collective security. Blum changed no votes. Yvon Delbos, who in six months became foreign minister in the Blum government, spoke for the Radical opposition. Although six Radical ministers sat with Laval, none spoke in this debate. Delbos denounced a policy that "upset everyone without satisfying Italy." This attack revealed how exposed the government was to Radical defection. But Delbos's speech was not enough to carry the Chamber against Italy.[104]

The most impressive address was delivered by Paul Reynaud, member of the Democratic Alliance and leader of the moderate republican group. Reynaud had just returned from London, where he attended the session of Commons that heard Hoare's personal defense and Baldwin's pronouncement that the plan was dead. France, Reynaud said, was in danger of isolation. He cited *Mein Kampf*. "Against whom is Germany arming?" The main obstacle to German expansion was an understanding between Britain and France. Italy would soon find Ethiopia too meager a mouthful. France's institutions could best be protected against the illiberal militarism of those states by close connection with liberal, democratic Britain. Hoare's fall showed that the British were now receptive to principles of international cooperation, France's traditional concern. Yet Laval had failed to seize the opportunity. Instead of cooperation, he pulled in the opposite direction. Without cooperation, France could come to isolation and mortal peril. The choice, Reynaud said, was between "Italy, the breaker of the Covenant, and England, its champion."[105]

Reynaud's speech surprised moderates with its force and was widely applauded. The British ambassador thought that if the Chamber had divided when Reynaud sat down the government would have been "easily defeated."[106] As it was, there was no vote until the next day, by which time feeling was less intense, minor speakers had dissipated policy arguments with party politics, and Laval made his own defense without leaving a chance for opposition reply. Laval carried the vote and one wonders if the French legislature was quite as taken up with Reynaud's argument as Clerk thought.

On 28 December Laval challenged the Chamber to do better than he had. The "basic question" was to decide whether or not his policies conformed to the interests of France. It was his job to protect French homes, not ameliorate British-Italian tension or go beyond what the Covenant demanded of each contracting state. He had followed the Covenant to the letter, had kept in step with Britain, and so warned Mussolini. Fudging the point, he declared that Hoare and he had agreed in September not to employ military sanctions. Nothing could be done about an oil embargo until the American Congress met in January, so he and the British waited on Washington. The British, his impression was, were the ones dragging their feet. Far from isolating Britain, Laval said staff talks were under way to implement, if necessary, the Covenant's provisions for military sanctions. What he wanted was European peace—hence the pact with Moscow, hence perhaps an eventual rapprochement with Germany. To the charge of personalizing foreign policy, he said he would not mind bringing to the Chamber the grave question of whether France should support an oil sanction. Responsibility would then lie with parliament for calling a general or partial mobilization.

Laval thus drew the sting of criticism. He threw responsibility for "the entire orientation of French foreign policy" back to the "representatives of the country," and there were precious few in that Chamber ready to vote for mobilization or war credits over Ethiopia. For the future Laval promised continued efforts at conciliation, he promised to maintain present obligations to the Covenant, and he did not foreclose further sanctionist action. Herriot admitted the speech was "very clearly favorable to the League."[107] Laval's revelations of staff talks had drawn breaths of astonishment. It was a ploy. The talks, as we saw, had little effect, and relations with Britain remained strained.

It was a well-done speech, stressing moderation and responsibility and, coming at the close of debate, precluded reply. Laval won the vote on 28 December, standing against Delbos's motion of censure by 296 to 276 and carrying the following motion of support by 304 to 261. It was an important victory, or so it seemed. Laval now held votes of confidence on three central matters: finance, the political *ligues,* and foreign affairs. Yet there were considerations that entered into the voting on 28 December but were not debated in the Chamber.

Some deputies did not want to upset the parliamentary calendar by a ministerial crisis just when bills on the political *ligues* (as amended by the Senate) and the budget for the next year still had to be put to the vote. For those whose primary interest was domestic affairs, Laval had credit for dispelling much of the threat of civil strife that had haunted France. For those concerned with avoiding devaluation, Laval and his 500 decrees had brought budgetary deflation, slight monetary inflation, and an improvement in public confidence. Alfred Sauvy notes that industrial recovery had begun before the decree laws and that deflation was not entirely successful, since there was something of a rise in prices, but demand and consumption did increase, and this benefited Laval.[108] This economic improvement may have been due, in part, to Laval's moderate and nondemanding foreign policy, for confidence grew with his assurances that France would be kept from war. Ambassador Clerk, surveying the scene in January, concluded that Laval's peace policy made him the most popular politician in France. The pope was reported to say that Laval's policy of moderation was the only comfort left to him on earth.[109]

Those who argued for a stronger connection with Britain in support of the League were in a minority. André Tardieu, elder statesman of the Center-Right, resigned from the group to protest Reynaud's call for a choice between Italy and Britain. Could Britain be counted on to the extent implied by Reynaud? More proof was needed. Meanwhile, said Tardieu, France should stay with Laval's prudent policy. Faced with this criticism, Reynaud resigned the presidency of the group, responding to Tardieu that France should at least do more to encourage British interest in collective security. Cooperation with London in support of sanctions, he said, "is our only chance for peace."[110]

Despite general support from the Right and the Center, uncertainty about Laval's overall policy, the loss of prestige at Geneva and to the small nations, the growing awareness of the contradictions and probable failure of his efforts to be all things to all men, the sense that France was moving away from traditional bearings, and Laval's reputation for intrigue bothered many, not least the increasingly distrustful Radicals and Socialists on whom his government depended.

As Radical discontent grew, as Daladier's Radical faction allied with leftist Popular Front opposition to Laval's domestic policies, Laval's coalition was undermined. The victory on 28 December was close, twenty votes, and only thirty-seven of the Radicals voted for the government. Had these conservative Radicals and the fourteen who abstained followed the ninety-three of their fellows who voted against, the government would have been out. Herriot himself wished this. But, although disliking Laval and alarmed by the increasingly precarious relations with the British, he did not want to bring the ministry down by his own resignation. Laval was much irritated by the way Herriot went along in the League Council while carping against him on the outside. But Herriot twice before had taken responsibility, and blame, for toppling coalition governments (of Poincaré and Doumergue) and, under bitter attack in the rightist press for his sanctionist position, he did not want to incur further opprobrium by bringing this one down. So he hoped the Chamber would do the overturning. After the foreign affairs debate he, as a minister, voted confidence for the government, but he walked the corridors counseling: "I can say nothing! But vote against us."[111]

The Radical party was divided. Not enough wanted to turn the ministry out. The defeat of Laval's government, wrote Peter Larmour, "was a dreadfully inefficient political operation. It took so long that the issues that had first aroused the hostility to it were forgotten."[112] This is not the place for chronicling the six weeks of confusion that opened with Herriot's resignation from the party presidency on 18 December, his replacement by Daladier, and the consummation of the Popular Front, whose electoral program was published on 10 January 1936.

While resigning party leadership, Herriot stayed with the ministry. In early January 1936, with the Chamber in adjournment, Daladier's left wing brought the militant Radical opposition to the fore. First attempts to enforce unity of opposition to the government failed, however, and with undisciplined Radicals voting for him, Laval won another vote of confidence, by sixty-four votes, on 16 January. It was his government's last victory. Three days later the Radical party executive, voting the election of Daladier as new party leader, condemned Laval's "ideas and methods" and demanded party unity. Radical participation in the ministry was no longer possible.[113]

On 22 January 1936 Herriot and three other Radical ministers resigned. Their joint letter of resignation said the demand of party loyalty made it impossible for them to supply the government with a working majority. There was no word of criticism of Laval or his policies.[114] Laval decided not to ride out these resignations. More were rumored to follow. On 20 January he told Aloisi in Geneva that he would dissolve the government on his return to Paris. He wanted out, he said, while he still enjoyed his string of five straight votes of confidence. To Eden he said that he knew he would be defeated on the next vote.[115] On 23 January Laval handed up his government, done in by party maneuvering in which opposition to his foreign policy played only a part. He thought no successor would do differently in avoiding provocation of Italy.[116]

Herriot was offered the premiership. He refused. Delbos also refused to form a cabinet. The president successfully called upon a third Radical, Albert Sarraut, behind whom stood Georges Mandel.[117] Radicals dominated Sarraut's ministry, but they forced no great change from previous lines. Laval had watched public opinion and national capacity, and the new government too chose to follow, not lead. Sarraut's was an interim government, to hold until the elections. He and his foreign minister, Pierre-Étienne Flandin, agreed with Laval's policy in the Italian-Ethiopian dispute, and it was continuity, not change, that marked the 100th ministry of the republic.

7 ITALIA CONTRA MUNDUM

The Day of Faith

Meanwhile, how fared Italy? We saw how the government minimized international pressures through diplomacy. Although the foreign ministry's excuse for war—that Ethiopia was a barbarous state—convinced no one, the prospect of a negotiated settlement kept foreign efforts at conciliation in play and prevented increasingly severe application of article 16. Most important in forestalling further sanctions was the reiterated warning of a European war. Three months after the invasion a ban on oil and other essential materials was still in debate. Successful in its short-run diplomacy, the government did not look beyond the war to Italy's international future.

Ethiopia had to be conquered as soon as possible. Further sanctions and the spring rainy season loomed ahead. But operations were stalled. At the beginning of 1936 the Italian fronts had not moved for six weeks. There had been no victory of strategic importance. Indeed, in mid-December the Ethiopian forces had mounted an impressive counteroffensive. Meanwhile, it was necessary to avoid economic dislocation and consequent social unrest in Italy. To offset the effects of bans on trade, while supplying the armies in Africa, the government intensified state control over economic and political life.

The government had to make popular a colonial war greeted in its preparatory stages with grumbling and indifference. It had to play up Italy's status as an isolated object of punitive action and keep the war from becoming a question of confidence. Sanctions were aimed at making the war too costly to continue, and this could be avoided only with public cooperation in antisanction measures. Internal solidarity was necessary to carry the regime through the troubles hatched at Geneva. A solid front would put the lie to those who thought foreign disapproval and punishment would undermine domestic support.

The government advanced to the populace a number of arguments in favor of the war. There would be revenge for Aduwa and pride in Italy on the march. There would be land and work, a frontier, settled under the Italian flag, to absorb Italy's excess population. Who knew what treasures of gold, oil, or precious minerals, lay beneath the soil? Enough, it was said, to warrant the cost of war. So went some of the rationales. In fact, after the conquest Mussolini showed no interest in Ethiopia's development. So indifferent was he when Lessona broached the subject that the head of the ministry of colonies concluded the land, as far as Mussolini was then concerned, could have been Syria or any other place.[1]

In any case, such propaganda was not enough to create disciplined, favorable public support. The lack of great victories in November and December 1935 discouraged the sentiment that all would go well. Workers found pay (forty-five lire a day) in the train of the army, and from the University of Rome a battalion of idealists (some of them of noteworthy antifascism later) joined the "civilizing mission" in Africa. But the war was fought by a conscript army. Few of the 176,000 metropolitan soldiers in the colonies on 3 October 1935 were volunteers.[2] With sanctions pressing down, with the British fleet on the way to Massawa, spirits were not to be bouyed simply by talk of renewing the Roman heritage of African glories and Mediterranean domination.

What dissolved indifference was the foreign opposition. What made the war popular was eventual military success.

The European threat was immediately understandable, so anguish and hostility could be turned into patriotic loyalty. Regardless of their views of the campaign, all Italians were affected by sanctions. A patriotic response was encouraged by the government as a safety valve for all sorts of discontent, as a nationalist affirmation that united Italians in a way the colonial campaign never could. Tensions of the months preceding the invasion were relieved in the call "Italy against the world." Italy, acting alone. Italians imbued with new responsibility. Italy, transformed, infused with Fascist energy and warrior spirit, would fight its battles on two fronts. The need for domestic discipline became as vital as the need for courage on the high African plateaus.

Sanctions, the League, Britain, and Eden were denounced in sadness, then in resentment, and then in anger. The Fascist Grand Council declared 18 November 1935, the day sanctions were applied, a day of "shame and inequity in the history of the world." It was a disgrace that Italy, with its great and noble past, trying now to realize its ideals and defend its right to live, should be singled out as the object of such a "test." Morally repellent, Mussolini said on 1 December, a "crude experiment" in which even the experimenters did not believe.[3] There were endless changes to be rung on a general theme. The League was made up of plutocratic anti-Fascists, out to get Mussolini's Italy. It was composed of egotistic Masons and laic mystics, influenced by decadent doctrines espoused by liberal democrats, Anglican bishops, Jews, and Bolsheviks. The League was the "extreme incarnation of the Enlightenment filtered through one and a half centuries of democratic romaticism."[4] This unholy coalition was led by the glutted and retired imperialist Britain, now playing dog-in-the-manger, fearful in its bloated weakness, represented by the ambitious, too handsome, anti-Italian minister for League of Nations affairs.

Xenophobia spread. A cigar brand under state monopoly became "Fiume" instead of "Britannica." Owners of establishments called "Hotel Eden" hung out new names. The king cancelled diplomatic receptions—the corps paid no visit to his palace at the new year. Austrians and Hungarians were favored in society, vexing the Swiss minister who, like his confederation, tried to stay neutral.[5]

To turn dissatisfaction to use, the government stressed the needs of a nation at war. "To economic sanctions," Mussolini said in his mobilization speech of October, "we will oppose our discipline, our sobriety, our spirit of sacrifice." Resentment was expressed on 18 November in the *Corriere della Sera* editorial reviling the Genevan coalition under the title "Against the Inhuman Siege." But Mussolini's article on that day of sanctions in *Il Popolo d'Italia* better illustrated the government's tack: "Unshakable and Admirable Resistance." The Grand Council, preparing for sanctions, declared Italians "ready to use through the agencies of the regime, all the moral energies and material resources of the nation" to show the world the "Roman *virtù*" of the Italian people.[6]

The party took up the task of mobilization. There were about two million men in the "fasci di combattimento" directly susceptible to Mussolini's orders for political action. A week after the war began the party secretary, Achille Starace, commanded each local secretary to intensify party activity "to the maximum." "Not a single minute of the day must be lost. During one's seven hours of sleep one eye must be kept open."[7] Party members gathered scraps of iron and wood, enforced economic measures, and insisted upon public patriotic behavior. A party committee watched over the prices now set for basic goods. It was party members who got out the audiences for the great patriotic gatherings, who draped the nation in flags on sanctions day, and who produced the Day of Faith in mid-December.

All agencies of the government cooperated. During the Ethiopian war the government made its first full-scale use of radio for a systematic propaganda campaign. About 30 percent of air time was devoted to political purposes. People were forbidden to listen to foreign broadcasts in public.[8]

General public cooperation was essential if inflation and the black market were to be held down. By the onset of winter, prices were gradually rising. People were urged to cut down on expensive items. Restaurants served only one helping of fish or meat—or at any rate were told to do so. Synthetic goods, substitutes for wool, cotton, whole milk, and coffee, made dramatic appearances. Transportation was cut back as the price of gasoline soared. Railroad traffic was reduced 10 percent to conserve fuel. Newspapers were reduced in size. Good soap was in short supply, as the limited amounts of chemicals and fats went into war production.

What the government lacked was new successes in the field. By mid-December the initial excitement over the early "victories" had worn off. Except for members of the party hierarchy who rushed to the war zones for the three months' service needed to qualify for ribbons and war crosses, few combat volunteers came from the middle class. Some war propaganda was even muted. The vainglorious aerial exploits of Ciano and the Mussolini boys, which caused such a commotion abroad, were censored from home consumption in October. On 9 December, Alfieri in the ministry of press and propaganda wrote to his minister Ciano: "Now more than ever international events are intimately tied to military operations."[9] The same held true for the popular mood. December war bulletins repeated a monotonous refrain: no change in the situation along the whole front. There was a revealing comment from this period by the federal secretary in Milan. "What interests people is the length of delay in offensive operations." What were the difficulties? Why, people wondered, did Badoglio want another 20,000 men? "A decisive military action is awaited with impatience, to clarify a political situation fraught with a degree of tension." This "sense of uncertainty," the secretary concluded, this "grey period of waiting," could "lead to discouragement."[10]

Years later, in July 1943, in the midst of another war going badly against Italy, fighting for his political life before the Grand Council, Mussolini made the defense: "The truth is that no war is ever 'popular' when it starts . . . it becomes popular if it goes well, and if it goes badly it becomes extremely unpopular. Even the war for the conquest of Ethiopia became popular only after the victory of Mai Chio [conclusive defeat of Haile Selassie's last force, March 1936]." The essential thing is not the "psychological fluctuations" of the "mass of people" but their discipline. The "people's heart is never in any war," he said. "War is always a party war. . . . it is always one man's war."[11] In 1935, as in 1943, what Mussolini needed was a show of popular support, and in 1935 he was able to create it.

On 18 December 1935 the party produced the "wedding-ring day," the day of allegiance. Mussolini spoke at Pontina, his new city in the reclaimed marshes, and there followed the ceremony of donation, of participation of the masses. Gifts of gold and precious metal from various cities and individuals had already arrived. Now donation was generalized to the nation at large. On the Day of Faith, throughout the kingdom—into flaming crucibles attended by uniformed Fascists, blessed by priests, and sited at the war memorials of the towns—the women of Italy cast their wedding rings.

What more precious gift, apart from a son or a husband, could a poor woman make to the national cause? Not all gave, nor were all the donations voluntary. The British ambassador reported that force was applied, in Pontina, of all places, to move reluctant older women to the offertory.[12] In Rome, 250,000 rings were collected; in Milan, 180,000. The Italian employees of the League of Nations presented a gold bar. Two and a half tons of gold were collected. All in all, in this and other donations throughout the war, the foreign exchange control was enriched by almost four tons of gold (worth some four and a half million U.S. dollars, 1935 value) and over five tons of silver. Over a two-year period the state expended the equivalent of about one billion U.S. dollars to conquer Ethiopia.[13]

The immediate value of the donations, of course, was political. Ruggero Zangrandi called the Day of Faith "the one true plebiscite held after 1922." The emotional loyalty those pledges of allegiance created bound the donor to the regime.[14]

The House of Savoy identified itself with the cause. The queen, in a singular and much remarked appearance, was the first to give her band, along with the king's, in Rome. Her eldest daughter and royal princesses and duchesses presented themselves at the crucibles in major cities. The prince of Piedmont, the crown prince, donated his highest decoration. Two royal dukes commanded divisions on the northern front. The king had already declared his solidarity when he inaugurated the new University City in Rome on 1 November 1935. His country, he said, was "engaged in events imposed upon it by the supreme exigencies of its life, of its security, and of its future. In every hour of her glorious history Rome has carried out her mission of civilization. Today, Italy is following along the same path, more than ever united by a spontaneous effort of faith and will."[15] When thanked for the queen's role in the ring ceremony, Victor Emmanuel replied (so Mussolini recalled): "Duce, no one more than I understands what you are doing for our country in these days. The Queen and I are grateful and proud to be of use, in any way, in this difficult time, as you request."[16] This public association of the royal family with the government, with its African ambitions, and with Italy's crisis under sanctions moved many to overcome their doubts and reservations and was thus of immense benefit to the regime.

There was much other evidence of support. The exiled Socialist Arturo Labriola and the old liberal Vittorio Emanuele Orlando overcame their anti-Fascism in love of country. Orlando's offer to serve, much-publicized by the government, moved Mussolini to sarcasm about overripe old men, but it was genuine.[17] Also from abroad came expressions of loyalty to Italy from Massimo Rocca, former Fascist, who defected after the murder of Matteotti, and Mario Bergamo, hostile to the League and viewing the conflict in terms of civilization against barbarism. Sanctions and the anguish of isolation brought forth patriotism that imperialism had not tapped. Luigi Albertini and Benedetto Croce, no friends of the Fascists, offered up their senatorial gold medals in honor of Italian soldiers, as did 414 of the 419 senators. Mussolini donated his collection of metal busts.

Nor was the clergy silent. Gaetano Salvemini, ever vigilant, compiled a list of 108 higher churchmen (7 cardinals, 27 archbishops, and 74 bishops) who spoke for the cause.[18] Circumspection might suite the pope, but not the cardinal archbishop of Milan, Idelfonso Schuster. On 28 October 1935, at high mass in the Duomo, he praised the new chapter of Italian history opened by the Fascist government (settlement of church-state relations by the Lateran agreement of 1929) and urged cooperation in the "national and catholic mission of good works, especially now when on the plains of Ethiopia the Italian standard carries forward the cross of Christ, smashes the chains of slavery, and opens the way for missionaries of the gospel." Schuster then prayed for the "protection of the gallant army that, in fearless obedience to the commands of the fatherland, is opening the gates of Ethiopia to the Catholic faith and Roman civilization."[19]

Schuster's exhortations came on the fifteenth anniversary of the March on Rome, the main Fascist celebration day, and the beginning of the new Fascist year—Anno XIV. On the same day the cardinal archbishop of Bologna, Nasalli Rocca, told the women of the city to take up the tasks Mussolini expected of them, to, "in this historic time," raise the spirits of their men, unite against sanctions, and lead the austere life of national resistance. On sanctions day, 18 November 1935, the archbishop of Amalfi, Ercolano Marini, discredited the League as acting under the occult forces—virulently anti-Catholic, of course—of "Masonry, Bolshevism and Anglicanism" and reviled those enemy camps trying to thwart Italy's "civilizing mission." On 8 December 1935, speaking before Mussolini, the bishop of Civita Castellana, Santina Mangaria, thanked God he was witness to "these epic days." He declared the solidarity of the clergy under Mussolini's leadership and attacked the odious ingratitude of Britain and France who, "in defense of barbaric slavery, against our rights, speak hypocritically of the sanctity of a pact, arbitrarily interpreted," ignoring Italy's sacrifice and alliance in the world war. Then, with a Fascist salute, the bishop presented Mussolini with his pastoral chain.

Such were typical judgments of the Italian hierarchy. The archbishop of Parma, Evasio Colli, did warn in a pastoral letter of 5 February 1936 against giving in to "waves of collective hatred, organized lies, and prejudices of every kind." For the most part, however, the clergy offered *te deum*s to soldiers, blessings to departing regiments, and nationalist encouragements to their flocks. On the Day of Faith, unity and sacrifice were lauded, and the inequitable siege was condemned. Schuster had invited churches in his diocese to send "superfluous" gold and silver to the local Fascist headquarters. On 7 December the Vatican's *Osservatore Romano* had argued that, since the main burden of sanctions would fall on the poor and the burden of war on those with sons in the field, parish priests should devote themselves to such needs as a matter of charity. The Vatican hoped that church donations to the cost of war would not be necessary. Still, a day later, the bishop of San Miniato told Mussolini that for the "victory of truth and justice" the clergy would melt down the gold of the churches and the bronze of the bells.[20]

It never came to that, but, as with the House of Savoy, the endorsement of the clergy legitimized the support of many people and encouraged the hesitant. Mussolini in due course acknowledged the "effective collaboration rendered by the entire clergy in the fight against the hordes of Ethiopia and the so-called civilized sanctionist hordes."[21] Daniel Binchy reported that the 60 bishops and 2,000 priests present chanted in response to this speech, with its further words of conciliation and praise: "Duce, Duce, Duce." Surely, Binchy said, this was one of the strangest demonstrations ever held in the capital of Christendom. Making allowance for the difficulties of the clergy's position during the Ethiopian war, Binchy concluded that some of their speeches "can only be described as war-mongering of the basest kind."[22]

Of course, most of the clergy merged support for the war into larger, more continuous themes. They spoke gratefully of the "man of Providence" who had ended the standoff between church and state, of the leader who kept bolshevism at bay. They believed in a missionary duty for Christians and a civilizing duty for Europeans. Now, as loyal Italians, they joined a nation deeply moved with anxiety, resentment, and pride. Winds of liberalism, internationalism, and ecumenicalism did not stir in the parishes of Italy in the pontificate of Achille Ratti, Pius XI, in Anno XIV, Era Fascista. In short, a reading of public statements by the clergy shows the intense, comprehensive nationalist sentiment emerging and being developed at this time. With the nation in danger, antisanctionism was a theme on which all could agree. Where some bishops saw a just war, more saw an unjust siege. And most were ready to speak out on the great events.

Not so the Holy See, and the ambiguous silence of the pope gave rise to increasingly harsh criticism abroad. There were two issues. One was the absence of papal comment since the war had begun. Second was the question whether the Vatican, maintaining a formal neutrality, was responsible for the strong statements of support emanating from the clergy. It was church practice to permit clergy free expression in national concerns as long as principles of Christian charity and the needs of the universal Church were not ignored. On the other hand, the pope was primate of Italy and intimately tied to that nation's clergymen. Binchy concluded that "even if the Vatican itself maintained a formal neutrality, its toleration of the chauvinist speeches and behavior of members of the Italian hierarchy and other prominent Italian ecclesiastics constituted a direct encouragement to the Fascist leaders and an implicit support of the Fascist cause."[23]

To be sure, the Vatican wished the war a swift end and pursued this goal beyond the public view. Meanwhile the Vicar of Christ, in his primary capacity as spiritual and moral leader, was failing to speak out either in support of a national crusade or against an unjust war.

Prior to October 1935 the pope had delivered some strong words against an aggressive war in Africa, some clear signs of his disfavor.[24] When the war began, however, and international opposition made resistance a national cause, Pius XI said no more. There were tremendous dangers on all sides. He did not agree with the liberal predicates or punitive action of the League. A loyal son of Lombardy would not turn his back on a suffering Italy. Any measure of support for Mussolini, however, was untenable, given Pius's early opposition and the certainty that it would provoke tremendous outcry abroad—and probably among many Italian clergy. To directly oppose Mussolini would be even worse. It might turn the Duce to a radicalized fascism, and terrible harm would come to the church. If Mussolini fell, bolshevism; liberal democracy was too weak to stand against the communist menace. Mussolini, for all his faults, had at least managed that. The cardinal secretary of state, Eugenio Pacelli, shared the pope's views. Just before his death in 1939 Pius XI said: "Late, too late, in my life, I have discovered that the dangers that threaten religion do not come only from one side; they come from the other side as well."[25] But in 1935, according to the Polish ambassador at the Vatican, Pius thought the Soviet Union was encouraging British opposition to Italian ambitions in Ethiopia so as to profit from general upheaval in Europe.[26]

Grieved by the failure of diplomatic negotiations, gravely upset by the drift of events, in an allocution on 16 December 1935 the pope responded to the charge, as he put it, that he "had not fulfilled the duties inherent in his divinely ordained office." He maintained silence, he said, because given the "uncertainty of events and men" there was danger that any remarks he made would become subject "to misunderstanding or deliberate distortion."[27]

In this war, the opposition of anti-Fascist émigré groups had little effect. Communists, joined by socialists, followed the Comintern line that preached sanctions and collective security but added its own calls for strikes, prevention of troop departures, and disruption of battle plans in the field. There was to be class conflict on the peninsula. The capitalist-imperialist war would end in military defeat, followed by the collapse of the bourgeois state and the triumph of socialism. The communists and socialists sponsored a

Congress of Italians Abroad, held in Brussels 12–13 October 1935. The League was urged to adopt sanctions and the "real" Italy was called upon to throw Mussolini out. There was no response. No coherent communist organization existed to heed the call. All that happened was to confirm conservatives in their moderation, for if sanctions pushed Mussolini to the point of collapse, the red menace might overtake Italy.

The *Giustizia e Libertà* group, itself internally split, stayed aloof from the socialist-communist left. Its leader, Carlo Rosselli, shunned the Brussels conference. Worried that international opposition would encourage a patriotic rally, placing no trust in the League, Rosselli argued for using the strains of war to stir up civil strife. The validity of this policy of individual acts of opposition was denied by the leftists, for whom the issue was class struggle. It also was fated to have no effect. The leaders of the *Giustizia e Libertà* resistance in Italy were arrested and, in February 1936, sentenced to prison.[28]

There was neither the organization nor the mood for strong resistance within Italy. The émigré groups continued their criticism throughout the war but, whether nationalist or socialist, they had no political impact. Their efforts in Zangrandi's words, "showed only the psychological distance between the exiles and the reality of Italy." In Rome the minister of the interior, reviewing the failure of the opposition in 1936, wrote that the communists and the members around the *Giustizia e Libertà* group made "colossal errors of judgment in the political situation." There was, he concluded, no mood for rebellion in Italy. The year 1936 "saw a severe setback to all anti-Fascists."[29] True enough, but it was more than the emergence of patriotism that neutralized calls for opposition—Mussolini's police state prevented the organization of any political opposition on the left.

Le contro-sanzioni

In addition to the political response to sanctions, there was the need to reply to the economic threat by economic means. Sanctions, Mussolini said on 23 March 1936, opened "a new chapter of Italian history." There was a lesson. "An independent foreign policy is impossible without the correlative capacity of economic autonomy." Henceforth, Mussolini said, Italy must be prepared for the eventuality of war by creating "in the shortest possible time the greatest autonomy in the economic life of the nation."[30]

Autarky, only approximately possible for a country as poor as Italy, meant regulation, and, as it turned out, the war unsettled the arrangement of hands-off between Mussolini and big business that had served both well. Mussolini did not start his governance as an economic radical. State interference, as with the founding of the Istituto Mobiliare Italiano in 1931 or the Istituto di Ricostruzione Industriale in 1933, sought, by and large, to facilitate private initiatives. Promulgating corporatism, a politically useful fiction, Mussolini took credit for social harmony between economic sectors, but unrest was reduced in fact by the difficulty of dissent in a single-party dictatorship. Business enjoyed managerial autonomy, profit, and labor peace in return for not interfering in politics. In 1935 and 1936 the private sector, having traded political influence for the benefits of stability, was unable to control Mussolini's radicalism, reemerged in an aggressive and expansionistic foreign policy. The demands of war economy, the needs of rearmament and protection against the effects of sanctions, meant a rapid increase in regulations over trade, finance, and production. These were acceptable in the patriotic fervor of the Ethiopian war and for the increasing profit and production it brought. But the growth of public enterprises and government regulations, with consequent limitations on private power, showed big business that there was no escape from the implication of a policy of autarky—the loss of autonomous authority for private enterprise.[31]

Italy suffered from weak finances and a dependence on foreign goods. Sanctions were imposed precisely to exploit this vulnerability. Members of the Coordination Committee counted on Italy's poverty to aid them in restraining the government's capacity to conduct war. There was in sanctions an implied advantage of strong nations over weak, a discrimination contrary to the egalitarian assumptions of the Covenant. Recognizing its weakness, the government applied controls to the economy.

The war had to be paid for without bankrupting the state or unsettling the population. Political gains—patriotic sentiment—could be measured off against economic loss—shortages and inflation—but only in the short run. The cost of armament in the fiscal year 1935–36 was ten times greater than civil expenditures.[32] The budget deficit, some 2 billion lire in 1934–35, soared in the next fiscal year to over 12.5 billion, and the public debt rose by 5 billion. Conventional revenue remained static. Half the state income in 1935 came from indirect taxes on consumer goods, meaning higher prices and lower quantities demanded if this source were used further, given the passive state of commerce.[33] This meant new taxes and short-term loans. In 1935 came levies of 10 percent on interest and increased taxes on estates, bachelors, automobiles, electricity, and above all those precious imports, oil and gasoline. Dividends were limited to 6 percent for three years, during which time excess profits had to be invested in state funds. Massive sales of bonds occurred, particularly in the conversion of 3½ percent government redeemables into 5 percent holdings on the consolidated fund, leaving the government to pay high interest, but raising some 7 billion lire immediately. Bank rates went up a point to 4 percent. On 27 November 1935 the Bank of Italy raised the price of domestically purchased gold, in effect taking the lira off the standard at home. There was a danger of inflation, with the cost of living index edging upward.[34] In the course of 1935 the government increased the circulation of convertible currency by some 4 billion lire, to 19 billion, and in the middle of the year (2 July) suspended the required 40 percent minimum gold cover held in the reserve, which was down to a dangerously low 3.4 billion by the end of the year.[35]

Economic restrictions did not, during the Ethiopian war, unsettle society, largely because of voluntary cooperation from all quarters. Felice Guarneri called the public spirit of the population Italy's secret of success.[36] Cooperation, but also surveillance. The party had responsibility for price control. During the war the center of party activity became price fixing at local levels and watching against violations.[37]

The greatest danger from sanctions lay in the area of foreign exchange. With the end of credit and loans from Europe, with the export trade cut by two-thirds, sanctions could in fact badly hurt the Italian economy. Such, at any rate, was the "rather dark picture" economic adviser Guarneri painted for Mussolini in September. This was the time of crisis, when Hoare spoke to the Assembly, the British fleet steamed about the Mediterranean, and it looked to Badoglio as if Italy's game was up. The problems were considerable, many antedating those raised by the war. Italy's soft currency had been dreadfully overvalued since the British and Americans left the gold standard. Pegged in 1927 at 19 lire to the U.S. dollar and 92.46 to the pound sterling, the lira in 1935 brought only about 12 to the dollar and 58 to the pound. It thus was hard enough to sell abroad, and harder still to get through foreign protectionist barriers. The persistent adverse balance of trade might have been worse, save that imports fell during the early 1930s almost as much as exports.

Responding to these problems, even before the uncertain needs of imperialism, the government created a foreign exchange control, the Istituto Nazionale Cambi, in May 1934. By February 1935 import licenses were required, an inconvenience to industry that was later a matter of considerable friction. To bring order to the preparations on the home front and to mount the economic resistance to sanctions, Mussolini, in the months before the war began, created two economic controllers. Felice Guarneri was named superintendent of the foreign exchange control in May 1935. General Alfredo Dallolio, as commissioner of war production, took up the task of organizing mobilization. They were the men for the jobs. They enjoyed wide-ranging influence and worked together well. Dallolio was the acknowledged expert in war production. Guarneri, sitting at the center of industry for fifteen years as head of the economic and statistical service of the general confederation of Italian industries, the highly articulated and very successful lobby of big business, had a knowledge of Italy's economy as good as, if not better than, that usually available to government bureaus.[38]

Both men saw the danger from sanctions, the danger that Italians might be unable to buy abroad, that industry might be stopped and the war effort paralyzed. They began a program of immediate stockpiling of essential materials: food, coal, oil, gasoline, aviation fuel, scrap iron, textile fibers, fat, and cellulose. Such stockpiling they, and the service ministries, saw as the first line of defense. The goal was for six months' worth of supplies, enough to keep up production at home, and enough war material in the colonies to continue the fighting in Ethiopia if communication with the peninsula was cut. Stockpiling accelerated during the summer months. In August 1935, for example, imports of wheat were more than eight times that of the August before, and imports of other cereals were about double. By the end of October estimates were that Italy could hold out against an oil embargo for three to three and a half months, thanks to the stockpile, and more oil was on the way.[39] Badoglio at this time reported enough fuel in Eritrea for two months.[40] This estimate was based on an assumed rate of use that, in the event, was high. The army consumed only some 300 tons a day.[41] With this lower rate of use, the colonial reserve by the end of 1935 was capable of being stretched three to four months. The cost of this stockpiling was a tremendous drain on the foreign reserve. Italy's balance of payments in the first ten months of 1935 showed a deficit of 2.5 billion lire. The adverse figure for October alone was 233 million.[42]

As sanctions approached, Mussolini held five meetings between 30 October and 8 November to review Italy's needs. These were attended by Guarneri, Dallolio, Finance Minister Paolo Thoan di Revel, Minister of Transport Alfano Benni, and, as Mussolini was the minister, the undersecretaries for war, air, and the navy, Federico Baistrocchi, Giuseppe Valle, and Domenico Cavagnari. From these meetings, under Guarneri's guidance, came the directives for the state of siege. To protect reserves, imports would be cut to a minimum. This meant economy in the armed services, greater care in ordering, better utilization of national resources, coordination of purchasing, and funneling all buying abroad through the offices of Dallolio and Guarneri. Waste had to be stopped, nonessentials eliminated, and priorities clearly established. Secret service information of inefficiency and waste in Africa, reinforced by the critical reports of Lessona and Badoglio after their inspection tour around the first of November, led Mussolini to promise Guarneri: "I will send to Africa a man who has money sense, a sense of economy," and on 14 November De Bono was removed, replaced by Badoglio.[43]

Imports, Mussolini directed, should be purchased from nonsanctionist countries. But the problem was not sources of supply. Coal, for example, constituting 13 percent of Italy's imports in 1935, could still be bought from British firms after sanctions were imposed on 18 November if there was hard cash to pay for it. When purchases in England fell off after sanctions, it was not because coal was an embargoed item (it was not) but because Italy, deficient in sterling reserves and now lacking credit facilities in London, found it easier to get coal from Germany and Poland and Belgium, where barter or other clearing arrangements were possible. Purchases from England were made as late as 11 October, when mine owners offered, and the Italian government accepted, favorable terms for coal purchases for the state railway.

"Economy" and "work" were Guarneri's watchwords. On 15 November a forty-hour week was instituted, to spread available work among the unemployed. Restrictions on imports meant cutting down purchases of nonessential consumer goods. On 24 October a decree forbade hoarding. Energy conservation was necessary. Taxes raised the price of gasoline. Theatres closed early to save electricity. In early November forty-seven trains were taken out of service to conserve coal. During the period of sanctions, November 1935 to June 1936, Italy imported 7.5 million tons of coal compared to 10 million tons in the same period of 1934–35. The Italian Red Cross organized paper drives and rag collections. A "buy Italian" campaign began. Factory discipline increased; workers were exhorted to produce more. Neglected land came into cultivation. Grain yields were surveyed. Antisanctionist activity became a national crusade: synthetic fibers, alcohol for motors, newspapers cut to four pages, meat limited to one meal a week. The Dopolavoro, a state-sponsored recreational organization, gave instructions on how to raise chickens and rabbits at home.

A state office for combustible liquids was established in October, directed by Ernesto Santaro, to serve the needs of aviation and shipping. A state agency to facilitate the use of alcohol as motor fuel was set up in November, and from January distilled products made from wine were regulated. There were control offices for the use of cloth, wool, and domestically available metals and minerals. Coal and iron came under government monopoly. Nowhere was state control more manifest, more rigidly demanded, than in the workings of Guarneri's foreign exchange control, which guided the most basic of all countersanctionist measures—the protection of the reserves, of Italy's purchasing power.

The exchange control had absolute authority over imports. Without such stringent measures, an imbalance of foreign trade might compromise the integrity of the state. Italy's financial isolation did bring the initial benefit of some limitation on foreign indebtedness, but this hardly helped credit. Exports were encouraged, but the 750,000 cases of lemons Guarneri proudly reported having sent to sanctionist countries made little dent in the great deficit incurred by the stockpiling of war materials. Proposal 3 prohibited receipt of Italian goods. While it took some time for this sanction to become effective, owing to the need to pass legislation and sort out allowable exceptions, by January 1936 it was at work. In that month Italian exports fell off by 46 percent compared to January 1935.

Imports too were down, by 39 percent, reflecting the careful watch on depleted reserves. The metallic reserves of the Bank of Italy, supplemented by the recall and demonitization of silver coinage, were to uphold the lira. The foreign exchange control was to make sure imports could be paid for. By far the greatest amount in its reserve came from gold drawn on the Bank of Italy. The 2.5 billion deficit for the first ten months of 1935 was covered by a 3 billion contribution of the bank. There were three other sources of the reserve. In May 1935 foreign securities were requisitioned. This amounted to some 700 million. There were the proceeds, another 700 million, from sales of bonds and funds, mainly through the forcible conversion of securities held abroad and the required investment of corporate profits exceeding 6 percent. Lastly, there were, in 1936, the donations of gold and precious metal, amounting to 500 million.

All foreign outlay was centralized. By the end of 1935 the exchange control had distributed abroad 3.9 billion lire to support the needs of industry and commerce and the capacity of the state to wage war. Such supervisory authority helped build confidence, encouraged rationality, and promised to alleviate the great strain of an adverse balance of almost 3 billion for 1935. At the end of that year Guarneri estimated needs and income for 1936 and predicted that he could cut the loss to 1 billion lire on projected foreign expenses of 6.25 billion.

At the end of January 1936, with stockpiling expenses behind and the domestic economy under rigorous control, Guarneri predicted that, if sanctions were not intensified and there was some reduction of industrial production, Italy could endure the existing financial and economic pressures for a year and a half, until the end of June 1937. In that same month the British consul in Turin reported that there were apparently sufficient stocks of raw materials to provide for industry for the next twelve months, with some reduction in the standard of living.[44] To be sure, there was some grumbling and a good deal of minor evasion of restrictions. The confederation of Italian industries complained that the government failed to compensate business for the loss of supplies from abroad. Yet business went along, carried by the patriotic wave.

The future of economic conservatism in the face of now massive state interference and possible political radicalism was not clear.[45] There were open questions in January 1936, the answers to which would effect the precious morale as well as the cold statistics. How long would sanctions and the consequent cost last? Were further measures to be directed against Italy? Above all, how far could the army advance before it was stopped by the rains or held up by Ethiopian resistance, or before the international pressures on Italians grew too great to bear? Meanwhile, although obliging Italians to live at least provisionally in a closed eeonomic system, *le contro-sanzioni* held the fort. A Japanese mission was sent from Tokyo to learn the secrets of Italy's resistance.[46]

De Bono

It seemed it might be a long war after all. The front lines had hardly moved in the two months since the October advances. To be sure, fear of a European conflict had receded. On 7 January 1936 the British told the Italian government that units of the Home Fleet at Gibraltar, including the massive *Hood*, would return to home ports and that a number of important ships would leave Alexandria for a spring cruise. Eden's promotion caused some worry, but could Eden, any more than Hoare, move the cautious and conciliatory French to stronger measures? Roosevelt irritated the Italians on 3 January 1936 by requesting Congress to pass broader, more discretionary neutrality legislation to "discourage the use by belligerent nations of any and all products calculated to facilitate the prosecution of a war in quantities over and above our normal exports of them in a time of peace." This hinted at a restriction on oil. In his speech Roosevelt denounced "the twin spirits of autocracy and aggression" and criticized militant imperialism, scarcely veiling reference to Italy.[47] In Rome, however, Ambassador Breckinridge Long predicted that Congress, dismayed over the apparent chicanery surrounding the peace proposals, would not approve an oil embargo.[48]

Delays in the time table for sanctions were a setback to the Geneva front. The Committee of Eighteen met on 12 December 1935 to consider the oil sanction (proposal 4-A) but adjourned without action on 19 December, demoralized and uncertain after the Hoare-Laval proposals. The length of time it took to put sanctions into effect meant that even on the question of oil there was time for Italy to continue stockpiling, to organize terms of use, and to cultivate potential suppliers. Still, the question of the application of proposal 4-A was to come again before the Committee of Eighteen at its session scheduled for the time of the League's Council meeting on 20 January 1936.

In Rome everyone's calculations were influenced by estimates of how long the war might last. The first war communiqué of the new year (number 27, of 3 January) repeated the refrain "Nothing of note to report." The Ethiopians refused to present themselves for "strategic battle." Badoglio continued to build up, not fight. Discouragement spread as, in the face of sacrifices demanded at home, the red pins remained stationary on the war maps maintained by citizens. Only fair-weather roads extended beyond the frontier, and

General Rain might bog down the troops in the spring, as General Snow had stopped Napoleon, if the march was not soon renewed. Dispatches to foreign offices in late December and early January described the Italian scene in terms of war weariness, mounting anxiety, pessimism, disquiet, skepticism, depression, and lack of confidence.

Three weeks after the Day of Faith and the collapse of peace hopes, the French chargé reported the press and government were becoming "breathless" in their efforts to keep up patriotic enthusiasm. Chambrun in early January reported that Mussolini appeared bewildered, lacking his former determination. Léger doubted he would survive the year as head of the government. Lessona saw him as shaken, discouraged by the unheavals of diplomacy and the slow pace of the war. Ciano concluded victory in the field was impossible.[49] A British appreciation of the military situation written on 16 January 1936 concluded there was "no important result foreseen before April, and short of killing the Emperor or engaging in large scale gas warfare from the air it is difficult to foresee what major successes the Italians can now hope to achieve before the rains."[50]

Publicly Mussolini made the argument that "all war, particularly colonial war, has its absolutely indispensible pauses," necessary for logistical regrouping. Privately he protested the loss of initiative and the sobering setbacks during the Ethiopian counteroffensive of December. He told the Italian commander on 14 January 1936 that Italians anxiously awaited a great battle. It was "essential" to retake the initiative. The army must have one aim: combat. The impression must end that it was dominated by defensive thinking. In the next week Mussolini forwarded intercepted telegrams in which the Ethiopian minister in Paris had advised the emperor that it was "absolutely essential" to avoid a pitched battle. Low Italian morale, the minister warned, would rise with a field victory. At the foreign ministry in the Palazzo Chigi diplomats kept to their rigid, instransigent stand but, as Guariglia recalled, placed "all their hopes" in military victory.[51] In Berlin, as the year 1936 opened, Hitler thought the situation in east Africa was very bad, possibly to become tragic soon, for Italy.[52] "We are sitting in a circle of fire," said Italo Balbo in January, critical of Mussolini's handling of the crisis.[53]

To understand the war front it is necessary to go back three months, to mid-October 1935. On 17 October the northern line still lay close by the Adigrat-Aduwa-Aksum border. There Emilio De Bono had stopped to regroup, a decision made in the face of repeated injunctions from Mussolini that he, or at least a column of Eritrean soldiers, should instead charge on to Makale, some fifty miles to the south. De Bono was not incompetent, blinded by corruption, or senile, as his enemies painted him. No one was more loyal to Mussolini and the Fascist cause. But the assumptions he and his officers had made about this war no longer met the political needs of the government, and therein lay his trouble.

When De Bono as minister of colonies planned and sponsored the invasion, and asked Mussolini for the command, the strategy was for a prolonged, cautious advance. Now Mussolini needed dramatic, highly visible, prestige victories, and he wanted at least to put Tigre under Italian control in case European disapproval forced a compromise settlement. Yet De Bono stuck to the border, while beyond Aduwa equally historic defeats awaited revenge. Forty years before, the Italians had been chased from Tigre. They had penetrated to Amba Alaji, forty miles south of Makale, to be defeated there in December 1895, only 300 surviving from a force of 2,000 men. The battle of Amba Alaji was followed by a dramatic three weeks during which the 1,500 men at the Makale garrison were held under siege, then forced to surrender in January 1896. These defeats broke Italian power in Tigre, ended the first dream of empire over Ethiopia, aggravated diplomatic isolation in Europe, and opened the way for the final humiliation at Aduwa. Now, with the international future again unclear, with the prestige of the government again on the line, with once again a massive political gamble hinging on success in an Ethiopian war, Mussolini could not tolerate a continuation of the leisurely plans of quieter days.

De Bono's enemies in Rome encouraged Mussolini's impatience. Imagine De Bono's dismay when the two most prominent of them appeared in Eritrea on 17 October 1935 on an inspection trip meant, he well knew, to evaluate his capacity for further command. That Mussolini decided, only four days after the invasion, to send out Alessandro Lessona—undersecretary of the colonies, De Bono's former ally, and now his archrival—and Pietro Badoglio—the kingdom's most prominent soldier, a marshal of Italy, and chief of the general staff—was insult enough to De Bono's dignity and pride.

De Bono had just, on 17 October, exacted Mussolini's reluctant agreement not to push on to Makale. It was true that military intelligence said there were no troops in the town and that Haile Selassie Gugsa, who had recently defected with 1,200 men, wanted to lead a force there to take the spoils. But De Bono refused to extend the line. His sense of military responsibility demanded progress by steps, pausing to place mobile detachments to protect the route and to bring up supplies along the way. The track was uncertain. Motor transport burned into the short supply of gasoline, and the unpaved roads, even in dry weather, would soon be rutted beyond use. A third of the mules were unusable. Gabba, chief of staff, estimated no advance was possible before mid-December. And two or three battalions sent out to Makale on the run would become an irresistible "easy mouthful" for the Ethiopians. If taken, the loss would grievously injure Italian prestige.[54]

Lessona and Badoglio were appalled by the field command's caution, the sense of slow pace. To their ears, a few of De Bono's senior officers spoke of a more aggressive stance. General Santini said the army could move in a month. Quartermaster General Dall'Ora was even more optimistic—a march to Makale could begin in the first week of November. But overall, Badoglio reported to Mussolini, De Bono's command was dominated by a colonial psychology, an "Eritrean mentality." Talk at headquarters was for a war of position, of two or three years' duration, of slow advance. The primary interest was in establishing strong defensive posts. To win, went the old saying, one only need stay still. It was an old theory that against such fortified strongholds the Ethiopian levies would wear themselves out. Italian casualties and costs would be minimal and progress, if slow, was certain. Authority and prestige would never be endangered, and this would benefit the eventual needs of administrative rule. So ran the colonialists' logic, the strategic assumptions of the northern front, exasperating to the visitors from Rome.

Exasperating, for it took no account of the needs of the government. Only a swift and smashing military victory could free Mussolini from his diplomatic troubles. De Bono's narrow, local perspective took no account of the problems posed by the tense international situation. His plans, far from guaranteeing safety and success, were, Lessona argued, "dangerous." The idea of victory without fighting simply did not correspond to the national need. Lessona told De Bono: "Either Italy wins the war in a few months or it is lost."

The northern command, Lessona and Badoglio concluded in their reports to Mussolini on 3 November, was not up to the job. The command exaggerated the difficulties facing it. While troop morale was high, the command staff was passive and disordered, lacking coordination and purpose. De Bono refused to impose central authority over the various units, and they went their own way without clear direction. There was demoralizing profiteering and corruption. Lessona's indictment concluded: De Bono's limited vision, his timidity and irresolution, made him unfit to command a "great decisive battle."[55]

Badoglio was equally critical. To him De Bono was a Fascist functionary, not a soldier of the king. Regular army generals would have taken the command gladly. Badoglio made his own case when he blamed Mussolini for selecting someone retired from active service since 1920—when De Bono resigned from the royal army "for reasons of personal and political nature," that is, to serve the Fascist party—when there was in Italy a marshal who had led Italian troops in the victory of Vittorio Veneto. Badoglio denounced De Bono's ignorance of the use of artillery. To Mussolini he reported on 3 November that the troops were ready—only the officers stood in the way of action. They stayed in comfortable quarters, never traveling the length of the front. "Saturated with the special Eritrean mentality, they behave like bureaucrats, not operational commanders." They were, in short, "static in spirit and act."[56]

These reports bolstered the argument made by Baistrocchi of the war ministry. De Bono had only the authority of the ministry of colonies, whereas conducting a war should be in the hands of the ministry of war. As high commissioner De Bono played a political and administrative role; as commander he had a military duty. The colonial responsibility hampered and confused the military purpose. The command structure, Baistrocchi recommended, should be reorganized.[57]

Pertinent as these criticisms were, fairness demands an appreciation of the logistical problems that dominated De Bono's thinking and influenced his military judgment. Between January 1935 and the invasion of October, his job as high commissioner was to build up Eritrea, improve the harbor and dockage of Massawa, and run roads from the port to the highlands to the front. Mussolini himself ordered in May that a three-year supply of food and munitions be on hand. In July he congratulated De Bono on the "roads, water, victuals, barracks, stores, hospitals and an infinite number of other necessities . . . successfully provided. . . ." Roads, above all. During the period of preparation, 38,000 civilian construction workers went to Eritrea, two-thirds on government salary and the rest on private contract.[58] There were reports of scandals, of favoritism, and these later compromised De Bono's name, but to understand his problems every book on this war should reprint photographs of soldiers pulling trucks through dust and ruts, fording streams, and dragging their vehicles through the mud.

Road building was not enough. From 20 October 1935 onward, Mussolini renewed his orders for movement toward Makale. Progressive sanctions meant war. He gave terms for settlement to the French on 16 October—these would be turned down. There would be a few weeks of quiet in Europe until after the British elections of 14 November. It was necessary to advance on Makale no later than 3 November.[59] De Bono swallowed his better judgment and complied. Makale was taken on 8 November. There was celebration in Italy, but the advance was indeed a dangerous overextension, as Badoglio was to find out in December. After Makale there was no further conquest for two months.

Three days later, on 11 November, Mussolini ordered De Bono to advance a division another sixty miles, to Amba Alaji, and to expand on other fronts. De Bono refused. Such action, he confided to his diary, would be "disastrous," and his judgments on Mussolini's conduct were no less harsh.[60] Refusal sealed De Bono's fate. His opponents carried the day. On Lessona's return to Rome in the first week of November, Mussolini began the search for a successor. Many wanted the job, among them Badoglio, Balbo, Bais-trocchi, Dall'Ora, and Graziani who, relegated to the secondary southern front, lobbied Lessona through his wife, arguing his relative youth (fifty-three years as opposed to De Bono's sixty-nine and Badoglio's sixty-three) and his proven colonial success. On 12 November Mussolini chose Badoglio.

For Badoglio the field command was an opportunity to establish his in-dependent reputation (the victory at Vittorio Veneto had been shared with others) and, with his vaunting personal ambition, he no doubt foresaw titular and economic advantages. The choice had advantages for Mussolini also. He was convinced that Badoglio would drive on to rapid successes. Badoglio told him that the next move forward—if all went well, the long-awaited great decisive battles—would come within a month.[61] Badoglio's criticisms of the previous conduct of the war assured a clean sweep of De Bono's command and the prevailing attitudes, and his rank and stature en-sured respect.

On 15 November 1935, agreeing to take the position, Badoglio extracted from Mussolini a promise of operational autonomy. Mussolini was to pre-sent no such interference as had bedeviled poor De Bono and undermined his command authority.[62] This Mussolini was willing to give. Military re-sponsibility would now rest on military shoulders. If Badoglio failed, it would not be a failure so much of the regime as of the army, a failure not of Mussolini's man but of his rival. Badoglio was not a party member. A Pied-montese, a professional soldier, his loyalty lay with the king. When talk turned to the question of a successor to Mussolini at the head of govern-ment, Badoglio's name was the first mentioned. In a way, in this difficult mo-ment, the command was an exile. Balbo, languishing in Libya, could testify to the fate of those whose light shone too brightly on the peninsula. On the other hand, if Badoglio succeeded, the improvement in Mussolini's domes-tic and international position would be immense. It was the prospect of success, not the anticipation of failure, that no doubt influenced Mussolini now.

De Bono was not surprised at his dismissal, but he was bitter at the in-trigue and the irresponsible falsification of his position. "They are content, but my heart is broken," he wrote in his diary.[63] He was let down with a marshal's baton, although ungraciously given. "I can never do that," Mussolini at first lamented. "De Bono advanced without fighting. I do not want to appear ridiculous in front of the English."[64]

In the month after De Bono's departure an Ethiopian counteroffensive almost cut through the extended right flank of the Italian line. The objective of the offensive begun on 15 December 1935 was to surround Makale, isolating it from the Italian rear. From the left Ras Imru came over the

Takkaze River at Mai Timkat, aiming at Aksum. He forced the Italians into a twelve-mile retreat, back behind the Dembeguina Pass. In the middle, Ras Kassa, now field commander in the north, linked up with an advance force of Ras Seyum in Tembien where, on 22 December, Seyum had retaken the provincial capital of Abbi Addi and moved up to the Warieu Pass. Troops of Ras Mulugeta advanced on Makale directly. There was great alarm in Rome. The last two weeks of December saw the darkest period of the war for Italians—hence the depression in official circles at the time of the Hoare-Laval proposals and around Christmas. The victories of Imru at the Dembeguina Pass and Seyum at Abbi Addi gave some life to the Ethiopian camp. Three weeks before, on 30 November, Haile Selassie had moved to field headquarters at Dessye. Now Seyum imagined it would be possible to hold Tembien.

But in January the Ethiopian counteroffensive was turned back. The troops could not follow through on the opening successes. In one of the most important engagements of the war, during the so-called first battle of Tembien in January 1936, the Italians held at Warieu Pass. Defeat here, it was speculated in a comparison to Aduwa of 1896, would topple Mussolini. For Badoglio the siege of the Warieu Pass, 21–24 January 1936, was the most anxious period of the war. Italian initiative was at stake. So was Badoglio's reputation. He had to live up to Vittorio Veneto and live down his responsibility for Caporetto, the great victory and Italy's demoralizing defeat of the world war. A relief column reached the besieged garrison at the Warieu Pass after the Ethiopian forces were routed in a mustard-gas attack. So, at least, stated Ras Kassa on 23 January, the day after he began his main attack against the garrison: "Suddenly a number of my warriors dropped their weapons, screamed with agony, rubbed their eyes with their knuckles, buckled at the knees and collapsed. An invisible rain of lethal gas was splashing down on my men." Gas was now the conclusive retaliatory weapon, its use approved by Mussolini six weeks before. Ras Imru had undergone a gas attack one month earlier, on 23 December, as he crossed the Takkaze during the December counteroffensive. "My chiefs surrounded me, asking wildly what they should do, but I was completely stunned. I didn't know what to tell them, I didn't know how to fight this terrible rain that burned and killed."[65]

There was dismay in Rome over the poor showing in December. And the use of gas compromised Italy's foreign position. On 3 January 1936 the Ethiopian government asked the League to inquire into "the way in which hostilities are being conducted." It accused Italy of breaches of international agreement in attacking with "asphyxiating and poison gases," beginning on 23 December at the Takkaze.[66] All this was bad publicity, especially followed as it was by allegations of bombings of neutral Red Cross hospitals and by a series of charges of atrocities leveled by both sides.

In Rome expectations that the new command would bring swift, conspicuous victories changed to expressions of irritation and impatience. De Bono and his friends in the ministry of colonies took gleeful comfort from the embarrassment and diminished reputations of Lessona and Badoglio.[67] The Ethiopian counteroffensive was proof of their warnings against an overextended and exposed flank. Mussolini was shaken enough in December to criticize Badoglio in the Grand Council and hint at a possible substitution, either Baistrocchi or Graziani.[68] Lessona defended Badoglio. Preparations, such as surfacing the road to Makale, took time, he said. Over 300,000 men were in east Africa, as well as hundreds of field pieces and 254 aircraft. All would be enough to ensure eventful victory. "By the end of April we will have either won or lost." Others were not so sure. Ciano and Mussolini's son Vittorio shared the defeatist mood of late December and early January. Badoglio could do no more than De Bono, Ciano said. The mountainous terrain would not permit a decisive military victory. Better to treat at once with Britain than to be strangled by sanctions.[69]

During January, as we saw, Mussolini urged Badoglio on. All Italians were anxious for a great battle. Badoglio, like De Bono, felt this pressure but dared not, could not, run the risk of further defeats. He was not discouraged. The lesson of the attacks of December and the battle of Warieu Pass was that the Ethiopians could not carry through to crush an Italian force if it were large enough and gas was in reserve. Badoglio tightened up camp. Already 200 correspondents who had followed De Bono were confined to Asmara and told there would be no news beyond the terse official communiqués. Faced with this restriction and the prospect of a pause as Badoglio grouped his forces, 180 of them left.[70] It seemed it might be a long war after all.

The Southern Front

In the south, on the secondary front, Graziani was under ambiguous orders. He was to defend Somalia, of course. For this he had in October 1935 some 60,000 men, 51,000 rifles, 1,500 machine guns, 2,000 motor vehicles, and 38 airplanes. Facing him stood strong Ethiopian forces. On the plateau of Bale, covering the central provinces and the southern approach to Addis Ababa, were 40,000 to 60,000 men under Ras Desta. Guarding Harar and Ethiopia's railroad connection with the outside world were 30,000 men under Dejazmach Nasibu, headquartered at Jijiga. These two commanders were young and progressive, in contrast to the hidebound leaders Mulugeta, Kassa, and Seyum in the north. Desta was married to the emperor's eldest child; Nasibu, widely traveled, was prominent among the young Ethiopians.

They were formidable opponents, but Graziani, following their intentions through the interception of every radio message they sent, was secure. He wanted more. An offensive attack against Harar would cut off Ethiopia's main supply line and communication route. This, argued Graziani, was "not only possible but necessary to speed up and definitely end" the war.[71] Such a plan was against the wishes of the ministry of war and the general staff, who wanted to concentrate all offensive capability on the northern front. Mussolini's general approval, however, kept Graziani's ambition alive. Thus his opening operations in October, a series of border penetrations, were mainly to the east, in the Ogaden. The target there was Gorrahei, located on the road from Belet Uen to Dagabur and Jijiga. Gorrahei, once in Italian hands, was to become a major supply depot and air base for the drive against Harar.

The Ethiopians recognized the importance of Gorrahei. If it is lost, the leader of the garrison force told Haile Selassie in July 1935, "it will be as if the Italians occupied all the Ogaden." Grazmach Afeworq, however, could not hold out against air attack. The first bombers hit Gorrahei on 4 October 1935. The garrison sent a frantic S O S to Harar, but the reply was "Courage, courage, be strong, be strong."[72] Reinforcements came too slowly from Dagabur. Afeworq fell on 4 November, wounded two days before while firing the fort's only antiaircraft gun, which he continued to man until he collapsed from gangrene. Without his leadership the garrison foundered. The southern Ogaden lay open. Graziani carefully described his action to Badoglio as a mere defensive operation, but the Italian front in the southeast now lay 180 miles into Ethiopian territory.[73]

The retreat from Gorrahei discouraged the Ethiopians, despite a victory when an Italian column of pursuit tanks was ambushed at Anale by the reinforcements meant for the garrison.[74] The emperor went to Jijiga and Harar in mid-November to stop the decay of morale. He ordered Nasibu to stand at the stronghold of Dagabur. There was no supply or transport facility capable of advance in the face of Italian air power. On 2 December 1935 the Ethiopian government told the secretary-general of the League that, to spare the civilian population of Harar the horrors of air bombardment, all troops would leave the city, which would thereafter be used by the military only for the wounded.[75]

Graziani did not retake the offensive in the Ogaden for another five months. He needed clearer approval from Rome; he needed more motor vehicles. Neither was easily secured. In Eritrea Badoglio was now installed as commander of east African forces and, together with the general staff and the war ministry, was intent on keeping the Somalian front secondary.

In his first telegram to Badoglio, on 17 November 1935, Graziani scouted the possibility of a Harar offensive as soon as he improved his transport. Badoglio sent no reply, but a conversation with his staff revealed his thinking. "It is not time for a great offensive [from Somalia]. Graziani has neither the troops nor sufficient supplies. An offensive in Somalia . . . must be made only when we will win a decisive victory."[76] Lessona took up the cause. In rivalry with Baistrocchi, his opposite number in the ministry of war, Lessona, like Graziani, depended on a flanking action direct to Mussolini to outmaneuver his opponent. First he asked Graziani how many vehicles were needed. Double the present supply of trucks and cars (another 2,850) and add 25 Caterpillar tractors to the previous consignment of 85, said Graziani. Then he could begin the offensive in March 1936, after eliminating the growing threat from Ras Desta in the Juba region. This was a formidable order, which Lessona manfully took to Mussolini. With this equipment, he argued, and a clear authorization, Graziani could cut Ethiopia off from Djibouti and British Somalia, assure Italy of the richest territory in the empire (Harar, among its other virtues, was held to be oil country), and put Italy in control of the main religious centers of the non-Amharic Muslim population.

Mussolini reserved judgment. Baistrocchi was furious. Such permission would alter radically the war ministry's strategy and give the initiative to his rivals in the ministry of colonies. Baistrocchi immediately wrote a tart note to Graziani recalling the defensive orders for the Somalian command. Strategic planning was the province, not of the ministry of colonies, but of the general staff and the ministry of war. Interference in military matters was intolerable: "As governor of the colony you depend on Lessona, but for operations, logistics and personnel on the ministry of war." Since Graziani addressed even his communications to Badoglio via Lessona, Baistrocchi added: "The ministry of colonies is an *address*, nothing else."

Graziani retorted angrily, raising an issue of confidence. Badoglio, warned by Baistrocchi, decided to reply, at long last, to Graziani's telegram of 17 November. On 6 December he restated the "unchanged general order" that the Somalian front should remain on the defensive. Such a stance was appropriate when Graziani faced a challenge in the opposite direction from the Ogaden, but Badoglio's long-range opposition to any southern offensive in the future was made clear in a telegram to Lessona on 8 December. Supply restrictions, he said, precluded forward actions on both fronts.[77]

These exchanges ended inconclusively. Mussolini, reading them all, did not intervene except to send out a vice-governor, Angelo De Rubeis, from the ministry of colonies to superintend Somalia, freeing the commanding general for combat and the organization of conquered territory. The decision in Graziani's favor was to be made, not in the ministries, but on the battlefield. Graziani freed himself of the burden of defense by removing the threat to the colony he was ordered to protect.

While Graziani had thrust toward Gorrahei, Ras Desta descended from the Bale plateau to stand at Negelli and then at Dolo, to draw pressure from Harar by challenging the frontier to the west. Against him, Graziani assembled a strong, mobile force of 25,000 men at Dolo. On 7 December

Badoglio reaffirmed the order to remain on the defensive so as to give any attacking force "the severe lesson" of a decisive defeat in set battle, the persistent, yet unrealized dream of the northern command. Graziani wrote in the margin a sarcastic "Bravo." He had his own, more aggressive, idea of severe lessons. He requested permission for "maximum liberty" to use asphyxiating gas against "barbarian hordes who are prepared to commit any horror." On 16 December Mussolini agreed—"for supreme defensive reasons." Desta told the emperor that on 17 December gas bombs "rained like hail." His men were forced from the trenches, the gas causing inflamed and readily infected wounds.[78]

Italian use of gas is not in doubt. In his "directive and plan of action" of 30 December 1934 Mussolini laid down that there must be "absolute superiority of artillery and gas."[79] There was plenty in the colonies. Shipments of 294 tons of asphyxiating gas, 45 tons of mustard gas, and thousands of tear-gas bombs, passed through the Suez Canal in 1935.[80] According to the British war office, 29 tons of asphyxiating gas passed through in the last five days of December alone.[81]

Gas was the most efficient way to break up mass formations. Graziani and Badoglio used it as the need arose, to soften up Desta beginning on 17 December 1935 and against Imru as he crossed the Takkaze on 23 December in the critical Ethiopian counteroffensive just before Christmas. The emperor claimed that gas, used first in bombs and canisters and later sprayed from the air, was Italy's "chief method of warfare."[82] It *was* important. Overall the war was won by overwhelming force and superior organization, but gas, spread on the ground to burn bare feet, to contaminate water and food, and to disperse men and animals, prevented frontal attack and turned retreats into disorganized routs. Gas demoralized the troops; fear of gas made the recruitment of reinforcements difficult; and above all, gas was, as at the Takkaze, a last resort when the outcome was uncertain. No doubt in the course of the war its use saved Italian and Ethiopian lives that might otherwise have fallen to metal or explosion. But chemical war from the air was a one-sided contest and in contravention of Italy's adherence to the gas protocol of 1925 (to which the Ethiopian government, in anticipation of the invasion, acceded on 18 September 1935). Sentiment throughout the world condemned its use.

The contest was too unequal. Italian arguments of Ethiopian barbarism did not lessen discredit for their conduct. In December, after the outrages of bombing civilian targets and the gas attacks, came the apparently deliberate bombing of clearly marked and neutral Red Cross ambulance and hospital units behind the front lines. There was an Ethiopian Red Cross National Committee, established in September 1935, and Italians contended military preparations went on behind the emblem, but other units were hit as well. To quiet the storm, on 16 January 1936 Mussolini sent a courteous letter to the head of the International Committee of the Red Cross in Geneva deploring "accidents" of aerial bombardment. Red Cross officials thought this meant Mussolini was becoming more responsive to world opinion.[83] To an extent he was, for diplomatic purposes. On 5 January 1936 he ordered the routine use of gas suspended until after the meetings of the League Council and Committee of Eighteen, scheduled to begin on 20 January. But on the nineteenth, Badoglio, then in harrowing battle in Tigre, was told he could use "all the means of war, I say all" for a "maximum decision."[84] Gas fell on Makale two days later and, as we saw, saved the day at the critical battle of Warieu Pass on the twenty-third.

In the south Graziani prepared to advance against Ras Desta. The battle of the Ganale Doria between 12 and 20 January 1936 was won by the application of superior mechanized force against a demoralized, depleted collection of foot soldiers. By the beginning of January the men of Ras Desta, centered in Negelli, had been reduced to less than 15,000, less than a quarter of the troops with which he had descended from the high plateau.[85] Desta was more complacent than was warranted by his desperate plight. The long desert march left his men hungry and thirsty—"walking skeletons staggering along in the dust," International Red Cross representative Marcel Junod described them.[86] Food was lacking; dysentery was rampant. Air attacks destroyed supplies. Men, fearful of gas, deserted at the sight of smoke bombs. By the beginning of January 1936 Desta's force had lost what impetus it once had for attack against Italian Somalia.

On 4 January 1936 Graziani judged that there was no longer any chance of an Ethiopian offensive in the region of the Juba River. Two days later Desta announced to Addis Ababa, in a message intercepted by the Italians, that his petroleum supply was exhausted.[87] If Desta was to be engaged, Graziani would have to take the initiative. There was no permission from Badoglio, but the northern commander could not interfere with the explicit permission of Mussolini that arrived on 7 January 1936. The "great animosities" among the east African commanders was the talk of official Rome.[88]

Graziani's advance began on 12 January and ended on the twentieth with unopposed entry into what remained of Negelli, capital of Borana, almost obliterated by forty tons of bombs. Graziani gave orders to an air commander on 24 January for mop-up operations: "Burn and destroy all that is inflammable and destructible. . . . bomb neighboring woods with gas and incendiaries." There was to be no truce, said Mussolini.[89] The rout was complete. Desta fled by mule toward Addis Ababa, barely escaping capture.

The battle of the Ganale Doria, coming a few days before Badoglio turned back the Ethiopians at the Warieu Pass and took the initiative in Tembien, gave Mussolini his first major field victory, at a time when he badly needed a battle success to lift depressed spirits in Italy. The occupation of Negelli, closing off the way for Ethiopians to get supplies from Kenya, was claimed as a great strategic prize. Mussolini saw it as a hopeful augury. When Ambassador Drummond saw him on 3 February, Mussolini said that Ethiopian armies, lacking provisions and sanitation, were incapable of prolonged resistance. That, he said, was the important revelation of Graziani's advance.[90]

With the occupation of Negelli, which advanced the southwestern Somalian front by some 250 miles, Graziani freed himself of his burdensome defensive mission. He was able to argue convincingly for forward movement toward Harar, defined now by Mussolini himself as "the principal and essential objective of Somalia's armed forces."[91]

8 WAITING TIME

Geneva

Mussolini watched the battlefields with one eye cocked toward the forthcoming sessions of the Council and the Committee of Eighteen. No action was expected from either, but they would show something of how the wind blew. With spirits in Rome raised by Graziani's push northward, Mussolini did not bother to give Aloisi any instructions for Geneva beyond a suggestion to stress the catalog of Ethiopian atrocities. The existing sanctions were more help than hindrance, he said, and if the oil embargo were applied—a decision on which was the ostensible purpose of the meeting of the committee—Italy would simply leave the League and go it alone, to the point of war if necessary.[1]

The Council was to take up where it had left off on the previous 19 December when, to calm the uproar generated by the Hoare-Laval proposals and to turn aside an Ethiopian request to call the Assembly into meeting, it had stepped away from the issues by deciding its Committee of Thirteen (all members except Italy) should examine the situation yet again. Meanwhile, the Ethiopian government applied for financial aid, and on 3 January asked the League to establish an inquiry into the conduct of the war, hoping both to clear the charges of torture and the use of dumdum bullets, by which Italy justified reprisals, and to publicly establish and thereafter prevent the use of gas.[2]

Both requests were turned down. Ethiopia's desperate need of financial help was obvious. In 1930 the Assembly had passed unanimously a treaty for "financial assistance for the victim of aggression," designed for cases precisely like this one and meant to guarantee aid by member states. But few governments ratified it. Now none was willing to advance anything. The Committee of Thirteen decided on 20 January that it could do nothing. Some were afraid that if financial aid were granted, Ethiopia might ask next for military assistance.[3]

The request for an inspection mission died in the Council, as had a similar request made at the outbreak of the war. There were, said Chairman Madariaga, too many "serious difficulties, both theoretical and practical." On the recommendation of Frank Walters, undersecretary-general, director of the political section, and later the League's historian, the request was simply dropped. The purpose of the League, it was said, was to stop a war, not to observe one.[4]

There was no mention of peace plans in the Council when it met on 23 January 1936. Earlier in the month Avenol had written to Eden suggesting it was time for Council intervention. It should organize an extended, highly regulated program of assistance to Ethiopia, and by these intercessions bring the war to an end. Laval supported this, but it ran into strong opposition in the Foreign Office. It was not yet time, said Vansittart. Soon, noted Patrick Scrivener, both sides would be "floundering in the mud." In the terms of the program of assistance suggested now, he continued, Ethiopia would be put "not only in a harness but even in a straitwaistcoat." Even if phrased as "effective guidance," Addis Ababa would surely refuse such an assistance program. There was a sense of time to spare in mid-January. Peterson could reflect: "If Italy fails to conquer her, Abyssinia will become an active menace." Then, he imagined, the Ethiopians, "flushed with success," would have over 600,000 armed men, offering "grave dangers to her neighbours unless somebody takes her in hand." That somebody would have to be Britain. Avenol's job, Peterson concluded, was to "open a way for Italians" by bringing Ethiopia "to the bar." Yet British opinion made it impossible for the government to support any such attempt.[5]

The question of Council action was canvassed in the meeting of the Committee of Thirteen on 20 January. Eden said the League should take no initiatives. Laval thought conciliation should precede further sanctions —operatively the situation was the same as before the Paris plan. No, argued Eden, that water was under the bridge. Eden carried the debate.[6] The Ethiopian delegation was relieved. They feared having to choose between concession and loss of League support. Conciliation was a vain hope. Mussolini had told Aloisi he would accept no compromise unless Italy secured full sovereignty of all conquered territory. Opinion in Geneva, at least that of Aloisi, Eden, and Massigli, was that, after the French elections of April and May 1936 and when the fighting stopped as the rains began, public opinion would be cooled down enough to allow reopening settlement talks.[7]

Public attention was focused on the January session of the Committee of Eighteen. This group, directing sanctions for the Coordination Committee, had not met since the shock of the Hoare-Laval plan. A glance at the battle map showed that Graziani's success in the south was balanced by Badoglio's troubles in the north. It was, indeed, precisely as the Committee of Eighteen met that Badoglio, responding to the Ethiopian offensive against the isolated Italian garrison at Warieu Pass, drew up a panicked order to withdraw from Makale and other forward posts on the high plateau. Sanctions, slow to start, were now doing the job of depleting Italian gold reserves. If the pressure were kept up, said the sanctionists, Ethiopian resistance and the rains would help bog Italy down in an intolerably costly war and bring the Fascist government to its senses—and to terms.

The question was how far, and how fast, the Coordination Committee should turn the screw. Some thought the legitimacy of the League depended on strong and immediate action. Titulescu told Eden that the oil sanction now had symbolic value. Failure to apply it "would certainly be interpreted as a sign of weakness on the part of the League." Prior to the Paris plan, the League had been credited with Italy's embarrassing position. Now "Italy's impending fall was being attributed to natural causes, to Abyssinian resistance, and to every kind of reason except the action of the League." The need, said Titulescu, was to reassert the authority of the Covenant.[8]

But it was precisely "natural causes" that the governments in London and Paris counted on. The timetable for sanctions was long. Progress could be without haste, without undue risks. The cost and difficulties that restraint of trade imposed on small sanctionist states such as Yugoslavia could be alleviated by measures of mutual support. Meanwhile, existing sanctions would undermine the Italian economy until mud stopped the offensive, at least between May and October. This assumption explains part of the sanguine moderation maintained in January by the big powers. "Time is still playing into the hands of the Abyssinians," wrote the American chargé on 7 January. Eden was forced to reassess his thoughts somewhat when he was told in early January that the big rains came, not in April, but at the end of May or the beginning of June. "This change of date is important," he noted, but the assumptions remained intact.[9]

It seemed that the rains were helping already. Unexpectedly late rains had hampered Italian operations in October and November 1935, an unseasonably early start of the little rains at the end of December frustrated Graziani, and the big rains in the south were due for March. January was usually completely dry in Addis Ababa, but in 1936 the city was the wettest it had been in that month since 1907. These unseasonable downpours, the British minister said, "proved far more useful to the Ethiopians than the efforts of the League of Nations." His French counterpart, however, thought the January rains "more troublesome" for the Ethiopians than for their enemies, stopping wagon transport beyond the capital.[10] A cabinet paper of 20 January by the British secretary of state for war stated the supposition that lack of roads would force the Italians to withdraw from positions as far forward as Makale in order to maintain communications during the big rains. A War Office appreciation circulated to the Dominions on 16 January stated that, short of killing the emperor or starting large-scale gas warfare from the air, it was difficult to imagine a major Italian success before the

rains. It was reported to the Quai d'Orsay on 16 January that foreign correspondents and most of the foreign military observers at Asmara thought
the northern campaign was a failure.[11]

Not much credit was given contrary opinions. In January an American,
Colonel William Donovan (during the Second World War the head of the
Office of Strategic Services), concluded from a visit to the northern front that
victory before the rains was inevitable. Eden thought this was an exaggeration, at odds, he said, with "what we know elsewhere." He told the
cabinet that Donovan's impressions were "generally felt not to be of much
importance."[12]

On 22 January Duff Cooper presented to the cabinet the evaluation of the
War Office that a long period of inactivity and lowered morale lay before
Italians in Ethiopia, and that it would be a test of Mussolini's capacity to
maintain Italy's determination. The prevailing mood of letting events take
their course was expressed by Vansittart on 14 January: "The worse the campaign in Africa goes, and it is going worse, the more superfluous do these
[further sanctionist] measures or contemplations become at this stage. They
involve a certain amount of provocation or risk without materially altering
the real results."[13]

In this vein the cabinet on 15 January agreed that immediate action was
not necessary at the forthcoming meeting of the Committee of Eighteen. Not
that Britain would oppose a proposal for the oil sanction. But a final decision would rest on an expert report of probable effectiveness and on the extent to which collaboration of the armed forces of other League members
could be counted on in case of war. Keeping in step with the French, as Vansittart wrote, "made valour safe."[14]

Eden

It was Eden's first League meeting as foreign secretary. Many at Geneva
thought he would compensate for the damage done by Hoare. Eden,
however, while he spoke much in favor of the League, was above all a dutiful
member of a government in which opinions were unchanged after Hoare's
fall.

Eden was thirty-eight years of age. He had earned his rewards by good
behavior. Championship of the League made him a political asset—hence his
two successive elevations to cabinet posts. By and large he stayed in the rings
carefully drawn by his elders. There was in the cabinet, Eden observed, "no
lack of former Foreign Secretaries and other aspirants to the office."[15]
Simon, Neville Chamberlain, and Halifax, and, outside of the cabinet, Vansittart and, in the Treasury, Warren Fisher—these men treated Eden with
some wariness, which he returned. Eden was not quite the dashing Galahad

of the Covenant, as represented in the press. It was a tempting picture, given his youth and undoubted elegance, but it provided him with a reputation for hewing to a determined, unswerving pro-League policy, when in fact his position was as conditional as was Hoare's. Eden was not, in January 1936, a wave maker. A recent biographer states that when he came to office Eden had "scarcely said a controversial thing in his life; he had created no precedents, and his reputation as an idealist, which was by now well established, had no basis in anything he ever said."[16] One is struck, reading the cabinet minutes of these months, by his deference. Yet he could be stubborn. In a secret note to Hitler in January 1936, the Duke of Coburg, who knew Eden at Eton, wrote: "He has to be handled with especial care, as he is apt to jib."[17]

Eden was a reserved man. Once, discussing his character and judgment after the disastrous Suez crisis of 1956, Lord Moran said to Churchill of Eden's father: "Sir William's uncontrolled rages terrified his children, who were always on tenterhooks, fearing that they might say something that would start an explosion. . . . Anthony did not inherit his father's instability, but it must have been a handicap to be brought up in such an atmosphere."[18] After courageous action at Ypres in the Great War, Anthony Eden found calm first in the rarified atmosphere of the study of Arabic at Oxford and then in the elite corps of men who ran Britain's international relations. His attraction to the League came from his sense, as a survivor of the "lost generation," that an alternative to war must be found and from the affinity, perhaps, between a rather stiff and formal personality and the stiff and formal logic of the Covenant. Geoffrey McDermott, in 1936, was a newcomer in the Southern Department of the Foreign Office and shared the "high hopes" of his young colleagues at Eden's promotion. Later, critical of his performance over the years, McDermott concluded that Eden's weakness was a lack of "knock-about common sense," a lack of knowledge or interest in the fundamental concerns of economics, and too traditional a focus on Europe and the Near East. A month after Eden took office he was already criticized as no organizer, as inexperienced in running a great department —the Foreign Office was "under-machined."[19]

Eden's immediate concern in January 1936 was to repair the damage to Britain's connections with Europe. He did bring a perspective to the task different from Hoare's and Vansittart's. He did not much like Mussolini or Italians—a sentiment vigorously reciprocated. While he bought part of the "mad dog" argument, he thought Mussolini's threats were largely bluff. He wanted to continue to play the League hand against Italy, for a future value that remained to be seen. He did not dismiss it offhand as too weak a reed, too uncertain a tool. And he was not ready to deal around Geneva. The Ethiopian affair was to be kept formally bound up in the framework of the

League. This, if nothing else, would allow Britain to meet, and to be absolved of, its responsibility for collective security in Europe.

In all this the cabinet concurred. Eden's appointment served a political need; his policy was basically the old one. Eden would right the dual policy Hoare had thrown out of balance. In his first speech as foreign secretary, on 17 January 1936, Eden repeated the refrain that the League must have the elasticity to remove grievances that led to war as well as the strength to discourage aggression. This speech, on the eve of the meetings of the Council and the Committee of Eighteen, did not call for a new determination to press sanctions. All the Council should do, said Eden, was to "take stock." The American chargé said Eden's speech was "eminently 'safe.'" While the government thought Hoare's methods were faulty, the chargé concluded, they agreed with the aim of his policy.[20]

Eden, then, carried on the established British policy in the Italian-Ethiopian war, and he did it skillfully. A Swedish diplomat, Gunnar Hagglof, wrote of Eden's work at Geneva: "I saw for myself how he could change the atmosphere of a conference from deep pessimism and general distrust to mild optimism and willingness to co-operate." Eden, Hagglof said, was above all a "diplomatic artist."[21]

Vansittart, too, had good words for him. Reviewing Eden's first three months in office, Vansittart congratulated him on his handling of the Rhineland crisis of March 1936. Vansittart was thinking too of Italy, to which his comments applied equally—and as commendation and recommendation for what was Vansittart's own line.

> You have extricated your country, with great skill, from a position in which it might have been either dishonoured and isolated, or forced into dangerous courses. You have avoided, with equal wisdom, a head-on collision with old associates. . . . You have had the foresight and firmness to grasp the central fact. We have *got* to be cautious, and not be carried away prematurely, or we may pay for it with our national existence.[22]

Two months later, in May 1936, looking back over Eden's handling of the Ethiopian affair, Thomas Jones asked whether Eden's eloquence on behalf of the League had served the association and Britain well. Eden had played out his hand, Jones wrote, in behavior that was "magnificently consistent but was it diplomacy? Did he fail to foresee the debacle or did he prefer to be consistent [even to the point of League failure]?"[23] The answer is: both.

The Committee of Eighteen met on 22 January 1936. Laval led the French delegation. This was his last League meeting. At Geneva he confided he would resign his government on returning to Paris. At the meeting of his Council of Ministers on 14 January he had barely touched upon the Ethiopian question.[24] Leaving Paris he asked Cerruti to send to him at Geneva any suggestions for a negotiated peace that the ambassador might pry from his government.[25] Nothing came of this. Mussolini told Aloisi to take no initiative. On the other hand, Mussolini did not disagree with Aloisi's idea of some kind of mandate for Italy, as long as full sovereignty over conquered territory was left to Italy. On 23 January Luigi Cortese, Aloisi's secretary at the foreign ministry, approached Eden's aide, Lord Cranborne. Cortese said Mussolini was ready to put forward proposals that left the emperor sovereignty over the "Amharic" territories, reserving only the "Ethiopian colonies" for Italy and leaving open a settlement in Tigre. A full Italian proposal would be brought to Geneva only after British approval. Cranborne turned the idea down. Britain would not go behind the League. Even the Paris proposals had had a semblance of authorization from the Coordination Committee.[26]

Laval, therefore, in these last hours, was not to be budged beyond agreeing to refer the oil question to committee. He saw no reason to stiffen French policy in the last moments of his ministry, with the additional cost to defense that a hostile Italy would involve. Since the British cabinet, too, decided to commit nothing to an oil embargo before receiving an opinion from experts, this killed any chance for immediate application of the sanction. Delay was encouraged by other concerns. The king of England, George V, had died on 20 January, overshadowing international affairs for the British delegation. In Washington the future looked dim for Roosevelt's proposals for increased export controls. On 10 January the Senate's Foreign Relations Committee had cut them back drastically. Eden, meanwhile, was playing on a second string, getting expressions of mutual support in case of war over oil, and these were just coming in. Finally, there was the expectation that the war would be long and costly, that the rains would come, and that the existing, moderate sanctions would be enough. Italy might not, after all, be able to buy American oil if there was no money to pay for it.

All these considerations hung in the background as the Committee of Eighteen took up proposal 4-A, which Riddell had put forward on 9 November 1935 and which sought to extend sanctions to oil, coal, steel, and iron "as soon as the conditions necessary to render this extension effective have been realised." What the committee decided was to refer the question of the effectiveness of an oil embargo to a committee of experts. A study followed and was submitted on 12 February. Meanwhile, on 22 January, the Committee of Eighteen dropped altogether the possibility of extending sanctions to iron, steel, and coal, based on the argument that on "information collected by the Secretariat . . . the probable efficacy of an embargo on those products was not known."[27] What was in store was another wait. Eden had not saved the day.

Mediterranean Security

For those who felt let down disappointment was all the keener because on 22 January 1936, the same day the Committee of Eighteen reduced the scope of proposal 4-A and again deferred a decision on oil, the chairman of the parent Coordinating Committee received letters stating that, in the case of war arising from the application of article 16, mutual assistance as called for in the Covenant would be forthcoming among the following states: Britain, France, Greece, Turkey, Yugoslavia, Czechoslovakia, and Romania.[28]

These assurances stemmed from a British initiative. Under Eden as under Hoare assurances of support were sought, not to consolidate a *system* of collective security, but to help in case of war, to restrain Italy by presenting a united front, and, for Eden, to restore confidence in Britain among Mediterranean sanctionist states.

The earlier British expectation of bilateral security agreements with the French had not led far. Naval talks had been adjourned since 9 November 1935. Little came of conversations in December between their air and military staff officers. It seemed unlikely that there would be specific agreements between the two governments. Flandin told Simon in early January that the public supported the present republican form of government precisely because it promised to keep France out of war. If France went to war now, Flandin warned, the republican regime would be finished.[29]

This was a sobering judgment. And, as the French refused to take any steps to prepare their army or air force for action—as earnests of good faith or of their capacity to act—Laval's old assurances of support were put even more in doubt. On 14 January the British decided in this circumstance to do nothing to reopen military or air conversations and not to send troops for a joint defense of Djibouti, the railroad, and British Somaliland, at least not until French troops fit for battle were established there. Each country would have to take its own military responsibility in those areas.

There was, however, a flicker of life on the naval side. The French naval staff continued some planning. This was done without the knowledge of the minister, who instructed officers in the Mediterranean not even to meet with their British counterparts. While ministerial hesitation and reluctance depressed British officials, they decided on 14 January 1936 to have another go at naval talks. The Naval Conference was being held in London, providing a useful cover for the French staff, who could send officers to London without revealing their purpose. That the representatives, when they arrived, were not members of the naval staff was distressing, but talks were held on 15 January. A verbal agreement was reached: in case of war arising from sanctions the British would protect the transport of two divisions from French north Africa, not to Spain, but to Bordeaux; the commanding staffs

would establish liaison; France might send a destroyer force to aid antisub-
marine work off Gibraltar (to be the province of the Home Fleet); and the
western basin would come under French responsibility.[30]

This was as far as Anglo-French naval conversations progressed during
the Italian-Ethiopian war. It was not far, but it did create a precedent. The
principle of joint talks was established. The Germans worried that such talks
could be turned against them should they violate the Locarno agreement on
the Rhine.[31] And some French naval maneuvers occurring directly after the
talks were taken as manifestations of cooperation—a squadron from Brest
went to Casablanca and a squadron from Toulon went forth on Mediterranean exercises.[32]

Meanwhile, the British carried on conversations aimed at getting
statements of mutual support from other Mediterranean states. In January
they asked the governments of Greece, Turkey, and Yugoslavia what preparatory naval, military, and air measures were being taken and what the
policy of their armed services might be in the event of an Italian act of war
resulting from the application of sanctions. The British did not propose
specific measures. The previous month, in December 1935, when an oil sanction seemed imminent, the chiefs of staff in London had formulated, quite
precisely, what aid they expected from each country. But soundings in
December and early January led to return inquiries that would have
broadened possible areas of military involvement, and this caused the British
to back off. The king of the Hellenes, for example, was alarmed that Italian
bombers might hit Athens and surrounding industrial centers as a warning to
other small states to mend their relations with Rome. Yugoslavs feared in-
cursions by Italy's client Albania. Greeks fretted about a danger from
Bulgaria. Perhaps Albania and Bulgaria would take advantage of a Mediterranean conflict to act in the Balkans. So, the question went to London,
Would the British reciprocate with assurances of support? But the British
emphatically wanted to avoid anything beyond the specific matter of an
Italian belligerent response to the sanctions in the immediate Ethiopian
situation. On 14 January it thus was decided to begin talks with the assumption that an immediate Italian attack was not likely and with the object, not
of applying pressure toward the fulfillment of earlier British desiderata, but
merely of making general inquiry about anticipated action and policy. It was
not the intention to "make arrangements for everyone to 'contain' everyone
else," noted Cranborne on 7 January. "We want to keep the atmosphere of
war out of Europe as long as possible. Will not the conclusions of all these
private arrangements [such as a Greek-Yugoslav pact against Albania suggested by the prince-regent in Belgrade] conduce to a state of nervousness
which may go far to produce the result we wish to avoid?"[33]

The Greek government gave the guarantees for which the British hoped. It had been shocked by the Hoare-Laval revelations, which seemed to members of the Little and Balkan ententes like a change of British policy that would leave them exposed to Italian wrath just when they were being approached with requests for support. Now cooperation seemed a chance to stiffen Britain's Mediterranean policy. In early November, when it was a question of either conceding the use of Navarino as the alternative anchorage to Alexandria or having it taken by the British navy, the king promised the use of harbors, docks, and repair facilities in case of war. This the Greek government now, in mid-January, reaffirmed. It added a promise to cooperate in a Naval Control Service Organization based at Athens for regulation of shipping in the eastern Mediterranean and to cooperate in overseeing the Aegean from Salonica. Another item: in case of war the British envisioned an air strike at night on the Italian fleet in the Taranto harbor. Because of the short range of their carrier-based aircraft, the British planned to send their planes on to an airfield at Janina in northwest Greece, to return the next day to the carriers standing off Zante Island west of the Peloponnesus. Greek approval was necessary for this operation.[34]

In the event, preparatory measures by the Greek government were few. Some destroyers were refitted; there was some training. But past economizing and lack of foresight left Greece short of mines and depth charges, without net defenses, and utterly deficient in antiaircraft equipment. In all of the country, with the Piraeus open to air attack, there were only four antiaircraft guns, unsupported by searchlights or sound detectors. British aid was needed to buy more guns; the British air force would have to protect Athens.

Earnest promises the Greeks made—much help they could not give. They worried about a Bulgarian incursion. Prolonged operations would involve reinstatement of some officers implicated in the rebellion of May 1935 (which in August had resulted in the dictatorship of General John Metaxes), and this would mean serious political disruption.

The Turks played up well. Britain's stock had risen steadily in Ankara, for the movement of the fleets in September 1935 seemed to indicate a firm British stand in the Mediterranean. Foreign Minister Rüstü Aras and Ambassador Nicolas Politis were firm supporters of the Covenant. Like the Greeks, the Turks wanted stability in the eastern basin. This was impossible, opinion in Ankara went, as long as Italy held, and fortified, the Dodecanese Islands and so menaced southwestern Anatolia. Efforts to appease Italy by granting possession of the islands in return for a promise of nonfortification had come to nothing. What remained was suspicion and distrust and, consequently, support for any British move that rendered Italian aggression less likely. In November Aras spoke to the British ambassador of an identity of interest in the Mediterranean. Any reduction of British naval influence, he said, would be a calamity for Turkey, as would any Mediterranean settlement that left Turkish interests out of account.[35]

Like the Greeks, the Turks agreed to cooperate in a naval control service, acting from Istanbul. In addition, they would close Smyrna to shipping. The British would have privileges of anchorage, docking, and repair facilities. Considerable preparatory activity went on. Leaves were canceled; lookouts and port defenses were reinforced; stores were laid in. The Turks had something to gain by war. Infantry and planes were readied to attack and recover the Dodecanese.

Like the Greeks, the Turks asked for help: munitions, equipment and training for minesweeping, intelligence data on the Dodecanese. To these requests London replied with nonspecific assurances of support in case of a League war. The British, the Turks were told, "would fulfill their obligations in whatever form most practicable if and when the case arose." And the unstated policy was to give no cooperation to any action aimed at recovery of the islands.

Yugoslavia was in a more difficult position. Austria was in danger from the Germans. Albania, leaning to Italy, was a constant threat. France could not be counted on for military assistance. There were no staff conversations with the French during this tense period of the Ethiopian war. The Dalmatian coast was vulnerable to Italy. And Italy was the best customer of Yugoslavia, buying 20 percent of its exports. It was the Yugoslav delegate who argued most impressively to the Committee of Eighteen that sanctions demanded economic assistance among participating states. Small and exposed countries should not have to bear a disproportionate share of burdens and opprobrium, all the more so as Yugoslavia proved a loyal adherent to Genevan decisions.

On 4 December 1935 Eden asked for "authority in principle" to render such economic aid to Yugoslavia as the Foreign Office, the Board of Trade, and the Ministry of Agriculture and Fisheries might approve. The first measure proposed was to ease import restrictions on bacon, eggs, turkeys, and chickens from Yugoslavia. This was not much, and only limited quantities were involved. No member of the cabinet wanted strong competition with domestic production. But it was some help and was prompted both by the argument of equity and the recognition that without substitute lines of trade the logical replacement for Italy's economic influence along the Danube and in the Balkans would be Germany.[36]

And economic support, as recommended by the Coordination Committee's proposal 5, was the counterpart to military support. At first, in December, the British chiefs of staff had proposed a number of lively requests of Yugoslavia. They wanted Yugoslav ships to engage the Italians in the Adriatic. The Yugoslav army was to invade Istria, preventing the transfer

of Italian divisions from there to Libya, and was to resist any attempt by
Italian forces to land in Albania. And there were to be active measures by
the Yugoslav air force. On 14 January 1936 the Defence Policy and Requirements Subcommittee decided not to make these requests. The
Yugoslav army would take twenty-five days to mobilize and Yugoslavia was
understandably reluctant to irritate its neighbors with preliminary action.
Replying to the January inquiry about plans proposed in the case of war, the
Yugoslav government noted the weakness of its navy, the defenseless nature
of its sea and land frontiers, the need, because of Bulgarian unreliability, to
use its force to safeguard communication lines to Salonica, and the difficulty
of taking action against Italy. Without French aid, Yugoslavia could turn no
more than half its force against Italy. As with Greece and Turkey, mutual
support depended largely on how much assistance came from Britain.
Yugoslavia needed aircraft and submarines for coastal defense and loans or
credits for war matériel, for gas masks, helmets, ammunition, tanks,
horseshoes, and saddlery.[37]

Apart from secretly determining possible military assistance, the British
wanted also to associate the Mediterranean states in a joint, and public,
statement of collective support. This would reinforce the rationale of collective action against Italy, bolster morale among sanctionist states, define the
terms of assistance as Mediterranean in scope and limited to action arising
from a response to sanctions, and generalize the criticism that Britain was
hectoring Italy. The French too wanted such a statement, and Eden and
Laval agreed it should take the form of a letter to the League. The British
would approach the states for confirmation. Publication would counter
Italian protests of November 1935, let Italy know where everyone stood, and
quiet German concern that the military conversations were directed against
them.

The diplomacy involved in getting these letters—diplomacy undertaken
simultaneously with the military inquiries just described—is noteworthy in
two regards. One was the failure of the Italian diplomatic counterattack. The
other was the unexpected degree of cooperation revealed between the states
of the Little and the Balkan ententes.

What was asked in January 1936 was that Greece, Turkey, and Yugoslavia
affirm in public their obligations under article 16, such as had been given in
private the month before. Against this the Italians argued that the British
request was juridically unsound. Questions such as an Italian war, not discussed at Geneva, could not be raised by member governments under the
cloak of the Covenant without appearing provocative. Britain was using the
League to play its own game. British naval demonstrations in the Mediterranean, with their attendant anxieties, were made unilaterally, without

reference to members of the League. Time and time again the Italian government had proclaimed it had no intention of broadening hostilities to Europe or of threatening any European imperial interests. For governments to associate themselves with the British initiative would be an act of enmity toward Italy, out of accord with various pacts of neutrality, conciliation, and friendship. These Italian démarches, which the governments of Athens, Ankara, and Belgrade reported immediately to London and Paris—no doubt to stiffen nerves there—had no effect. In every case the governments took care to coordinate their replies with Britain.[38]

And with each other. Collaboration among Yugoslavia, Romania, and Czechoslovakia (the Little Entente) and among Yugoslavia, Romania, Greece, and Turkey (the Balkan Entente) was at its height. The threat from Hungarian revisionism, the economic troubles of the depression, concern about Germany, and now the cooperation at Geneva all strengthened the ties. By and large these states were led by convinced internationalists, men who had almost a free hand in their conduct of foreign policy and who were determined to protect the antirevisionist interests of their small nations. Aras, Beneš, Titulescu, Politis—each was familiar with western capitals, each fluent in the French language, in which meetings of the ententes were conducted. Titulescu, in 1935, acted as president in meetings of both ententes. He held as an article of faith that the groups must act together in the Italian question and in support of Britain. Only thus would the League have any substance with which to restrain aggression.[39]

These men were motivating spirits on the podiums, in the committees, and along the corridors of Geneva in the 1930s. There was regular contact between their foreign ministries. When the British refused to become engaged over Albania in December 1935, military talks opened between Greek and Yugoslav military staffs. When Yugoslavia, Greece, and Turkey were now approached by Britain, they composed their statements in consultation with Romania and Czechoslovakia, which states thus associated themselves further with support of article 16 and sent their own, similar, letters to the Coordination Committee. When the Turks pressed the British for a statement of reciprocal assistance, the British complied and extended it to Greece and Yugoslavia.

So on 22 January 1936 letters went to the chairman of the Coordination Committee stating that, in case of war resulting from the application of sanctions, Britain, France, Greece, Turkey, Yugoslavia, Czechoslovakia, and Romania would offer mutual assistance as foreseen in article 16 of the Covenant. The Italians protested that such representations were unjustified and illegal. The hypothesis of Italian belligerency in Europe, the notes of protest read, was "not only arbitrary, but completely nonexistent." In Rome and Berlin the agreements were seen as the first steps in hostile military alliances.

The Romanians' and Czechs' involving themselves in a Mediterranean quarrel was entirely uncalled for, said Suvich to the German ambassador.[40]

Hugh Wilson wrote to Hull on 27 January that the statements of mutual assistance, "of the highest importance," could not "fail profoundly to affect the future relationships and political development of Europe."[41] This made too much of the matter. In December the British had indeed wanted to tie Mediterranean states down to exact military assurances. On 14 January, however, the crisis was declared past, and the government decided to confine conversations to general inquiries as to what measures the states were contemplating, without trying to get specific assurances about what actions would be taken in case of hostilities. Apply too much pressure, the argument ran, and one would get in return unwanted requests for help. These general statements of mutual assistance could or could not be interpreted as fulfilling the condition laid down by the cabinet on 15 January 1936 that a decision on British participation in any oil sanction would be guided not only by the predicted efficacy of such a measure but also by the "extent to which collaboration of the armed forces of other members could be counted on."[42] Eden declined, both in London and in Geneva, to use the assurances as an argument in favor of swift imposition of the oil sanction. His lack of leadership led to disappointment at the meeting of the Committee of Eighteen on 22 January. Titulescu had urged immediate imposition as vital to the authority of the League. Instead the decision was once again postponed. The experts were sent to do a feasibility study.

The conversations about mutual assistance, then, were not a British attempt to strengthen the machinery of the League. Likewise, they were too general to determine the extent of collaboration in case of war, as information the cabinet needed. Instead, they can be taken as a diplomatic activity, after the loss of confidence caused by Hoare, meant to show continued British concern about collective action *in this case*. To cabinet members there seemed time for measure and moderation. This opinion was shared most emphatically by the new French foreign minister, Pierre-Étienne Flandin.

Flandin

Flandin represented the government of Albert Sarraut, a caretaker regime meant, in Sarraut's words, to give France "calm, peace, tranquility, security, and self-confidence" until the general elections of April and May. The foreign policy implications of this were not clear. On 30 January 1936 Herriot gave a mighty speech to the Chamber in favor of the League, collective security, and the rights of Ethiopians. The next day Sarraut announced that those sentiments represented the inclination of his government. He declared himself "obstinately faithful" to the League. Joseph Paul-Boncour, holding an open portfolio as minister of state, was put in charge of League of Nations affairs. This reassured Léon Blum and the Left, who knew Flandin was not an enthusiastic Leaguer. In a vote of confidence on 31 January, Sarraut carried the Chamber by 361 to 165, supported by the Center, the Left, and the Socialists, the Communists breaking their policy of opposition and abstaining.[43]

No one expected Sarraut's government to do anything except hold the ring for 100 days while the deputies campaigned and until the elections of April and May clarified the political scene. The ministers were anti-Laval. Their policies were not. Laval's approaches to various problems would not be reversed by a short-term government. It had, in any case, no real alternatives to put forward. Dismayed by Laval's conduct Sarraut's ministers might have been, but they worked with the same issues and goals. Continuity and safety for three months were what Frenchmen expected.

Flandin came to office amid reports that Germany planned to remilitarize the Rhineland, using as the excuse that the Franco-Soviet pact of 1935 and the British and French staff talks described above were incompatible with the Locarno Treaty and threatening to the Reich. This the French denied, but such was the anxiety in Paris that Flandin made this his first item of business when he met with Eden on 27 January 1936.[44]

Flandin stressed that his policy was different from Laval's. Flandin, it was true, looked different. Towering, blue-eyed, pipe-smoking, tweedy, he was far more to English taste. He wanted, Flandin said, to improve relations with Britain. And instead of a direct understanding with Germany he wanted to return to a plan of encirclement such as the late foreign minister, Jean Louis Barthou, had recently pursued. Paul Bargeton, director of political affairs at the Quai d'Orsay, added one significant change—that Italy, tied up in Africa, was for the present to be left out of the projected new alignments in Central Europe and the Balkans.[45] Over the Rhineland Flandin got little comfort and even less help, then or later, from Britain. Just as the French had refused to be drawn far over the matter of Italy in the Mediterranean now, with Germany the issue and French interests touched directly, the British stood aloof. The resentfulness concerning withheld support and cooperation that filled London earlier now moved to Paris.

Mussolini gave a critical estimate of Sarraut's government: "Composed almost entirely of Freemasons and people with similar ideas." He evaluated Flandin as a "shrewd and calculating man," at heart opposed to sanctions and certainly opposed to war.[46] This was an accurate assessment, and satisfactory to Mussolini. Laval's minister of war, Jean Fabry, might lament that "Italian-French understanding was buried with us" when his government left office, but its value was already much reduced by this time. For example, as one of his last acts in office, Fabry met on 18 January 1936 with the military command to discuss French defense and consider a report showing that, as Italy was now considered a danger zone, precautionary measures had deprived the northeast frontier of fourteen divisions, a fifth of divisional strength. These divisions were kept in the south, while the German government increased its army size and contemplated remilitarizing the Rhineland.[47]

Flandin did not seek a cordial or a special relationship with Rome, but without British assurances against Germany he saw a value in ending an embroilment that made the immediate German challenge more difficult to meet. He suggested to Eden that all the troubles related to Ethiopia might be drowned in a comprehensive Mediterranean settlement which would ameliorate tension and lead, perhaps, to an end of the war. This idea was not followed up. Instead, Flandin and Eden ended their conversation on 27 January 1936 with the comforting conclusion that Mussolini's position was "deteriorating" and patience was in order until "financial strain, together with the advent of the rains, might create another opportunity for settlement."[48]

9   STOP AND GO

American Neutrality

On 22 January 1936 the Committee of Eighteen created a Committee of Experts for the Technical Examination of the Condition Governing Trade in and Transport of Petroleum and its Derivatives, By-Products and Residues. Oil was all that remained of proposal 4-A, as iron, steel, and coal were unceremoniously dropped by the Committee of Eighteen on the consideration that League members could not significantly restrict Italy's supply. Of the thirteen countries producing over a million metric tons of oil in 1935, however, twelve sat on the Coordination Committee and supplied most of Italy's normal petroleum imports.

The Committee of Eighteen was scheduled to meet again at the beginning of March to decide the question of an oil sanction. This decision, the British government held, must wait until the experts brought in their report. Meanwhile, existing sanctions continued. Badoglio on 11 February 1936 began his southward offensive. Everyone wondered how far he would get before the rains. And much attention turned to the complicated controversy surrounding the new neutrality legislation in the capital of the largest oil producer and transporter of them all.

The neutrality act of August 1935 had been a temporary measure meant to keep America uninvolved during the congressional recess. It made it mandatory for the president to prohibit shipments of arms, ammunition, and implements of war to all belligerents once he had declared the existence of a state of war. Roosevelt and Hull, meaning to give some implicit support to the League, lost no time, as we saw, in applying this act in advance of actions at Geneva. But the Department of State recognized that the narrow definition of prohibited products said nothing of raw materials and other finished goods necessary to the conduct of modern warfare. Roosevelt and Hull, therefore, resorted to appeal, requesting businessmen to keep shipments of such essential materials to prewar levels. Trade beyond those levels, the administration argued, was against the spirit, if not the letter, of neutrality. The moral embargo had some measure of success. Hull thought it kept the rise in exports from being "many times greater" than it was.[1]

Figures show that total American exports to peninsular Italy for 1936 were below the 1934 level and that a decline from the prewar surge began in

November 1935, as the moral embargo was stressed. Much of this reduction, however, can be accounted for by stockpiling done before or in the early weeks of the war and by the imposition of stringent foreign exchange controls in Italy. American exports to Italian Africa, for example, reached the high of $1.7 million in August 1934, as stockpiling hit its stride, and then dropped to $22,000 in January 1936.[2] Goods that went directly to the east African colonies were needed for desert warfare, items such as water-refining equipment, cars, trucks, tractors—Badoglio entered Addis Ababa in an American automobile and Graziani's forces depended on Caterpillars—and oil, oil for the army, the navy, and the merchant marine.

Americans took advantage of Italy's war needs to increase trade. It was legal to do so, and many businessmen rejected the notion of a moral embargo. Sanctionist states also varied in how far their nationals held down commerce with Italy. The terms of sanctions took a big immediate bite, of course. From December 1935 to March 1936, for example, British trade with Italy fell to 9 percent of prewar value, and French trade fell to around 40 percent. Romania—Italy's main supplier of oil, which continued to flow—went to 61 percent, mainly petroleum. The Soviet Union, despite sanctions and proclamations of principle, maintained a lively trade in nonembargoed items—83 percent of its prewar export volume to Italy.[3]

But exports from the United States increased—above all in oil. In 1934 America supplied 6.4 percent of Italy's petroleum imports, the monthly average of this American oil being worth about $500,000 in 1934. In the last three months of 1935, oil worth about $5.5 million was shipped to Italian ports, including some, worth $828,000, sent directly to east Africa for war use. January 1936 saw oil worth $1.7 million sent; the figure for February

OIL IMPORTS TO ITALY

	1934		1935	
	Metric Tons (thousands)	%	Metric Tons (thousands)	%
Romania	973.5	33.2	1,699.4	44.6
Soviet Union	814.4	27.8	577.2	15.2
Iran	301.1	10.0	263.5	6.9
Netherlands East Indies	17.6	0.6	8.9	0.2
United States	186.3	6.4	476.8	12.5

SOURCE: League of Nations, *Official Journal,* Special Supplement no. 148, pp. 80–84.

NOTE: France supplied less than 2 percent of Italian petroleum imports.

was $1.8 million. March showed a decline to a more normal $663,000. State Department officials thought the great increases in the first months of the war had come from filling orders placed earlier, during stockpiling.[4] Other countries, above all, Romania, continued unsanctioned exports of oil. In 1935 the increased American total was still only 12.5 percent of Italian imports of petroleum. Depots sited at the Suez, Port Said, and on the Red Sea and the Gulf of Aden were supplied by the Anglo-Iranian and Royal Dutch Shell companies, in which the British, by the government in the first case and through private investment in the second, held influential or determining shares. But from the growth, and above all the potential of the American market, many argued that it could act to neutralize an embargo by League states.

In 1935 the United States produced more than half of the world's petroleum, a stupendous 134,521,000 metric tons of the total 224,237,000. While the flow from countries represented on the League's Coordination Committee would stop with an oil sanction, the flow from America would go on if it were not restrained by Washington. Italy's entire import for 1935 was, after all, less than 4 million metric tons. The questions in Europe were: What, if anything would Congress and the president agree on for control of this trade? And how might this affect the states of the League? Waiting for an answer to these questions was another excuse to go slow. On the matter of the oil sanction, declared Laval, "everyone knows that it is above all a question of America."[5] And the committee of experts was established precisely to estimate the effectiveness of an embargo with and without American cooperation. Its report was something else to wait for. Eden told the cabinet on 29 January that there was nothing to do until the experts reported.[6]

The arms provisions of the neutrality bill expired at the end of February 1936. From October 1935 onward the State Department had planned for a new bill. The job, wrote Joseph Green of the Office of Arms and Munitions Control, was to find "the impossible compromise between what the administration wants and what we can presumably get through the Senate."[7] What the administration wanted was wider discretion in judging what to embargo, when to exercise its authority, and against whom to apply such provisions. It was just such discretionary provisions, however, that neutralists and isolationists in Congress wished to keep out of any legislation.

Congressmen William Borah, Hiram Johnson, Gerald Nye, Bennett Clark, and Maury Maverick were against aggression no less than was Roosevelt. But, they argued, it was not the business of the administration to designate aggressors in distant wars, to restrain trade accordingly, and so get America embroiled in foreigners' problems. Senator Nye (then engaged in his investigation of arms dealers) realized that modern warfare involved more than guns and tanks. This understanding was clearer now than it had been in the debates on the first neutrality act back in 1935, when shipments of arms alone were prohibited. Through the experience of the Italian-Ethiopian war, isolationists saw that loans and raw materials permitted wars to continue; they saw the need to widen the embargo—as long as it was mandatory, affected all sides, and involved America for or against no one.[8]

The State Department drew up a bill to submit to Congress when it reconvened on 3 January 1936. The first draft, by Joseph Green, R. Walton Moore, and Green Hackworth, carried over the existing impartial arms embargo but gave the president complete discretion to place any restriction whatever on other trade items, as long as it applied equally to all belligerents. Hull thought, despite the impartiality, that Congress could not accept it. He sought the opinion of his major embassies in Europe. Should an embargo be on all commodities, just on essential war materials such as oil, steel, iron, and copper, or on such materials in excess of normal trade? Breckinridge Long, in Rome, favored the last alternative. The others, he said, following the Italian line, might provoke European war. Jesse Straus, in Paris, favored prohibiting only credit. William Dodd in Berlin, Hugh Wilson in Berne, and Robert Bingham in London pressed for as much executive discretion as possible.[9]

The administration's final draft, submitted to Congress on 3 January, was a compromise. Concessions were made to the isolationists. All restrictions, once instituted, would apply to all belligerents. No distinction would be made between just and unjust causes, between aggression and defense. War was war and the United States was neutral. The arms embargo and a ban on loans were mandatory. The discretionary provisions permitted the president to select the moment to impose the embargo, continuing current practice, and to name the articles of war. These, now, would be more than arms. If he thought it would lessen the length or intensity of the conflict, the president could prohibit certain exports in excess of prewar averages as determined by the administration. Food and medical supplies were exempted, but oil, metals, and perhaps cotton, could all be included—as the president determined. The president could also, at his discretion, loosen the credit embargo with short-term loans and declare that trade with belligerents was at a citizen's own risk.

The broadening of the embargo framework to include the possible addition of oil and essential materials was potentially of immense significance to the future of sanctions. Equally significant was the possibility of restraining trade by withdrawing protection. In a press conference on 3 January 1936, Hull called the bill "one of the biggest developments in foreign policy within some generations," as the government had now waived "a standing policy of one hundred and forty years relating to the right of our nationals to trade directly with the belligerents, except as to contraband."[10] Laval and the Quai d'Orsay saw its importance. In abandoning the principle of freedom of the seas, the administration had removed the major difficulty with a blockade of an aggressor state and had thus removed the principal objection of the British to this aspect of collective security. No longer would mention of a blockade expose states to a conflict with America.[11]

These features of the bill, together with Roosevelt's strong speech against aggression on 3 January 1936, were taken in Paris as an indication that America, while retaining its "neutrality," would coordinate its measures with the League. The French ambassador thought this was confirmed when on 9 January Hull spoke to him regretfully about the current passivity of the League. It was embarrassing, Hull said, that just when the United States had started to take a firm stand, the League was marking time. The diplomats at Geneva should stop waiting for America. If the projected law were passed and the League made a firm decision on oil, Roosevelt would use his discretionary power to coordinate American action with a League initiative.[12]

There was a sharp tone to the president's message to Congress on 3 January. "To say the least there are grounds for pessimism," Roosevelt said as he surveyed foreign affairs, and he launched into an attack on the "twin spirits of autocracy and aggression."

> Nations, seeking expansion, seeking outlets for trade, for population or even for their own peaceful contributions to the progress of civilization, fail to demonstrate that patience is necessary to attain reasonable and legitimate objectives by peaceful negotiation or by an appeal to the finer instincts of world justice. They have therefore impatiently reverted to the old belief in the law of the sword, or to the fantastic conception that they and they alone, are those chosen to fulfill a mission. . . . [13]

Roosevelt's remarks, with the simultaneous introduction of the administration's neutrality legislation to Congress, caused much perplexity in Europe. Hitler was surprised by the vehemence of Roosevelt's language —there were no dictators outside of the Soviet Union, he contended, as other leaders were popularly supported. But he welcomed the renewed declaration of neutrality and the absence of any supportive reference to Britain's championship of the League.[14] The Italian press wrote resentfully of the harsh comments about aggression and of Roosevelt's insinuation that his words would "not prove popular in any nation that chooses to fit this shoe to its foot." The neutrality bill, Virginio Gayda wrote in *Il Giornale d'Italia,* implied "obvious intervention by the United States in the conflict" and its "adhesion to the League and direct submission to British policy." But expressions of relief or fear or conclusions of any sort about the future were premature. *Le Temps* rightly pointed out that American actions would not be predictable until the text of the legislation was voted on and applied by the administration.[15]

Opposition to the administration's position gathered on Capitol Hill. On 3 January 1936 another bill was presented by Senators Nye and Clark and Congressman Maverick, denying the president any discretionary authority. The neutralists' alternative bill required the president to impose a trade embargo at once, not at some unspecified time "during the progress of the war." Commercial credit would be severely restricted. Trade would be cash and carry. The purchaser, not the American sender, would take the risks, since American vessels were barred from war zones.

The fundamental issue was, Who should control policy in case of a war in which the United States was not directly involved? Congress by means of the mandatory provisions or the president at his discretion? A month and a half of debate ensued. Hiram Johnson, to the point of threatening a filibuster, opposed any infringement of freedom of the seas. Intense criticism was leveled at the notion of traders' taking the risks. Oil, cotton, and maritime interests lobbied strongly against the administration measure. Groups of Italian-Americans campaigned against it. Isolationists argued that anything other than rigid mandatory neutrality would lead to foreign entanglement. By early February it was clear that the State Department's bill had no chance of passage, and on 7 February the administration conceded defeat, hoping to raise the issue again after the November elections.

The alternative legislation, drawn up now by the Senate's Foreign Relations Committee, was basically the existing neutrality act "bob-tailed."[16] The committee reported on 12 February, the same day the committee of experts reported in Geneva on the oil situation. As presented, the bill recommended extending the standing neutrality legislation with the following modifications. The embargo on arms, ammunition, and implements of war would go into effect toward all belligerents "whenever" the president determined that a war existed. Removing the option of issuing such a proclamation "during the progress of the war" meant this possibility for tactical maneuvering was removed. Banning loans to belligerents was made mandatory, an application of the Nye committee's thesis that such loans had led to American involvement in the Great War. The money and arms market was now closed automatically to those at war, regardless of the justice of their case or America's interest in the outcome. Belligerents were belligerents, and no arms or loans would come from America. This fact was understood in Europe and made the cautious ever more so. Such withholding of support, this "getting in the policeman's way," wrote Vansittart, could be "quite fatal" to Britain in case of war in Europe.[17]

The second neutrality act passed overwhelmingly in the House on 17 February 1936 and in the Senate the next day and was signed into law by Roosevelt on the last day of the month. It was to run to May 1937 and was to be applied at once to Italy and to Ethiopia. Its passage was a bitter defeat for the administration. The bill said nothing about oil, nothing about quotas or normal prewar levels of trade, nothing about raw materials or finished products other than "implements of war." The president was allowed no control over such trade. Roosevelt made the old appeal to a moral embargo when he signed the bill. This was all that was left to the administration. Congress wished to isolate America from overseas quarrels, and one way to do this was to tie the president's hands.

The Experts' Report on Oil

The report of the expert committee on the technical conditions governing trade in and transport of petroleum was delivered on 12 February 1936. The experts were not expected to give an opinion on the oil sanction as an instrument of collective security, its possible effects on the Italian economic or political scene, or whether it might slow down the invasion or stop the war. These were to be evaluated by the member governments of the Coordination Committee on the basis of the experts' technical report and their own political and military considerations. The committee's opinion related only to how an oil embargo might affect Italy's *ability* to "cover the whole or the greater part" of its oil requirements.

The report estimated that Italy had in stock or en route oil sufficient to its needs for the next three or three and a half months. An embargo applied by all members of the Coordination Committee—if American oil exports were held to a normal prewar level—would be "effective," drastically reducing Italy's ability to procure petroleum. If there were no limitation in the American market, the "only effect" would be to make gas and oil more difficult to obtain and more expensive. What this implied, whether the Italian government could afford the more expensive purchases and the political effects of increased costs, was not discussed. The experts rendered a similar conclusion regarding transportation. If sanctionist states withheld tankers, 50 percent of the needed capacity could be supplied by the Italian merchant fleet, and the rest on charter from nonsanctionist states—but again with "greater difficulty" and "greater expense" for Italy.[18]

Frank Walters, viewing the report from the Secretariat, thought it was "clear, conclusive, and encouraging," even though a simultaneous report of the Senate's neutrality bill killed all hope that the American government would restrain trade to a prewar level.[19] At least uncertainty about America was no longer an excuse to avoid a decision on the embargo. Yet, once again, there came the familiar dispiriting delay. The report had to be considered by the governments. The embargo was to be discussed at a meeting of the Committee of Eighteen scheduled three weeks later, on 2 March 1936. During this time Badoglio began his major offensive southward. The chill of failed pur-

pose—brought on by the news of the Hoare-Laval plan—a sense of lost opportunity, a sense that the tide was turning against the League, increased in
Geneva. Talk grew of the necessity to reform the League, regardless of how
the Italian affair ended. Those who see fullest flowering at the moment when
decay begins might note that it was just at this time, on 18 February 1936,
that the Secretariat took possession of permanent headquarters, the huge
new Palace of Nations, the largest public building in Europe, with its lovely
park and breathtaking vista of Lake Geneva and Mont Blanc.

Three weeks to think about the choice. The experts indicated that Italy
might obtain oil from Albania and Latin America. Albanian petroleum was
discounted—poor quality and limited supply. Mexico and Colombia had oil,
but they exported to the United States. Venezuela deserved special attention.
Its large supply of crude oil was refined elsewhere, about 20 percent in the
United States and 80 percent in the Dutch West Indies. About 15 percent of
Italy's oil import normally came from these islands. If the Dutch joined an
embargo, said the experts, there was no technical reason why Venezuelan
crude could not go directly to Italy for refining. The problem was transport.
Italy would have to rent or buy considerable shipping for the carriage, add-
ing to the strain on its domestic economy.

The British tried to get Latin American states to stand up for the embargo.
For chairman of the experts' committee, the British sponsored the Mexican
League representative, who in his initial enthusiasm said that, if needed to
keep down the flow to Italy, Mexico would reduce its oil shipments to the
United States. The Latin American delegates by and large, however, worried
about being caught between League action and American neutrality. Who
knew what might develop from some reassertion of the Monroe Doctrine?
The delegate from Venezuela had another problem. A separatist movement
existed in the Caribbean oil areas, and revolutionary disturbances might
emerge with a change of Dutch policy there.[20]

Titulescu, foreign minister of Italy's major oil supplier, Romania, remained at the forefront of the sanctionist cause. On 22 January he told Eden
that the League's future authority depended on immediate imposition of an
oil embargo. No friend of Italy, he suggested in other conversations that the
Soviet Union replace Italy as a party to various Danubian understandings.
For Titulescu the economic loss from sanctions was as nothing compared to
the political gain of cementing ties with Britain and crippling "the enemy of
all the Balkan peoples."[21]

Positioning in Britain

When the Board of Trade sent its petroleum experts to the study committee,
it gave them a list of the technical problems to set out in the committee's

report. The effect of such a string of reservations worried the Foreign Office, so its representative was instructed to keep in touch with the press in Geneva to counter any charge that the British were trying to sabotage the inquiry with multiple objections.[22]

After the experts' report was in, Gladwyn Jebb on 18 February reviewed for the Foreign Office some possible sanction courses, to be discussed prior to the meeting of the Committee of Eighteen on 2 March.

1. The most obvious course was to combine an embargo on oil exports with a prohibition on the use of tankers. A variation on the latter could be to prohibit Italian ships' use of bunkering facilities in ports of call belonging to sanctionist states. This measure had not been discussed by the experts committee because the Board of Trade thought it close to a blockade, hence a provocation. Jebb agreed that it went further than circumstances warranted.

2. There could be a general embargo of all goods to Italian east Africa by sea or land. Since most shipments went to Eritrea and Somalia in Italian bottoms, however, this would not add to Mussolini's difficulties.

3. Italy could get coal and steel from Germany, so there would be no point in resurrecting those items as initially recommended under proposal 4-A.

4. The tanker sanction could be applied by itself. A month before when Jebb advocated this Vansittart had commented tartly: "I have some sympathy with the [opposing] Board of Trade view. The worse the campaign in Africa goes, and it is going worse, the more superfluous do these measures or contemplations become at this stage. They involve a certain amount of provocation or risk without materially altering the real results." But the campaign did not get worse, and Jebb now made a stronger case for the tanker sanction.

Italy had enough carriers to accommodate about half of its consumption at the time. Some, however, were in use for transport to Africa, and at least one had been converted for water transport. With a tanker sanction, Italy would have to arrange transport for an additional 1.8 million tons of oil, involving leasing or buying a quarter million tons of shipping. They might on an emergency basis barge Romanian oil up the Danube to Vienna and then send it by rail, but this would be very expensive. And shipping oil from across the Atlantic would likewise be costlier than getting Romanian oil via the Black Sea route. Furthermore, a tanker sanction would not offend the Americans, as it would seem in line with the moral embargo. Still, Jebb concluded, the most efficacious way to apply pressure on the Italian economy would be to combine a tanker prohibition with the oil embargo itself.[23]

The tanker sanction had a further virtue in British eyes. It would spread the sanctionist burden to the Scandinavian nations, particularly Norway. The standoffishness of what Vansittart called "the little eunuch-states" was always a sore point in London. In mid-January, for example, when questions of military support were much discussed, the Danish foreign minister said his country hardly could be expected to participate in mutual assistance because of its great distance from the Mediterranean. Denmark should be treated similarly to a South American state. This infuriated the British Foreign Office. Peterson wrote: "No conception more prejudicial to the whole idea of collective security could be entertained than that it is open to any member of the League to use its influence, and to vote at Geneva for the imposition of sanctions against an aggressor while at the same time leaving the possible military consequences of this action to be borne by one or two fellow members." Stanhope said the matter was of "supreme importance," going "to the whole root of collective security." Vansittart insisted: "We must continually press this theme. If we fail to do so the League will fail in disaster and the entire future of the continent will be imperiled." But the smaller northern states wanted to avoid risk. "Norway will not tamely allow itself to be driven into a new war policy," its foreign minister told the Storting on 11 February 1936, as the oil report was about to come in. The League was of no use, he said, if it could not find a solution to the threat of disorder. "An active peace policy must be pursued, and there is no time to be lost."[24]

Eden, as he began to prepare for the sanctions meeting of 2 March, showed slight determination to push for the oil embargo. To the cabinet on 19 February he said he was inclined toward it but that if the cabinet decided against it he was ready to propose alternatives, as outlined in the Jebb memorandum. Additionally, he would then propose, as the "best course for the League," a resolution reaffirming League willingness to apply the oil sanction but also, in line with the evidence in the experts' report, stating that the matter now had to be referred to the United States.[25]

This was a remarkably disingenuous suggestion. It played loose with the evidence, shifted responsibility for a matter of collective security to a government outside the League that could in fact do nothing to help, and did so in a manner precisely and repeatedly warned against by Hull. Ambassador Lindsay showed up Eden's fatuity. The Congress is eager to have done with the controversy, Lindsay wrote on 21 February. The administration had scarcely mentioned the moral embargo for two months (on 29 February Roosevelt made one last call in its behalf). Prompt application of an oil sanction, Lindsay said, "would do more than anything else to restore League prestige and to influence American opinion in favour of collective security." To evade this decision at Geneva on 2 March and then plead with the United States for independent action so as to encourage League members would be taken as an inept attempt to shift responsibility to or entangle the United States, and it would be resented accordingly. With this dispatch came to an end any thought in the Foreign Office that the Roosevelt administration would or could do anything to reduce American oil exports.[26]

Eden next asked Barton in Addis Ababa how far the military and political situation in Ethiopia had deteriorated since Badoglio had begun his advance on 10 February. Was Ethiopia in danger of collapse? No, replied Barton on the twenty-fourth. The government was not in despair nor weakened in its overall control. There was no shortage of food, and the army would be active for "some time to come." What Ethiopia needed, said Barton, was money.[27]

Yet things were not going well, and the Ethiopian government grasped at every straw. On 20 February the minister in London appealed to Eden for direct assistance, noting that the League, for all its moral value, gave Ethiopia no material aid.[28] More poignant and more revealing was the plea the emperor himself had made the day before in a personal appeal to King Edward VIII. Sanctions were not enough to stop the war, he said. What was needed was direct British intervention. Mussolini had offered, Haile Selassie said, to negotiate peace terms. He asked the British to "decide a place where the two countries may meet and negotiate the matter, in the meantime an armistice being called."

If nothing else, this was a plea for time, time to stall the Italian offensive until the rains. It is true there was much talk in Rome at this time of a bilateral agreement with the Ethiopian government. Italian agents had three separate initiatives under way. In his message to the king, the emperor referred to terms brought to him by the Italian wife of the Ethiopian minister in Rome. Only some form of British guarantee, the emperor's argument ran—and it was pressed by Barton—only some specific acceptance of responsibility, could protect Ethiopia if it entered into negotiations with Italy. France and the Vatican were not acceptable mediators. If possible, the emperor's message concluded, and the request was made again two weeks later by his minister in London, might Ethiopia become part of the British dominion? Might Britain take over the country as a protectorate or as a mandate?

The cabinet discussed this appeal on 24 February. British help was categorically refused. There could be no question of a mandate or protectorate. Any negotiated or conciliatory settlement had to come from or through the League. Britain would not facilitate talks. The old report of the Committee of Five, Eden stressed in his reply to Barton as well as in a speech to Commons on 24 February, must be the foundation of any settlement terms. Haile Selassie could, if he wished, make his request to the League and ask that the Committee of Five be reconvened. Meanwhile, Britain would do nothing. A unilateral guarantee of the security of the country, already rejected when the issue was discussed in London in previous years, was all the more out of the question now that foreign troops occupied much of the land.

The emperor, once again, had asked for more than the British would give. Eden sent the British reply on 24 February. It was not, however, until 12 March that the military attaché delivered it to Quoram. This delay was perhaps the result of difficulties in arranging transportation, or it may be that Haile Selassie knew the futility of his request. He received the reply without comment and then spoke at length of the inadequacy of the League, wherein all his hopes reposed.[29]

Ethiopia's geopolitical insignificance to Britain was revealed to the world on 20 February 1936, when Mussolini published in *Il Giornale d'Italia* the gist of the Maffey report of June 1935, purloined from the safe of the British embassy in Rome, with its clearly stated conclusion that "no such vital British interest is concerned in and around Ethiopia as to make it essential for His Majesty's Government to resist an Italian conquest." Mussolini meant by this exposé to prove prior to the March meeting of the Committee of Eighteen that Italy neither meant to nor could harm British interests in Ethiopia.

On 24 February Eden spoke to the Commons, his first parliamentary address as foreign secretary. To criticism about dilatoriness toward the oil sanction, he spoke of the need for a judicious determination of its effectiveness. Oil, he said, should not take on "symbolic quality." It was "a sanction like any other and must be judged by the same criterion, whether its imposition will help to stop the war." Sanctions were a means, not the end. "The end is a settlement in accordance with League principles which will establish normal relations between neighbors on a lasting basis."

It is clear that the double policy lived on with Eden. On the eve of the meeting of the Committee of Eighteen, on the eve of a presumably final determination of the oil sanction, Eden unexpectedly raised the hope that the settlement plan of the Committee of Five would "be neither forgotten or set aside." The machinery of the committee, he said, was still available to the disputants, if they wanted to use it.[30]

Grandi was behind the idea of reinvoking the Committee of Five. He told Eden a few days before his speech that Mussolini was agreed to the "possibility ultimately of negotiation within the framework of that committee's report," a concession the Italians had never before made. This influenced the reply Eden made to the emperor as well. It is hard, however, to imagine that Eden thought anything could come of his suggestion, and it is hard to see much purpose behind it. Eden said in his memoirs that the reason he supported the oil sanction two days later in the cabinet was that Mussolini failed to respond immediately. Yet Grandi had stated clearly that "such negotiation was not possible at the present time."[31]

Reaction in Rome to Eden's speech was generally favorable. Eden was seen as indecisive. All his stress on effectiveness, which Italians thought disproved by the experts' report, and his holding out the suggestion of further negotiations slowed down the sanctionist momentum. Some in the Palazzo Chigi wanted to contest Eden's assertion that existing sanctions were working well. Grandi, whose moderating influence was still felt in the ministry, argued to the contrary. Instead, Grandi said, Italian diplomats should deplore how the boycott caused economic difficulties. This would give an excuse for Britain and France not to advance to further measures. Grandi put his idea to work on 28 February, lamenting at the Foreign Office the "very serious effects" sanctions had in Italy, what with the eroding of reserves, and the problems of a campaign likely to last several years.[32] The tactic worked.

But, all in all, Eden only confused the Italians. Despite the moderation and conciliatory tone of the speech, two days later Eden supported the sanction in the cabinet and surprised Italian officials when the British delegation at Geneva came out in favor of the embargo on 2 March. These events further embittered Italians toward Eden, toward his disingenuousness and his apparent hostility and intransigence.[33]

Yet the British decision to support the oil sanction was not determined by anti-Italian sentiment or by the criterion of effectiveness. In the cabinet on 26 February 1936, political considerations set the British course. Most of the cabinet thought an oil sanction would *not* do much toward ending the war. As Eden told Commons in April, "While admitting the ineffectiveness of the oil embargo, we thought that such an embargo should be put on." To Barton on 4 March he was somewhat more detailed: "It cannot be expected that the embargo will have any immediate effect: the most that can be hoped for in present conditions is that it will increase the Italian difficulties. If it is applied, it will be applied less by reason of its probable effectiveness than as a means of demonstrating the determination of members of the League to persist in the policy upon which they have embarked."[34] Two cabinet members recorded dissent to the decision on 26 February. Walter Runciman, president of the Board of Trade, and Monsell, first lord of the Admiralty, held that an ineffective sanction should be dropped, a position, Monsell tartly pointed out, "held in the past by many of his colleagues and by the Cabinet itself." But the matter was seen somewhat differently now. An oil sanction would be safer, unlikely now, of itself, to provoke a Mediterranean war. Some cabinet members did hold out hope for limited effectiveness, as the cost of purchase from alternative sources could not help but add to the strain on the Italian economy. Arguments about the political merit of the sanction went back and forth. The soon-to-be concluded conference on naval limitation might be jeopardized. Response: no reliance could be placed on Italy's signature anyway. Mussolini might withdraw Italy from the League and denounce the Locarno agreements. Response: these actions, if they occurred, would be for reasons largely independent of the oil sanction. The Admiralty wanted to recommission some ships, end the state of emergency in the Mediterranean, and bring some major units home. Response: since the danger zone of war seemed passed, this could be done even if the oil embargo was applied. The military situation in Egypt was good. A Chiefs of Staff report concluded there was no risk of invasion through the western desert.[35] The sanction, all agreed, would not extend to shipping or constitute a blockade. Some urged the government not to yield to "left wing" opinion. But, in the end, political considerations clinched the decision of support.

It was impossible to go back either on all that was said at the time of November's general election or on the assertions in support of the League at the time of the Hoare-Laval plan. The embargo did indeed have symbolic value. Refusal to support it now, Baldwin said, would have "a disastrous effect both now and at the next General Election," would jeopardize the government's authority, and would throw into question the prestige of his position as prime minister. He had his personal prestige in mind, too. A few days before, Thomas Jones had found him tired and feeling "rather sorry for himself." Baldwin talked to Jones about senility, about "old and tired men" who "carry on too long." He wanted, Jones wrote, to "hand over to his successor [Neville Chamberlain was his choice] when his own prestige was not too far declined and with the Party in good heart," which it clearly was not in the wake of the Hoare-Laval disaster.[36] So, Baldwin told the cabinet, since public opinion was in favor of working through the League, the British citizenry and "the whole of Europe" were "entitled to know whether collective economic sanctions would work so that every country could make up its mind as to how far it would cooperate in a collective system." And there was something to be said for a concession to left wing sentiment. The carrying out of rearmament plans depended on industrial mobilization, for which cooperation with the Trades Union and the Labour party was essential. If the government opposed the oil sanction, opposition to government defense programs "would have a moral basis it at present lacked." This "labour side of the question," said Baldwin, was vitally important. "With that cooperation, this country in five years time would fear no one."

The Dominions for the most part favored the measure. There was a sense of common purpose within the empire over upholding the Covenant. And the alternative was to do nothing, inaction which, in the face of world expectations, would be a "fatal blow to the League," with great repercussions in America and Germany. Lastly, there was a fear that, should the emperor publish the appeal he had sent to the king and the British government had done nothing, its reputation would sustain a further blow.

The conclusion, then, was that Eden would make it clear to the Committee of Eighteen on 2 March that the government favored the oil sanction. Eden was to try to secure its application as soon as possible, in order to postpone consideration of the shipping sanction or an embargo of port facilities. The decision was a major one for the British government, and it came as a surprise when announced at Geneva. A "coup de théâtre," Aloisi said.[37]

Morally Insupportable

On the first of February Mussolini published in *Il Popolo d'Italia* an appeal to "the students of Europe." Italy wanted peace in Europe, he wrote. The Ethiopian undertaking was a simple colonial matter. Yet sanctions would lead to blockade, and a blockade meant war. It would be "the most terrible and most unjustified war that humanity ever saw . . . a war of slaughter in Europe . . . a war of vengeance" for which Italy would not be responsible. All Italy wanted was to protect its possession from Ethiopian aggression and barbarities. That was why the verdict of Geneva was a "fraud." Ethiopia, not Italy, was the aggressor. So much for the League's claim to honor and justice. The association in fact was led by lying, incendiary, bloodthirsty imperialists. They were the ones who would bring destruction upon Europe. And who would fight in this horrible war? Who would be facing machine guns and gas for a mistaken cause? Students, Europe's young men, not the politicians of the Left (he mentioned Léon Blum by name) who had brought about the war. It was, therefore, up to the youth to stop these intrigues against Italy.[38]

On 13 February 1936 Charles Maurras, in a column in *L'Action Française*, called for "the knife" to be used against deputies who supported sanctions. That very day Léon Blum was set upon by students and cut on the head, suffering serious shock and loss of blood.[39] In February the most serious of the incidents of the ongoing Jèze affair almost closed the faculty of law at the University of Paris. This episode, inflammatory newspaper articles, and the attack on Blum showed the bitterness and violence of political passions. Widespread sympathy went to the injured Socialist leader, and indignation against his assailants. Sarraut's government moved rapidly, showing a spirit and decisiveness few had anticipated. The government dissolved various rightist organizations, including the national federation of students of the Action française. These actions, with the ministry throwing its lot with the Popular Front, enhanced the prospects of the Left in the days before the two-stage general election of April and May. On 16 February the Popular Front held its largest public demonstration to date. None of this influenced the foreign ministry. Flandin, as adamant and blunt as Laval ever was, remained firmly set against any French participation in the oil embargo. Flandin was the object of an Italian campaign to delay, if not to discourage altogether, the imposition of that sanction.

Italian diplomats brought out their repertoire of carrots and sticks, with the usual successful result. Suvich said that the U.S. Congress, by limiting embargoed items and denying Roosevelt discretion in applying neutrality legislation, had made it easier for Europeans to renounce the oil embargo. Mussolini declared the decision of Congress "a precious service in the cause of world peace."[40] The experts' report, said Suvich, showed that an oil embargo would have little short-run effect. Italy had reserves enough to finish the war, more than the estimated three or three and a half months' worth. Worse yet, the estimate was not a technical conclusion, but a figure meant to influence the United States government by showing that its cooperation would help. Finally, in Italy's view, an oil sanction would be morally insupportable.[41]

The Italians dropped the threat of war. That old bluff, if bluff it was, had served in its time, but had also prompted alarming precautionary responses among sanctionist states. Nor does it seem that there was much concern in Rome about the likelihood of war. On 7 February Aloisi talked with Salvatore Denti di Piraino, newly appointed commander in chief of the Italian fleet. Denti was eager to be at sea, but he was kept in Rome, without instructions as to what might be a cause for war or, in case of war, what action was expected of the fleet. The British forces, said Denti, were overwhelmingly superior, and he was very doubtful about how Italy would emerge from a conflict. Ten days later Admiral Ranieri Biscia reported that at the Naval Conference in London the British Admiralty acted as if sanctions and the present concentration of British naval strength in the Mediterranean were not features of their planning.[42]

In February, the French government was warned that support for an oil embargo, while not bringing an immediate war, would irreparably damage relations between the two states. Italy would denounce the Gamelin-Badoglio military understandings and reject the talks concerning air cooperation begun by Ministers Denain and Valle. Italy would refuse to sign any treaty proposed by the naval limitation conference. Italy would withdraw from the League of Nations. Worse, Italy might turn toward Germany and denounce the security agreements made at Locarno. Could France afford to lose Italy just now, officials asked, when chancelleries buzzed with talk of possible German remilitarization of the Rhineland? Italy had always been faithful to the Stresa front against German violations of the Versailles Treaty, Mussolini told Chambrun on 27 February, but any new sanction would be a final straw, pushing Italy into isolation from which his government would have an "imperative need" to get out, turning then toward Germany.[43] These were strong threats, made to a susceptible government, and they confirmed Flandin's opposition to further sanctions. Ingram, holding down the British embassy in Rome, thought Mussolini's warnings should be taken seriously, although the cabinet, as we saw, discounted them in its decision to support the embargo.[44]

Mussolini made clear what he expected. France must stop the oil sanction at Geneva on 2 March before the "small, irresponsible nations, with no direct interests," pushed the embargo through. There was no point to further sanctions anyway, for military events were turning in Italy's favor.[45] Mussolini said the end of the war would come swiftly, not just from a series of Italian victories, but also from the progressive wearing down of Ethiopians' ability to resist. That was the lesson he had learned from the collapse of the forces of Ras Desta in January during the battle of the Ganale Doria in the south.

On 29 February, on the eve of the meeting of the Committee of Eighteen and after the Italian victories of Amba Aradam and the second battle of Tembien, Chambrun wrote to Flandin that Italians were predicting a rapid end to the war—two months, perhaps and Mussolini thought it would be over in six weeks. A great offensive on both fronts was set for the early days of March. The successive defeats of Ethiopian troops and the famine that would menace the countryside would lead the emperor to treat directly, with the Italians. Italian morale, Chambrun said, was at its highest point since the war had begun. This should be kept in mind, he concluded, in thinking about any aggravation of sanctions, for Italians, imagining that a victorious end was at hand, might be excited to dangerous fanaticism if it seemed they would be deprived of the fruits of their efforts.[46]

Flandin heard also from Minister Bodard in Addis Ababa, whose dispatches painted a correspondingly bleak picture of Ethiopia's prospects. His reports were far more pessimistic than those sent to the Foreign Office by his colleague Barton. A feature of our story is how the divergent views of agents abroad influenced policies of the governments of France and Britain and account in some measure for the differences between them. On 29 February, for example, Chambrun mentioned the danger of famine. Five days before Barton had cabled Eden that there was no shortage of food. Bodard stressed disorder in the armies, their inexperience in modern war, and the lack of arms. Barton said there was little danger of collapse. Flandin, increasingly anxious anyway, found Bodard's information a confirmation of the case presented by Italian diplomats. Time seemed short now, at the end of February, as it had not in earlier months. To the French, conciliation seemed all the more necessary as an alternative to sanctions. Ethiopia would go under if something was not done at once. As Flandin wrote later, it was "not only events in Europe but also those in Abyssinia that made us search with all haste for an honorable solution to the conflict."[47]

Battles of Annihilation

Diplomacy moderated interference. Domestic mobilization, a nationalist response, overcame the effects of sanctions and disapproval. But it was the generals who won the empire for Italy, won it fast and won it sure. In the battles of February and March in Tigre, which provided the backdrop of diplomatic maneuvering in Europe, the northern command conclusively defeated the Ethiopians in set battle, routing their forces so completely as to make impossible any regrouping into organized opposition.

The Italian lines had held against the Ethiopian counteroffensive of January, which was broken in the first battle of Tembien. In this engagement Badoglio saw the inadequacy of the Ethiopian command structure and the extreme deficiencies of training and supply among the troops. He learned that he could stop what had been most feared of the Ethiopian, impetus of attack and maneuverability of men, the first halted by modern weapons and the second controlled from the air. By the second week in February 1936, with his front reorganized, Badoglio was ready for a drive toward Addis Ababa. On 10 February he launched an attack against the perhaps 50,000 men of Ras Mulugeta entrenched in the region below Enderta upon the looming bulk of Amba Aradam, fifteen miles south of Makale.

The battle of Amba Aradam (or Enderta, as it is also called) lasted from 10 to 19 February and showed the pattern Badoglio used confidently and successfully in every subsequent engagement. Against a hopelessly un-prepared foe he brought the strongest armed force ever mounted in a colonial war. On the eve of the attack Badoglio boasted: "We shall win this war with a campaign of the utmost brilliance, a campaign unequalled since the days of Napoleon. In less than two months, beneath the weight of the assault, you will see the Ethiopian empire crumble to dust."[48] Badoglio took no chances. His first requirement was overwhelming firepower. He com-plained that De Bono was ignorant of the proper use of artillery. Against Amba Aradam, against the 10 cannon commanded by the Ethiopian minister of war, Badoglio used 280 field pieces and fired 23,000 rounds. The defenders of the mountain were crushed beneath a mass of flying metal. There was no help for Mulugeta. The emperor ordered the troops of Ras Kassa against the Italian flank, but his message took three days to arrive. Kassa received it on 15 February, the day Mulugeta gave up Amba Aradam.[49]

After winning a battle of position Badoglio sought to ravage the fleeing warriors, so turning retreat into rout. Badoglio knew that the unregimented forces were unlikely to regroup for further operations once they were demoralized and scattered into the countryside. To ensure dispersion, Badoglio had at his disposal 170 aircraft, unopposed in the sky and able to refuel at Makale, a scarce fifteen miles from the mountain.

When Badoglio talked about a battle of "annihilation" he referred to a destruction of the will to fight as well as of life itself. In the early days of planning the role of air power in the Ethiopian war was seen by Air Minister Valle as primarily defensive, a means of interdiction, a way to break up an attack.[50] Badoglio, like the theoretical pioneer Giulio Douhet, saw its offensive potential as well. In 1928 Douhet wrote that an air attack on a city was not merely to destroy things—what was important was to "discourage social life," and for this he recommended the use of "aggressive chemical means."[51] Badoglio's conception of air power in war, first put into practice on a vast scale in Ethiopia, followed Douhet's closely. "I relied," Badoglio wrote, "upon a continued and persistent air bombardment varying in intensity at irregular intervals of time—comparable to the pounding, harassing uses of artillery in the Great War. . . . By this means I expected to affect especially the morale of the enemy and to lower his fighting spirit." And, once the battle of position was over, and the foe in flight, he "handed over to the Air Arm the task of continuing the battle with the pursuit of the enemy. . . . At first the Abyssinians had put up a lively reaction to the action of our airmen; later, finding there was no escape, they resigned themselves to their fate, passively enduring the continuous, violent, hammering onslaught, which went on without a pause from dawn to sunset. . . ."[52]

The follow-up of the battle of Amba Aradam lasted four days, through 19 February 1936. "The brilliant exploits of the Air Arm during the pursuit may be summed up in the following figures, which are a proof of the energy we expended in following up our success: 546 raids, during which 396 tons of explosive and 30,000 rounds of machine-gun ammunition were used."[53] George Steer wrote of the consequences of such air attacks:

> The most cruel effect of aviation on the Ethiopian was that it destroyed his traditional response to his leaders. Instead of assembling for mass security around their leader . . . they scattered now in a frantic dash for individual security. . . . Italian air supremacy made of the Ethiopians a rabble which could not think for itself. It demolished, in fearful explosions and vibrations of the solid earth, the aristocracy which was the cadre of their military organization.[54]

The tricolor of Italy was atop Amba Aradam, the troops of Ras Mulugeta scattered, and the Ethiopian minister of war himself fallen to a hostile population in the region. The way stood open to breach the passes of the watershed of Amba Alaji, where the troops of Pietro Toselli had been routed forty years before. These passes Badoglio's men took on 28 February 1936. Meantime, Badoglio turned against the remaining Ethiopian armies in the north: Ras Kassa and Ras Seyum to the west in Tembien, still facing the

Warieu Pass, and Ras Imru in Shire, further west, near Aksum. Badoglio mounted his assault on a grand scale. Proud of its scope, he wrote: "For the first time in colonial military history, there were to be employed simultaneously in a general attack, five corps on a front 150 miles long. . . ." In fact, of course, it was not a colonial campaign, but was, for the Italians, "an overseas war in colonial territory."[55]

Mulugeta's defeat greatly alarmed the Ethiopian troops to the west. His army was the best of the imperial force. His stand on Amba Aradam was considered impregnable. His defeat was thus a crushing blow to morale, now further discouraged by defeatist propaganda leaflets dropped from Italian aircraft and announcing the exposed and hopeless position of the western armies.

The situation of Kassa and Seyum was critical. The Italians were heading west to cut off their line of retreat. Both commanders, and the emperor, realized they must withdraw from a sure deathtrap. This is what Badoglio expected—the defeat at Amba Aradam would disrupt the entire front. But Kassa and Seyum did not move, hoping, perhaps, for aid from Imru and beset by a crippling dysentery epidemic in their ranks. On 27 February Badoglio set out against them, launching the second battle of Tembien.[56]

Strong Ethiopian counterattacks were broken by the superior firepower of a pincer movement of two Italian army corps, one of which, "for the first time in history," was supplied by parachute drop.[57] The charge of brave men, barefoot and in cotton shammas, was of no avail against the mass of matériel used in this battle: 7 million rounds of ammunition, 48,000 artillery shells, and 195 tons of bombs. What remained of food and supplies, already scarce in January and now almost gone, was destroyed. By the evening of the third day, 29 February, except for some pockets of resistance, the Ethiopian troops were fleeing southward. The correspondent of *Corriere della Sera* described the scene for Italian readers on 3 March 1936:

> The Ethiopians straggled along in disorder. There was only one road open to them, and the fords were so narrow, the rocky walls of the ravines so precipitous that they were soon jammed together in a solid mass. Even though we were flying at 1,000 meters, we could see them quite plainly. Our plane swooped down, zigzagged along the defile, sowed its seeds of death and zoomed upward.[58]

One Ethiopian army, that of Ras Imru, remained in the north, in Shire, close to Aksum. Imru was greatly disheartened by the news from Amba Aradam, but, like Kassa, stood his ground despite urging from the emperor to withdraw. The Italians attacked on 29 February and encountered the most determined opposition yet. Here was the bitterest fighting of the campaign.

Italian casualties were usually on the order of one out of ten—in the battle of Shire they were one out of four. Mussolini himself admitted the losses were serious.[59] Yet, once again, what chance had the Ethiopian against the machine gun? In three days an Italian corps fired 50,000 artillery shells and 10 million cartridges, against probably no more than 25,000 Ethiopians. The Italians, in this one battle, expended more ammunition than the entire Ethiopian northern line possessed at the start of the war.[60] On the morning of 3 March 1936 the last Ethiopian army in the north was in retreat.

But Imru escaped with half his men, and pursuit again took on great importance. Imru withdrew toward the Takkaze River. It was, Badoglio wrote,

a retirement which, with every link broken under the constant onslaught of our aircraft, very quickly turned into a disorderly rout. On his reaching the fords, difficult in themselves because sunk between high, steep, and thickly wooded banks, his passage was rendered even more terribly critical by continued air activity. In addition to the usual effective bombing and machine-gun fire, small incendiary bombs had been used to set on fire the whole region about the fords, rendering utterly tragic the plight of the fleeing enemy.[61]

Imru faced more than firebombs. Gas was used once more on the banks of the Takkaze. Imru led 10,000 men to the fords. Within days he was left with only his personal bodyguard of 300; the rest had deserted or been hunted down.[62] For two months this most capable of the northern commanders hid in the west trying to raise force. It was a hopeless task, for defeatism and regionalism prevailed. "The greater part of the [Gojam] troops," he reported to the emperor, "have deserted and refuse to fight except in their own district; the few who remain have worked to disintegrate even our own personal soldiers, so that we have not been able to carry out our plan."[63] It was through Gojam that the Blue Nile flowed from Lake Tana into the Sudan. In mid-February 1936, to encourage defeatism, Mussolini instructed Badoglio to spread the word in Gojam that the emperor had removed all his gold from Ethiopia and sent it to an Egyptian bank.[64] The local chiefs lost authority as well as heart, and they dallied with the Italians, unable or unwilling to rally their own men. Gojam, by March 1936, was in revolt. At the end of March Imru left Gojam and headed east to joint Haile Selassie.

News of the great victories in the north, coming on the eve of the fortieth anniversary of Aduwa (1 March) and on the eve of the meeting of the Committee of Eighteen and a decision on the oil sanction, made Italians exultant. The mood of the peninsula turned around. And, sitting at his headquarters on 1 March amid stacks of messages of congratulations, Badoglio reflected: "The curtain has fallen on the second act. . . . Now we must think of the third. The enemy has suffered such a shattering defeat that for the first time in his history he has lost all desire to go on fighting."[65]

10 THE WORLD LOOKS ON

An Appeal

Italian diplomacy made its case in Paris. Field victories meant the end of the war was near. It was now or never for a peace by settlement. The alternative was a full Italian conquest. An oil sanction would be useless provocation. It would cost France dearly and should be stopped at Geneva on 2 March. Flandin accepted those conclusions. He was not, however, inclined to bargain on Italy's behalf to end the war regardless of the fate of Ethiopia. Unlike Laval, he fancied no personal connection with Mussolini. On the first of March 1936 Flandin sent him a rather cool message implying that hints of a reversal of policy toward France constituted an egregious threat and that Italian complaints were unjustified. France was faithful to Stresa, had used its influence to temper British and League action, and never denied Italy a rightful place in European affairs. Hectoring talk from Rome only threw doubt on the true intentions of the Italian government.[1]

Flandin's doubts would have been confirmed had he heard Aloisi tell the German ambassador two weeks before that for Italy "Stresa was dead and done with." Once the Austrian matter was out of the way the "force of events would, quite naturally, bring Germany and Italy together." Spelling it out more clearly, Mussolini told the ambassador on 22 February that whatever Cerruti was saying in Paris to encourage favorable League action toward Italy, he, Mussolini, could state that "Stresa was finally dead." As for Locarno, "It was an appendage of the League of Nations and would disappear of its own accord the moment Italy left the League. . . . France was passing more and more into the hands of the Left and in the not very distant future Léon Blum would be the uncrowned king of France. Relations between Italy and France were consequently deteriorating steadily."[2]

The year-long association with France was being phased out. French moderation would of course be encouraged—the war, and sanctionist pressures, was not over—but, as France moved toward the Left and Flandin put renewed emphasis on the connection with London, the French would share the fate of the British: as useful a foe as valuable a friend. In the early spring of 1936 Mussolini looked for self-sufficiency. The African war was coming to a close. The old hope of a future in the Balkans awoke. Increasingly self-confident for having bested the League, he felt less need to maintain more than formal connections with governments who seemed hostile to him, to Fascism, and to his expansionary visions.

Flandin could not so readily give up his ties to Rome. He had taken office "to rebuild the dam against Germany." What if Hitler advanced on Austria? Then, Flandin told Eden on 7 February 1936, "everything depended on Italy." Alone, France was powerless to help Yugoslavia or its allies in the Little Entente. To move French troops to the Adriatic by sea took too long. And French public opinion "utterly excluded" a retaliatory strike against Germany.[3]

France's dependence was shown in the decision of the Council of Ministers on 27 February 1936. In the case of German remilitarization of the Rhineland, France would take no isolated action. France would respond only together with the other signatories of the Locarno Treaty, Belgium, Italy, and Britain, "in execution of the stipulations of the Covenant of the League and the Locarno agreements." This, apart from possible preparatory measures, would be a "collective action that would be decided by the Council of the League and by the Locarno guarantors."[4]

But on whom could the French count? The Ethiopian war ended what there was of the Stresa front and eroded Locarno. One could not rely on the Italians, who threatened to cut remaining ties if the oil sanction was applied. Yet to introduce the League would mean relying on precisely the effectiveness of sanctions, this time against Germany. The British had turned aside Flandin's appeal for bilateral collaboration. It had to be collective action or nothing. At the forthcoming meeting of the Committee of Eighteen, therefore, despite Italian warnings, the French should not undermine the League. This did not preclude showing some goodwill toward Italy. It seemed best, in a fluid situation, to preserve international attachments, however fragile.

An oil embargo would be both ineffective and dangerous. Flandin had this out with Eden when they met in Geneva on 2 March. The danger lay in Mussolini's "categorical" assertion that if the sanction were applied Italy would leave the League, refuse to sign a naval agreement, and renounce the military accords with France. Flandin said that these unequivocal warnings determined French policy—the Council of Ministers would not agree to the oil sanction.

If the sanction would in fact be ineffective, why all the fuss? Eden asked. Because Italians saw themselves "flayed alive," Flandin answered. Each additional aggravation endangered peace and rallied Italians behind Mussolini. Since the oil embargo could not end the war in a short time and hence not deprive Italians of their victory, it would merely make the League look "ridiculous." But, Eden replied, the League would look more ridiculous if it did nothing. The sanction front would crumble. A designated aggressor would be permitted to call the moves. If nothing were done, "people's thoughts" might turn to alternative sanctions, such as a shipping embargo. This, said Eden, was "much more dangerous." In addition, to do nothing would expose the League to devastating discredit in the United States. But, important as it was to Eden, American opinion was not clearly significant to France and thus had little influence on its policy formulations.[5]

The only honorable solution to this vexing Ethiopian business, as far as the French government could see, was a negotiated settlement. Prompt liquidation of the conflict was the recommendation of Flandin's minister of war, fearful of repercussions in the Islamic world. The turmoil in east Africa encouraged nationalist foment in French-controlled territories, troubled Mediterranean peoples, and created fusion groups opposed to French hegemony, groupings preyed upon by communists. At the very least, Minister Joseph Maurin warned, the current tension sowed seeds of internal trouble should the need arise to mobilize troops in France's Islamic empire. This, by extension, posed a problem for the national defense of France itself.[6]

On 27 February Mussolini told the French he did not care to go on killing Ethiopians. The time was ripe, he said, for some solution to the conflict. "Anything is possible if new sanctions are not applied." But what Mussolini seemed to have in mind was a settlement, not within the context of international authority (as with the recommendation of the Committee of Five), nor even directed by colonial officials in London and Paris (as with the Hoare-Laval proposals), but through some form of direct negotiation between his government and the emperor's.[7]

For the French government what was important was the indication that settlement might be possible. Thus the "new peace move" that Flandin pressed on Eden when they met in Geneva on the morning of 2 March. Italy had now won the war in the north and controlled the passes at Amba Alaji that opened to the south. Only one army stood between Badoglio's forces and Addis Ababa. Officials in Rome thought the war would be over by the rains—six weeks was Mussolini's guess. An article the previous day in *Il Popolo d'Italia* stated: "With the occupation of Amba Alaji the old scores between Italy and Ethiopia are now militarily and morally settled."[8] All this was enough for Flandin. It might, he said, be the last chance for settlement.

Eden gave in without objection. Who knew whether there was hope? What Eden saw was that only a wrenching row could force a decision on oil at this session of the Committee of Eighteen. And Eden, with the cabinet decision of support a secret in his pocket, could show it was not the British who were letting down the League. Furthermore, he intended to avoid any of the direct involvement in peace planning such as had discredited Hoare. Any approach to the parties must be left to the League, to the agency created to follow the dispute, the Committee of Thirteen. The report of the League's Committee of Five gave plenty of room for manuever and, with its provisions for League assistance and a frank exchange of territory, was more acceptable than anything like the Hoare-Laval proposals, which conceded large areas to barely disguised Italian occupation.

Meanwhile, said Eden, it would be appropriate to combine "some step toward the oil sanction with a step along the path of reconciliation." The Committee of Eighteen might set a date—"say three or four weeks ahead" —when the embargo would go into effect should the two parties not agree to negotiate on the basis of the report of the Committee of Five. For the committee to fix a date, Flandin warned, "was too much like an ultimatum to Italy," and he asked if Eden intended formally to *propose* the embargo at the meeting. Eden said he hoped this would not be necessary. "It would be best to arrange matters privately in advance and not have any difficulties in public." Working with Avenol, Eden and Flandin agreed to postpone any decision on the oil sanction by the Committee of Eighteen for "say forty-eight hours," while the Committee of Thirteen called for a cease-fire and for a prompt reply accepting negotiations. Only then, if there was no satisfactory response, would the Committee of Eighteen meet to decide on the application of the oil sanction.[9]

No one foresaw, of course, how disastrous this delay was to prove for the League. The Committee of Eighteen met on 2 March 1936. Before discussion on the question of oil, Flandin recommended that the committee adjourn to let the Committee of Thirteen make "another urgent appeal" to end the war. He proposed no date for a later decision. The peace appeal was to get under way, as Flandin wanted, without reference to sanctions. It was thus with shock that the French delegation heard Eden state that the appeal procedure "need not cause any undue delay" in imposing the oil embargo. He had to "make plain" to the committee that the British government favored "the early application of such a sanction if the other principal supplying and transporting States who were Members of the League of Nations were prepared to do likewise."[10]

Eden's revelation of the British position took everyone by surprise. In view of his moderate speech to the Commons exactly one week before and his accommodating tone with Flandin, a strong stand was not expected. His declaration—so the alarmed French delegation said to him—constituted a threat to Italy that would jeopardize the success of the appeal.

Delegates asked themselves three questions. Why did the British government, at last and after such lingering uncertainty, decide to come down on the side of an oil sanction regardless of the probable noncooperation of the United States and in the face of French opposition? Why did Eden keep this decision a secret for five days, permitting the impression of a more equivocal stand? Why did he choose that moment for his announcement, bringing together without warning what the French wanted to keep apart—the threat of the oil sanction and the hope of a negotiated settlement—knowing as he did that such an implied ultimatum risked nullifying the peace appeal to which he had agreed?

Flandin was bewildered and angry. Eden had let him down. He tried to take the sting out of it for Rome. To Bova Scoppa, heading the Italian delegation, Flandin said Eden's rigid position found little support among other delegates. It was hard to swallow Eden's instransigent remarks, he said, but if Mussolini accepted the general principle of negotiation while his "prestige was in full glory following the recent victories"—which both Flandin and Avenol assumed were enough to assuage Italian pride—then Italy would have the support of France.[11]

Puzzled over the motivation of the British cabinet, Flandin cabled his ambassador in Washington, saying he was struck by Eden's emphasis on the need to keep the sympathy of American opinion. Was there some development there that had moved the British to such a resolute stand? Probably not, replied the ambassador. It was just that the British, worried about the future, wanted as a general practice to keep on the good side of the Americans.[12] At the moment, however, stress on this theme only confused the French, who were given no reason to value it.

Eden's handling of the situation at the Committee of Eighteen was maladroit. One explanation for it was that recent Italian military victories, after so much belittling of Italian prospects, had frightened the British and set them to using the League to defend the empire. On this view, the delegates' resentment arose from being misled for so long over what was revealed now, after all, as the true British interest.[13] Some in Geneva thought Eden's declaration was just for domestic political advantage, able to be neutralized by success in negotiation. In that case, however, did not Eden's announcement compromise the states who followed Britain? The Russian decision on oil, for example, was still not made. Now, if the embargo was proposed, the Soviet Union would have to accede to it.[14] Grandi gave much of the explanation, however, in a dispatch to Rome. The cabinet decision was related to rearmament policy. Trades Union support was to be won, by an anti-Fascist policy, through the League. Eden, borne to office on the wave of protest against Hoare's secret dealings, would risk his position if he went along with Flandin without a clear stand on the oil issue.[15]

In London, dismayed senior Foreign Office officials had been told neither of the cabinet decision nor that Eden might make such a declaration. These "reflective and prudent men," as the French ambassador, Charles Corbin, called them, thought Eden was carried away by the sanctionist atmosphere of Geneva, where, they held, heroics led to disaster. These officials thought Eden was influenced, not by experience or a sound overview of his department, but by his direct entourage, in Corbin's words, "younger men, imbued by theory and lacking practical experience."[16] There is a point to this. Eden, at thirty-eight, was an outsider to the department. He stood self-consciously aloof from the influence of Vansittart and Vansittart's friends, upon whom Hoare had so greatly depended. His "team" was made up of like-minded Leaguers—his parliamentary secretary, Lord Cranborne (then forty-two and later marquis of Salisbury); his diplomatic adviser, William Strang (forty-two); his private secretaries, Robert Hankey (thirty, son of Cabinet Secretary Maurice Hankey) and, after January 1936, Oliver Hardy (forty-two).

Eden's behavior at this meeting on 2 March ("nervous, unpredictable, and 'un-English,'" Swiss Foreign Secretary Motta called it),[17] raised the most hackles for the failure of advance notice. Eden might have gone along with Flandin's appeal; he might have seen fit to make his announcement even at the risk (or with the intent) of compromising this appeal. But he might also have avoided the confusion and resentment felt by many delegations—above all those from the states of the Balkan and Little ententes—who were loyal supporters of British moves at Geneva. Eden's statement to the committee was the first they heard that the British government would adhere to an oil sanction. The decision had been made on 26 February, five days before. Not until 2 March was anyone given news of it. Yet advance warning was needed to prepare positions of support for the committee meeting. It would only have taken a few telephone calls. It is hard to understand why these were not made. The cabinet had instructed Eden to "avoid taking the lead" and to act "with as little publicity to himself as possible," but it had also stressed that cooperation with other members of the League was essential.[18] Delegations at Geneva would learn of the cabinet's decision in any case. That they were not given it in advance, that they found it out only when it took the form of a threatening ultimatum to Italy, was particularly galling to the representatives of those states who had recently concluded agreements of military assistance with Great Britain, envisioning precisely that the oil sanction might lead to war. These delegates, treated to satisfactory explanations of British policy in the conversations leading to the military agreements, were now kept in the dark.

Eden's explanation to the cabinet was that, with Flandin set against the sanction and for a peace appeal, the situation was different from that envisioned by cabinet instructions directing him to take no initiative. He agreed to an appeal, but it was clear from talks with other delegates that something must be said *in the committee* about "intentions on the subject of sanctions, otherwise the world at large, and Italy in particular, would assume the oil sanction was dropped." Some comment on his part was "unavoidable."[19]

The peace appeal was the work of Flandin. Eden shared neither his fear of further sanctions nor his hope that much could come of the appeal. Despite these reservations, Eden went along. The French draft spoke of opening negotiations "within the framework of the League of Nations and in the spirit of the Covenant with a view to the cessation of hostilities." Only later was added the phrase "and the definite restoration of peace." When Eden noted there was no mention of the Committee of Five's report—the only existing League-sponsored settlement proposal—Flandin replied that Eden's ultimatum-like statement on 2 March to the Committee of Eighteen had so lessened the chances of success that Italy must not be further provoked to turn down the appeal. He went along with Flandin's request to extend the time for reply to one week, despite his position that the limit should be forty-eight hours. When Eden asked about a shorter time period, Flandin's League representative Paul-Boncour said this would be a "final effort at conciliation" and Italy should not be given the excuse of lack of time for refusing. Eden made no objections. He had no alternative proposals. On 3 March 1936 the Committee of Thirteen issued the appeal, setting 10 March as the day to consider the replies.[20]

Flandin, Frank Walters wrote, was left "in possession of the field."[21] Italian diplomacy had turned the trick. The oil sanction was again postponed. In return, Flandin said that Mussolini must now make "a European gesture" and accept the principle of negotiation. If he did that, Flandin promised, he would call a subcommittee to examine possible terms, but even this would be postponed until the middle of March. In the meantime, Flandin asked Italy to suspend hostilities. If Italian pride was satisfied, if the old issues were truly settled, such suspension was in order. A cease-fire would be of little practical importance, he argued, since the rainy season was almost upon the Italian armies and operations would soon stop. During a cease-fire as well as during the rains, roads and supplies could be prepared for later warfare.[22]

Oil sanctions were not yet dead. Eden said the appeal procedure "need not cause any undue delay." If both parties did not reply affirmatively the Committee of Eighteen would meet immediately after the 10 March deadline. A second session of the petroleum experts was in the works. Having first examined the efficacy of an oil sanction, they now, pending a decision on whether such an embargo would be applied, were to study methods of application. This committee met three times between 4 and 7 March and on the seventh issued its report (lost in the confusion of the Rhineland crisis), recommending that the tanker sanction be added to the oil embargo.[23]

The debate on oil would soon resume. Thanks to Eden's threatening statement before the Committee of Eighteen on 2 March, Flandin pointed out to him the next day, the chance of success for the peace appeal was "notably diminished." If the embargo were applied and Italy withdrew from the League and from Locarno, Germany would be "tempted to profit by the situation in the demilitarized zone" of the Rhineland. Then, Flandin asked, would the British government be "ready to support France, even alone, in the maintenance of the demilitarized zone?" Before the French made a decision on the oil sanction they had to have an assurance from Britain over the Rhineland.[24]

The Rhineland

Flandin's request was predictable, with a predictable result. Ever since the beginning of the Italian-Ethiopian affair the French had asked the British for assurances of support on the Continent in return for cooperation against Italy, and these they never secured. The cabinet on 5 March merely set up a committee to examine the extent of British obligations under Locarno. Remilitarization of the Rhineland was not of major interest to the British. Italian imperialism was not of major interest to the French. Leaders of each state made little effort to envision how cooperation on either issue might serve for the future. So neither government helped the other much.

By March 1936 the threat of Mediterranean war seemed over. At the end of February the Southern Department in the Foreign Office circulated a memorandum, "Mussolini's Future." The question was: Did Britain want a weak or a strong Italian state? The answer was: British interests were best served if Italy was weak. Italy was an unreliable international actor. "The only constant element in Italian policy during the past fifteen years has been its inconstancy." The pattern would continue. "It follows that the relegation of Italy to the position of a second-class power need not be regretted by the governments whose interests lie in stability." "Even friendship with England is an argument in favour of a weak Italy," which would place "higher value on financial and political cooperation." Such cooperation would be more likely if Mussolini fell. So, the report concluded: "Though we should do everything we reasonably can to reestablish friendly relations with Italy, and though it is not our business to punish Italy or to punish Mussolini, yet it is not on balance a British interest to protect Mussolini from the consequences of his own acts, to preserve the Fascist regime, or to safeguard the threatened status of Italy as a first-class power."[25]

Neither Laval nor Flandin would have drawn such a conclusion. The French ambassador Corbin, on 6 March, pointed to a further divergence of views on Italy. The recent "blackmail" practiced by Mussolini, Italy's flirtation with Germany, and Mussolini's pressure on France with the threat to denounce Locarno and the League were judged "intolerable" in Britain and contributed to the increasing hostility. There was, said Corbin, a tendency among the British public to group Hitler and Mussolini as dictators responsible for Europe's troubles and to call a plague on both their houses.[26] In France officials worried about the one and sought cooperation with the other—much different from the British moods of indifference or rejection.

On 3 March 1936 the Committee of Thirteen sent the peace appeal to the governments of Italy and Ethiopia. Eden asked Barton to apply some gentle persuasion, but not anywhere near the degree Hoare had recommended in December. Now, said Eden, it would be "both improper and imprudent for us to volunteer any advice." On the other hand, he told Barton, Haile Selassie "lost nothing in the public estimation by placing himself in the hands of the League."[27]

What else, indeed, could the Ethiopian government do, with its northern armies defeated and the invaders poised in Tigre? On 4 March the Ethiopian delegation at Geneva sent a telegram to Addis Ababa stating that Ethiopia's only hope was to "accept conciliation immediately since an interval of time would help us in our reorganization."[28] The next day the emperor agreed to open talks.[29] On the sixth the Ethiopian minister in London told Eden that Haile Selassie could no longer accept the terms of the Committee of Five if that meant Italian advisers on Ethiopian soil. Such a concession was ruled out by the invasion. Again he asked if Britain would give Ethiopia dominion status, and again this idea was turned down. Anything done for Ethiopia had to go through the League.[30]

Italian diplomats, of course, were elated by the possibilities for delay and obstruction. They wanted to stall until Badoglio's renewed offensive could "clarify the situation" in the north and until Graziani got an offensive under way in the south. The play was to accept the invitation "as we had always done in the past," in Aloisi's words, but without any degree of commitment. To make use of the volumes of nauseating documentation on Ethiopian barbarism, they could recommend that as part of any negotiation the League should investigate these Italian charges (a new installment of which was presented to the League on 28 February 1936), claiming that uncivilized Ethiopia should be put under European control. That should take enough time. "Moral: Eden played the hypocrite; imitate him," wrote Aloisi on 3 March.[31]

The pope sent Tacchi Venturi to Mussolini on 4 March to recommend prompt acceptance. Mussolini turned the priest aside with a reference to Eden's threatening statement. He could never agree to an appeal presented as "an ultimatum, an imposition, a humiliation . . . a pistol at the throat."[32] Suvich said that if the League encouraged Italy to deal directly with the emperor some solution might be reached, but negotiations at Geneva could present insuperable difficulties.[33]

Mussolini was hardening. He rejected the string-along tactics proposed by the Palazzo Chigi. On 5 March he drafted a reply to the League, which he intended to submit first to his Council of Ministers due to meet on the evening of 7 March. His reply was simple: he would not accept the appeal under threat. Attolico claimed Mussolini decided on 7 March to withdraw from the League altogether.[34] Yet one day later, on 8 March, within the prescribed deadline, an official reply was handed in at Geneva stating that the Italian government agreed "in principle to the opening of negotiations."[35]

What happened to change the Italian response was not that Hitler sent German troops into the demilitarized zone of the Rhineland on 7 March 1936, but that he did so without advance notice to Mussolini and accompanied the move with a speech before the Reichstag meant to conciliate the western democracies and prevent a Locarno front against him. Mussolini was in the midst of a flirtation with Hitler. He hinted a closer move to Berlin as he prepared to cut his ties with the west. It was of use to his diplomacy that this prospect agitated the British and French. Thus, Hitler's conciliatory words to Italy's enemies were viewed in Rome as a rebuff, a stab in the back, causing extreme anxiety and complicating Italian diplomacy. This was, in a way, what the British wanted. Eden told Harold Nicolson that to prevent another German war he was "prepared to make great concessions to German appetites provided they will sign a disarmament treaty and join the League of Nations." Contention between Germany and Italy meant, for Eden, that he need not soft-pedal in regard to Italy.[36]

Hitler's excuse for occupying the Rhineland was that the mutual assistance treaty between France and the Soviet Union violated the Locarno agreements, after which Germany would not hold them binding. The treaty was ratified by the Chamber of Deputies on 27 February, proposed to the Senate for swift action, and passed on 12 March. The Chamber's action prompted Hitler's move. There were other reasons for this striking riposte, among them domestic political considerations, the wish to anticipate any agreement concerning Locarno by the British and French, and the fear of an eventual reconstitution of the Stresa front. War Minister Werner von Blomberg gave the deployment order to the German army on 2 March, and on the next day he set 7 March as the date for the advance. The Italian-Ethiopian affair had been watched closely from Berlin, and, in particular, its effect on Italy's behavior as a cosigner of Locarno played a part in the decision to act.

Hitler was not sure how far he could trust Mussolini. Some German officials worried that Mussolini might accept the peace appeal, conclude the war with the approval of Britain and France, and thereby open the way for a reconciliation with Britain and the sudden reconstitution of the Stresa front.

The advantages they counted on from a long African war and the resulting European tension would disappear. So, ran the conclusion, it was important to act while dissension among Locarno powers was still strong.[37]

On 28 February, discussing what Italy might do, Ambassador Hassell wrote from Rome:

> Any resolutions that may be adopted by the Committee of Eighteen, which is to meet on March 2, will naturally be of decisive importance for future Italian policy. Perhaps it may be possible to take our decision as to how we will react to a ratification [of the Franco-Soviet treaty] only after the question of whether more drastic sanctions are to be applied has become clear. In case of more drastic sanctions we need have no doubt that Italy will remain completely passive in the event of proceedings by the Locarno Powers against the German "sharp reaction"; indeed an active attitude against Locarno [on the part of Italy] would be entirely possible.[38]

On 28 February Hassell talked with Mussolini. Italy would leave the League if another sanction were imposed, and Mussolini would end his support of Locarno. Italy "would not participate in any counter-reaction which might be called for by a German reaction to the ratification." The expression sent to Berlin was: "Italians would stand at the window and be interested onlookers."[39]

This was a relief to Hitler, who was genuinely fearful that some sanction might be placed against Germany.[40] Mussolini's assurance, it appears, encouraged him to act. But in the process he undercut what he knew was the Italian position of opposition to the League of Nations, just at the delicate moment of the peace appeal from the Committee of Thirteen and the imminent decision on the oil embargo, and this is what made the Italians so furious.

In his speech before the Reichstag on 7 March, Hitler spoke of Germany's "unchangeable longing for a real pacification of Europe." He spoke of cooperation in Europe, cooperation with those very states arraigned against Italy over Ethiopia. He offered to conclude "new agreements for the creation of a system of peaceful security in Europe" on the basis of a number of proposals that included new arrangements in the west, an air pact, non-aggression pacts with states bordering in the east, and, lastly, "now that Germany's equality of rights and the restoration of its full sovereignty over the entire territory of the German Reich finally have been attained, the German government considers the chief reason for withdrawal from the League of Nations removed. They are therefore willing to re-enter the League of Nations."[41]

This was the heavy blow to Mussolini. At first, and later, the Rhineland seemed a fortunate event. The pope said Mussolini was "lucky, very lucky."[42] The Germans pointed out the advantages of an action that so completely diverted attention from Africa, from Italy, and indeed from existing sanctions. But these advantages were obscured, at least for the moment, in the news that Germany had offered to rejoin the League and associate itself with Italy's foes in new European arrangements. This news, delivered to Mussolini, only minutes before he entered the Council of Ministers prepared to turn down the peace appeal, had a shattering effect. Here he was about to propose a reply implicitly threatening, at the very least, withdrawal from the League if the oil sanction were imposed. This threat had strength precisely because the other two great revisionist powers, Germany and Japan, had themselves withdrawn to take up a free hand. Now Germany turned the tables, seemed ready to cooperate with the enemy camp, and the Italian threat lost its sting.

Suvich said anything had been expected from Germany—except that. Mussolini thought his most important weapon was struck from his hand and that Hitler had betrayed him. Italian officials, including Mussolini, were sure that Germany, once in the League, would vote in favor of sanctions against Italy.[43] Grandi said Hitler's overtures for new settlements were part of a "brutal program for the Germanization of Europe," and Mussolini saw Europe facing an entirely new situation.[44] As Hassell said, the "psychological effect" on Mussolini "at this critical moment for Italy was extraordinary, but it might have been 'catastrophic' in the true sense of the word if he had received it an hour later."[45]

It was a close call. As it was, despite Mussolini's initial response of truculent anger and his predilection to press ahead regardless of the danger, the moderates in the Palazzo Chigi got their hands on his draft reply to the Committee of Thirteen and recast it to state agreement "in principle" to talks. There was no mention of the spirit of the Covenant or of negotiating within the framework of the League, on which Eden set so much store. On the other hand, there was nothing of reservations, such as that sanctions must cease before talks began, or of conditions, such as no withdrawal from conquered territory, or of charges, such as Ethiopia's unfitness for membership in the comity of nations. The Rhineland occupation, and Hitler's speech, restrained the Italian diplomatic hand. Hitler, however, forced European states to reckon directly with Germany, and the ongoing action against Italy seemed much less important as attention turned north of the Alps. This unexpected breathing space, Italian diplomats hoped, could, with the help of France, be used to get rid of sanctions altogether.

On 8 March Flandin and Van Zeeland called an urgent meeting of the Council of the League for 14 March, in London, to discuss the Rhineland situation. At issue were the effectiveness of the collective security mechanism to deal with this treaty violation, the possibility of applying sanctions, the utility and strength of the connection between Britain and France, and, fundamentally, the worth of the League itself. For France, *this* was now the test case. And, to their dismay, French officials found the British more lukewarm on the question of the Rhine than Frenchmen allowed themselves to feel over Ethiopia. Hence, French interest in the Ethiopian matter declined sharply, becoming mainly the wish to end the war as quickly, if not so honorably, as possible. The British insisted that the Rhine and the Mareb represented two distinct issues and should not be confused. This was no comfort to the French. The Rhine was on their doorstep. If the League could not stand up against a European treaty violation at least as much as it stood up against one in Africa, what value was there in maintaining a "test" that could not be applied further?

Walters summed up the demoralization and lack of purpose at the Council on 14 March: "The meeting in London seemed to be, for the first time in the history of the Council, a gathering of individual States possessing no common legal or moral basis of action; but each concerned with its particular interests in relation to the resurgent German power."[46] The cause of collective security made no advance. After the meeting the Belgians and the Dutch began a return to neutrality. The British and French went at one another, requesting and withholding pledges of mutual security, neither clear of the other's intentions and, in the event, letting each other down. Italy, without a policy, attended and held aloof.

"The question of the moment is to learn if Europe will or will not become German," Massigli warned the British.[47] No decisive results in land operations against Germany were possible outside the framework of a coalition, said the French general staff. Yet the British did nothing, so nothing happened. The French concluded they were abandoned and betrayed.[48] The Council likewise took no action. No sanctions were placed against Germany. Advocates of collective security, in the spring of 1936, were left disillusioned, suspicious, and aware of seemingly insuperable weakness.

The British Chiefs of Staff received a report on 16 March entitled "Condition of Our Forces to Meet the Possibility of War with Germany." Naval and air forces at home, the report went, "are denuded to an extent almost unparalleled in the past. The despatch of military reenforcing units to Egypt has resulted in a situation which will prevent us from sending overseas any further formations of any kind without mobilization." The crisis in the Mediterranean left the island exposed: "We have at present no naval forces in Home waters which could take any effective action to protect our trade routes or prevent German forces from bombarding our coasts." Almost all ammunition was in the Mediterranean. Only sixteen antiaircraft guns and twenty-five search lights were on the south coast. It was possible to man only one-third of the stations considered necessary to defend London. As of 16 March 1936, "the R.A.F. could produce no offensive or defensive effort whatever." There was only one way to immediate improvement: peace "guaranteed in the Mediterranean" and return of the force assembled there.[49] The implications of this judgment for British policy in the Italian-Ethiopian affair are obvious.

Concentration on the Rhineland and preparations for the Council meeting in London resulted in postponing the meeting of the Committee of Thirteen scheduled for 11 March to consider replies to the appeal for negotiation. Eager to have at least a semblance of negotiation under way so as to defer even further the decision on the oil sanction, Flandin and Van Zeeland suggested that the Committee of Thirteen (the Council without Italy) meet in London when the Council (at which Grandi represented Italy) met to discuss the Rhineland and Locarno. The Italians hinted that despite their obligations under Locarno they would take no action in Europe so long as they were exposed to sanctions. Flandin and Van Zeeland scouted the idea of direct negotiations between the belligerents, with a simultaneous suspension of fighting and sanctions. Flandin suggested to the British that Italian support in Europe was worth the direct withdrawal of sanctions. Negotiations and the suspension of sanctions would lead to the reconstitution of the Stresa front.[50]

To these ideas the Italian government replied that it had decided to negotiate directly with the Ethiopians. It would keep the League informed. It would not get involved, in any case, in questions of general policy, conditions, or cooperation with the League. No League observer or intermediary could be present at the bilateral talks. As to the suspension of hostilities and the concomitant lifting of sanctions, this would be possible only after progress in preliminary bilateral talks. Otherwise, the benefit of stopping the fighting would fall entirely to the Ethiopians.[51]

As to Flandin's suggestion of lifting sanctions altogether, that depended on British approval. Throughout the month of March 1936 the cabinet took no stand, although the issue of dropping sanctions was raised, exacerbated by the problem of what to do about Germany. On 16 March the cabinet heard First Lord Monsell warn that the only ships in Europe capable of dealing with the German pocket battleships were the battle cruisers *Hood, Renown,* and *Repulse.* The last was in dock, the first two in the Mediterranean. British shipping was exposed. Air Secretary Swinton said that with so many aircraft and airmen in Egypt the position at home was "deplorable." It would, he said, "be difficult to imagine a worse situation so far as the Air Force was concerned if any emergency should arise." From this came the suggestion that if no oil sanction were imposed some forces could be brought back from the Mediterranean, but there was no decision.[52]

The Rhineland crisis gave the service chiefs a chance to press their case as never before. On 17 March, approving the report "Condition of Our Forces," they concluded: "If there is the smallest danger of being drawn into commitments which might lead to war with Germany, we ought at once to disengage ourselves from our present responsibilities in the Mediterranean, which have exhausted practically the whole of our meagre forces." With ships, planes, and troops locked in the distant sea, the country was so defenseless there was little point in staff conversations with the Locarno powers, as Britain had so little to contribute. On 1 April the service chiefs repeated their conclusion. "If we seriously consider the possibility of war with Germany, it is essential that the Services be relieved of their Mediterranean responsibilities, otherwise our position is utterly unsafe."[53]

A political decision was not made. And nowhere was there mention of recalling the Committee of Eighteen to make a decision on the oil embargo. To the cabinet on 19 March Eden warned that if sanctions were removed, as the French wanted, they would never be reimposed. The instructions he sought at this cabinet related only to the meeting of the Committee of Thirteen, set now for 23 March, not to discuss sanctions, but to consider the replies to the negotiation appeals sent out three weeks before. Before sanctions were dropped, Eden said, some prospect of a settlement more tangible than a mere armistice was needed. He wished to propose that the chairman of the Committee of Thirteen and Secretary-General Avenol get in touch with both sides—given their affirmative replies—and examine the prospects for negotiation. Once a viable peace seemed in sight, then further decisions about sanctions could be made.[54]

The Committee of Thirteen met on 23 March and resolved to do as Eden suggested. This, to Italian relief, was not accompanied by deadline threat of an oil embargo, by any conditions, or by a direct demand to stop the fighting. Meantime, the diplomatic scene was darkened by renewed Italian suspicion of British intentions as Italian forces reached the shore of Lake Tana and the source of the Blue Nile, by the uproar about attacks on undefended Red Cross units, and by an intense use of gas on the northern front in late March and early April. The war was back in progress as, in mid-March, Badoglio prepared for what he hoped would be a final drive southward.

Mai Chio and Ashangi

On 7 March Mussolini announced that Badoglio's victories over the armies of Rases Mulugeta, Seyum, Kassa, and Imru, the conquest of Amba Aradam, and the posting of the Italian flag at the pass of Amba Alaji had "broken the Ethiopian northern front."[55] Badoglio then set out to occupy all of northern Ethiopia and impress upon the inhabitants the strength and permanence of Italian rule. Should there be a settlement, Italy would have at least the north under firm control. And before starting the final act, before an advance on Dessye and thence on Addis Ababa, it was well to have the area to the rear organized.

During March Badoglio pushed out from Tigre. A column led by Colonel Vittorio Ruggero, the leading political agent of the secret service in the field, was sent to occupy Sardo, near the border of French Somaliland on the Dessye-Djibouti road. Ruggero was to make political accommodation with the sultan of Aussa. He was to be in a position to threaten, if the need arose, the Djibouti railroad and Ethiopia's eastward line of communication. He was to be ready to move westward against Dessye. And, perhaps above all, he was to be on the spot to arrange any corridor to Assab that might be made part of a peace settlement in negotiation with the emperor.[56] The occupation of Sardo caused great anxiety to Haile Selassie, and he was powerless to stop it.

At the other end of the line of operations Badoglio sent a mechanized column 200 miles to Gondar, the capital of Gojam. As the province was practically denuded of Ethiopian troops, the forces would thus have an open road to Debra Markos from which to threaten Addis Ababa. Gondar was also close by Lake Tana, and it would be an easy move to occupy the borders of the lake and press against the frontier of the Anglo-Egyptian Sudan. The move to the Gojam region was completed in the first week of April. It was seen by some as a test of British intention, for it touched for the first time an area of imperial concern: the headwaters of the Blue Nile. On 2 April General Enrico Caviglia wrote in his diary that if the British protested "it will become clear they are following their own interests, and not a principle, that is, of the League of Nations. This will make them act." Aloisi wrote on 1 April: "One begins to see the danger in our military victories."[57]

The fear that Britain wanted war resurfaced. Why else did they strip the island to concentrate their forces in the Mediterranean? Aloisi likened the danger to another Fashoda.[58] The initials "S.d.N.", went the joke, stood less for "Société des Nations" than for "Source du Nile," as Britain manipulated the League for its imperial purposes. Yet nothing was very clear. In Rome Drummond was at a loss. "I ask myself what I am doing here and if it would not be just as well if I left."[59]

On 3 April Grandi gave emphatic assurances from Mussolini that the Italians were "more than ever conscious of their obligations" and "had no intention whatsoever of overlooking or repudiating them." Eden relayed these to Egypt with the comment that he saw "no reason to suppose that Italian policy towards or activities in Abyssinia threaten to invalidate" commitments to respect rights on the Nile watersheds. On 7 April Suvich gave direct assurance to Egypt that Italy "has not, nor ever can have in the future, any designs of conquest or colonisation in Egypt." Italy would respect Egyptian rights at Tana.[60]

Certainly the move of the Gondar column worried the Egyptians, who, reflecting that they had not been a party to the Anglo-Italian agreements of 1906 and 1925 concerning Lake Tana, wanted assurances now that the flow of the Blue Nile would not be interrupted. The prime minister of Egypt on 4 April asked if the British intended to send troops to occupy Lake Tana, now that the Italians were nearby. The answer was no. Back in August 1935 the general staff had warned that such an expedition would be "costly and difficult" and "unsound strategically." The Maffey report confirmed that such action was not necessary so long as British rights were not invalidated. So Eden replied to Cairo on 7 April that as "Gondar and Lake Tsana are Abyssinian territory . . . there could be no question of the occupation of this part of Abyssinia . . . for the purpose of blocking the road to the Italians." Tana was not an issue.[61]

The Italian soldiers reached Sardo and Gondar without incident. These were the end points of an arc, 360 miles long, that formed the Italian front and behind which lay 100,000 square miles of newly occupied territory. Lines of communication and supply were ready for the final drive. In the center, due south of Makale, past Amba Aradam, and along the edge of the high plateau toward Dessye, an Italian column stretched out, at the end of March, thirty miles beyond Amba Alaji to Mai Chio.

On 19 February Haile Selassie had moved north from his headquarters at Dessye to the region of Quoram, just south of Mai Chio on the Makale-Dessye road. There he waited with the last of the Ethiopian armies of the north. Gone was his hope that Kassa and Imru would fall back to the Alaji Pass to join him in defense of Dessye. Imru was in flight, trying vainly to raise a force in the west—vainly, for Gojam was in revolt and imperial control over the empire was disintegrating. There was much desertion and betrayal. Kassa and Seyum reached Haile Selassie in mid-March, without a single armed man. On 23 March, the emperor acknowledged his desperate situation to Imru. "Our army, famous throughout Europe for its valour, has lost its name. . . . From the League we have so far derived no hope and no benefit."[62]

23 March was the day the Committee of Thirteen met, at long last, to acknowledge the replies to its appeal for negotiation issued three weeks before. Its decision was that Chairman Madariaga and Secretary-General Avenol were to get in touch with the two governments. Nothing was said about a further meeting of the Committee of Eighteen. Nothing was said about oil. There was no time limit. The emperor was right—there was no hope from Geneva. That same day, speaking in Rome, Mussolini announced

a new policy of economic autarky for Italy. While the sky was not yet completely clear, he said, what clouds remained would be rapidly dispersed.[63]

Haile Selassie, self-admittedly no soldier, was on his own. He commanded 31,000 men, all that stood between Badoglio and Addis Ababa. Several courses were open to him. He could refuse to give battle and move off into the fields, restricting himself to guerrilla action against Italian lines of communication. He could move southward, to Dessye or beyond. That he had these alternatives tormented Badoglio. If the emperor took to the countryside, as he had long advised his commanders, the opportunity for a conclusive battle would be lost. The northern war would drag on. If the emperor, undefeated, moved southward, Badoglio would have to organize a large-scale battle perhaps hundreds of miles in advance of his bases. In either case, there were great logistical difficulties. Caution and delay would mean the issue would not be clear before the rains. And Graziani might get to Addis Ababa first.

The emperor decided on yet a third course: to confront the Italians in direct battle at Mai Chio before they became any stronger. In the middle of March he moved his forces northward, beyond Lake Ashangi. Badoglio's relief was immense. He wired Mussolini, "Whether the Negus attacked or whether he awaited my attack, his fate was now decided: he would be completely defeated."[64]

The Ethiopians had more than the ground force with which to contend. In preparation for their advance the Italians in mid-March 1936 began to use gas, in what was to become the most intensive use during the war, against the population and encampments on the plains of Ashangi and Quoram and against the emperor's emplacements in the Quoram hills. There was no defense against the planes, dropping bombs and cannisters of gas and fitted with sprayers to distribute the poison more widely. The emperor had only one or two, largely symbolic, antiaircraft guns. Again, all that remained was to protest to Europe. On 17 March Ethiopia filed with the League a formal complaint that Italy was in violation of international conventions and agreements, and the same complaint was sent to signatories of the Hague Convention number 4 of 1907 and the Geneva Protocol of 1925 (to which Ethiopia had acceded on 18 September 1935 as the war approached). On 20 March direct appeal was made to the British government to stop Italians from using asphyxiating gases and bombs on civilian populations.[65]

Although on 30 March 1936 Lord Halifax told the House of Lords he had slight information on the matter—a statement received in Addis Ababa with "pained amazement"—vivid reports were appearing in the press, the public in Britain and France was greatly shocked, and governments, in fact possessing plenty of evidence, took somber note.[66] The Foreign Office had received "conclusive proof" on 30 January 1936 that gas was in use on the southern front. The British military attaché had picked up that evidence in December 1935 at Dagabur. What could be done? Not much, said the Palazzo Chigi, for the Italian foreign office noted that the Geneva Protocol did not permit interference by a signatory state unless directly touched by a violation.[67] Yet indiscriminate use of gas was hard to justify. Talk of its use as a form of retaliation or reprisal convinced no one. What, after all, then became of "the civilizing mission"? There was a distinction to be made between irresponsible atrocities of undisciplined warriors and the use of gas, which was a responsible act of a government.

On 6 April 1936 the British cabinet discussed "this great historic fact," the use of gas against civilians and contrary to international agreements. There were imperial consequences, the Ethiopian foreign minister warned: the adverse effect such warfare had on "relations between white and coloured races everywhere."[68] And, while the cabinet decided it was inappropriate to make a direct approach to Italy on behalf of Ethiopia, there was Britain itself to think of. Vansittart told the French ambassador that "the future existence of Europe would depend to some extent at least on not allowing the use of gas . . . to pass in silence."[69] The British public, the point was made in the cabinet, could justifiably ask "how, if poison gas could not be prevented in this war, it could be prevented elsewhere, e.g. in Europe." But the cabinet felt the only appropriate recourse was to propose an impartial inquiry through the League and call upon respect for the laws of war. Existing conventions did not contain enforcement mechanisms. International prohibitions could be rendered effective by stopping manufacture of such weapons, but, the cabinet concluded, "if all the countries of the world were democracies this might be easier."[70]

Gas was now a weapon with which to reckon. Italy, Germany, and the Soviet Union had it ready. Italy was putting it to use. The democracies must have some too, or risk the fate of hapless Ethiopia. During 1935 and 1936 the *Revue internationale de la Croix-Rouge* ran monthly articles on protecting civilian populations against chemical warfare, detailing measures for "passive defense" undertaken by Red Cross chapters, concerned citizens, and governments. The French government, for example, regulated the manufacture and sale of gas masks by a decree-law of 30 October 1935. And after Mai Chio the French government decided to go ahead with gas production. On 4 April 1936, at a meeting of the service ministers and chiefs, Premier Sarraut approved construction, on a trial basis, of a factory to manufacture mustard gas.[71]

The British took a bit longer. On 4 April Eden told the Belgian ambassador that, great as the danger was to the democracies, since dictators could go ahead regardless, "British opinion would not tolerate the manufacture here of poison gas." Three months later, on 10 July, with the note that the Geneva Protocol forbade the employment but not the production and storage of gas, the War Office received permission to produce, in the words of the new chief of the Imperial General Staff, Sir Cyril Deverell, the "most potent form of gas which was now available."[72]

The emperor, facing the gas attacks, decided on a final stand. He would lead the one remaining army of the north against the invader. This decision, which led to his defeat, was later much criticized, but it seemed to Haile Selassie that he had little choice. If he, personally, did not act, he would lose his authority and honor. His chiefs, whose feudal powers he could not ignore, advised him to go into battle. He announced his decision to his entourage on 21 March, two days after Kassa and Seyum arrived with reports of the total collapse of the northern front. He saw there was to be no help from Europe. There were no acceptable terms for peace—and the horrors of gas warfare made prospects for a negotiated settlement unlikely. His army was in distress. There was no choice but to risk what remained to him or retire in dishonor to a crumbled heritage.

Haile Selassie had no false hope. He was exhausted, withdrawing into religious contemplation. He knew the risks. "The defeat of my personal army would be the end of everything," he said to his aide, Theodore Konovaloff, the last European in his camp. To take the offensive was "indispensable" for his honor. It was a political act, mainly. He admitted that "he never hoped to vanquish the Italians at one blow or reoccupy Dabare, Amba Alaji, and so on," said Konovaloff, but for the expectations of his people and to maintain personal authority he had to act. He worked with feeble materials. Against the advice of Konovaloff, he gave leading roles to incompetent feudal chiefs and he was unable to refuse their repeated appeals for delay. Haile Selassie wanted to start the offensive on 25 March, hoping to enlist some of the aroused (and bribed) local population. The days dragged on. "I know myself that it is wrong, but there is nothing to do about it," he said sadly.[73] It was not until the thirty-first that the Ethiopians advanced.

The week's delay had given Badoglio time to fortify his position and bring up reinforcements. On 29 March Mussolini authorized the use of gas at "any time and on any scale."[74] On 31 March the Ethiopians attacked, and at dawn the next day Haile Selassie ordered retreat. The battle of Mai Chio was over.

On 2 April the Ethiopian minister of foreign affairs sent a message to the legation in Paris, intercepted, of course, by the Italians.

> The military situation will become impossible. There are only 5,000 men at Lake Tana to oppose the advance, via Gondar, toward Gojam and the capital. The Italian troops have already advanced halfway between Assab and Dessye and there is not a single soldier to stop them. Ras Imru's army is much re-

duced. As to the remainder of the armies, which have dissolved, they have
joined the Emperor's army. The Emperor's army is in danger of being surrounded. Impossible to find reinforcements. Get in direct touch with Eden ex-
plaining confidentially to him the gravity of the military situation and the
immediate danger. Let us know his opinions on the immediate measures to be
taken.[75]

This was a plea in extremis, and Eden turned it down the next day. Ask for
an early meeting of the Committee of Thirteen, he told the Ethiopian envoy.
Britain also would ask for its meeting on 8 April. Meanwhile, the emperor
started south to Lake Ashangi and to Quoram, toward Dessye, with the
Italians in pursuit. He was exhausted, uncertain. Konovaloff saw him at
lunch the day the retreat began and asked what he intended to do. "I do not
know," Haile Selassie replied. "My chiefs will do nothing. My brain no
longer works." As for the Italians: "It is beyond our power to hold them
back."[76]

The retreat began in disorder and ended in demoralization and disintegration. Badoglio sought to destroy all semblance of opposition, all will to do
anything but submit. Two army corps made the pursuit, one of them
supplied by airdrop. The air force, wrote Badoglio, "sent up its aircraft,
regardless of their type, even to the last machine, in order to carry the attack
to its utmost limit and pour down their part of it from above."[77] He pressed
his advantage more ruthlessly than at any other time in the war. Bombs, and
gas of a volume yet unexperienced, rained on the survivors of Mai Chio,
trapped on the shore of Lake Ashangi.

For four days running, 4–7 April, the town of Quoram was "literally
drenched with gas." Haile Selassie said Lake Ashangi was deliberately
poisoned. John Melly, physician and leader of a volunteer British ambulance
unit wrote on 12 April: "This isn't a war—it isn't even a slaughter—it is the
torture of thousands of defenceless men, women and children with bombs
and poison gas. They're using gas incessantly, and we've treated hundreds of
cases, including infants in arms—and the world looks on—and passes by on
the other side.[78] Melly, when he wrote these words, was lucky to be operating
at all. Two weeks before, his unit, displaying the Red Cross emblem, was
almost completely destroyed by Italian bombers. While the gas did not touch
European nationals, hence there was no protest by European governments
under the Hague or Geneva conventions, the bombing of British and Swedish and Ethiopian Red Cross units in March caused considerable public
indignation in Europe. The Ethiopians formally protested to the League.
The Italians countered with another allegation of Ethiopian atrocities, and
protested in turn against "misuses of the Red Cross emblem."[79] The furor
over these incidents gave Mussolini some pause. Max Huber, president of
the International Committee of the Red Cross, went to Rome on 25 March

to explore terms for an investigation of the charges. On the twenty-eighth Mussolini told Badoglio to avoid damage to any British Red Cross units in the sensitive Gondar region.[80]

The only aid available to Ethiopian wounded came from the fourteen Ethiopian Red Cross ambulance units and the foreign volunteer units, together with some hospital facilities of greatly varying quality, run by the government and charitable institutions, in Addis Ababa, Dessye, Harar, Diredawa, and Debra Tabor.[81] An Austrian physician, with an Ethiopian unit attached to Ras Kassa's army, attended to 50,000 cases, mostly of dysentery, before the unit was destroyed by bombs in January at the second battle of Tembien. Melly, with remnants of his unit sheltered in a camouflaged grotto near Quoram, treated 3,000 wounded in the last three weeks of March. A Dutch ambulance unit there was treating another 200 patients a day. An Egyptian ambulance united treated 73,687 cases from its Harar section alone, of which 1,378 were surgical. Another 18,000 patients were attended to by five other sections. The Swedish unit, which was bombed on 30 December 1935 during Graziani's advance on Negelli, had treated 10,000 patients. Of this incident Marcel Junod wrote: the "deliberate destruction" of the Swedish unit meant the loss of "the only source of any assistance for that whole southern army. . . . Nowhere along the whole route had I seen any spot which had been bombed with such concentrated fury.[82] The doctors, nurses, and staff of these units performed heroically. Most units were destroyed or captured. A number of volunteers lost their lives—John Melly was casually shot by an Ethiopian looter during the sacking of Addis Ababa in May.

A delegation from the International Committee of the Red Cross, composed of Sidney H. Brown and Marcel Junod, a medical doctor, was sent to help the Ethiopian Red Cross chapter, to help the foreign ambulance units, and to check on the observance of international conventions. Brown and Junod each wrote a book about his experiences. To provide scenes of the war front it is enough to conclude with one or two of their observations and some sentences from the published report of this delegation.

Junod visited the front at Mai Chio, Quoram, and Lake Ashangi. After a fourteen-hour air attack the plain at Quoram, he told Brown, looked like a scene from the *Inferno*.[83] Junod wrote:

> Men were stretched out everywhere beneath the trees. There must have been thousands of them. By this time I had only one idea: to get as far away from this exploding hell as I could as quickly as possible. . . . As I came closer, my heart in my mouth, I could see the horrible suppurating burns on their feet and on their emaciated limbs. Life was already leaving bodies burned with mustard gas. . . . Who was to help them in their suffering? There were no doctors available and our ambulances had been destroyed.[84]

And, from the published report:

> Almost all the wounded were untended, without doctors, and died. The ambulances were immobilized in their shelters in the grottos, and could attend only some 200 or 300 wounded per day, i.e., those who had the strength to come to them. Relief of the wounded on the field of battle [the purpose of the Red Cross envisioned by its founder] was non-existent. It would have been necessary to treat all these wounded, bring them to the main road, and evacuate them to Waldia and Dessye; but transport was quite impossible by day owing to air attack, by night owing to the brigands.[85]

Later, in Addis Ababa, Badoglio told Junod: "The International Red Cross would have done better not to interfere." But as Brown wrote earlier, "If we are not able now to force a so-called civilized nation to respect the Red Cross, there is no hope it will be respected in further, larger wars." Eden asked what would help Ethiopia. On 7 April Barton replied: "Elimination of gas from the Italian armoury."[86] This, as we saw, was far beyond what the cabinet thought it wise to press for.

It is now after the massacre of Ashangi. An air-supported Eritrean division marched 150 miles to Dessye. They reached the town, wasted under torrents of bombs, on 14 April 1936. The emperor was in parallel movement southward. Opposite Lalibala, apparently on sudden impulse, he left the body of his column and went off to that city of worship, where he stayed for two days, 12–14 April, in solitary meditation. It was Lent.

11 CONQUEST

A Mechanism of Restraint

The crushing victory at Mai Chio and the rout at Lake Ashangi put the war in new perspective. All the general staffs had guessed wrong. A campaign of two years, they judged. "Everybody made a mistake," Flandin told Eden on 8 April. The War Office, Vansittart complained, underrated the Italians. The sanctionist time-table was overtaken by events. "It would not be prudent to count on Italian military difficulties," Paul-Boncour warned at Geneva, either to make a peace settlement more likely or to hold off victory much longer.[1]

These conclusions were the basis for French arguments in April for moderation toward Italy, for opening bilateral peace negotiations, and for insisting on no extension of sanctions, hoping that existing measures would be lifted as part of a truce. Only moderation would keep Mussolini out of Hitler's arms. The French government was bouyed by optimistic reports from Chambrun about the prospects for settlement and Mussolini's readiness to pursue a western orientation. Mussolini wanted "absolutely to reconstruct the Stresa front," Chambrun said on 3 April, and would enter into direct negotiations with Ethiopia if sanctions were lifted. Mussolini told Chambrun specifically that gas had not been used.[2] The French government was equally influenced by the pessimistic reports of Minister Bodard on the worthlessness of support to the disintegrating Ethiopian cause. The French refused to permit transport of an arms shipment on the Djibouti railroad. The pretext was that the shipment, although of Czech origin, was transshipped through Hamburg—and Germany was forbidden by the Treaty of Versailles to export arms.[3] In reality, they did not want to prolong the war. The Ethiopian cause was lost; the emperor should seek peace. The best way to prompt liquidation of the conflict was negotiated settlement. It was too bad if Ethiopia had to make a sacrifice. The only alternative was submission to a conqueror. So Flandin had proposed the peace appeal of 2 March, postponing consideration of the oil sanction and putting the matter in the hands of the Council's Committee of Thirteen, beyond the ambit of the sanctions-directing Committee of Eighteen.

Beyond this the French could not go, for the British were not ready to raise sanctions or to put pressure on Ethiopia to compromise. Ambassador Corbin warned from London on 30 March that if his government maneuvered too blatantly to these ends "the mass of British opinion would see this as a sign that France is not interested in collective security or the League except as an instrument for use against Germany." Reasonable as this seemed in Paris, in Britain it would result in a call for isolation from the Continent.[4] So, tied to cooperation with Britain, the French lamented as relations between Britain and Italy deteriorated in the weeks after 23 March.

The use of poison gas was a source of British outrage. On 4 April Eden warned that gas warfare "introduced a new element, which at one and the same time makes the continuance of war more intolerable by obviating any prospect of associating Italy with League assistance to Abyssinia. It will, in His Majesty's Government's view, be one of the primary duties of the Committee of Thirteen at its next meeting sharply to condemn Italy's violation of the Hague Convention and the general protocol."[5] This message to the French government, which additionally rejected a suggestion that the British bring pressure on Haile Selassie to consider a compromise, indicated that the next meeting of the Committee of Thirteen would not facilitate settlement as much as the French hoped. The Italians would hardly take kindly to a new condemnation. The committee, instead of accommodation, might end up issuing more ultimatums, calling for a meeting of the Committee of Eighteen, renewing the threat of the oil sanction or the closure of the Suez Canal—to end an "intolerable" war—or fanning public wrath over the issue of gas.

Perhaps there would be a call for a full-scale investigation. Already on 23 March Madariaga was instructed to express concern to Italy about allegations of the use of gas. Suvich replied with the usual complaints of Ethiopian atrocities. The conduct of the war had become an issue. On 25 March the president of the International Committee of the Red Cross, Max Huber, went to Rome to discuss a Red Cross investigation of the bombing of the ambulance units. Aloisi demanded stiff conditions: the question of gas would be excluded, no Ethiopian could participate in any investigation, and Italy must not be made to appear to stand trial. Huber went to see Mussolini. The Duce promised to respect the Red Cross flag and, as we saw, told Badoglio to avoid damage to the emblem in Gojam.[6]

But a day of reckoning might be close. In the wake of the disaster at Mai Chio the Ethiopians appealed to Eden who, on 4 April, asked for a meeting of the Committee of Thirteen for 8 April to consider both conciliation and the use of gas. Eden took a fairly stiff line in the cabinet and in the Commons on 6 April. Conciliation could not be pursued indefinitely. If there was no ready result the Committee of Eighteen would have to consider further sanctions. Five weeks had gone by since Britain agreed to postpone the decision on the oil embargo. Both parties consented in principle to negotiate, but not until 2 April had the Italians invited Madariaga to Rome for preliminary talks. This in itself was awkward. The chairman of the Committee of Thirteen could hardly go likewise to Ethiopia.[7]

On 6 April the cabinet considered what sanctions there were to impose, and to what purpose. The only swift way to stop the war was to close the Suez Canal. This would mean war with Italy, however, and the option was not taken. There was oil, but an embargo would not save Ethiopia, for it took time to work and the French resisted immediate application. Still, the government could not raise existing sanctions, given public opinion. Sanctions, if they had not stopped the Italian offensive, did keep pressure on Italy so as to prevent, possibly, the imposition of untenable terms on Ethiopia.[8]

One could search in vain for a French official with the view, but some Englishmen thought the Ethiopians might hold out until the rains. They would begin in six weeks, and Italy's gold resources would be near exhaustion by the end of the summer. On 23 March Mussolini had declared an economic policy of autarky for Italy. On 25 March a prospective budget deficit of over 1.6 billion lire was announced. This cost, Jebb wrote on 9 April, enabled Mussolini to make in six months internal changes that otherwise would have taken six years, but the cost, the domestic impoverishment and international complications, was so great that Italy, autarky or not, might not be able to finance a renewed campaign after the rains.[9]

On 21 April the committee assigned to follow the application of sanctions reported that existing sanctions had had considerable effect. In January 1936 Italian exports had fallen by nearly 46 percent and imports by 39 percent compared to January 1935. Preliminary figures showed continuing declines for February and March. An imbalance of trade meant a continued heavy gold drain. It was estimated that the Bank of Italy now held half the amount of gold in store when the war began.[10]

Even if Italian troops reached Addis Ababa, British thought went, and formal offensive operations stopped, the Italians would be occupying a resentful and vindictive country and would be forced to maintain a large, expensive garrison there and to apply national resources, not in Europe, but to maintain its position in Africa against a guerrilla war of yet unknown dimensions.

Eden seemed determined to keep the pressure on. Barrington-Ward of the *Times* saw him on 7 April, before he left for Paris and Geneva and the meeting of the Committee of Thirteen.

> I found him tired but not dismayed. . . . He told me he was going to stick to his guns. If the Italians break an agreement in order to use gas in war, what agreement is safe? Nor can they go on using the League offer of conciliation as a means of delay and prolonging the war. If they won't come to terms then oil sanctions must follow. He is right and most of public opinion will be with him.[11]

British, not French, opinion would be with Eden. The day before the
Council of Ministers in Paris had reaffirmed its opposition to further
sanctions.

Was there anything else that could be done for Ethiopia? Money, perhaps.
On 6 April the cabinet decided the Treasury was not justified in refusing a
loan, but that it should be postponed a week or two until the situation
cleared. That was no help. The chancellor of the exchequer was given approval to facilitate, with great discretion, a private loan on the London
money market. But in mid-April 1936, in the aftermath of the Italian victories, no one wanted to make an uncovered loan to Ethiopia. The Foreign
Office on 8 April decided that the Royal Mint could contract to strike Maria
Theresa thalers—the silver coin widespread in northeast Africa and the
region of the Gulf of Aden. Thalers struck in London would be made accessible through the Sudan, but the Ethiopian government was in no position to take advantage of this liberality. (The only effect of the decision was a
slap at Austria, which, the British held, had forfeited its monopoly on striking the coin when its government had given permission to use the dies to Italy in the months before the war began.)[12] All this was very little. The cabinet
was willing to make some general expression about possible future economic
or financial help, but the intent of this was only, in Eden's words, to "satisfy
British public opinion."[13]

One sees the point of Madariaga's statement that the European problem
now was to reconcile Italy's existing position in Africa with popular opinion
in Great Britain.[14] There was confusion and resentment on the Continent.
Did the British government have a foreign policy? Aloisi said the cabinet had
let itself become "prisoner of a parliamentary situation of its own making."
How could the government approve any settlement, which surely must recognize the Italian victories? How could the French cooperate in such confusion? The cabinet's "ideas are fashioned day to day, according to events and
possibilities," Corbin told Flandin and a meeting of French ambassadors on
3 April. Goals were formulated, not with any clear vision of the country's
future needs, but from the prevailing "illusion and optimism" of the
electorate.[15]

To continue a rigid line only to please consummatory expectations, or to
punish or pressure Italy by continuing sanctions, went beyond the original
instrumental function of bringing a quick end to the war. The argument for a
test case of collective security had been negated, as far as the French were
concerned, when collective action proved a futile hope in the Rhineland
crisis. Flandin was quite clear to his ambassadors. If the British gave no
satisfactory bilateral assurances over the German question, assurances such
as they had requested in October with their movement of ships in the
Mediterranean, or if they made dilatory response to French requests, France
then had "the liberty of saying there will be no more sanctions against

Italy."[16] These assurances the British would not make. The cabinet on 8 April insisted that the two cases were distinct. In the Rhineland the call for sanctions pertained to the Locarno powers which, excluding Italy, meant France and Britain, and this prospect was insupportable. Baldwin thought it was time to review the whole matter of collective security.[17] Throughout the month of April, with little confidence in Britain and with less in collective security, the French sought to pull back. As the British would not agree to lifting sanctions the French could at least urge moderation to keep the diplomatic position toward Italy from deteriorating.

The Committee of Thirteen met on 8 April in a mood of profound pessimism. Leaders of several delegations were absent. The reason for the session was not clear. Madariaga had nothing to report. Since 23 March all that had developed from his charge to bring the two parties together was a bland invitation to visit Rome and ever more eloquent pleas from the Ethiopian legation in Paris. Was the session convened to give Madariaga authority for a trip to Rome? Suvich disingenuously asked Drummond, ignoring the issues raised by the battle at Mai Chio, the use of gas, and the desperate Ethiopian appeal to Eden that prompted the call to meet.[18]

Mussolini's intransigence left him with the initiative and left committee members in a quandary. The Yugoslav delegate said his country was ready for "great sacrifice" to prevent an Italian triumph, which would end with Italy becoming an "intolerable neighbor" in Europe, but what he recommended was that Britain close the Suez Canal.[19] The other delegates, worried about Germany, said little. Litvinov instructed the Soviet delegation to take no initiative. The French goal was stated in Massigli's memorandum for the minister: the prompt conclusion of peace; "no time must be lost." It was not that the French were worried any longer about a Mediterranean war. Léger called the navy general staff on 10 April to say that no matter what sorts of further sanctions the British might propose, "the mechanism of Geneva will act as a restraint. England cannot act alone. We will prevent an oil embargo that might push Italy into a hostile act against the British." Thus, Léger concluded, the French navy need take no measures in anticipation of a conflict. France would not be drawn.[20]

At the Committee of Thirteen, Flandin blocked an investigation into the use of gas. He refused to condemn. He insisted on legal opinion. And, stopping all discussion, he insisted that any investigation of Italian conduct simultaneously consider alleged violations of laws of war by the Ethiopian government. Eden responded that the use of gas was a matter of government policy, whereas the alleged Ethiopian atrocities were "irresponsible" acts by "undisciplined military forces." Eden found little support in the committee, and the matter was dropped. All that emerged was a request to the International Committee of the Red Cross for its information, Junod's reports from the front. This request was turned down. The International Committee said its material was gathered and held in its capacity as a neutral international body, not to be shared beyond what was called for by its own needs and by the Geneva Convention.[21]

Eden wanted also to raise the threat of a meeting of the Committee of Eighteen and a decision on further sanctions. Five weeks, after all, had gone by since the committee had suspended its work for this try at negotiation. No results were in evidence, and it was no longer tolerable to postpone the committee's meeting. "If once an armistice were arranged," Eden said to Flandin, "conciliation might go on as long as the parties liked." The rains, he thought, and continued sanctions, would work against Italy, making peace terms easier for Ethiopia. He thought it "doubtful" Italy could recommence hositilites in the autumn, but to postpone the Committee of Eighteen further would bring only discredit on the association.[22]

Flandin would have none of this. For the British it was as bad as dealing with Laval. Eden said Flandin obstructed all serious action and presented "the Italian case with confident cynicism." Flandin defended himself. He wanted to calm the Italians. Concessions were possible—Mussolini wanted only immediate satisfaction, which could be accommodated to the long-term needs of Britain and France. But Italy gave Flandin no help. Flandin warned Aloisi he would soon have to choose between Italy and Britain. He probably did not know it, but precisely at this time orders went to the Italian army to prepare defenses on the French frontier.[23]

What was urgent, Flandin told Eden on 8 April, was to "give the impression that negotiations were being taken seriously." This meant approval of direct negotiations between the two parties outside the framework of the Covenant, away from Geneva, unobserved by any third party. The emperor should be pressed to cooperate. Sanctions should be raised if hostilities stopped during the talks. It was an article of faith in French and Italian circles that British support for their continuation was the main encouragement for the Ethiopians, keeping them from accepting Italian terms.[24]

On 9 April the Committee of Thirteen instructed Madariaga and Avenol to contact the Genevan delegation of both sides. A trip to Rome was postponed. There was no "threat," and little hope. The committee agreed to meet again in a week, on the sixteenth. It was argued (and taken by the Italians as an implied ultimatum) that if no concrete results were reported, the Committee of Eighteen would be called at once. A Council meeting was in the offing. The issues could be aired there. The next two weeks, then, were important for any final try. No organized force stood between Badoglio and Addis Ababa. The emperor was in flight. If some sort of terms, substantive or procedural, were arranged, face would be saved. That was all the French wanted.

Direct Talks

The victories brought an explosion of joy to Italy. Mussolini told his Council of Ministers on 9 April that Mai Chio made certain "the first objective" of the war, "the total annihilation of Ethiopian military formations." Mussolini was convinced that nothing short of a European war could now stop a sweeping success. The problems faced by Britain and France were of no concern to him. Before Aloisi left for Geneva on 7 April, Mussolini gave his three conditions for a settlement: maintenance of conquered territory, no corridor to the sea at Assab, and unconquered Ethiopia under a strong Italian protectorate on the model of Iraq or Morocco.[25]

Italian officials constantly kept in mind the possibility of some form of settlement. Discussion of terms was the core of an immensely successful diplomacy that had mitigated the strength and urgency of calls for collective action. This strategy had led to the prewar Paris proposals of August 1935, the report of the Committee of Five in September, endless palaver and hopeful overtures, the Hoare-Laval proposals, and now the protracted decision on an oil sanction. There were additional reasons for considering terms of settlement. In his directive of December 1934 Mussolini had said the Ethiopian matter would have to be resolved by "the destruction of the Abyssinian armed forces and the total conquest of Ethiopia." Prior to the victory at Mai Chio there was the danger that the war might drag on another season, that sanctions might become too costly to bear, or that changes in the European scene might make a swift conclusion of hostilities necessary. And even if it were a peace after conquest, it would be to Italy's benefit if the settlement sat well with Europe. The first advantage would be the swift lifting of sanctions. The problem, of course, was that Ethiopians refused to give up what Italians wanted.

For some time—since Hoare's fall showed that no new peace terms were likely to be proposed from Geneva—the Italians had scouted the prospect of direct negotiations with Ethiopia. A number of moves were made, some by interested individuals, some by agencies of government. These moves lacked coordination, to the extent that Aloisi in late February 1936 feared the settlement would be bungled as badly as the diplomatic preparations for the war.[26]

The most enterprising, although the least important, of the schemes was hatched by a Palestinian adventurer, Chucry Jacir Bey. In early December 1935, claiming friendship with Ethiopian dignitaries, Jacir Bey approached the Italian military secret service with a plan to negotiate directly with Haile Selassie. Terms involved the maintenance of the Tafari dynasty with the title of emperor, direct subsidy by the Italian government, and continuance of Ethiopian sovereignty and diplomatic rights over an independent but reduced state in Shoa with a sea corridor to Assab. In return, all of Tigre and border areas of Eritrea and Somalia would be ceded to Italy, and the army, police, and central ministries would be put under Italian control. Jacir Bey signed an agreement with Colonel Emilio Faldella of the secret service. One hundred million lire (convertible to Swiss francs) was deposited in a sealed account in the Bank of Naples. Jacir Bey was given until 30 January 1936 to bring about a halt in the fighting and two weeks more for the emperor to send word accepting these conditions to Italy, to the League, and to states that were not members of the League. Jacir Bey was given the option of cooperating with the general staff to organize a rigged battle if the emperor thought a decisive defeat was necessary to justify his concessions. If all else failed, he could kidnap Haile Selassie in the course of an air journey and spirit him behind the Italian lines.

This contract set in motion elaborate activity on the part of the secret service. Agents went to Alexandria, Jerusalem, Djibouti, and Brussels. Monies were sent about. Special ciphers were devised. Plans were set to ready an aircraft and instruct a pilot for the kidnapping. Among other things, the secret service agents in Brussels undertook sabotage, selling to the Ethiopians rifles rendered useless. Nothing came of Jacir Bey's plan. He never made contact with the emperor. The deadline of 15 February 1936 came and went. The money stayed uncollected in the Bank of Naples.[27]

Other individuals, less well-sponsored, tried to act as intermediaries to end the war. Charles Collier, a Scotsman, governor of the Bank of Ethiopia, absolutely loyal to the emperor, went to Rome in November 1935 to scout the ground. When Grandi warned he might threaten Mussolini's life, however, he was not received. Came February 1936, and Collier was invited to Rome. He talked with Suvich and even more with Giuliano Cora, former Italian minister to Addis Ababa. To Cora he suggested that if Italy was ready to end the war Cora might make a special mission via the Sudan to see Haile Selassie, with whom he was in good standing. Nothing came of this, but Collier was invited to keep in touch, upon his return to Addis Ababa, with the Italian consul in Djibouti, the nearest Italian representative.[28]

Probably the most significant contact between representatives of the two governments took place at the end of February 1936—significant because it came after the battle of Amba Aradam (Enderta) and the death of Ras Mulugeta, while Badoglio was preparing to launch the second battle of Tembien and the battle of Shire, which broke the northern fronts of Rases Kassa, Seyum, and Imru. These overtures led Haile Selassie to direct an appeal to King Edward VIII on 20 February, saying that "Mussolini has offered us to negotiate directly with her [Italy] for peace" and asking the British government, "before any more blood is shed and any more harm done," to "decide a place where the two countries may meet and negotiate the matter, in the meantime an armistice being called."[29]

Both sides brought proposals to Djibouti. Down from Addis Ababa on 24 February went Medogras Afework, biographer of Menelik and, until the outbreak of hostilities, the Ethiopian minister in Rome. Afework was virtually Italianized. He spoke Italian fluently, knew Rome intimately, depended on the Palazzo Chigi for communication with his government, and was married to an Italian woman. Perhaps with the help of Collier, and claiming full authorization from the emperor, he formulated a proposal that involved the cession of some territory that the Italians held (Aduwa and Adigrat in the north, Walwal in the Ogaden, and Negelli in Galla Borana) and provided for some economic advice and assistance from Italy. In return Afework's proposal asked Italian cession and recognition of sovereignty over Assab, payment of war damages of 1.5 billion lire, and a mutual assistance pact. When Mussolini read these terms he rejected them flatly, noting, however, that they gave evidence of an encouraging willingness to enter into the direct bilateral negotiations Italy preferred.[30]

Afework received the Italian terms on 24 February from his wife, to whom they were given on her sea passage to Djibouti: a corridor along the existing British and French frontiers to assure Ethiopia would march with Italian territory only; cession of Tigre, of the Ogaden up to Harar, of Borana up to Negelli; economic concessions; and all advisers to the government to be Italian. To sweeten the blow the emperor could keep his dynastic throne and would be given an initial and substantial gift of lire to distribute to his chiefs.

The emperor considered the terms. His minister of commerce and valued adviser, Makonnen Habtewold, recommended he open discussion, conciliation giving "more time for preparation" for defense. His foreign minister, Blattengetta Herouy Wolde Selassie, warned that if a report of direct dealing with the Italians were leaked to the League it would destroy the Ethiopians' case, so he advised against responding. Everett Colson suggested just a general reply, with no commitment to particulars. The Italians intercepted these messages between the ministries in Addis Ababa and the emperor in Dessye. The emperor decided against negotiation, turning down the terms in the second week of March.[31] The British did not like the terms either, when they learned of them in April. Geoffrey Thompson in the Foreign Office noted: "I don't like the idea of making Ethiopia into an island in an Italian sea. It would mean inter alia complete territorial separation of the Tsana watershed with the Sudan." This would have deplorable effects in Egypt.[32]

There was one more attempt at direct talks that is worth noting. The intermediary used by the secret service was Jacir Bey. The foreign ministry used Afework's wife and also helped the colonial ministry to work through Dr. Adrien Zervos, the Greek consul in Addis Ababa and the loyal personal physician to the emperor. Contact was made with Zervos in Athens (ostensibly in a visit with the son of Foreign Minister Blattengetta Herouy) by

Enrico Cerulli, adviser to the colonial ministry and long-time student of Ethiopia. Their talks continued intermittently through the month of March, during which time Zervos was in contact with Addis Ababa by telegraph. This puts in slightly dimmer light the formal Ethiopian denials of 13 and 20 March to the League that "it is not true that direct negotiations have been opened or are about to be opened. . . . The Ethiopian Government will always refuse to enter into any direct negotiation; it will only agree to negotiate within the framework of the League. . . ." Strictly speaking, this was true. Yet the government, tied though it was to the authority of the League, can hardly be faulted for trying to ease the painful fate of the country. The Afework exchange and the Zervos talks were, after all, highly tentative and preliminary. Even more so were other attempts at intervention. Francis Rickett traveled to Rome, Khartoum, and Djibouti hoping to smooth a path. Another informal intermediary looked up Colson in Alexandria. The fact that Colson, in ill health, was absent from the emperor's entourage and from Addis Ababa during the grave days of April and the first two days of May meant there was no one watching over these exchanges for the government.

On 28 March, at any rate, after a month of sparring, Zervos asked for guarantees for the Tafari dynasty, compensation of 300 million lire, help in the development of the country, and a treaty of alliance such as the Italians had with Albania. Cerulli offered some vague encouragement. The two parties set up a special cipher system to continue correspondence, and Zervos left for Addis Ababa to report. A week later, in the wake of the disaster of Lake Ashangi, Zervos sent a message to Cerulli saying he was ordered by the emperor not to return to Athens to continue the talks. This was enough for Rome. On 4 April Suvich, Aloisi, Guariglia, and Cerruti decided to suspend all further communication with the Ethiopians.[33] There was nothing to fear from the request by the Committee of Thirteen for negotiation "within the framework of the League." Military victories settled terms better than talks could. On that very day, 4 April, aircraft bombed Addis Ababa for the first time.

Thus by 9 April, when the Committee of Thirteen instructed Madariaga and Avenol once again to get in touch with the delegations of the two governments, both sides had decided to drop direct contact with each other. The Ethiopians were on the run. Mussolini brimmed with confidence. Far from inclining him to moderation, the recent victories left in him a mood of increasing truculence. As for Europe, when in early April he saw an aircraft fly to the height of some 30,000 feet, he observed: it could fly over London without being seen.[34]

From now on settlement was to be on Italian terms. Giving orders to Aloisi on 14 April, Mussolini was in an expansive mood. Ethiopia was lost, he said, defeated and on the verge of internal disintegration. The League was incapable of leadership in international affairs. Thus one could give a little to the League. Italy would consent to the League appeal on the condition that procedural questions be settled directly with the Ethiopians, without intermediaries or observers, without mediation by the Committee of Thirteen, and not at Geneva, but in a new venue, perhaps at Ouchy. Hostilities would be suspended only when procedural questions were resolved, when actual peace talks were under way, and only after conditions were established to protect the Italian military position. Addis Ababa could be conquered as all these preliminaries dragged on.

Italy, Mussolini said to Aloisi, was ready for anything. Cartridge production was up to 100 million per month. There were 800 million rounds in Eritrea. Twenty-five divisions were on the line, six in reserve. There were 2,800 aircraft for military use, and in east Africa were 423,000 soldiers and 100,000 workers.[35]

But what about substantive conditions for peace? After all, even with conquest something had to be done with the emperor, the dynasty, the great lords. This was a vexing question. First, Italy must have direct authority over all conquered territory. An appearance of Ethiopian sovereignty somewhere was permissible, but the power of the state would have to be in Italian hands. The emperor could have something about one-third the size of the present territory, and Italy could give him some 150 million lire. After all, Mussolini laughed, he had paid a 1.8 billion settlement to the pope.

At the field command in the north General Gabba, thinking ahead for when the war was over, put together a project of territorial adjustments meant to break up the present "artificial" empire. Some parts were to be annexed, others given protectorate status, and for Gojam and the Blue Nile area, a type of mandate. Shoa would be left autonomous. It was here the existing dynasty could reign, disarmed and under Italian control. Alessandro Lessona rejected the thinking behind this plan. Lessona went out from the colonial ministry in April 1936 to take care of political arrangements, for instance, for Badoglio to negotiate with the crown prince if he was captured in Dessye. For Lessona, and for Badoglio, Gabba's plan was much too cautious, too old-fashioned, too preoccupied with being acceptable to the League of Nations. This was hardly the "radical" stroke to be proposed with the prospect of overwhelming victory. For Lessona political issues would be settled on the war front, not at Geneva. Military success should have its rewards. Lessona's plan envisioned a little Shoan state for Haile Selassie under an Italian protectorate and surrounded by Italian territory. The rest of Ethiopia would be Italian, pure and simple, with Victor Emmanuel as emperor. This was Lessona's "integral solution." Why should Italy try to satisfy Europe with mandates and corridors?[36]

One last try to get in touch with the emperor should be mentioned, for Badoglio carried with him a plan as he moved to Dessye. When Badoglio and Lessona arrived at Dessye on 20 April the crown prince had fled before the Italian column arrived a week earlier. His father was in retreat toward the capital. On the twenty-first Lessona and Badoglio proposed to Mussolini the following: they would send Haile Selassie a message announcing they were going to march on Addis Ababa, that no defense was possible, and that to avoid shedding "more Christian blood" he should send emissaries to treat directly with Badoglio. This was an ingenious idea. There were considerable advantages to having the emperor concede before the final blow. He would not have to be run down. A final arrangement could be made in advance of conquest. Guerrilla opposition would be reduced. Removal of the government to the provinces would be thwarted. It was a tidy idea. For the last ten days of April, during all the march from Dessye, Badoglio sent wireless messages "in friendly and respectful terms" suggesting a meeting to discuss "a reasonable peace."[37] There was no response.

A European Poison

There is a pro-League criticism of Avenol as secretary-general of the League that is typified in the view of the French feminist and League enthusiast Louise Weiss, who interviewed him in these years. "Neither prophet, nor judge, nor apostle" of the League, Avenol was "a complete technocrat," without ideological commitment to the founders' vision of the association he served. Here is Weiss's charge against him, delivered in 1935: "You are the passive liquidator of the hopes our generation invested in the League of which you have charge, the administrator of its failings, the anonymous official who seeks the irreproachable execution of contradictory instructions."[38]

There is something to this. Avenol did have a view of the League very different from its founders and from those who now pressed article 16. Avenol thought the enforcement machinery of the Covenant was insufficient for a system of collective security. In a crisis, to avert problems the League could not control, a better alternative was preventative diplomacy of the traditional sort. The future of the League lay in nonpolitical humanitarian activities. But it was now deeply immersed in a vexing political matter that threatened to tear it apart. Italy must be drawn into talks because only by settling the Ethiopian issue quickly, and with Italian cooperation, could the association be saved.

Avenol was gravely worried for Europe. He revealed his fears in a letter to Léger on 14 April 1936. The danger came from Britain, he said. Italy had disrupted Britain's arrangements in the Mediterranean and threatened its empire. At first the British had used the League to thwart the challenge to empire, masking its attempt with a claim of disinterest, of obligation to the Covenant. This had not worked. The Italians now had 400,000 men in east Africa, flushed with victory. If the League were shown to be impotent, however, Britain could come to a Mediterranean settlement directly with the Italians. To this end they might use the threat of calling the Committee of Eighteen—for France could not support further sanctions—the League would thus be declared bankrupt. Eden would not be surprised. Indeed, Avenol surmised, "might I not even say that could be his objective?" A declaration of insolvency from France, bankruptcy for the League, and to the following end: justification for a total reorientation of British policy. British policy was *not* fixed as pro-League. Such a stance was a mask catering to electoral opinion. British leaders were undecided, sluggish. For them a satisfactory solution might be an arrangement whereby Italy controlled the Mediterranean with the support of France, leaving the League out of the picture. This combination would end British fears of German hegemony on the Continent. Indeed, it would open the way for an understanding with Germany itself. But this would be of gravest consequence for the rest of Europe, including France and Italy. Thus, said Avenol, was the Ethiopian affair "a European poison."[39]

These were mighty fears, enough to justify one last try to stave off further sanctions. So broad was the scope of Avenol's anxiety that it is not enough to see him just as a reactionary French nationalist playing the Laval-Flandin delaying game. At bottom Avenol worried that the entire political complexion of Europe might change through reversal of British policy.

Avenol's initial optimism that the Italians would see value in cooperation was dashed on 15 April when Aloisi arrived carrying Mussolini's instructions. Procedural agreement must be bilateral and precede discussion of peace terms; talks must be direct, must not involve the League, and must be held outside Geneva. There was to be no cease-fire until peace talks were under way, and then only with safeguards approved by Badoglio. These were hard demands. Avenol argued they were only an initial position, subject to modification after an Ethiopian rejection. Time must be allowed. The Committee of Thirteen, Avenol said, should postpone its meeting set for 16 April.[40]

The French delegation pushed both ways. To the Italians it argued for a more conciliatory stance, a greater show of willingness to call a cease-fire. To the British it urged pressure on the Ethiopians to accept the Italian terms as the only way to save the country. These entreaties were to no avail, of course, given the disagreement between Britain and France on questions of urgency and terms. On 16 April the Ethiopian delegation absolutely refused to consider the Italian conditions, which went, they said, beyond the framework of the League, against the spirit of the Covenant, and contrary to the Committee of Thirteen's original (3 March) appeal for talks, which Ethiopia and Italy had both accepted. The Ethiopians thought their cause was now abandoned. The emperor sent a telegram on 17 April: "Ethiopia is now entitled to ask herself whether the principle of collective security is not really a dead letter."[41]

This question hung over the Committee of Thirteen on 17 April when it heard Madariaga's report of failure. It was on the minds of members of the Council on the twentieth as they abandoned hope of a cessation of hostilities by agreement. It seemed answered when no delegate urged intensification of sanctions or raised the issue of gas. Eden, it is true, and delegates from Denmark, Romania, and Turkey, indicated a willingness to consider further "economic or financial" sanctions, but no proposal was made to this end. "It is slipping badly," Eden said of the collective front. "We have done our best but I fear it is going to crumble."[42]

The French were willing to write off Ethiopia, to write off the sanctions experiment, because they needed Italy in Europe. Paul-Boncour, head of the French delegation, put it to the Council: "If we are to meet the present threats to Europe, we need peace in Ethiopia. The situation of a great country in relation to the League must be regulated so that that country may participate in the work of European reconstruction." He did not endorse further, did not call for the lifting of, sanctions. He ended his remarks affirming a "community of feeling" with Britain.[43]

That remark might have been different. There had been, after all, much earlier talk of the need to consider further sanctions to satisfy the honor of the League. Eden, two weeks before, seemed ready to "stick to his guns" and put additional pressure on the Italians. There was talk around London of a threat to close the canal. There was much worry in Geneva that the Council session might end with a rupture between Britain and France if Eden pressed the point.

Nothing like this happened. Once again, in reality, the positions of the two states were close enough to make compromise possible. Each stayed in step with the other. Moderation was the premise. No precipitous decision by either side. No call to lift sanctions, no call to intensify them. The common ground of postponement served both governments. The British could save face; the French could claim to save Italy. As a member of the British delegation said, "League failure" was preferable to "British failure."[44]

Paul-Boncour argued partly that the French government could not make decisions of such magnitude until after the elections set for 26 April and 3 May. When he left Geneva on the twenty-first, it was with assurances to

Eden that once the elections were over the government would be "willing to participate in a determined effort" to end the conflict, whatever that meant. He had made it clear to Sarraut, he said, that Eden "only consented to agree to the moderate programme now being adopted at Geneva on the condition this effort were seriously made." Sarraut "fully understood and approved." Wilson, however, noted that lesser members of both delegations said that the election issue was of little consequence, that French policy would be the same regardless of the outcome, and that Eden knew this when he accepted Paul-Boncour's line.[45]

In the meantime, how to avoid that appearance of bankruptcy? It was in the interest of not breaking up the sanctionist front that Eden decided to abstain from pushing the oil embargo, a tightening of credit restrictions, or the issue of gas warfare. With the exception of the delegate from Ecuador, whose government raised sanctions on 17 April on the ground that Italy had accepted (in principle) the invitation of the Committee of Thirteen to begin settlement talks, the Council voted to continue existing sanctions. As for the Committee of Eighteen, it was decided that "if circumstances did not demand an earlier meeting" the committee would meet during the ordinary session of the Council in May.[46] To counter charges of inactivity, Chairman Vasconcellos of the Committee of Eighteen called the committee of experts for 21 April, declaring, "Sanctions are not dead." Following this announcement, in which Vasconcellos dilated upon the effects of sanctions in reducing Italian trade, the Italians protested to Lisbon and his government rebuked Vasconcellos. Adding insult to injury, Bova Scoppa told him: "Your committee has done great service." Sanctions gave Mussolini popular support as solid as "a block of granite."[47] Meaning to confirm Vasconcellos's statements, the committee of experts told the press on 21 April that Italian imports for January were off a third from the year before and a substantial gold drain was under way.

Eden was satisfied. The farce of conciliation was over. At the Council the Italians underwent "the ordeal" of adverse world opinion. The sanctionist front was "still intact," and it was, Eden claimed, "the best we could do."[48]

Flandin was relieved. He had expected Eden to make more of a scene, given his statements to Commons that, while the oil embargo would not be effective it should still be applied, and his threats of condemnation over gas warfare. As it was, all the Council did was to express a generalized dismay at any violation of international agreements. Flandin took Eden to task for making comments that were misleading and risky.[49] If the British raised the sanctions question again at the Council meeting in May, the French might argue that the present measures should be lifted instead. As long as the war went on, the danger grew that Hitler might move against Austria. Only a few days before the Austrian foreign minister had said the last hope of his land

lay in solidarity between France and Italy.[50] From Chambrun came word of
Mussolini's determination to "intervene with all his forces to defend the line
of the Danube against the German menace." Yet the French decided against
reinforcing their Alpine division for possible use in aid of Italy in an
Austrian crisis, fearing the Italians would misinterpret the move as a British-
inspired act of pressure arising from the Ethiopian affair.[51]

The Italians left the Council on 20 April satisfied. Mussolini asked Aloisi
to thank Paul-Boncour and tell Eden that, as requested, press attacks on
Britain would stop. It was held widely in Rome that the British cause was
lost, the advantage had passed to Italy, and perhaps now relations with Britain might improve.[52]

As for the League, Léon Blum's lead in *Le Populaire* on 22 April said it
all—"It is over." The League merely plays with words. Behind its lines
"there is an admission of impotence, abandonment, the acceptance of the accomplished fact." Ethiopia can no longer count on the League. Whatever
happens, resistance or rain, "Geneva will not act further, content to watch in
silence." The French government assumed a heavy responsibility. "When the
new Chamber meets, will Ethiopia still be there? Will it be possible to
reestablish an understanding with Britain? Will it be possible to revive the
confidence of people in the League, the confidence of the League in itself?"[53]
Blum asked these questions in the middle of the election campaign. After the
balloting he stood in command of the largest party in the Chamber and
within six weeks of his editorial was premier of France.

Holding Action

The sanctions front held at the meeting of the League Council on 20 April
because nothing was demanded of it. The British agreed not to push the
issues of oil, credit, or gas. The French, foreseeing swift conclusion of the
military campaign, excused themselves on the plea of the upcoming elections. Few thought a change of government would bring a change of policy.
Blum, in an election address on 21 April, said sanctions meant peace, but the
decisive parliamentary victory of the Popular Front in the balloting of 26
April and 3 May turned mainly on domestic concerns, and Sarraut's government still would speak for France at the meetings of the Council and the
Committee of Eighteen scheduled for 11 May.

In London two Foreign Office memorandums set forth alternatives on the
question of continuing sanctions. The first, dated 24 April, by O'Malley,
Peterson, and Strang, concluded that only radical action at the May meetings would save the League. Radical action meant a League decision to
prohibit or control Italian war-related traffic through the Suez Canal. Much

was at stake. If Mussolini got away with armed aggression, if war was shown to pay, if the League was discredited, general disillusionment with collective security would destroy the League and what value it had for Britain. Only this drastic measure could save the day. The canal sanctions would give heart to Ethiopian resistance, strike effectively at Italy's capacity to wage war, and, even if it was too late to stop the defeat of the emperor, could be used to force the transfer of sovereignty to the League as a trustee until the future status of Ethiopia's government was determined. If the French vetoed this plan, the British government could disclaim responsibility for the failure of collective security.

Against this proposal came, on the twenty-eighth, a countermemorandum drafted by Victor Wellesley, Lancelot Oliphant, Reginald Leeper, Ashton Gwatkin, and Ralph Wigram. This group cited Drummond's warnings that Mussolini would prefer national suicide to defeat over Ethiopia. Indeed, the very day this memorandum was circulated, Mussolini, referring to the possible closing of the canal, said: "I do not want war, but if England wants it, she shall have it."[54] It was the presumption of war that dominated the argument against closing the canal, war which might encourage Hitler and the Japanese. British prestige abroad, damaged, to be sure, by Italy's success, would ultimately depend on the speed of rearmament. War with Italy would do more harm to British influence in the Mediterranean than would doing nothing. Nor would Britain have the support of other powers. The counterargument concluded: "We believe national interest and not natural sympathy must dictate foreign policy." To push the Italian issue, forcing a break with France, would be to "sign our death warrant." A breach with France would be a "physical danger to our existence."

On 5 May O'Malley, Peterson, and Strang issued a strong rebuttal. They flatly disagreed with the presumption that a League-sponsored closure meant war. They stressed moral factors ignored in the countermemorandum, referring to a statement by the bishop of Durham, no pacifist, that Mussolini had committed an "enormous crime." It is true, these authors said, that such an approach left the political sphere for the moral, but this was the way political issues were increasingly viewed by the British public. So much to the good, for the tendency was "as much the result of a profound political instinct as of a moral revival." Such an approach, in fact, was the only road "to the preservation of civilization."[55] It was the bishop of Durham who had written in a letter to the *Times* on 30 August 1935: "Justice is a higher concern than peace: for while justice can never be abandoned, peace can never be unreservedly pursued. Not first peace, and then justice: but first justice and then, at whatever cost, peace—that is the inexorable law for man."

These were fine words, and against them the head of the Southern Department threw his weight. The League, Orme Sargent said, was a lost cause, long since discredited. There could be no further disillusion if a simple maintenance of existing sanctions was proposed. Cooperation with France was essential. The navy needed some relief in the Mediterranean, so good relations with Italy should also be pursued. Italy's "fear of Germany will make her anxious to bury the hatchet if only we don't insist on driving her to extreme Anglophobia." Vansittart commented on the original memorandum: "The heart speaks for it and the head against it." The canal sanction would "of course" lead to war, Vansittart said, and the impotence of the Mediterranean states, the disarray of anti-German forces, made war out of the question. Keep existing sanctions, was his advice. "If we can't carry the League with us in that, and it is doubtful," there would be "little hope of its following us effectively into a war."[56]

On 28 April Ambassador Clerk reported from Paris that sanctions were very unpopular. Regardless of the elections, the French would probably not go along with any extension on 11 May. Vansittart drew the lesson. "We should not attempt the impossible." Any further measures would lose the French who, "in their anxiety," would take the "opportunity to run out on *existing* sanctions." British policy on 11 May should be as it was on 20 April—concentrate on existing measures "and see how much we can make that hurt." "It is the least we can do for unhappy Abyssinia," Cranborne agreed.[57]

It is worth quoting at length from these Foreign Office minutes to show how firmly established in late April was British determination to hold on to existing measures even though the end of the military campaign had swept away their purpose—ending the war. With the war over, the French argument ran in May, sanctions should be lifted. British reluctance to do so put an additional strain on relations with France.

Stanhope, Cranborne, and Eden made their agreement with Vansittart. Here is Stanhope on 30 April:

> If we can hold a united front on existing sanctions, I feel the month of May may well be Italy's strongest and the League's weakest moment. If so, this is *not* the time to put forward peace proposals. I deprecate very strongly the defeatist attitude which has taken over part of the F.O. The Abyssinian war is not yet over and Italy is far from being out of her difficulties. If the League is going to take off its pressure now, it deserves to die.

And Cranborne on 1 May: "We should not take any initiative with a view to defining peace terms. Things cannot be worse for Abyssinia than at this moment. They may conceivably become better." And Eden, in a comment that would bear weight even if conquest ensued: "We must press for the maintenance of existing sanctions until peace is signed," a peace amenable to the League, that is.

Much the same conclusion was taken across Downing Street by the cabinet on 29 April and 6 May. On the twenty-ninth the main concern was the Admiralty's request to relax the state of readiness and concentration of the Mediterranean Fleet, on war footing since August. In the naval view the danger of war was past. The strain on the fleet was showing. There had been almost no leaves, no reliefs, no recommissioning of ships, and the hot summer weather lay ahead. To maintain for much longer the present "concert pitch," the Admiralty would have to ask for "some measure of mobilization," perhaps the calling up of 6,000 reservists. Such a step might be tantamount, in Italian eyes, to a hostile act. Beyond this, the general stability of Europe demanded "recovery of relations with Italy," with Italy back in cooperation with France.

The cabinet decision went against this, on political grounds. Any redistribution of force at the moment would be "disastrous," interpreted abroad as "admission that our policy had failed, that we were abandoning Abyssinia to her fate, and washing our hands of the whole affair." Further, it would make Eden's position "impossible" at the League meetings in May. Pending the meetings in Geneva, then, the fleet would stay where it was, with some relief and "unostentatious movements" of ships permitted, "provided these were not on such a scale as to reflect on our foreign policy."

No decision was taken that day as to British policy for the May meetings of the Council and the Committee of Eighteen. It was acknowledged that with the Italian military victory Britain's position there would be both humiliating and crucial. Delegates at Geneva were interested in Europe; attention no longer focused on Ethiopia or Africa. Britain, Eden said, was in for "a long period of strain."[58]

On the evening of 29 April Grandi talked with King Edward, considered in Rome one of the few Englishmen genuinely sympathetic to Italy. Edward saw no point in closing the canal. "To what end?" he asked Grandi. "To prevent victorious Italian troops from returning home?" He hoped an understanding would be speedily reached between Britain and Italy. The League, as presently organized, was dead, he thought. Edward's comments made a great impression on Mussolini and Suvich when Grandi sent his report down by special courier.[59]

A sense of resignation to the fate of the League is seen in minutes about a letter from Walters, in the League Secretariat, urging a rally to the cause before the Geneva meetings. Peterson said Walters wanted a "whip-up" before the Council met. All to the good, if the British government meant to take active steps. But if all that was to be done was to argue for continuing existing sanctions, it would be a mistake to get further embroiled "by once again taking the lead in flogging a dead horse." Eden sounded the tired refrain—let others do it: "The League must really show some vitality of its own." Neville Chamberlain showed greater definiteness. He wrote on 2 May: "The Italians' success will encourage the French to urge that, now everything is finished, we ought to lift the sanctions, let bygones be bygones, and get Italy back to the Stresa front at once. That seems to me intolerable. . . . I am sure the time has not come for the League to own itself beaten. All the same, it is beaten."⁶⁰

On 6 May the cabinet instructed Eden for the upcoming meetings. Moderation and postponement was the plan, with Eden to play a passive, reactive role. He was to call for a "stock-taking of the present position of the Covenant," probably to take place at the Assembly in September. Over Ethiopia, he was to turn down the French request for a joint approach to Rome. Italy could inform the League of what it proposed for the empire. Britain would then respond. As far as the future of sanctions was concerned, Eden was to advocate nothing new.⁶¹

Voices were now heard in England in favor of abandoning sanctions. On 6 May Austen Chamberlain said it was futile to continue. Of this speech in the Commons he wrote:

> I really did not want to make it, but I felt it would be cowardly to shirk saying what J thought and that it might help Eden and the Government if I belled the cat. They are in an extraordinarily difficult position with a public opinion that is all sentiment and passion and will not face realities. . . . I don't believe public opinion will at present allow us to pursue the only wise policy, which is to call off sanctions, to restore what is called the Stresa front and then to sit down seriously to try to come to terms with Germany if possible, and to fortify peace against her if it is not.⁶²

On 2 May Eden had made this defense of the British position: "We had an obligation, a signed Covenant obligation, to play a part. We have sought to play that part to the full, and, so far as we have done this, we have nothing to reproach ourselves with, nothing to apologize for." Aloisi greeted Eden's comment as "avowing the failure of sanctions," and signifying the beginning of "a complete turnabout" in British opinion. "The crushing diplomatic-military victory of Mussolini is unanimously recognized."⁶³ This went too far, however. The British were sticking. But to what? Before the House on 6 May Eden spoke of the need for realism. What, however, asked Frenchmen, was his reality? *Le Temps* blamed the current difficulties on the fact that for the past decade the British had refused to accept the responsibilities of leadership which went with the role the country could not avoid playing in Europe.⁶⁴ This is a fair criticism. "Eden has played his hand out," wrote Thomas Jones. "It has been magnificently consistent but was it diplomacy?"

This was a prevalent question. Massigli, a friend of Britain, saw Eden in Geneva on 10 May and said his embarrassment was equal to his indignation. The impression everywhere was that British policy was at a dead stop.[65]

Sarraut's government felt an urgency that was little appreciated in London. Flandin disagreed strongly with the contention that sanctions should be maintained as punitive measures or used to influence peace terms. Arguments to such ends, the French thought, were irresponsible, further alienating Italy and upsetting Europe without helping Ethiopia or the League. Above all, before Blum and the Popular Front took command, Flandin wanted to bring the British around to cooperation in an overture to Rome to conclude a "reasonable" settlement. Blum, Flandin thought, would never consent to terms satisfactory to Italy, and the poisoning effects of the war would drag on and on.

There was something to this argument. Blum recognized that Italian victory and Britain's antisanctionist position over the Rhine had set French opinion against any further sanctions. The most he might do as premier was to maintain existing measures, saving what was possible of the League's reputation. Like Eden, Blum was a moderate and not particularly keen on sanctions now. But, if he could help it, he did not want to raise them as his first act as premier, and that meant he would allow their being drawn on into the summer.[66] This gave the urgency to Flandin's call for settlement before Sarraut's ministry left office on 4 June. The fact of conquest must be recognized before then and, if possible, something definite decided with Britain on the conditions for lifting sanctions.

Larger policy concerns went begging. What, for example, did the British see as a future role for Italy in Europe? What was the exact value the British gave to the continuation of the sanctions front relative to further alienating Italy? London could not respond to such questions, for the government did not know. Diplomacy demands direction. The French seethed in frustration as Flandin's overtures for a joint policy at the May meetings met one rebuff after another. Aloof immobilism characterized the British stand.

It will be recalled that Eden acceded, willingly enough, to inaction at the Council on 20 April on the promise that once the French elections were over a decision would be called for from the Committee of Eighteen. On 23 April Flandin suggested that promise no longer held. Paul-Boncour's speech to the Council that Italy must not be further alienated represented the recognition that the Ethiopian affair was overshadowed by the German problem. In the event of a war with Germany, France could not afford a neighbor with grievances. And Italy might be able to keep Germany in check over Austria. All Mussolini wanted, Flandin argued, was immediate satisfaction, and Britain and France could afford concessions if they but recognized their

long-term interests in Europe. The reply he received was that concessions of
principle were the most difficult to make. France's Ambassador Corbin put
it in another light. It would take "real courage" for the British government
to avow the failure of the policy on which they had won the election in
November.[67]

The collapse of Ethiopian resistance confirmed the French in their
urgings. They asked that Britain join in a direct approach to Italy outside the
League, perhaps using as an excuse that the 1906 treaty made them interest-
ed parties in Ethiopia's future. This was the right moment to approach
Mussolini, Flandin said, while he was full of success and the future status
of Ethiopia was undeclared. It was imperative to open talks immediately.
Otherwise, what would happen at Geneva on the eleventh? Otherwise, how
would the League get out of its impasse? That was the reality of the situation.
None of the smaller powers knew where to turn or what to do. Britain and
France would have to take a lead, beginning immediately with joint talks to
set up the approach to Italy. There was this complication. Flandin had just
suffered an automobile accident and was in bed pending an operation on his
arm. But, he told Clerk on 4 May, he was determined to go to Geneva in a
week, unless his doctors forbade it, and he wanted to talk to Eden first.
Could Eden stop in Paris for a private meeting on his way to Switzerland?[68]

Eden turned down all suggestions. He would deal with France in the normal diplomatic way or see Flandin in Geneva, but a Paris meeting was out. It
would mean a compromise, would mean dealing outside the League, and
would bring forth the criticism that had put out Hoare. British opinion held
principles above this particular interest. Mussolini could not conclude a
peace treaty with a nonexistent government. British policy itself was not yet
determined. So what was there to talk about?[69]

Such blithe irresponsibility infuriated the French. There was plenty to talk
about. If the British would not cooperate, France would approach Italy
alone. Chambrun warned Suvich on 2 May to avoid "the grave political
error" of a unilateral proclamation that Italy would annex Ethiopia or take
it as a protectorate. Such an act, Chambrun said, would give rise to an international crisis of "extreme gravity." Moderation would pay better for the
Italians.[70]

The same day Flandin laid it on the line. Referring to a comment by
Suvich that the Italian government was inclining toward a "radical solution"
that would "totally" resolve the Ethiopian question, Flandin said such a
declaration would not be acceptable to the League. There was no way
around this. Reconstitution of the Stresa front—the fond hope of the
French—depended on a solution Britain could accept and against which the
League would not protest. The peace of Europe depended on prompt settlement. The decisive advantages to Italy, both in Europe and in Africa, would

not come through narrowly conceived dramatic acts for the sake of prestige. If the Italian government took the narrow view, France would have no further justification for trying to moderate international opinion in Italy's favor.

The hour had come, Flandin said, for Mussolini to state the conditions under which he was prepared to treat. The emperor, Flandin thought, would go west to the provinces to set up his government. In the face of conquest, if Italian demands were moderate, Britain might agree to influence him toward negotiation. Mussolini must reveal his intentions to the French before 11 May. If Flandin decided they were not viable, he would return them, and if Mussolini would not accommodate, the French policy of moderation would change. If they seemed workable, he would inform the British and try to open talks.[71]

By the time Chambrun received these instructions the emperor had fled, not west, but east, to exile abroad. This transformed all aspects of the crisis. For the Italians, victory in Ethiopia meant victory in Europe.

Addis Ababa

On 14 April the Eritrean column under General Pirzo Biroli reached the imperial field headquarters at Dessye to find the crown prince just departed. The same day the emperor left his prayer at Lalibala to renew his flight south, and in the Ogaden Graziani at last launched his attack on Ras Nasibu and toward Harar. On 20 April Badoglio moved his advance headquarters to Dessye and prepared for the final run to Addis Ababa.

Barton put the Ethiopian dilemma bluntly: "League action [that is, inaction] towards the use of gas superimposed on League attitude towards sanctions has reduced to a minimum Ethiopia's power of resistance. . . ." He made a personal appeal to his government to make £100,000 available to Ethiopia, to reinforce Gambela, and to complete a road from the Sudan frontier through Gambela to Gore. A political officer should go to Gambela for liaison; rifles, machine guns, and ammunition should be sent to Khartoum for Gambela; and the Ethiopians should be told that if they moved their government to Gore support and communication would be available.[72]

Nothing came of Barton's plea. Eden applied "the test of collective action"—as ever, the kiss of death. Financial assistance is "nowhere enjoined by the Covenant." No arms from the government. No road making inside Ethiopia. The Sudanese enclave at Gambela would stay open only on a normal basis, being however, like Berbera in British Somaliland, open for Ethiopian purchases of supplies.[73] As a matter of fact Eden was paying more attention than he let on to Barton to the movement of Italian troops in the

Gojam area and to the possibility that the Ethiopian government might relocate in the west.

The advance, with the possibility of Italy's creating a native army in the land it controlled, was taken now as a genuine imperial threat. Eden told the cabinet on 22 April that despite diplomatic agreements and Italian reassurances he doubted there would be peace for long over the question of rights around Lake Tana. A week later he reported that at Gallabat, on the Sudan frontier, the Italians had concentrated a much larger force than stood opposite on the British side. "The Italian triumph," he said, "was already reacting on the situation in the Mediterranean." Further disturbing was "the effect on the black races in Africa and on the situation in India." In Egypt delicate negotiations were going on to regularize the British position on the Nile. Initial nationalist reaction to the war, which threatened to hem Egypt between Italian armies in Libya and east Africa, had been to recognize a value in British protection. Now, at the cabinet on 29 April, Eden raised the possibility that Italy might "sooner or later attempt to take our place in Egypt," offering for example, "to adopt a more conciliatory attitude towards Egypt in regard to the Sudan than we could ever give."[74]

The Italians took advantage of the turns in their favor. The notorious propaganda broadcasts to the Arab world from Bari, which had caused so much irritation at the beginning of the conflict, were renewed on a scale equivalent to the height of their intensity in August and September 1935. This campaign, aided by a large population (54,800) of Italian residents in Egypt and by subsidies to the nationalist press in Cairo, stirred anti-British sentiment with charges that Britain used Egypt only for purposes of empire, that they would desert Egyptians as they had let down Ethiopians, and that Italians, denying imperial ambition, were natural allies.[75]

Badoglio merits notice for the methods of warfare he introduced in Ethiopia, soon to find application in Europe. There was, of course, his use of aircraft to support ground troops, to provision advance columns, and to seek and destroy and, above all, in this colonial context, to demoralize with machine guns, bombs, and gas. The use of bacteriological warfare was rejected as unnecessary and imprudent.[76] In his deployments Badoglio struck at important targets, sending columns forward to take full advantage of speed and mobility without traditional precautions for covering the routes. In this way he smashed into the heart of the kingdom, taking strategic centers and leaving the extremities to wither. Badoglio in seven months brought to an end a war most people thought would last for several years.

Neither he nor Mussolini saw the war through colonial eyes. Neither saw it as a progressive gaining of control over the population or suppressing of irregular opposition en route, as a preparing of administrative structures as the army moved forward, as a process of organizing the rear *pari passu*, not only to better supply the front, but to stabilize the country as part of a new Italian holding. For both of them, all that could wait. What was at stake was immediate benefits, the political advantages to be gained from victories in the field. The Ethiopian war was, for Mussolini, significant only in its European light. Once his empire was won, Mussolini lost interest in it. Badoglio viewed his mission as a conqueror, a military chief, only in the slightest sense concerned with colonial responsibilities. Once he entered Addis Ababa he lost all interest in the country. Not for him the problems of government, of putting down resistance in the countryside, of winning people to Italian rule, of populating the land with colonists, of putting the soil to work for Italy. Two weeks after he arrived in Addis Ababa, Badoglio left for home. His job was done.

Badoglio was able to achieve his success—and the titles and honors he avidly sought—because the forces under his command were in every respect except personal bravery overwhelmingly superior. It was a European campaign in Africa. Badoglio could conduct a war of movement because his troops were well led, well equipped, and tied together by a thousand radio stations. They had no need to rely on signals, on landlaid wire. This helped the deployment of the air force, its use as a "logistical instrument rather than as a fighting force," which, along with wireless communications, Badoglio considered the most important reason for his victory.[77] Every message the Ethiopians put to the air was immediately intercepted. Of opposing air power or effective antiaircraft protection they had none.

As to the Italian superiority in modern weaponry, in May 1936 the Italian command in east Africa had 30,000 motor vehicles, 2,000 radio sets, 30,000 field telephones, 200,000 tons of fuel, 3.2 million hand grenades, 4.2 million artillery rounds, 845 million cartridges, and provisions to sustain a half million men.[78] And all this was smoothly supplied by sea. The army was well served by the navy and the Italian merchant marine, who took due pride in transporting the men and over two million tons of goods to Massawa and Modgadishu and in handling all communications between Italy and east Africa. The navy also took credit, along with the diplomatic service, for moderating international pressure—the Italian fleet in the Mediterranean forced caution on the British and so circumscribed international action against Italy.[79]

Badoglio went to Dessye on 20 April. During the next five days General Dall'Ora brought 1,700 cars and trucks up to Dessye. The march from there to Addis Ababa, a thrust of 250 miles, started on 24 April. In the next two days some 10,000 Italians and 10,000 Eritreans moved off in three columns at greatest possible speed. The only question was whether supplies could keep up with the pace. Badoglio counted on being able to use the Djibouti railroad for provisions when he reached the capital. On the twenty-seventh Mussolini sent a telegram to Paris stating that the Italians would take control of the railroad in Ethiopian territory and keep it running.[80] It caused considerable bitter feeling in London when the French government, who had refused to allow war matériel for Ethiopia to pass along its stretch, now instructed the railroad's French manager to yield to superior force and permit Italian use.[81]

The need for speed governed Badoglio's thinking. While Italian diplomats strung along the Committee of Thirteen on the question of negotiation, he was anxious lest some premature agreement rob him, and Italy, of the glory of taking the capital. On 8 April he had cabled Mussolini from Makale that he needed only until the end of the month to reach Addis Ababa. Rest easy, Mussolini had replied, you will have the time—a tip-off that no serious peace talks were likely. Badoglio had little fear of organized opposition. The Ethiopian force was "pulverized," but speed was important before any resistance could be put together. On 24 April Mussolini suggested that, ideally, the capital should be reached before 11 May, when the "Genevan Sanhedrin" was scheduled to meet, "but if not possible it is not important, for time works for us." (The Sanhedrin was the high court of justice and the supreme council in ancient Jerusalem before which Jesus was condemned.) As to the taking of the capital, "Britain begins to be resigned to the fact, Europe awaits it, and Italy is certain." Badoglio replied, "I will be in Addis Ababa before 2 May."[82]

The 20,000 men, two columns on foot and one mechanized, found the "march of iron will" demanding but uneventful. With the flanks entirely exposed, the outskirts of Addis Ababa were reached on 4 May, the same day on which the emperor embarked upon the British ship of war *Enterprise* in the Djibouti harbor.

Haile Selassie, profoundly depressed, left Lalibala on 14 April for his capital. He had hoped to go to Dessye. Now he had to stay east of the Italian column in possession of that city. It was a miserable trip south, for he was beset by sniping from local tribesmen and reports of further desertions and betrayals. Discredited by defeat, traveling in hostile country, he was lucky to avoid assassination. He headed for Warra Hailu and its telephones to the outside world, only to find that it too was occupied by Italians. His party was strafed by an air patrol. He got to Fiche, near the northern road, boarded a car, and, weary to the bone, arrived in Addis Ababa on 30 April, facing a most uncertain future.[83]

The threat of imminent Italian occupation put the city in a panic. Steps were taken to remove the empress and part of the imperial household to

Jerusalem, if the British agreed. The cabinet in London consented on 22 April, as long as the empress took no more than six persons in her entourage. When the emperor arrived on the thirtieth his ministers posed three alternatives: immediate resistance, retirement of the government to the remote city of Gore in the west and the mounting of a guerrilla war, or flight to Europe. Blatta Takale Wolde Hawariat, whom Haile Selassie had left responsible for Addis Ababa, had formed a patriotic association for guerrilla warfare. Move to Gore, he urged, for the rains would immobilize the Italians, and internal disorder, such as the open revolt in Gojam, meant the Italians could not easily impose their rule. Takale spoke of the beneficial effects of a possible war. Supplies might be obtained through Sudan and Kenya. The empire might be reconquered. Few spoke of a flight to Europe, although a train waited for the empress and the *Enterprise* stood by to receive her.[84]

Haile Selassie was tortured by indecision. Fatigue, spiritual misery, irresolution—these are the sorts of descriptions made by observers. Steer saw him on 1 May. "His aspect froze my blood. Vigour had left the face, and as he walked forward he did not seem to know where he was putting his feet. His body was crumpled up, his shoulders dropped; the orders on his tunic concealed a hollow, not a chest."[85]

Haile Selassie met with his Council of Ministers on 30 April. He approved the plan to move the government to Gore. A caravan was organized, some boxes of archives gathered up. The emperor told the American minister he would go on fighting as long as there was one Ethiopian soldier left to help him. He asked the British minister if his government would permit him to purchase arms and supplies through the Sudan and if, as a last resort, he could escape by air by that route. Barton answered ambiguously, saying existing communications with the Sudan would not be altered.[86]

On the afternoon of 1 May the Council of Ministers met again. The Italians were 100 miles to the north, expected in a day or two. The emperor had to leave the capital. Ras Kassa, the most powerful nobleman of the land, argued, not that the government remove to Gore, but—to the horror of those who supported Takale's plea for continued struggle—that the emperor board the special train and flee to Europe. The vote went twenty-one to three (Takale, Foreign Minister Herouy, and Dejazmach Yigezu, minister for domestic affairs). The Council's judgement was that Haile Selassie should leave for Djibouti.

The emperor hesitated. He considered a final battle for the capital. The war drum sounded at the palace, stirring for the last time what fervor remained to the army. Haile Selassie said all was not over. They could still fight, still meet Badoglio before the city, and he too would carry on. At least the fighters could delay the Italians, to cover a westward move to Gore. The

soldiers cheered, some parties of the imperial guard encamped on the outskirts of town, but no orders for attack came. Resistance was in fact impossible. The chief of the one remaining force (5,000 men) announced his troops
would not fight. That was demoralizing news, and perhaps more than
anything else influenced the emperor to take flight. "They are prepared to
die for you," said Takale of the cheering troops. No, replied the emperor.
"They shout like this with your machine-guns behind them but no one would
fight for us. The masses would betray us."[87]

Kassa and the Council pressed their case. The emperor was at the limit of
his endurance. He conceded, deciding to take Ethiopia's cause to Geneva,
not to Gore. He thought, he wrote later, "that the horrors we had endured
would furnish the clear proof of our determination to preserve our independence." Early on the morning of 2 May, with Kassa and Seyum,
without informing even his private secretary, he boarded the train for
Djibouti. Takale was beside himself when he learned the Elect of God had
left his people for foreign asylum, and he suggested that Addis Ababa be set
on fire to defy the Italians and to turn the inhabitants out to become guerrilla
fighters.[88]

Haile Selassie stopped at Diredawa, prey to second thoughts. He talked
with the British consul for several hours. He said he did not want to leave in
Ethiopia's moment of agony, that he was beginning to regret his departure.
Perhaps there was still a chance to go south, join Desta, and continue the
fight somewhere between Harar and Jijiga. "It took me some time to dissuade him, but it had to be done," the consul recalled. "The military situation at this time was quite hopeless. If the Emperor had attempted to
continue the fight I do not think he could have escaped death or capture."[89]
The train continued to Djibouti, and on the afternoon of 4 May 1936 Haile
Selassie boarded H. M. S. *Enterprise*, bound for Jerusalem and what was to
be an exile of five years to the day.

Meantime, Addis Ababa fell apart. There was shock at the emperor's
flight. Takale went to the railway station to confirm the news. "My country,
there is no one to defend your cause," he cried. Government collapsed. Ras
Imru, reached by telephone in Debra Markos, was asked to be viceroy.[90] In
the capital, looting and riot spread unchecked. Foreigners took refuge in
barricaded legation compounds. The French took in 2,000, and 1,500 sought
protection at the British legation, defended by a regiment of Punjabis sent
there in December. The soldiers of this guard made sorties to various sectors
of the town to relieve besieged foreign missions. An American S O S was sent
by wireless to Washington, relayed to London, and then back to Addis
Ababa because it was impossible for the Americans to call the British for
help five miles across the town.[91]

On 2 May Flandin made a humiliating plea to Mussolini for help, asking that Badoglio advance his troops as swiftly as possible so as to lift the siege of the French legation and restore order in the capital. "Do what you can to get to the aid of the threatened foreign community as soon as possible," Mussolini ordered. On the evening of the fourth advance troops of the Eritrean brigade reached the outskirts. The next afternoon Badoglio took possession of the city, having prepared a triumphal entry.[92] On 9 May Mussolini proclaimed an Italian empire, naming Victor Emmanuel as emperor and Badoglio as viceroy.

What disturbed Eden about the Italian victory was that "so much was incalculable." What, for example, was one going to do with the emperor? And the government, if it went west to Gore? The emperor's flight answered the first question. As to the second, the governor-general of the Sudan feared that a "semi-bandit center masquerading as the Ethiopian government, created by "desperado ex-soldiers drifting southwest," might be established at Gore. As little British involvement as possible was the rule, but in May 1936, 30 troops disguised as police and 100 men of the Camel Corps infantry, along with a British officer, joined the police contingent already on duty at the enclave of Gambela, the upper limit of steamer traffic from Sudan on the Sobat. For political concerns a British consulate existed at Gore. This connection was kept up. A representative there might prove useful.[93]

Gambela was secure for the moment, but Eden's doubts about the future continued. In May, told that Italy had no intention of raising an army in Ethiopia, Eden replied: I don't believe it. This was wise skepticism. On 7 May Mussolini declared he would not train Ethiopians except for a small police force. But the following day Aloisi noted the plans Mussolini had: organization of an Ethiopian force of a million soldiers, creation of fifty airfields, a metallurgic industry sufficient for Ethiopia's military development, the eventual establishment of a territorial connection with Libya through the Sudan and Egypt, and the liberation of the Suez Canal to Egypt, then presumably under Italian influence. With it all, racial purity in the new east African empire.[94]

Empire, for Mussolini, was for swords, not plowshares. Not that much was done, in the event, but ideas were grand. In October 1937 he told his Council of Ministers, "I want a black army with which we will dominate all of Africa." In Libya there should be ready 100,000 men, for it would be "Italy's strategic base." Similar principles applied at home. "To make a warrior people there is only one way: to have always greater masses of men who can make war, and who want to." Hence the Ethiopian war, and hence the later involvement in the civil war in Spain. As for the empire, here is Ciano in early 1938: "My conception of the Fascist Empire is not of something static. We must go on advancing. And it is reasonable enough that the haves should be worried."[95]

Diredawa

Badoglio won the race to Addis Ababa, won the lion's share of glory. This was a bitter blow to Graziani on the southern front. If he could not get to the capital first, at least he had hoped to have a hold on Harar and the railway line at Diredawa. But, plagued in the preceding months by bad weather and lack of supplies, he was still, on 5 May 1936, only at Jijiga. Graziani, always second in Italian planning, had to count also among his disappointments that he was, on 2 May, distant from the railroad on the day the emperor escaped to Djibouti.

Harar had been Graziani's goal from the beginning, but not until he defeated Ras Desta and occupied Negelli in January was he freed from the burdensome command of the defense of Somalia to turn to the Ogaden, to Harar, which Mussolini then agreed was to be "the principal and essential objective of Somalia's armed forces."[96] The Ogaden was not entirely neglected during preparations for the battle of the Ganale Doria against Desta. Air attacks were kept up against the troops of Ras Nasibu in their fortress towns. For example, on one day at the end of December, seven airplanes dropped 5 tons of bombs, including 500 pounds of liquid mustard gas, on Dagabur and Sasa Beneh. It so happened that the British assistant military attaché was then at Dagabur, the field headquarters of Nasibu. He collected a sample of the yperite, had it analyzed in Aden, and sent it on to London where, on 30 January 1936, the Foreign Office received its first conclusive proof of the Italian use of gas.[97]

Bombing runs were something, but to undertake an offensive across the Ogaden, Graziani needed trucks, tractors, and trailers. After Negelli these, and permission for forward action, were no longer withheld. Graziani was technically under the authority of the colonial ministry. Undersecretary Lessona, attentive as he was to Graziani's wishes, helpful as he was in getting a colonial division sent from Libya, was supplanted after January by Baistrocchi in the ministry of war. Questions of rival authority aside, it was the undersecretary of war who controlled supplies.

Supplies came, but slowly. Thirty thousand men would advance toward Harar, 300 miles away, and to support them roads had to be built and supply networks established. Essentials of life and warfare were collected at Gerlogubi, Gorrahei, and Badu Danan. Preparation went on through February, through March, and into the first two weeks of April. These were bitter months for Graziani, for from the north came malicious taunts from his rival and naïve exhortations from the Duce. Badoglio, scooped against

his will by the victory at Negelli, made up for lost time in February with victories at Tembien, Amba Aradam, and Shire. From Tigre, fresh from his
successes against Mulugeta, Kassa, Seyum, and Imru, noting the war was
now at a decisive point, Badoglio asked when Graziani would be ready to attack Ras Nasibu. "Audacity will pay off," he said. Graziani mustered congratulations, adding: "I am bitterly aware that, had I been believed a year
ago when I pointed out the advantage of an offensive on the southern front, I
could have annihilated both the Ethiopian armies in the Ogaden and so have
brought the Italian-Ethiopian war to an end. History will attribute this
failure to its proper source. My own conscience is completely clear."[98]

Badoglio did not let up, nor did Mussolini. A few days later Badoglio
replied: "Tell me when you plan to attack Ras Nasibu. If you have already
launched the offensive, tell me where you will receive my telegrams."
Graziani was beside himself with fury. Unable to move, he shot back: "I
have no intention of leaving anything to chance." He stepped up air strikes.
On 29 March, for example, thirty-three planes flew to Harar to drop twelve
tons of bombs on the town declared by the Ethiopians on 2 December 1935
to be an open city devoid of military activity.[99]

On 1 April, as Badoglio was in the midst of the great victory at Mai Chio,
Mussolini wired: "Instinct tells me the time is ripe to give Nasibu the flogging he deserves." The next day Badoglio crowed: "The army of the Negus
is in retreat southward. . . . The moment has come from this situation."
Mussolini urged Graziani to immediate attack. Did he not have force
enough at hand? But he ordered a stop to the bombing of Harar. "Catastrophic" reports in Europe were producing a bad impression. On 5 April
Badoglio reported the rout at Lake Ashangi. "Graziani, my old comrade in
arms, start now that we will have another victory."[100]

Poor Graziani. On Mussolini's telegram he wrote: "This time I am inferior
to a secretary." He wired back that he needed at least until the fifteenth. His
commanders needed time; water and food must be assured; vehicles had to
be readied. Worse than that, in the first week of April torrential rains began.
Until the sun dried out the land, General Guglielmo Nasi noted on 6 April
from Badu Danan, all traffic except by tractor would stop and operations
might have to be suspended. Three days later, when he learned that a ship-
load of forty Caterpillars had arrived in Mogadishu, Graziani sighed: "The
freight train!"[101]

On 14 April Mussolini warned that the advance column was at Dessye, the
international situation demanded a faster pace, and Graziani should "in-
dulge himself" no longer. He awaited, Mussolini said, announcement of the
march to Harar. That was the last straw. Graziani sent back a long ex-
culpatory telegram, ending with the request for his recall. He was an honest
soldier, he argued, ready to fight, loyal to the end, but he could not go

against his better judgement. To provision 30,000 men along an advance of 300 miles in the worst part of the rainy season was an undertaking that could not be rushed. It might appear in Italy that he was inactive; the truth was different. His problem was that the support he was given came little and late. That was that. If Mussolini did not like the situation as it was, Graziani would leave the command.[102]

As it was, Graziani moved at once. Prompted by the beginnings of Nasibu's offensive, three columns started toward Dagabur on 14 April against the last intact army of the Ethiopians—28,000 men, better-equipped than those defeated in the north, better-provisioned from Jijiga and the Berbera road. Zamanuel Nasibu was a brave soldier and competent leader. He had stretched a line to protect the southern approaches to the capital and the railroad, from which he now began lightning attacks. It was a bold conception, and Graziani thought he would have to cross lines of trenches, fortified caves, emplacements of barbed wire—elements with which Nasibu and his three foreign advisers hoped to create a second Verdun.[103]

Nasibu lacked supplies to do the job, however. Men in the trenches had less than sixty rounds apiece. The barbed wire ran out beyond Jijiga. The Ethiopians lost the initiative. Emplacements and sorties were exposed to Italian aircraft and machine-gun fire. On 27 April, after two weeks of hard fighting, Mussolini authorized the use of gas, except yperite. On the twenty-ninth the Italians occupied Sasa Baneh; on the thirtieth, Dagabur.

Nasibu fell back toward Harar. Then, unexpectedly, what remained of the Ethiopian army collapsed. On 2 May the emperor left the capital for Djibouti. On the third the southern commanders, completely unnerved by his departure, followed. That was the end of the southern resistance. Graziani flew at once to Dagabur, intent on getting to Harar before Badoglio entered Addis Ababa. To the disgust of regular army chiefs, Mussolini told him: "At Harar you will find your marshal's baton." But a sea of mud met him and bogged him down.[104] Badoglio rode into the capital on 5 May. On the seventh Graziani fell into a twenty-foot hole while visiting a dimly lit church and broke some bones. Nasi's column, without Graziani, arrived in Harar on the eighth. The next day, in Diredawa, Graziani stood on the station platform to receive Badoglio. It was another great day for Italians. With the ceremony in Diredawa, with the handshake of the conquerors, with men of the two victorious armies presenting arms to one another, the campaign in Ethiopia was over.

12 ETHIOPIA IS ITALIAN

Empire

When the emperor left Djibouti for Jerusalem, Italian diplomats sighed with relief. "This ignominious flight solves all our problems," wrote Aloisi. It ended the persistent concern of how to deal with Haile Selassie if he remained in the country. It relieved pressures created by the appeals from Flandin and sympathetic Englishmen such as Austen Chamberlain and Winston Churchill that the terms of peace be moderate.[1] Mussolini responded to such suggestions in a conciliatory interview given on 4 May to George Ward Price of the *Daily Mail*. He had no desire to exploit or oppress the Ethiopians. Instead, the country would be open to "the economic initiatives of friendly states, since our aim is to increase the prosperity of Ethiopian peoples and the wealth of the world." There was no threat to the British empire. Italy was now a "satisfied" power. "We shall become sound conservatives, indeed." On the matter of political settlement Mussolini was less obliging. It was impossible to state the nature of the peace, since the emperor's flight created "a new and completely unexpected situation." Peace would be on Italian terms, as the Ethiopian question was settled by Italian "sacrifices alone, by our blood alone, by our money alone, without asking anything from anyone."[2]

It was indeed a solely Italian victory—over Ethiopia by arms and over legalistic, sanctionist Europe by patriotic self-discipline and strong leadership. Italy was a colonial power of consequence now, the main rival to Britain in the eastern Mediterranean and in northeast Africa. On the afternoon of 5 May Badoglio entered the collapsed city of Addis Ababa. Mussolini called a rally of the nation for that evening, an *adunata* such as had greeted the invasion seven months before. That evening he appeared on the balcony of the Palazzo Venezia to announce the end of the war, proclaiming, "Ethiopia is Italian!"[3] Few Italians were immune to the outpouring of nationalist emotion, the patriotic jubilation, this called forth. In his speech Mussolini made no reference to the king, but as soon as he finished the crowd flocked to the Quirinale. It was Mussolini's great moment, and it was with some resentment that he saw he had to share the triumph with Victor Emmanuel.

Mussolini declared "l'Etiopia è italiana," and the war was over, on 5 May. On the ninth Badoglio and Graziani met at Diredawa. Of course, Italian control of Ethiopia was not sealed with their famous handshake. Badoglio estimated it would take ten years to put down brigandage and impose order on the countryside.[4] He wanted no part of that laborious task. In two weeks time, laurels secure and his hand out for further honors, he was on his way back to Rome, leaving the administrative problems of Ethiopia to a resentful Graziani.

Two things bothered Graziani when he arrived in Addis Ababa. One was the exposed position of Italian troops in the capital. Graziani was holed up in the city with less than 9,000 men, on short rations, without supplies of gas or food, without reserves of men or ammunition, without road or air contact, in heavy rains, while in the surrounding eucalyptus woods were a hostile population and what remained of the Ethiopian soldiery. Mussolini exhorted him to "lance the boil" of the putative government at Gore, but Graziani's immediate concern was simply to protect his vulnerable force. He felt, he told the British chargé, "like Gordon at Khartoum." And, his second grievance in this strait, his work was not helped by the way Badoglio reinforced the celebrations in Italy, claiming the job was done in Ethiopia and Addis Ababa was a garden of delights.[5]

Such problems did not trouble Mussolini greatly. He was ready to be as ruthless toward rebels as he was against armies. He told Badoglio that any who opposed the occupation should be summarily shot and gave Graziani permission to use gas if necessary.[6] He had his victory, and he turned now to Europe. The issue there after 5 May was the nature of the political and juridical settlement. The British and French warned against a unilateral declaration of annexation. But the British opposed everything he did, and with the Socialist success in France—confirming Mussolini's view that the rot was spreading—he discounted equally French offers of support and threats to withdraw it.

Mussolini's argument for annexation was that the emperor had fled because the country was in rebellion against him. Italy was moving into a vacuum left by a discredited and now absent central authority. By his defeats, his flight, and the revolution of his subjects, Haile Selassie had forfeited his right to govern. The turmoil of the various peoples of the land was proof enough for the League that "Ethiopia never constituted a state." Many of these peoples welcomed the Italian advance, "an act of self-determination . . . in favor of Italian rule." Mussolini had told Ward Price: "Ethiopia is a complex of tribes of differing races, while the capital is in the hands of robbers. It seems obvious that the best thing in the interests of all concerned would be the rapid establishment of Italian authority throughout the country." Having conquered for prestige and, in success, the attendant diplomatic and geopolitical benefits, Mussolini would be satisfied with nothing less than total control of all political organization.

Mussolini hinted at this condition in the *Daily Mail* interview, in the balcony speech of the fifth when he declared Ethiopia Italian by rights of conquest and civilization and asserted "the manifold races of the former empire . . . wish to live and work tranquilly beneath the Italian tricolor," and when he warned that Italy would defend its "brilliant victory." He knew there would be opposition abroad to annexation and that this would prolong sanctions. But neither could last forever, whereas an empire might.

When Chambrun came on 6 May to plead Flandin's case for moderation, Mussolini said nothing definite about Ethiopia's future status, noting only that the Italian army filled a political vacuum. He was quick with assurances that he would never raise a native army and would respect the agreements of 1925 with Britain and 1935 with France. Henceforth "we must concern ourselves with Europe." He did drop one threat: the war was over; if sanctions were not lifted he would leave the League.[7]

Two days later Cerruti told Flandin that Italy would proceed to annexation, pure and simple. Gone were the old assurances of a kernel of independence maintained in an Amharic state. But this idea—on the model of Morocco—was the basis of Flandin's offer of support, which stressed the importance of form, of not suppressing all semblance of independence. Flandin said he could not accept annexation. The League could not recognize the total disappearance of one of its members wrought by aggressive military force. Nor could France accept violation, not only of the Covenant, but of the treaty of 1906 and the Rome agreements of 1935. Direct national interest was also involved. What guarantee did France have that Italy would not build a new railway to compete with the French-dominated Djibouti line? As for the League, it was no longer possible to lift sanctions at the May meetings.[8] Flandin's hope to arrange the affair lay shattered, and the turn of policy Flandin threatened had come about. A meeting of the Council of Ministers on 9 May decided the French delegation would *oppose* any raising of sanctions, and if any proposal was made to extend them, the delegation would vote with the majority.[9]

None of this affected Mussolini as he pushed his advantages to the limit. There was to be more to his triumph than conquest and annexation. Another *adunata* was announced for 9 May. There, amidst enthusiasm raised to fever pitch, with his words broadcast throughout the peninsula by radio, Mussolini announced in a famous speech, not only annexation, but an empire. And not only an empire, but a new emperor—the king of Italy.

This last step took some doing. Mussolini would have preferred not to share the spotlight, accepting chants as "founder of the empire." It was, after all, his doing. This the king had recognized two days before when he invested Mussolini with the highest military decoration in Italy, the Grand Cross of the Order of Savoy. Its designation, drafted by Baistrocchi, read: "Minister of the armed forces, he prepared, led, and won the greatest colonial war in history, a war that he, head of the government of the king, undertook for the prestige, life and greatness of the Fascist fatherland."[10] And on the ninth the Grand Council of Fascism voted "the gratitude of the nation to the Leader, founder of the empire." It was to be a Fascist empire, an *impero* to stand against the *regno* of the royal state. Mussolini made this clear in his speech on the ninth: "Italy has its empire at last: a Fascist empire." An empire was more than previous ministers of the king had achieved. But if Ethiopia was also to be a national victory, the nation, as was evident on the night of 5 May, would have the king share in it.

The Negus had fled. The title, the Amharic designation "Negus Neghest," "King of Kings," was suppressed. Mussolini wanted to limit the gift of Victor Emmanuel's new title. In the drafting of the original announcement he omitted mention of succession within the House of Savoy. Once Victor Emmanuel died, the title would die too, or have to be redesignated. Thus the gift would seem all the more in Mussolini's usufruct. It took considerable tact on the part of Giacomo Medici del Vascello, secretary of the Council of Ministers, to convince Mussolini to attribute the title to the king and "his successors." It is reported that after the wild acclamation beneath his balcony on the night of 9 May, when the crowd began to move to the Piazza del Quirinale to cheer the new emperor, Mussolini banged his fist on the table and shouted, How does the king fit in? "He did not want to go; I had to force him." Luigi Federzoni said that on that day Mussolini decided to abolish the monarchy.[11]

But there was great political value in associating the royal house first with the war and now with the conquest. The king himself was grateful. A simple man, easily moved, tears came to his eyes when the crowd hailed him as emperor. Mussolini's wife said the king offered her husband the title of prince and, when he refused, pressed him (also unsuccessfully) to accept at least a peerage. She herself received a bouquet of roses from the queen—not much, but such a token never came before, or after.[12]

There were medals and honors for everyone. Graziani was made a marshal. Badoglio became Duke of Addis Ababa and the city of Rome supplied a lavish villa. He wanted more, succession and an annual stipend for his title, for example, and (it was said) Mussolini vetoed the suggestion that his heraldic motto be "veni, vedi, venci."[13] According to Ciano, Badoglio wanted to take his vice-regal designation home when he left Addis Ababa on 21 May and exercise the position from Italy, leaving Graziani, as a sort of intendant, with all the problems. Graziani deserved more, and the vice-regency transferred to him when Badoglio left. What about De Bono? His diary after his replacement is a record of his nervous and depressed state. Following Mussolini's victory speech on 5 May he wrote: "I hope he remembers that, for three years, only he and I thought possible what has come to pass." When the empire was declared he wrote: "For the future there is nothing for me." What he got was a promise to head a committee for the formation of a colonial army.[14]

Mussolini could afford to share some glory. Standing there on his balcony on the night of 9 May, with Italians supporting him as never before, Mussolini was at the apex of his career. In the face of the hostility or disapproval of most of the world, he carried, it seemed, all before him. He once bragged that he had solved "all the problems which baffled Cavour—the problems of Church and State, State and Empire, and of the economy at home and abroad—now there remains only the elimination, the elimination by fusion, of the rivalries between north and south."[15] And this might be accomplished through emotional unity around the figure of the Duce. An unstressed aspect of the Ethiopian war is Mussolini's expectation that the creation of a warrior and imperial state would educate Italians in a sense of common purpose, responsibility, and sacrifice.[16] The insistence that Italy act alone, that the empire be won by blood, that defeats be avenged, the stress on will and power—these and the call for national unity in the face of the external threat of sanctions were used to overcome internal division.

Lessona took these ideas more seriously than his leader. When he returned from Ethiopia in the middle of May he expected that Mussolini's foreign policy—so successful—would become less propagandistic and that public life would be inspired by ideas of austerity and reflection. The empire, for Lessona, signified "not only the conquest of African land . . . but . . . the wish of the Italian people to attain a higher level of national discipline, of education, and of public morality." Lessona decided to set an example of the new style. Instead of inflated rhetoric about future promise and great achievement, the undersecretary of colonies wanted to "establish a line of serious and sober conduct." He did not grant an interview on return; he made no public declarations. Lessona, however, was a minority of one and doomed to disappointment.[17]

Instead, the victory was generally described in the terms used by Mussolini, who in 1941 looked back on it as a "golden age" for Italy. One of the most intense, most luminous periods of its history, an epic, he called it. "All that was done was firm, decisive, manly, popular, and all, seen from a distance, seems romantic, as was the beauty, the poetry, the splendor revealed by the soul of the Italians. Never was a war felt so deeply. Never was

enthusiasm more genuine. Never was a spiritual unity more profound." The
night of 9 May saw the "full harmony of the collective spirit of the Italian
people."[18]

Mussolini did little to convert the moment of national exultation into concrete and stable expressions of national well-being. He cared nothing for
colonial development. He gave the foreign ministry to Ciano. Shrewd as that
young man was, he was certainly not the austere, reflective type Lessona envisioned. Instead of stable social direction, Mussolini gave Italians more
rhetoric and more militarism. What worked in Ethiopia might work in
Europe. Involvement in Spain, Albania, and world conflict followed in the
next six years. In 1943 Mussolini complained that Italians had all the virtues
except moral courage. "For that, we need generations and generations, and
terrible times like these," like war. Ethiopia was not a terrible war, which
partly accounted for its popularity. Less than 3,000 Italian nationals were
killed conquering the empire. Less than 1,500 died defending it against the
British in 1941. "Too few," regretted Mussolini.[19] As for moral courage,
Mussolini never went beyond the call to authority, autarky, and racism. He
once held his hand in front of De Bono. "This [his index finger] is the party;
this [his thumb] is the militia. In between is Italy."[20] So much for moral
leadership.

In May 1936 all seemed fine. There was full, honest civic rejoicing
throughout the land. The annexation decree was turned into law on 14 May
by the Chamber of Deputies, to shouts of "Long live the founder of the empire," and on 18 May by the Senate, which placed a plaque in the hall com-
memorating the event. On 12 May came a public statement by Pope Pius XI.
Opening an exposition of the world Catholic press in the presence of twenty-
four cardinals and the diplomatic corps, the pontiff, speaking in Italian, said:

> May this Exhibition be blessed by Almighty God, Who allowed it to begin in
> such an unexpectedly propitious atmosphere, general and local, near and far,
> to the point of almost exact coincidence with the triumphant joy of an entire
> great and good people over a peace which, it is hoped and intended, will be an
> effective contribution and prelude to true peace in Europe and the world.[21]

Pius's statement, coming as the League Council met in Geneva, was greeted in the Fascist press as a devastating blow to the League. Catholic circles
suffered in embarrassed silence, seeing, quite accurately, that this effusion
undermined the carefully tended pose of noninvolvement and encouraged
the charge of collusion. Despite the pope's concluding invocation of "Peace,
peace, peace," despite the fact that the Vatican's bells had stayed silent the
week before when steeples throughout Italy rang in the victory, his words
seemed to many unwarranted in the circumstance, unaccompanied as they
were by any pronouncement on the justice or injustice of the case.

Daniel Binchy explained the pope's words as an emotional expression let slip by a loyal Italian. But the speech was not extempore. The French ambassador explained it thus. Following the proclamation of empire, the pope and Cardinal Pacelli were greatly disturbed by the collapse of the international order. On the other hand, Pius thought he should make some obliging allusion to the elated mood of Italians, even to the point of associating such words, despite his own preoccupation and disquiet, with the call for world peace.[22] Mussolini drew the lesson, all the more readily when, while the pope would not crown the new emperor, the Vatican was among the first to recognize the king's additional dignity. Mussolini told Giuseppe Bottai: "I want to make a cynical declaration to you: in international relations there is only one morality—success. We were immoral, they said, when we attacked the Negus. We won, and then we became moral, completely moral."[23]

As for world peace, it was not lost on observers that the spectacle of the proclamation of empire was watched from inside Mussolini's office at the Palazzo Venezia by the representatives and military missions of non-sanctionist states—Germany, Japan, Brazil, Albania, and Hungary. This prompted Paul-Boncour to speak to Eden about "the dangers of a new constellation of dissatisfied states." The chargé of the United States was informally invited, but did not go, sending instead the embassy's military and naval attachés.[24]

Council Meeting, May 1936

The Council's delegates gathered in Geneva. On 10 May they received a telegram from Haile Selassie in Jerusalem. He had decided, he said, "to put an end to the most sweeping, the most unjust, and the most inhuman war of modern times by leaving the country in order to avoid the extermination of the Ethiopian people." He appealed to the League not to recognize "territorial extension" resulting from "illegal recourse to armed force." The next day the Ethiopian delegation was more explicit.

> The crime has now been consummated. The Convenant has been torn up. Article 10 had been outrageously violated. Article 16 is not applied. . . . The abandoned Ethiopian people felt infinite despair when, at the beginning of March 1936 it realized that it must renounce the hope and faith which it had placed in the support of the League of Nations. . . . Will the League of Nations, which is also a victim of Italian aggression, bow its head to violence?[25]

There was a saying: "Whatever the League took up, it adjourned." The maxim fit perfectly the question of further sanctions, postponed from the first of March to the end of April, then to May, by which time it was a dead issue. There was talk at the end of April that existing sanctions might be raised at the May meeting, perhaps as part of a settlement or, after 2 May, because the war was over. Ecuador had lifted them on 17 April, the first breach in the front. But Italian intransigence, the uncompromising pronouncement of empire on 9 May, and the declaration of annexation delivered to the secretary-general on the tenth, caught the delegates off-guard. Eden had admitted failure in his speech to Commons on 6 May, a collective failure, he called it. Some blamed Haile Selassie. Here is Vansittart: "The Emperor ruined everything. Had he played for time and kept on his feet until the rains, sanctions and the gold drain . . . would have done at least part of their work and we should have had a very different situation."[26] Most delegates at the Council now wanted to avoid exposing the League to harsh humiliation by raising sanctions at once. The Chilean representative made the exception with his argument that since the war was over sanctions no longer had any purpose. But the rest of the delegates thought it best to put aside consideration of the future of sanctions until the June meeting. Existing measures would stay in force—no more, no less.

The declaration of annexation raised other problems. Acting alone, es-chewing diplomatic consultation as to the disposition of the land, the Italians had decreed the unilateral suppression of one of the League's members. There followed the question of recognition and, more immediately, of the Italian claim that, as Ethiopia was no longer a state, it no longer deserved a seat at Geneva.

A decision on recognition could be postponed. It was, in any case, up to individual governments, who were just (12 May) receiving copies of the annexation decree. On the point of Ethiopian representation, in the grave if not black mood at Geneva, everyone agreed that the Council should not con-cede. Titulescu summed up the sentiment: "The Italians want us to eat shit. So be it. We will eat it. But they want us also to declare that it smells like roses. That is too much."[27]

Having been brandished with such contempt, the Italian threat to with-draw lost some of its force. A depressed Paul-Boncour, chief French dele-gate, told Eden, who was sitting uncomfortably as president of the Council at this meeting, that if the break had to come, better on a point of procedure, with Italy unmistakably in the wrong, than on a point of substance, where there might be room for argument.[28] The Ethiopian case, bleeding fresh, could not be denied. That state, its delegate told the Council, was "not the author but the victim of aggression." It was Italy that should withdraw. And if Aloisi refused to sit at the same table, claiming that "the only sovereignty in Ethiopia is Italian sovereignty," that was too bad. The Ethiopian delegate, Wolde Maryam, was called to the table. Aloisi left the room. On 12 May the Council voted to resume deliberation on sanctions on 15 June. In the mean-time, existing measures would remain in force.[29]

What did the Italian withdrawal from the Council table mean? Aloisi, with no instructions, gave no explanation. Did it mean Italy was leaving the League, or just refusing to take part in these discussions of the conflict? On 11 May Aloisi wrote in his diary that the day marked "the end of the Italian-Ethiopian debate on a diplomatic level." Aloisi was in fact back at the Council table within minutes of his gesture to present a report on the world court. On 13 May, however, Mussolini said he definitely intended to leave the League—perhaps not at once, no date was set. Mussolini waited to see what would happen at the June meeting. In the meantime, Aloisi smoothed over the trouble. He told Chambrun on 14 May that his departure from the Council table was part of a "momentary interruption" of Italian collaboration meant to preserve Italian dignity, but that it was also "advance notice" that formal withdrawal would follow if sanctions were not raised shortly. The Covenant never intended a punitive role for sanctions, and the war was over.[30]

The May meeting of the Council did not, any more than those of March or April, quiet the anxieties of delegates faithful to the League. The future of collective security was at a crossroad, and no guidance came from Britain or France. Lesser states had to trust on faith, or give it up.

That the French should mark time was understandable. Sarraut's government did not reflect the composition of the new Chamber elected on 3 May, and the Quai d'Orsay awaited policy direction from the new parliament. But how to explain the irresolution of the British? the cause of great concern to the smaller states. Eden seemed "disoriented" and pulled uncertainly between the humanitarian-collectivist sentiments of those whom Madariaga called the "vegetarians" and a more "realistic" view of international relations.[31] Mussolini thought this irresolution was another indication of British decadence, of enfeebled, superannuated pacifism and the low intelligence of Britain's leaders.[32]

On 14 May, in his last days at the Ethiopian desk in the Palazzo Chigi, Raffaele Guariglia tried to counter the anglophobia with a memorandum arguing the long-term need for Italy to return to good relations with the British and to reenter the framework of collective security. He predicted the British would give de facto acceptance of the conquest. France's value to Italy was diminished by its internal divisions. Cooperation with the British in the Mediterranean would reinforce Italy's new position there and lead to greater influence with Greece and Turkey, for instance, at a straits convention to be held in June (which, in the event, the Italians did not attend). The Ethiopian issue could simply be allowed to die at Geneva. Guariglia sent his thoughts to Grandi, who did not reply, and to Ciano, who was to be foreign minister after 9 June and who replied only that Guariglia was to go to Buenos Aires as ambassador. Guariglia's ideas were out of date.[33]

Britain was the one state at Geneva that could halt the general drift toward neutralism and disengagement. France, in the short run, would be of no help to the entente groupings in Central Europe or to the low countries. If Britain would not join in their protection, these countries were on their own. The French minister in Prague scolded the Czech foreign minister when he said on 12 May that the Little Entente would follow France and Britain if those two powers worked out a common policy; otherwise they would take an independent line. What has Britain to do with it? the Frenchman replied. Everything depended on British-French harmony, Camille Krofta responded, otherwise Czechoslovakia, Romania, and Yugoslavia could count on nothing. But from the Rhineland it was obvious that there was no common line, so France's former clients hedged their bets.[34]

A similar conclusion was drawn by states stretching from Norway to Iraq. The shock of annexation pulled wavering states to the Council meeting in May, but a centrifugal trend could be countered only by the most resolute action on the part of Britain. Belgium, for instance, was in the midst of a political crisis. Elections in late May strengthened extremes at Right and Left, benefiting those who wanted a policy of nonalignment and undermining those, like Van Zeeland, who supported the League. Belgian foreign policy changed accordingly, becoming neutral. Paul-Henri Spaak, foreign minister after 13 June, said the independent line was the "only way to maintain national unity and insure the country's survival." So much for internationalism and collective security.[35]

Within the Little and Balkan ententes, separatist interests took hold as guarantees of mutual assistance lost their credit. As in Belgium, foreign policy was increasingly influenced by internal concerns. The latitude of internationalist foreign ministers disappeared, and this weakened the League. The Yugoslavs worried less about Germany and more about Italy, against whom they scouted possibilities of a preventative war. Arguing for continued sanctions, they thought that if Italian expansion was to bring war to the Adriatic and Mediterranean, better now with the British to help than later, perhaps without British aid. The Greeks refused to join the Balkan states in any action against Italy unless Albania cooperated, which Albania never would, of course. Titulescu, the champion of the League, of ties with France, and of collaboration with the Soviet Union, was dismissed by King Carol, who moved closer to the Right and the anticommunism of Joseph Beck's Poland.[36] Beck, returning from the Council meeting in May, summed it up: "He had never seen Geneva in such a state of chaos. . . . No one had known what was to happen. Among the smaller states there was lively dissatisfaction on all sides."[37]

The behavior of the Soviet government attracted a good deal of attention and shows the transitional nature of the period's international politics. From

1933 on, the Soviets had supported collective security on the line that peace was indivisible. The aim was to keep up Western connections that, if they did not prevent a German war, might provide allies if it came. The Soviet delegation supported sanctions. Litvinov eloquently defended the Covenant in his speechs at Geneva. Hoping a determined British stand would tell against Hitler, he was at first ready to go as far as closing the Suez Canal. As time went on, in the face of British indecision and Italian success, he modified his stand, and in March and April Soviet reluctance to join in the oil sanction was one of the reasons it was not pressed. During the sanction period the Soviets did not let their relations with Italy deteriorate. Ideological differences were ignored in diplomatic and commercial spheres: the Soviet Union was a supplier of oil; the overall level of goods exported to Italy actually increased; ships of the Soviet merchant marine were hired for Italy's African transport.[38]

With the feeble response to the Rhineland, the Soviet foreign ministry thought it would be best if Italy were drawn back into association with France and, under the good auspices of the Franco-Soviet pact, kept out of Germany's reach. Thus, at the May meeting of the Council, Litvinov took on a mediator's role, arguing, as did Ambassador Boris Stein in Rome, that it was impossible to save Ethiopia and that if Italy gave guarantees to cooperate with the League, to stand watch over Austria, and to return to Geneva to play an active role in Europe within the context of collective security, sanctions should be lifted as soon as decently possible. This was the sort of thinking Avenol appreciated. He hoped the Russians might exercise a moderating influence on Blum with regard to Italy.[39]

Most states at Geneva in May 1936, however, disappointed and puzzled as they were, looked to Britain for a lead. In May it was obvious Britain had no policy. If collective security was to have a future, Eden had to make that clear at the Council meeting of 16 June.

There remained, after the May council, the questions of the future of sanctions and recognition of the new empire. More broadly, brought on by the events recounted here, there was general concern about Italy's future European role and, now much in the air, "reform" of the Covenant. These last two issues are beyond the scope of this book. Like the question of recognition, on which relations of various states with Italy soon came to depend, these were active diplomatic problems for the next two years. They were interwoven with Italy's new spirit of defiance and its involvement in the Spanish civil war, with whether or not there would be agreement in the Mediterranean, with the growth of an appeasement policy toward Italy, and with response to the Axis. Talk of reforming the League showed that support for obligations as defined by article 16 was insufficient and confirmed the League's political impotence. Flandin told Eden on 15 May that he was sure article 16 would be applied again by France only where vital national interest was involved. And to protect such interests, which among the great powers needed article 16 anyway? Let us determine, Flandin said, the extent of Mediterranean interests and then, instead of generalizing around a principle, deal exclusively with them and include Italy in a regiònal pact.[40]

Here was a lesson of the Ethiopian war. It was not so much that the League, or sanctions, failed, but that Britain and France did not apply to Europe the expressions of support for the notion of general obligation. With the existing framework of security rejected, and cooperation with smaller states shucked with it, the diplomatic history of Europe after 1936 was marked by particular understandings, neutrality, regional grouping, and specially bargained agreements. The vision of an effective League disappeared, given up for the advantages of direct negotiation. Appeasement became convenient.

What about sanctions? Could something be decided before the June 16 meeting of the Council? By mid-May thirteen countries were reported in breach of their undertakings. The rationale for sanctions diminished when they seemed like simple reprisal. Flandin's foreign ministry sought a way out. In return for calling quits over Ethiopia, the Italians would give an assurance recognizing a limited application of article 16 to Europe, give a Mediterranean guarantee to quiet the fears of Yugoslavia, Greece, and Turkey, and, with France, make some statement indicating defense of some of the states of Central Europe. With such assurances in hand by mid-June, and with British collaboration, no one at Geneva would oppose the call to lift sanctions, and Italy would be back in Europe. Blum, talking to Eden on 15 May, spoke vaguely about prolonging sanctions until the Assembly met in September, saying he did not want to raise them in June as his first act as prime minister, but that he would go along with the League and, above all, with London. On 23 May, in a message drafted by Paul-Boncour, the British were asked to join a diplomatic action to pursue these assurances in Rome. Time, and British-French concern, was essential if the matter was to be resolved by the Council meeting. The stakes were high. What was lost in Ethiopia might be saved for Europe. That, for France, was the vital point.[41]

Corbin approached Eden on 25 May, suggesting the joint overture to Rome. Eden presented him with a list of pros and cons, but no sign of how the British might move. The British stuck initially over the terms of disposition for Ethiopia. They worried about African dimensions that the French ignored. To be sure, for protection and as bargaining counters, France asserted the value of the railroad and argued the number and composition of the guards along it and at the legation in Addis Ababa. British apprehension was of a larger scale, however. Britain took as granted existing rights concerning Tana and Gambela, as well as certain grazing patterns followed by subject peoples from British Somaliland. Two main concerns for Britain were the question of an Ethiopian army under Italian control and the rights of access by non-Italians to trade and commerce. If Mussolini declared that Italy would observe the duties of a mandatory (providing for an open door and prohibiting a native military force) and would send the Council reports on its administration, the vexing issue of annexation and recognition could be made to disappear—and the League would reassume a standing in the affair. This was the sensible line, Corbin thought. He wanted to express it directly to Italy, if just to get talks started. Eden refused. That would smack too much of a deal.

Furthermore, Eden insisted on tying these African considerations directly to a liquidation of all issues of the conflict, not smoothing over certain features and hoping the others would disappear in time. One can see his point—What had the fuss been all about? Sanctions and recognition were at stake in Europe, not grazing rights or economic opportunities. The French wanted to isolate the Ethiopian issue, give Mussolini most of what he wanted, cut the issue off from discussions of the future of Europe and the League. No one except Italians had a vital interest in Ethiopia. Eden stubbornly disagreed. At bottom, Eden thought Mussolini responded more to pressure than to favor, so if one wanted Italian assurances there was no particular rush to raise sanctions.[42]

Sanctions *were* increasing Mussolini's domestic difficulties, Eden told the cabinet on 27 May. They had caused a progressive economic deterioration that would be serious by mid-September and grave by the end of the year; stocks would be exhausted and gold reserves depleted, ending with a complete breakdown of all credit facilities. This crisis would be solvable only by some "thorough-going socialization and demilitarizing of the country," or "by a war." Implication: by the time of the September Assembly meeting, Mussolini might be in a more amenable mood, so keep the sanctions on. Nor was Italy out of the trouble in the empire. To a June dispatch reciting some of the difficulties, Vansittart wrote: "The Italians will stew in this juice long and painfully. It will be interesting to learn whether the French hear the sizzling quite so clearly."[43]

Eden told the cabinet on 27 May that the purpose of maintaining sanctions at the June Council "would be to show a continuous respect for international law, though the immediate object would be to maintain them until Italy was willing to come to Geneva to discuss a permanent settlement and to recognize the authority of the League." It was pressure that would do it, and, after a time, France could find out Mussolini's intentions and ask him for a declaration. Meantime, Eden said he was "impressed with the dangers for the future if Italy escaped from all the consequences for her action." If sanctions were lifted in June, it "would prejudice future negotiations with Italy on many points."

Opposed to Eden's line in the cabinet of 27 May, Neville Chamberlain put forward the supposition that Mussolini "would probably respond if we offered to raise sanctions and come to terms, and that he might be very ready to cooperate again with France and ourselves in Europe." Chamberlain's position was similar to Flandin's. Put it to Mussolini directly: If sanctions were lifted would he stay with the League and stand against Germany? The responsibility to determine this should not be sloughed off on France. "To decline to acknowledge the position of Italy in Abyssinia would be a mistake." Two former foreign secretaries in the cabinet offered opinions. John Simon asked, If sanctions were kept on, what definite return was likely? If this was not easily determined, better to drop them at once. Ramsay MacDonald agreed. Would three more months yield sufficient additional pressure to justify Mussolini's buying off at a price acceptable to the League? MacDonald thought "Mussolini was friendly" to Britain and, if approached, would probably come to terms.[44]

The cabinet made no decision on the twenty-seventh, although most members leaned toward Chamberlain's reasoning. At its next meeting on 29 May Baldwin asked the opinion of each member. All agreed that sanctions should be raised as soon as possible. The questions were whether to do so at the Council in June or at the Assembly in September, what might be got out of Mussolini in the meantime, and, whether, in the interim, it was best to conciliate or irritate him. At the poles again were Eden, who wanted to do nothing on 16 June, and Chamberlain, who said inaction would be misunderstood as indefinite continuation, thus encouraging defection of League members.

Chamberlain also wanted to press Mussolini for an accommodating declaration, and there was now more wind in his sails. The *Daily Telegraph,* trying to break the stalemate by reviving talks and changing public opinion, and acting at the request of leaders in the Conservative party, sent its diplomatic correspondent to Rome for an interview with Mussolini. This was printed on 28 May, the day between the two cabinet meetings. What could be more conciliatory than Mussolini's words? "The end of sanctions will mark the entry of Italy into the ranks of the satisfied states." Italy would continue to observe its treaties of friendship with Greece and Turkey, implying a stable eastern Mediterranean. "Sanctions once ended, we shall examine [the matter of a Mediterranean agreement] with the desire to reach an understanding and in a spirit of collaboration and of peace." "We have no need of a black army either in Africa or Europe." "We are still studying the problem of the commercial relations of our empire with foreign states and we shall find for this a moderate and acceptable solution." "The interests of

Britain, insofar as the water rights of Lake Tana are concerned, will be strictly respected." The whole of [the force in Libya] will be brought home as soon as [British] ships are withdrawn." "Not only is an Anglo-Italian rapprochement desirable, but it is necessary, and I for my part will do everything which lies in my power to bring it about." "The League can go on, if it reforms itself." "If sanctions are continued, the problem of remaining in the League or leaving it will become urgent." "The end of sanctions will produce a general easing of the position and will open up a favorable prospect for stabilization and collaboration in Europe."[45]

What, indeed, could be more encouraging? Eden, suspicious as he was, thought the approach genuine to the extent that Mussolini wanted a détente. Neville Chamberlain and Baldwin were confirmed in their optimism. Britain could ask, Chamberlain suggested, that Mussolini say to the League what he had said to the newspaper. If he refused, then the cabinet could reconsider. But before a conclusion on sanctions was made, an approach to Mussolini should take place. This was the decision of the cabinet on 29 May.[46]

It was a stroke in Italy's favor. It seemed in Rome that all Mussolini had to do to raise sanctions was to make a public statement along the lines of the interview. But Mussolini was not in such an accommodating mood. He stood firm against calls from Aloisi and Suvich for moderation, against the recommendation that he satisfy foreign opinion by organizing the new empire so as to maintain some kind of international personality for Ethiopia. If the state continued to be designated as Ethiopia, the League could not complain of the elimination of one of its members. That was the moderating advice of his foreign ministry. Instead, Mussolini followed Lessona and the colonial office. Ethiopia *was* Italian. On 1 June he had the Council of Ministers declare the existence of "Italian East Africa," comprised of five regions, each under a separate governorship: Eritrea (capital, Asmara), Amhara (capital, Gondar), Borana and Sidamo (capital, Gimma), Harar (capital, Harar), and Somalia (capital, Mogadishu). A governor-general and a separate municipal administration was established in Addis Ababa. Ethiopia, as a state, disappeared.[47]

The End of Sanctions

A decision on the future of sanctions was influenced in an unexpected way. Immediate planning was in terms of a meeting of the Council on 16 June. By the first of June a decision had not been made either in Paris or in London. Paris awaited the arrival of Blum's government, which took office on the fourth. In London the cabinet was ready to lift sanctions, but deferred decision, hoping for some gesture of conciliation from Mussolini to ease the way. In Rome Mussolini let matters hang. On the third he left for his home at

Rocca delle Caminate, where his youngest child lay seriously ill with polio-myelitis. "They might leave me at peace by my child's bedside," he said when the diplomatic problems followed him there.[48]

What altered the situation was an unexpected request on 2 June by the Argentine government that the Assembly of the League be called at once, in-stead of waiting until its scheduled gathering in September. The purpose of the call was for the entire membership of the League to have their say on the question of sanctions and the "situation brought about by the annexation of Ethiopia."

The Argentinian move irritated the Italians. At first sight it appeared to complicate what Suvich and the moderates in the Palazzo Chigi had foreseen as a two-stage process. First, the Council, dominated by Britain and France, would meet on 16 June and propose the end of sanctions on the ground that the reason for their original application no longer held. The question of recognition would be reserved and not be prejudiced. Then, following some sign of Italian goodwill—some declarations of fair treatment for natives, for instance, and some statement of readiness to cooperate in Europe such as the British wanted—negotiations about recognition could start, be concluded during the summer, and when the Assembly met in September, the League would accept annexation and Italy would go back to Geneva. The call for an immediate sitting of the Assembly threatened this schedule. Even though sanctions might be raised, arguments to defend the authority and credit of the League might close the door to eventual recognition. If this happened, Italy would leave the League for good.[49]

Suvich himself did not have long to worry about the matter. On 9 June Mussolini gave up the ministry of foreign affairs to Ciano, who brought in Guiseppe Bastianini as his undersecretary. Suvich was the only un-dersecretary who did not move up to ministership as Mussolini divested himself of some portfolios taken up in 1932. Alessandro Lessona became minister of colonies, Dino Alfieri advanced to Ciano's former job as minister of press and propaganda, and Ferruccio Lantini took over the ministry of corporations. It was another changing of the guard in the Palazzo Chigi. The "purge" of 1932 had sent Grandi to London, Guariglia to Madrid, and Rosso to Washington. Now up again went the *tono fascista* of the foreign ministry. The diplomats who had (unconvincingly) covered the Ethiopian war with claims of legitimacy and who had (successfully) spread the bluff of war, who, to the end, were the "westerners" who saw Italy's future in cooperation with Britain and France, were sent off. Guariglia went to Buenos Aires, closing the Ethiopian desk. Aloisi gave up his position as secretary-general and was shunted to a stand-by post as minister of state. Mussolini considered replacing Grandi in London (with Guariglia), but changed his mind when Grandi argued that to remove him for political reasons would create a bad impression. Suvich gave up his power in Rome and went to Washington as ambassador. Ciano, cautious, even hesitant as he was at first, cared less about Geneva.

Suvich was correct in recognizing that the Argentine initiative was meant to bolster the League's prestige. However inconvenient, the Argentine case for a meeting was valid. When the Assembly had adjourned the previous October, it had endorsed the Council's judgment that Italy was in violation of the Covenant. The president of the Assembly, together with the secretary-general and the president of the Council, were to reinvoke the body when it seemed necessary. The Assembly had been mute since the outbreak of the war, and many states in the Western Hemisphere had come to think the League no longer held meaning for them. They resented that their voices went unheard as the great powers sought settlements on their own. Now the fate of the League was at stake. Before sanctions were dismantled by understandings between the big powers, the Latin American states—or so the government of Argentina claimed—wanted a say in the debate. If ignored, they would soon drop their connections at Geneva.

The Argentine government itself was dead set against recognition, which would be a blow to the League and to its mediating role in the Chaco dispute between Bolivia and Paraguay. The Argentinians wished to generalize to Italy their stand in the Chaco affair of nonrecognition of illegally annexed territory, or at least to prevent that position from being undermined at Geneva pending the Chaco conference in Buenos Aires. If the Assembly did not condemn Italy's annexation, Argentina would leave the League, and the rest of the South American states would follow.[50] The Argentine government was worried also about the active propaganda campaign against the League being carried on by Italy in South America. This campaign, aimed at Italian residents in the Western Hemisphere as well as at hesitant governments, in fact had small success in Argentina, where the government supported sanctions and where most Italians, to Mussolini's distinct annoyance, seemed indifferent or even hostile to the struggles of the motherland. Anti-Fascist sentiment grew during the Ethiopian war.[51] The Argentinians did not want to see Latin American states divided further on the Ethiopian issue, at least not because of neglect of their opinions at Geneva. The Assembly was a chance to pull them together, to renew their confidence in collective action and the principle of nonrecognition, all the more useful coming just in advance of a Pan-American conference.[52]

The Argentine government made the call on its own initiative. Both Avenol and Assembly President Beneš saw an Assembly meeting as an impediment to quick settlement. Both feared an upsurge of anti-Italian sentiment might drive Italy away before mediating diplomacy could get to work. Both thought the troublesome affair would be more easily wound up if the search for solution was kept in fewer hands. They had to accept the call. Yet, if the meeting could be put off long enough, there might be time at least to develop the arguments for removing sanctions. Accordingly, after consulting Eden as president of the Council, on 5 June the Assembly was called for the end of the month, 30 June, to resume consideration of the Ethiopian question it had turned over to the Council seven months before. It was also decided to postpone the Council set for 16 June to a day or two before the gathering of the Assembly.

The Italians continued their usual mixture of threat and concession. As usual, too, it was clear that if France and Britain could coordinate a policy, that would carry the day at the Assembly meeting. The heads of states of the Little Entente met in Bucharest from 7 to 10 June. They supported continued sanctions, but made it clear they were ready to follow any firm British-French lead if one were offered. The Italian minister said this meeting was the entente's "swan song." Central Europe was at "the point of death," with salvation only in association with Italy.[53] Mussolini's self-confidence flowered. Out came the threats of war, of leaving the League, of turning toward Germany. On 1 June he made a bellicose speech to divisional commanders in the army. Italy would go to war if sanctions were not soon raised. Sanctions, arguments in Italy ran, while not starving Italy into submission, would, if prolonged, deprive the country of materials needed for war, just as potential enemies were rearming. Rather than wait indefinitely, Italy might have to fight its way to freedom and access while the army was prepared and popular sentiment was aroused and militant.[54]

A time schedule existed. On 26 May Suvich had said a continuation of sanctions past June might cause Italy to "entirely revise its European political position." Two days later the military attaché in Paris said if sanctions continued there would be "grave consequences" and denunciation of the previous year's military arrangements. There were reports in the first fortnight of June of stockpiles of asphyxiating and vesicant gas being laid in at Benghazi on the Libyan coast, of stepped-up production of war materials, of a possible general mobilization of two million men on the peninsula, of increases in the armed strength on the French frontier, of plans for great maneuvers for 1936 in provinces bordering France and Yugoslavia. It was said that the reason Badoglio had returned from Ethiopia was to be on hand, as head of the general staff of the armed forces, before the Geneva meetings. All this thoroughly alarmed Chambrun—"time works against us"—and Drummond, both of whom stated that the alternative to raising sanctions was an Italian-German rapprochement.[55]

So much for the stick. As for the carrot, there was play in the reassurances sought by the British. The cabinet, on 29 May, told Eden to sound Grandi "as to whether Signor Mussolini would be willing to make a contribution towards a settlement by making a statement to the League on the lines of the statements he had already made to British Press correspondents" in the *Daily Telegraph* interview, an assertion, that is, that Italy would join in a Mediterranean agreement, not raise a native army, respect the imperial interests of others, and stay in the League as a stabilizing force in Europe.

Eden made this inquiry on 3 June, asking for a spontaneous declaration to "prepare the ground for a favorable examination of the situation at Geneva." Grandi said this paid no account to Italian sensibilities, whereby Italy was first victimized and now victorious. Eden came away discouraged, but this did not stop the cabinet from the chase. It was too convenient a scheme to drop. On 10 June Eden was told to tell Grandi that, "failing a statement to the League of Nations, it would be helpful if Signor Mussolini would make a solemn statement on appropriate occasion addressed to the nations of the world on the lines of the statement he had already made to certain newspapers."[56]

Ciano followed this up only tardily, and then in changed circumstances. The English saw an Italian declaration of good intentions as related to sanctions, softening the embarrassing act of raising them. Sanctions had to go sooner or later. Italy could ease the way, and all would benefit. By the time Ciano got around to making use of the request, sanctions were dead. And when the Italians then brought out recognition as their quid pro quo, the matter had moved to an entirely different plane. A simple statement was not enough to win that round.

The suggestions from the cabinet at its meetings of 29 May and 10 June show the drifting quality in British policy toward Italy. Baldwin was tired and preoccupied with other matters. Eden gave little direction. The usual spur from France was absent. Blum's new government wanted only to tie its League policy to London's. To find what this might be, Blum requested a private meeting with Baldwin and Eden. This the cabinet refused on 10 June. Whereas the French wanted to harmonize views, Eden said it was inappropriate to proclaim a joint sanctions policy beyond the purview of the Assembly and its fifty members due to meet at the end of the month. There could be talks at Geneva then, but prior consultation would only give rise to charges of deals or pressure tactics. In the Foreign Office two weeks before there had been talk of the need to "educate" Blum in the realities of foreign affairs.[57] Now Eden kept aloof, perhaps seeing that with his own course so indefinite, he and Blum would be of little support to each other.

Again there was no hurry for a decision over sanctions, with the meetings put off to the end of the month. How they might be ended—simultaneously, partially, allowed to peter out—had yet to be thought out. But, Eden said to the cabinet on 10 June, in the hesitant way his expressions are recorded often in the cabinet minutes, "he himself was rather veering towards the view that

if sanctions were to be removed there was something to be said for our taking
the initiative." The French were not going to give a lead because, according
to Foreign Minister Delbos, they did not want to give the British government
a way to save face at home by throwing that responsibility on France and the
French people.[58]

Eden's cabinet statement was enough for Neville Chamberlain, Baldwin's
heir presumptive, who was emerging as the strongest and most influential of
the ministers in a cabinet that, by 10 June, included three former foreign
secretaries with the return of Hoare as first lord of the Admiralty. Chamberlain wrote in his diary: "The party and the country needed a lead, and an indication that the government was not wavering and drifting without a
policy." He had another worry. "My fear is that the public belittle the
military power of Italy. . . . I know Badoglio well, and look upon him as one
of the best and greatest of living soldiers." Impatient with Baldwin's
dilatoriness and Eden's indecision, and to show there was life in the government even though sanctions had failed, Chamberlain acted. The night of 10
June, after the cabinet, in a speech to a large dinner of the 1900 Club of the
Conservative party, he gave his "conclusion" that it would be "the very mid-
summer of madness" to imagine that the independence of Ethiopia could be
preserved by the pursuit or intensification of sanctions. Common sense, he
said, showed that "we have tried to impose upon the League a task which it
was beyond its power to fulfill." As long as sanctions raised the risk of war,
"it is apparent from what has happened that in the presence of such a risk
nations cannot be relied upon to proceed to the last extremity of war unless
their vital interests are threatened."[59]

This speech, published the next day in the *Times,* aroused tremendous interest in Europe, not the least in London, where the rest of the government
read it with surprise. "I did not consult Anthony Eden, because he would
have been bound to beg me not to say what I proposed." Chamberlain was
not, despite common interpretation, trying to change policy or to defeat
Eden, and he was not advocating simple raising of sanctions. "At the same
time as I was urging on Anthony the reform of the League, I said sanctions
must come to an end, but we ought first to have from Mussolini a statement
of his intentions about Abyssinia and the Eastern Mediterranean," and this
was Cabinet policy.[60]

Chamberlain lacked government responsibility for his words, although he
reflected its thinking. But there had been an official silence of six weeks, and,
as he wished, his speech forced decision. Debate on sanctions was set for 18
June in the Commons. On the seventeenth Eden presented his proposed
speech to the cabinet. It recommended the immediate raising of sanctions.
He said he had "reason to believe" from Grandi's remarks to Vansittart that
Mussolini would give the League the assurances requested. This was hardly

the sort of evidence the cabinet had in mind on 29 May or 10 June, when assurances were seen as *preliminary* to lifting existing measures. Grandi was an unreliable source for such an optimistic promise. Vansittart spoke out of turn when he let Grandi think such a cabinet decision was a foregone conclusion. And, as it turned out, Eden's expectations were proven false. But such hope served; no one looked closely; and the cabinet agreed without a discussion to lift sanctions.

To give early is to give twice. The British delegation was told to take the lead in proposing their abolishment at Geneva. The French would be informed, but not consulted, before the announcement. Nor was there any advance warning to the other states of the League. British was asserting its leadership, by example and in retreat. Assurances of mutual assistance from the Mediterranean states under article 16 would continue for an indeterminate time in the period of "uncertainty." What was important now was that a sanctions decision had been made.[61]

Eden made his speech to Commons on 18 June, in "a tone of regretful frankness, which, however, suggests an embarrassed apology," as Harold Nicolson described it. Eden developed Chamberlain's arguments on the danger of war, the impossibility of restoring Ethiopia short of military action, and the instrumentalist contention that sanctions no longer had a purpose. It was best they stop quickly, rather than rotting away with consequent additional demoralization. As for international cooperation and authority, that would have to await a reformed League.[62]

It was a bad day for the government, with sharp Opposition attacks. Baldwin, under criticism for inactivity and want of leadership, saw his prestige drop to an all-time low. The government rode out a vote of censure on the twenty-third, with some young moderates such as Harold Macmillan voting against them. "Every mongrel is yapping," a friend wrote to Baldwin on 30 June, "believing that a very tired fox has gone to ground at Chequers, with no fight left in him."[63] That was the view of the government as a whole held by many.

As far as the practical needs of officialdom went, the matter of sanctions was about over. As Britain led, other states followed. The Council of Ministers met in Paris on 19 June, the day after Eden's announcement, deciding that as a practical matter sanctions should be raised and that the French would follow any decision of the League. In a foreign policy statement of the new government, read simultaneously on 23 June to the Senate by Prime Minister Léon Blum and to the Chamber by Foreign Minister Yvon Delbos, sanctions were dealt with in a strikingly terse and sober way that assured acceptance of their termination. "Maintenance of sanctions would only be a symbolic gesture without effect. What good does it do to continue aggravating measures to which one can no longer give definite objectives?"⁶⁴ On 18 June the governments of Australia and Canada, on the twenty-second, Belgium, on the twenty-third, Haiti, on the twenty-sixth, Chile, Honduras, Uruguay, and Poland, gave an antisanction judgment. On the eve of the Assembly session, the verdict of Geneva was unambiguous.

Since war was never formally declared by Italy, Mussolini's unilateral declaration that it was now over was not enough for international lawyers, nor was Haile Selassie's statement that his flight was meant to end the war. Ever since the occupation of Addis Ababa the question of the end of belligerency had concerned Americans. For them, and for the British, it revolved around the completeness of Italian control, the degree of Ethiopian resistance, and the effort to establish a government in western Ethiopia. The State Department took the position of "watchful waiting," trying not to add to Europe's difficulties. In mid-June its chargé in Rome argued that the arms embargo should be dropped to simplify the "already overcomplicated" European scene and to enforce the American claim of independence. But from Addis Ababa on 18 June the minister resident, Cornelius Engert, argued for keeping the embargo precisely to avoid influencing Europe and to avoid giving up that bargaining counter in the increasingly difficult problem of recognition. Yet with the British decision to drop sanctions a policy of maintenance became unrealistic. "Guerilla war is not real war," was the State Department's legal advice. On the nineteenth Hull advised Roosevelt that a state of war no longer existed, so the next day Roosevelt pronounced it over, and the embargo was lifted.⁶⁵

"No Assembly had ever come together in such a mood of ill humour, discouragement, and anxiety as that which gathered at Geneva on June 30th, 1936." "These were wretched days at Geneva." There was "a greater feeling of pessimism and defeatism than I have observed before in Geneva."⁶⁶ Even sideline incidents were sour and unpleasant. In the Council, a Nazi representative from Danzig made insulting gestures to the press. In the Assembly, Italian journalists hissed, catcalled, and blew abusive whistles when Haile Selassie ascended the podium, and they had to be removed by force. Three days later there was a suicide by gunshot in the Assembly hall by a Czech journalist whose suicide notes, one addressed to Avenol, pleaded the cause of Jews and small nations.⁶⁷ It is reported that as Van Zeeland was told on the podium of the suicide he remarked: "This is a show-place of fatal events. We are bound to witness fatalities."⁶⁸ The disarray of public manners emphasized the incoherence of international politics.

Assembly President Van Zeeland opened the session with a letter from Ciano. This was the response to the British suggestion that Italy smooth the way to lifting sanctions. It was full of assurances of cooperation and good behavior. The "sacred mission of civilization" would go on "according to the principles of the Covenant." Religious beliefs would be respected, slavery abolished, taxes levied only for local needs. There would be no native army. The door was open for "equitable treatment for the trade of all countries." Italy "would consider it an honor to inform the League of the progress achieved in her work of civilizing Ethiopia." With "the immediate removal of such obstacles as have been and are in the way of international co-operation," Italy would join in the search for a stable European peace.[69] None save the Austrian delegate expressed any confidence in the sincerity of the Italian note, despite the fact that Drummond appeared optimistic as he watched it being drafted and Avenol coached its presentation. There was no way to hold Italy accountable. It was only what the British had requested, a cosmetic dressing, and Vansittart asked his colleagues, "Did anyone expect anything much better?"[70]

What is significant about these assurances is that, in Italian eyes, they were not directed toward easing the lifting of sanctions, the purpose of the original British suggestion. That battle was won. Ciano's letter, dated 22 June, moved the diplomatic contest another step forward. Its intent was to make resumption of cooperation with League powers dependent, not only on their removal of sanctions, but on their abandonment of the principle that situations created by force cannot be recognized. Yet an affirmation of nonrecognition was one purpose of the Argentinian call. In an interview on 22 June, Mussolini was blunt about what he wanted. He did not insist that the Assembly recognize the new empire, but he would not accept any resolution that excluded eventual recognition. This, he said, would be worse than existing sanctions, for it would appear as a "moral sanction" and would be profoundly felt by the Italian people. What he expected from the Geneva meeting on the question of recognition was "*no decision* one way or another."[71]

It was precisely nonrecognition, however, that the Ethiopian delegation insisted upon. The League showed no hesitation in admitting the Ethiopians to the session, despite an Italian boycott as a result. Haile Selassie was in fact the second speaker. The figure of the emperor at the rostrum, recorded for the world in motion picture, a slight man, wearing a dark cape, speaking, after the abusive interruption of the Italian journalists, in the unusual-sounding Amharic—this sight lives vividly in the minds of those who saw the event or the films. Surely it was a poignant scene: the exile, taken from Djibouti to Palestine and then to Gibraltar in a British man-of-war (for fear of a rash act against him by some Italian naval captain), then on to England to a cool welcome and an uncertain future, standing there, the first head of state to address the Assembly, with a speech drafted by Jèze and Colson, by his very presence a rebuke to the League, asking what it was willing to do now for Ethiopia.

Sanctions? Declared dead in every speech, they were wrapped in a winding-sheet of formalism: an Assembly resolution "that the Co-ordination Committee should make all necessary proposals to the Governments in order to bring to an end the measures [proposals 1–4] taken by them in execution of Article 16 of the Covenant." On 4 July 1936, forty-four delegations approved, four abstained, and only Ethiopia voted against.

Enough was enough. No one wanted to worry about Ethiopia any longer. That was clear in the vote on two resolutions proposed by the Ethiopian delegate. One asked the Assembly "by an unambiguous vote" to proclaim it would "recognize no annexation obtained by force." The second: that the Assembly recommend to individual governments a loan totaling 10 million pounds sterling to Ethiopia, "that it may defend its territorial integrity and political independence." Money, in other words, to take up the war again. This was exactly what no state in Europe wanted to see. There was no discussion of the resolutions. Van Zeeland refused to bring the question of recognition to a vote, claiming it was implicitly provided for in the sanctions resolution, in which a preamble left Italy condemned as an aggressor state. This was barren formalism. On the matter of loans, twenty-three states declared against, twenty-five abstained, and only the Ethiopian delegate voted in its favor.[72]

The votes were a verdict on the League. That old sheet-anchor dragged. On 1 July the foreign ministers of the six European states neutral in the Great War, together with Finland, went on record disapproving of the application of article 16 as long as other articles, such as the call for disarmament, went unfulfilled.[73] The common cause was gone. To base a state's security on a Covenant applied incompletely no longer made sense. It was a retreat from collective security by all states, a retreat into neutrality, isolation, regional groupings, or appeasement.

Prentiss Gilbert noted the lack of incisiveness in any policy and the discouragement and suspicion regarding Britain and France. For example, Eden's statement to the Commons on 18 June on the continuation of the Mediterranean mutual assistance agreements during the period of "uncertainty" was not elucidated to the Greeks or Yugoslavs at Geneva. They naturally concluded it was merely convenient phrasing preparatory to a withdrawal of such arrangements. The ministers of the Balkan and Little ententes decided that in view of the "equivocal attitudes" of Britain and France they would not speak at the Assembly at all.[74]

Such a crisis in confidence greatly diminished Blum's authority, as did disunity and troubles at home. France, in Socialist hands, paralyzed by strikes, its financial and military weakness exposed before all, counted for less than ever. Blum and Delbos were unable and unwilling to cut loose from the policies of their predecessors. Léger told Cerruti he was bringing Delbos around to a moderate line toward Italy. The Portuguese foreign minister told Eden that "everyone knew that France did not count for much in Europe now." The atmosphere at Geneva was "bloody," Eden told Baldwin. Blum was rattled, the League in collapse.[75] To the cabinet Eden described the Assembly as the "most exacting and most depressing" he ever attended. The international situation, beset by the quarrel over Danzig, Germany's overtures to Austria, incipient trouble in Spain, anxiety in the Far East, the disarray of the League, and doubts and weaknesses that persistently undermined relations between Britain and France, meant that "from day to day there was the risk of some dangerous incident arising, and even the outbreak of war could not be excluded."[76]

No time was lost finishing off sanctions. The Coordination Committee met on 6 July and before lunch proposed to participating governments that measures be lifted on 15 July. On that date they did come to an end.[77]

Efforts were under way to resolve other areas of contention with Italy. The Mediterranean was defused. To reassure the Greeks, Yugoslavs, and Turks, Eden on 18 June said mutual support assurances "should not end with the raising of sanctions, but should continue to cover the period of uncertainty which must necessarily follow any termination of action under article 16." This declaration was viewed with considerable suspicion in Rome. It contributed to the decision of the Italian government not to participate in talks between the eastern Locarno powers planned for Brussels on 22 July. Italian diplomats noted that the decision to raise sanctions, taken by the Coordination Committee on 6 June, related only to proposals 1–4. No provision was made for terminating proposal 5, which concerned mutual support. The Italians formally protested on 7 July against the continuation of the military assurances.[78]

To alleviate tension, the British on 8 and 10 July told its fleet units that it was no longer necessary to maintain existing war-readiness in the Mediterranean and Red seas. Hoare told the Commons on 9 July that the government proposed to "release, at a very early date, those units which were sent temporarily to the Mediterranean from the Home station and from other stations abroad." On 18 July the main body of the Mediterranean Fleet left Alexandria, reinforcements from the China station returned to the East, and the Admiralty ended its prolonged state of war-readiness. Mussolini reciprocated. On 16 July it was announced that equivalent demobilization would take place "as soon as possible" in the Libyan contingent.[79]

These steps did not resolve the contention over mutual support, however. Eden told the Commons on 15 June that the withdrawal of fleet units had "no connection with the unilateral and provisional assurance of continued support to certain Mediterranean powers." The French, with a narrower perspective, put a more strict construction on their assurances. Delbos said

that the exchanges with Britain were tied directly to the application of sanctions and would be canceled whèn sanctions were withdrawn. The British
were not eager to maintain the assurances much longer either. Ciano told
Drummond on 12 July that resumption of normal relations in the Mediterranean depended on their cancellation. Drummond and Vansittart thought of
a way out: spontaneous assurances to Yugoslavia, Greece, and Turkey that
Italy had no intention of attacking them and desired normal relations in the
Mediterranean.[80]

Italy delivered such an assurance in mid-July, and on 13 July Mussolini
told a journalist that war between Italy and England was henceforth entirely
out of the question. Italy was now "among the satisfied peoples." On 15 July
sanctions ended, eight months to the day after they had begun. To a cheering
crowd below his balcony Mussolini said: "Today . . . a white flag is hoisted
in the ranks of world sanctionism. We would like to see it not only as a sign
of surrender but also as a symptom of the return of commom sense."
Civilization and justice had triumphed, he said, "both in Africa and in
Europe." That was enough for the British. Unilaterally they declared mutual
support arrangements over. On 27 July Eden said that in view of Mussolini's
declarations there was "no further need for the continuance of these
assurances."[81]

Let a final word come from Arnold Toynbee. "Thus, before the end of
July 1936, the grave in which the dead sanctions against Italy lay newly
buried had been ploughed over with such effect that, for an artless eye,
it already might have been difficult to detect that there had been an
interment."[82]

13   CONCLUSION

International affairs in July 1936 were more unstable than at any time since 1919. Ciano was feeling his way in the foreign ministry. Italians rejoiced in a "two-front victory," but Chambrun noted a fear of isolation in the Palazzo Chigi. Few Italian diplomats looked forward to the prospect of collaboration with former sanctionist opponents.[1] That left Germany, toward which there was growing a sense of common interest, manifested in the concession of Italian claims to influence in Austria. Mussolini welcomed the German-Austrian "gentlemen's agreement" of 11 July as eliminating "the last and only mortgage on German-Italian relations."[2] Germany, on 24 October 1936, was early to recognize the empire.

There seemed less reason to play along with the western democracies any longer. Mistrust of Blum, the complications of the Spanish civil war, and recognition of France's political weaknesses made it easy to break with France. In December 1936 Mussolini denounced the Stresa agreement and the military accords Laval had so carefully fostered. It was not long before claims on Nice, Tunis, Corsica, and Djibouti were heard from Rome. Britain and France drew apart. In June 1936 the minister of war, Alfred Duff Cooper, made a speech in Paris, approved by the Foreign Office, stating that close cooperation between Britain and France was a matter of life or death, but this sentiment was subjected to strong anti-French criticism in the Commons. It was clear that the two states were not working to a common end. The British government, and most members of the Conservative party, hoped that conciliation would bring improved relations with Italy. This policy was formally adopted by the cabinet in November 1936 and was to dominate British relations with Rome thereafter (a cause, incidently, of Eden's resignation from Chamberlain's government in 1938).[3] At the moment there was one item from the Ethiopian war making conciliation difficult, however.

This was the question of recognition, the "mortgage" still outstanding with the democracies. Recognition became an acute issue with any change in diplomatic representation. When Chambrun resigned in the summer of 1936, for example, the French refused to credit his replacement to Victor Emmanuel as king-emperor, and the Italians would accept no less. After 1

October 1936 the French were left without an ambassador in the Palazzo Farnese, and one year later the Italian ambassador left Paris. The British avoided the issue of de jure recognition by keeping Drummond on with his original letter of credence. The subsequent story of recognition belongs to a history of the later 1930s.

The matter of an Ethiopian delegation sitting at the League arose with the Assembly in September 1936. After anguished soul-searching, and an extraordinary journey of dubious propriety Avenol made to Rome to mediate the issue, the Credentials Committee of the League let the Ethiopian delegation attend. Many feared this would provoke Italy to leave the League, but it did not. As Ciano said, "We are keeping quite calm and we really don't care. . . . There are certain situations which only deserve to be treated with contempt."[4]

From July onward Ethiopia and collective security were lost causes, as the following events in Britain illustrate. The leadership of the League of Nations Union broke up in the early summer over the question of what to do about sanctions. The emperor lived on slender means in virtual seclusion in the town of Bath. His presence was an embarrassment to the government. The Duke of Windsor records this story. Once Haile Selassie went onto the terrace of the House of Commons while sight-seeing. Baldwin noted him approaching and, to avoid meeting the exile, ducked around the tables with his face buried in his hands. On 23 June John Simon said in the Commons that not a single ship would be risked to restore Ethiopia's independence. That, said Robert Cecil, doughty champion of the League, showed "the Covenant meant nothing to us. It was a death blow to collective security and indeed to the League as a guarantee of peace." Cecil exaggerated. In that capacity, the League was already dead.[5]

Yet, collective action had been a working reality for over seven months. Fifty states participated. People throughout the world gave their endorsement. The initial show of muscle made an impression in the United States and Germany. Within the existing terms of the Covenant, whether from honor, fear, hope, or diplomatic pressure, states applied, even if only partially, the provisions of article 16. An operational time shorter than plans envisioned, emphasis on the reconciliationist mode, and technically argued insistence on avoiding war weakened, but did not destroy, this achievement. Strong if not absolute economic power was arrayed against an aggressor state, and that power was coupled with the potential for decisive military action and a potentially reinforcing political ideology. This fulfilled the operational demands of collective security.

What is significant is that this support was not consolidated or extended, as was the official rationale—the idea of a test case. In the course of the war, interest in the future effectiveness of some collective system largely disappeared. Nothing important came of talk about the reform of article 16. States drifted apart. Albert Speer records the lesson Hitler learned. "Hitler concluded that both England and France were loath to take any risks and anxious to avoid any danger. Actions of his which later seemed reckless followed directly from such observations. The Western governments had . . . proved themselves weak and indecisive."[6]

Mussolini saw this hesitance first, and made it the guiding principle of Italian diplomacy. His perception of this fact and his willingness to act on it guaranteed him his empire. In 1943, at the time of Mussolini's overthrow, Eden wrote in his diary: "Looking back the thought comes again. Should we not have shown more determination in pressing through with sanctions in 1935 and if we had could we not have called Mussolini's bluff and at least postponed this [second world] war? The answer, I am sure, is yes."[7] Perhaps. Stronger action against Italy, stemming from support of article 16, might have forced Britain and France into cooperation and drawn in other states favoring the status quo. Out of sanctions came some official awareness of the potential of the League and a good deal of popular support for it. Rearmament was under way. All this might have served to restrain Hitler and create effective defense arrangements in Europe. As it was, the patent irresolution of the leaders of the sanctionist front discredited collectivist possibilities. Smaller dependent states lay exposed. Disintegration was complete.

Governments of great states are the centers of gravity in international relations and cannot eschew this responsibility without causing doubt and confusion. Because of an uncertain definition of national security, the British government did not decide either to lead at Geneva or to support the realism argued for by Laval and Flandin. Its actions were ambiguous, its cues unclear. Waiting upon the initiatives and resolve of others weakened the collectivist line of its dual policy of sanctions and conciliation. The oath of service to the League restrained what some judged to be the proper realpolitik of appeasement. In neither course were the British people well instructed by their government. Not leading, and unable to stand wholly on either policy, the government fell between them. There was no war in Europe, but Ethiopia was lost. And so was Italy.

While collective action was discredited, it seemed in London that accommodation was not. The failure of conciliation in the Ethiopian war was explained by unexpected events: premature publication of the August and December peace proposals, Hoare's resignation, the Rhineland occupation, the success of the Italian army, the flight of the emperor. But reconciliation in the Ethiopian affair would have been possible only if it had not denied the values of those who supported the ideals of the League and at the same time had accommodated the Italians. Reconciliation in fact failed because the government of Italy was informed by a nationalism that was not amenable to liberal accommodations.

Mussolini saw appeasement as a sign of weakness to be exploited, not a chance to share in a common cause. Sanctions, likewise—meant to put him into a mood for conciliation—were used instead to intensify militant statism and inflame national self-esteem. What was intended as nonviolent secular pressure was transformed into a cause for rapid intensification of integral nationalism. Far from creating a desire to reverse government policy, sanctions made the Ethiopian war popular. First they were used to provide a safety valve to release accumulated fear, anger, and frustration. Then isolation, condemnation, and shortage called forth positive reaction: pride in standing up to states hitherto patronizing or critical of Italy's ambition. Mussolini boldly seized his opportunity, and he won across the board. The summer of 1936 found him enjoying triumph on three fronts: conquest in Ethiopia, victory over the League, and Italians united behind him as never before.

NOTES

1: Test Case

1. Mussolini's "Directive and plan of action to resolve the Italian-Ethiopian question" of December 1934, first printed, with commentary, by Alessandro Lessona, *Memorie*, pp. 165–71, and more recently by Giorgio Rochat, *Militari e politici nella preparazione della campagna d'Etiopia*, pp. 376–79.

2. De Bono's memorandum of 19 November 1932 to the service chiefs, "Military preparations in east Africa," and Mussolini's directive (cited in note 1) in Rochat, *Militari e politici*, pp. 276–91, 378.

3. For the prewar period see George W. Baer, *The Coming of the Italian-Ethiopian War*, and Renzo De Felice, *Mussolini il duce*, pt. 1.

4. F.O. 401/35, pt. 22, no. 75, Public Record Office, London (hereafter cited as P.R.O.). Acknowledgment is made of the Crown copyright of material from the P.R.O., those documents cited here with F.O. or Cab. designation.

5. James C. Robertson, "The Origins of British Opposition to Mussolini over Ethiopia," *Journal of British Studies* 9 (November 1969):122–42.

6. Cited by Arnold J. Toynbee, *Survey of International Affairs, 1935*, 2:56.

7. F.O. 401/35, pt. 23, no. 70.

8. Keith Middlemas, *Diplomacy of Illusion*, p. 51.

9. Robertson, "British Opposition," p. 141.

10. F.O. 401/35, pt. 23, no. 73.

11. See the illustrations accompanying the revelations of the thief himself, Francesco Constantini, in "Gli occhi del SIM nell'ambasciata inglese," *Candido*, 10 November 1957.

12. F.O. 401/35, pt. 23, no. 70.

13. C.P. 166(35), 19 August 1935, in Cab. 24/256, P.R.O.

14. Bonzani to Baistrocchi, 17 March 1934, in Rochat, *Militari e politici*, pp. 311–12.

15. Emilio Canevari, *La guerra italiana*, 1:391.

16. F.O. 401/35, pt. 24, no. 146, encl.

17. Cab. Concl. 43(35)1, 24 September 1935.

18. Cab. Concl. 45(35)6, 9 October 1935.

19. League of Nations, *Official Journal, 1935*, p. 1226; F.O. 401/35, pt. 25, no. 53; Baron [Pompeo] Aloisi, *Journal*, p. 314.

20. John Fisher Williams, "Sanctions under the Covenant," in *British Year Book of International Law, 1936*, p. 132.

21. Ernst B. Haas, *Collective Security and the Future International System*, p. 11.

306 TEST CASE

22. A record of such disillusionment by journalist Edmund Taylor is contained in the chapter "Reflections on a Lost Crusade" in his *Awakening from History* (Boston: Gambit, 1969).

23. Frank P. Walters, *A History of the League of Nations,* p. 658.

24. Clara Conti, *Servizio segreto,* p. 269. Jules-François Blondel, chargé in Rome after 1936, claimed the French code was not cracked (*Au fil de la carrière,* p. 357). But Gianfranco Bianchi says Mussolini saw an interception from that embassy at the time of Laval's visit in January (*Rivelazioni sul conflitto italo-etiopico,* p. 42). The king's aide-de-camp also recalled Mussolini's intercepting a dispatch of Laval's (Silvio Scaroni, *Con Vittorio Emanuele III,* pp. 118–19).

25. The interceptions are in Carte Graziani, busta (b.) 67, fascicolo (f.) 230, Archivio Centrale dello Stato, Rome (hereafter cited as A.C.S.).

26. Fulvio Suvich et al., *Il processo roatta,* pp. 30–31, 81, 200–202, and Canevari, *La guerra italiana,* 1:412–13.

27. F.O. 401/35, pt. 24, no. 147, encl.; Raffaele Guariglia, *Ricordi 1922–1946,* p. 272.

28. Partito Nazionale Fascista, Ministero della Cultura Popolare, b. 185, f. 33, sottofascicolo (sf.) 6, A.C.S. (hereafter cited as P.N.F., Min. Cul. Pop.).

29. Rochat, *Militari e politici,* p. 26.

30. De Bono's memorandum of 19 November 1932, "Military preparations for east Africa," printed in Rochat, *Militari e politici,* pp. 276–91.

31. Rochat, *Militari e politici,* chaps. 1–3. Bianchi, *Rivelazioni,* prints much of De Bono's diary and other important documents. Badoglio, as chief of the general staff, received copies of De Bono's official correspondence concerning the Ethiopian preparations and campaign. These, concerning the planning period, along with other significant documents from the preinvasion period, are open in the A.C.S. Rochat's book, a reliable and convenient source, prints most of what is available in the Badoglio collection for the preinvasion period. What is open (as of 1973) does not go into the period of the war. Rochat also draws selectively on the massive Graziani collection, which contains almost all of Graziani's papers concerning Ethiopia, the Somalian front, and his viceroyalty. It is because of its completeness and openness, and in the absence of the papers of De Bono and Badoglio, that we know more of the workings of the southern Somalian command than we do of those of the northern, Eritrean, front.

32. De Bono's diary, 15 December 1932, in Rochat, *Militari e politici,* p. 31.

33. Emilio De Bono, *Anno XIIII,* p. 119.

34. Bianchi, *Rivelazioni,* pp. 95–99.

35. These themes are developed by Giorgio Rochat in "Mussolini e le forze armate," *Il movimento di liberazione in Italia* 21 (April–June 1969):3–22, and in "Il ruolo delle forze armate nel regime fascista," *Rivista di storia contemporanea* 2 (April 1972):188–99.

36. Badoglio to De Bono, 12 May 1934, and to Mussolini, 29 May 1934, in Rochat, *Militari e politici,* pp. 325–27, 349–51.

37. Baistrocchi to Mussolini, in Canevari, *La guerra italiana,* 1:400–402.

38. De Bono, *Anno XIIII,* p. 223.

39. Rochat, *Militari e politici,* pp. 285, 401.

40. Rodolfo Graziani, *Ho difesa la patria,* pp. 78–79, 83.

41. Lessona, *Memorie,* p. 223.

42. Badoglio to Mussolini, 12 March 1935, in Rochat, *Militari e politici,* pp. 408–11.

43. Carte Graziani, b. 7, f. 14. During Graziani's governorship (5 March 1935–31 July 1936) 135,115 men, 18,643 horses and mules, 810,000 tons of matériel, and 9,666 vehicles were moved across the docks (Graziani, *Il fronte sud,* p. 85).

44. De Bono, *Anno XIIII,* p. 126; Graziani, *Ho difesa la patria,* p. 83.

45. Here is how Graziani could address Mussolini (April 1936): "You who alone have penetrated and understood my spirit and who knows that for my country I would give my life 100 times . . ." (*Il fronte sud,* p. 310).

46. Graziani, *Il fronte sud,* pp. 88–89, 273, and an unsent letter of 10 October 1935 to Lessona, in Rochat, *Militari e politici,* pp. 474–80.

47. Rochat, *Militari e politici,* pp. 180–81, 416.

48. Ibid., p. 263.

49. Ibid., pp. 202, 489, reprints the exchanges. The post-Ethiopian feud between De Bono and Lessona grew to be one of the most rancorous and protracted of the regime, Lessona charging corruption and De Bono asserting that Lessona's claim to participation in the march on Rome was false.

50. Graziani, *Il fronte sud,* pp. 95–100; Rochat, *Militari e politici,* p. 239.

51. Rochat, *Militari e politici,* pp. 185–87, 196, 427–28. Graziani's complaint was addressed to Angelo De Rubeis in the colonial ministry to pass on to Mussolini.

52. Carte Graziani, b. 7, f. 14.

53. Federico Baistrocchi, "L'attività dell'esercito per l'esigenza A.O.," in *Le forze armate dell'Italia fascista,* ed. Tomaso Sillani, pp. 107–12.

54. Mussolini told De Bono of his intention to be present in a letter of 18 May 1935 (Bianchi, *Rivelazioni,* pp. 18, 62–64).

55. Enrico Caviglia, *Diario,* pp. 132–33. It was Malladra's plan that Badoglio presented to Mussolini in August 1935 (Rochat, *Militari e politici,* pp. 470–73).

56. De Bono, *Anno XIIII,* p. 223.

57. P.N.F., Min. Cul. Pop., b. 185, f. 34.

58. F.O. 371/20176, pp. 271–75.

59. Aloisi, *Journal,* pp. 311–12. Publication of Vittorio Mussolini's eventually notorious book of recollections, *Voli sulle ambe,* was held up until 1937 because of the hostile reaction abroad to the bombings.

60. Benito Mussolini, *Opera omnia di Benito Mussolini,* 27:277, 298.

2: The International Plane

1. Hoare to Eden in Geneva, 13 October 1935, F.O. 432/1, pt. 4, no. 36 P.R.O.

2. At the Committee of Imperial Defence Subcommittee on Defence Policy and Requirements (C.I.D./D.P.R.), 11 September 1935, in Cab. 16/36, P.R.O.

3. Cab. Concl. 47(35)1, 16 October 1935.

4. Cab. Concl. 44(35)1, 2 October 1935.

5. F.O. 371/19144, pp. 12–17.

6. Nils Ørvik, "From Collective Security to Neutrality: The Nordic Powers, the League of Nations, Britain, and the Approach of War, 1935–1939," in *Studies in International History,* ed. K. Bourne and D. C. Watt (London: Longmans, Green, 1967), pp. 385–89.

7. Frank P. Walters, *A History of the League of Nations,* p. 663.

8. F.O. 432/1, pt. 4, no. 36, 13 October 1935.

9. Ibid., no. 37.

10. Gunnar Hagglof, *Diplomat*, p. 98.

11. Great Britain, *Parliamentary Debates* (Commons), 5th ser., 313 (1936), col. 818 (hereafter cited as 313 H.C. Deb., 5th ser., col. 818, or with appropriate vol. and col. numbers).

12. Cab. Concl. 45(35)6, 9 October 1935.

13. Luigi Villari, *Storia diplomatica del conflitto italo-etiopico*, pp. 154, 160.

14. "Austria will not be disloyal to a friendship destined to last far into the future [the hope]. That friendship has been increased by a debt of gratitude—not provided for by the Covenant—which also implied obligations [the stand on the Brenner]" (League of Nations, *Official Journal*, Spec. Supp. no. 138, pp. 101–3, 113).

15. F.O. 401/35, pt. 25, nos. 67, 68.

16. League, *Official Journal*, Spec. Supp. no. 138, pp. 106–7. Motta's views on the need (without much suggestion for a solution) to "harmonize the idea of neutrality with the idea of solidarity" and the nature of the Swiss position in this dispute as set out in statements to organs of the Swiss government are collected in Giuseppe Motta, *Testimonia temporum*, pp. 140–62.

17. F.O. 371/19146, pp. 24–25, F.O. 371/19148, p. 138.

18. League, *Official Journal*, Spec. Supp. no. 145, pp. 25–26, 70–78, 124–40.

19. Walters, *History of the League*, p. 663.

20. Cab. Concl. 44(35)1, 2 October 1935.

21. Laval claimed in a note of 18 October 1935 that in these talks he and Hoare ruled out, "in any contingency, measures other than economic or financial arrangements" and excluded "any possibility of recourse to military actions, to a naval blockade, or to the closing of the Suez Canal" (F.O. 432/2, pt. 4, no. 47). In sum, he told the Chamber on 28 December 1935, they had excluded "everything that might lead to war" (France, Chambre des Députés, *Journal officiel, débats parlementaires*, 1935, p. 2863, 29 December [hereafter cited as Chambre, *débats*]). This overstated the general and provisional nature of Hoare's comments. Hoare could not, after all, bind his government, although this reflected its thinking quite accurately. What Hoare said (according to the British record) was that he was anxious to avoid an action raising the question of belligerent rights, not that the government would forbid this in advance, although any strong action depended on French cooperation, as Laval knew (F.O. 401/35, pt. 25, no. 147, encl.).

22. Chambrun speaking on 10 October 1935, F.O. 401/35, pt. 25, no. 54.

23. F.O. 401/35, pt. 25, no. 53; for Mussolini's dismay with economic sanctions see ibid., nos. 79, 82.

24. F.O. 371/19149, p. 8. In August 1935 Peterson was given charge of a new department in the Foreign Office dealing exclusively with the crisis as relating to Ethiopia.

25. F.O. 800/295, pp. 304–6.

26. F.O. 371/19150, p. 28.

27. Earl of Avon, *The Eden Memoirs: Facing the Dictators*, p. 283.

28. F.O. 432/1, pt. 4, no. 47.

29. Lord [Robert] Vansittart, *The Mist Procession*, p. 532.

30. F.O. 800/295, pp. 292–94.

31. F.O. 371/19144, pp. 72–78.

32. Général [Maurice] Gamelin, *Servir*, 2:179.

33. F.O. 432/1, pt. 4, no. 52, and pt. 3, no. 12.

34. Avenol, F.O. 800/295, pp. 292–94; Vansittart, F.O. 37/19147, pp. 56–58, and F.O. 371/19144, p. 78.

35. Note of 18 October 1935, a brilliantly worded document, F.O. 432/1, pt. 4, no. 47.

36. F.O. 371/19151, p. 99.

37. Alessandro Lessona, *Memorie,* pp. 188–89.

38. Quirino Armellini, *Con Badoglio in Etiopia,* pp. 251–55.

39. Lessona, *Memorie,* p. 190.

40. Enrico Caviglia, *Diario,* p. 136.

41. Gianfranco Bianchi, *Rivelazioni sul conflitto italo-etiopico,* pp. 103–5, 186–88.

42. F.O. 371/20176, pp. 271–75.

43. Leonard Mosley, *Haile Selassie,* p. 199; Angelo Del Boca, *The Ethiopian War, 1935–1941,* p. 49.

44. Emilio De Bono, *Anno XIIII,* p. 270; Lessona, *Memorie,* pp. 198–99, 207–10.

45. Partito Nazionale Fascista, Segretaria Particolare del Duce, Carteggio Riservato, b.3, f.8, A.C.S. (hereafter cited as P.N.F., Seg. Part. Duce, C.R.). Mussolini censored the proofs of De Bono's book in 1936, crossing out the second half of the last sentence when De Bono included this telegram.

46. F.O. 401/35, pt. 24, no. 188, 23 September 1935.

47. F.O. 401/35, pt. 25, no. 18, 4 October 1935.

48. Baron [Pompeo] Aloisi, *Journal,* pp. 314–15.

49. Emilia Chiavarelli, *L'opera della marina italiana nella guerra italo-etiopica,* pp. 92–97.

50. So he said to Hoare, 10 September 1935, F.O. 401/35, pt. 24, no. 147, encl.

51. Cab. Concl. 45(35)1, 9 October 1935.

52. F.O. 371/19143, pp. 15–19.

53. F.O. 401/35, pt. 25, no. 15.

54. Nino D'Aroma, *Mussolini segreto,* pp. 94–95.

55. F.O. 371/19556, pp. 1–47; F.O. 371/19154, pp. 35–38.

56. F.O. 401/35, pt. 25, no. 201.

57. Ibid., no. 16.

58. Ibid., nos. 53, 54.

59. F.O. 371/19144, pp. 169–70; F.O. 371/19146, p. 82.

60. F.O. 432/1, pt. 4, no. 39, 14 October 1935.

61. Aloisi, *Journal,* p. 315; Mussolini, *Opera omnia di Benito Mussolini,* 24:299.

62. F.O. 401/35, pt. 25, no. 82, 15 October 1935, and no. 79.

63. Mussolini, *Opera omnia,* 27:300.

64. Bianchi, *Rivelazioni,* pp. 107, 193–97.

65. Vanna Vailati, *Badoglio risponde,* pp. 238–39.

66. Mussolini's telegram to De Bono, 20 October 1935, *Opera omnia,* 27:300.

67. Full text of the terms, with Italian commentary, in F.O. 401/35, pt. 25, nos. 112, 113. Mussolini outlined them in a dispatch to De Bono on 20 October, urging him to have Tigre and Makale in Italian hands by mid-November (Mussolini, *Opera omnia,* 27:300).

68. F.O. 371/19151, p. 25.

69. F.O. 401/35, pt. 25, nos. 64, 71, 73.

70. F.O. 371/19154, pp. 108–9.

71. F.O. 371/19152, pp. 68–71.

72. F.O. 401/35, pt. 25, no. 92.

73. F.O. 371/19154, pp. 6–10.

3: Double Policies

1. Jules Romains, *Sept mystères du destin de l'Europe,* p. 295; Carte Graziani, b. 7, f. 18, A.C.S.

2. John P. Diggins, *Mussolini and Fascism,* p. 294.

3. Edgar B. Nixon, ed., *Franklin D. Roosevelt and Foreign Affairs,* 3:162.

4. For Matthews's reflections on the campaign (and upon himself) see *Two Wars and More to Come* (1938), *The Fruits of Fascism* (1943), *The Education of a Correspondent* (1946), and most recently—his opinions unchanged—*A World in Revolution* (1972). From the Ethiopian side, and for the most informative book to come from the war, see that of the correspondent of the *Times* (London), George L. Steer, *Caesar in Abyssinia.*

5. See Angelo Del Boca, *The Ethiopian War,1935–1941,* chap. 5. The some 200 of these communiqués are collected in Quirino Bosca, *Cronistoria dell campagna italo-etiopica dal 2 ottobre 1935 al 18 maggio 1936.*

6. Philip V. Cannistraro, "The Radio in Fascist Italy," *Journal of European Studies* 2 (June 1972):145.

7. Nicholas Pronay, "British Newsreels in the 1930's," *History* 57 (February 1972): 63.

8. Tony Aldgate, "British Newsreels and the Spanish Civil War," *History* 58 (February 1973):60.

9. Pool, *The "Prestige Papers."* For the United States, where the Gallup poll only began in October 1935, the nature and degree of interest is discussed in Diggins, *Mussolini and Fascism,* chap. 12.

10. Thomas Barman, *Diplomatic Correspondent,* p. 58.

11. [Stanley Morrison] *The History of the "Times,"* vol. 4, pt. 2, p. 8.

12. Series 15227, cartons R-3644–49, Archives of the League of Nations, Geneva (hereafter cited as A.L.N.).

13. *Collective Security and the Future International System,* p. 11.

14. Francesco Coppola, editor of *Politica,* on 19 January 1936, in *La ragioni dell'Italia,* ed. Gioacchino Volpe, pp.45–47.

15. F.O. 371/19166, pp. 71–76.

16. Emile Giraud, *La nullité de la politique internationale des grandes démocraties, 1919–1939,* p. 155. Giraud defines formalism as "a system that substitutes rite for action, that is satisfied with appearance and neglects reality" (p. 143).

17. League of Nations, *Official Journal,* Spec. Supp. no. 138, pp. 43–46.

18. Viscount Templewood, *Nine Troubled Years,* pp. 169–70; 9 November 1935, Sir Samuel Hoare, Private Papers, F.O. 800/295, P.R.O.

19. A biographer wrote: "Eden had scarcely said a controversial thing in his life; he had created no precedents, and his reputation as an idealist, which was by now well established, had no basis in anything he ever said" (Dennis Bardens, *Portrait of a Statesman,* p. 121).

20. *Times* (London), 2 and 3 October 1935.

21. Roy Jenkins, *Mr. Attlee,* p. 160.

22. F.O. 371/19148, pp. 189–94; *Times* (London), 9 October 1935.

23. Lord Cranborne, Private Papers, F.O. 800/296, P.R.O.

24. A. L. Rowse, *Appeasement: A Study in Political Decline, 1933–1939* (New York: Norton, 1961), p. 26.

25. Keith Feiling, *The Life of Neville Chamberlain,* p. 269. For a rebuttal of the claim that Baldwin tried to make rearmament a central concern of the voters, see James C. Robertson, "The British General Election of 1935," *Journal of Contemporary History* 9, no. 1 (1974): 149–64, and C. T. Stannage, "The East Fulham By-Election, 25 October 1933," *Historical Journal* 14 (March 1971): app., pp. 165–200.

26. From Chamberlain's diary, 2 August 1935, in Iain Macleod, *Neville Chamberlain,* pp. 182–83.

27. Jones, *A Diary with Letters, 1931–1950,* p. 155; *Times* (London), 5 October 1935.

28. 305 H.C. Deb., 5th ser., cols. 18, 149.

29. "Middle Opinion in the Thirties," *English Historical Review* 79 (April 1964):285.

30. Ibid., p. 290.

31. F. W. S. Craig, comp. and ed., *British General Election Manifestos, 1918–1966,* p. 76. See also Viscount [John] Simon, *Retrospect,* pp. 212–13.

32. *Times* (London), 12 October 1935.

33. *Times* (London), 21 October 1935; Mussolini, *Opera omnia di Benito Mussolini,*27:300; F.O. 371/19152, pp. 68–71; 305 H.C. Deb. 5th ser., cols. 29–31; F.O. 401/35, pt. 25, no. 114; Baron [Pompeo] Aloisi, *Journal,* p. 316.

34. Jones, *Diary with Letters,* p. 155.

35. Earl of Avon, *The Eden Memoirs: Facing the Dictators,* p. 280; Macleod, *Neville Chamberlain,* p. 188.

36. Alfred Sauvy, *Histoire économique de la France entre les deux guerres,* 2:178.

37. Chambre, *débats,* 1935, p. 2395, 6 December.

38. Geoffrey Warner, *Pierre Laval and the Eclipse of France,* p. 115.

39. *Le Populaire,* 8 October 1935; Blum, *L'Oeuvre de Léon Blum, 1934–1937,* pp. 125–28.

40. Chambre, *débats,* 1935, p. 2811, 27 December.

41. Jean Fabry, *J'ai connu . . . 1934–1945,* p. 86.

42. Personal Papers of Benito Mussolini, together with Some Official Records of the Italian Foreign Office and Ministry of Popular Culture, 1922–1944 (hereafter cited as Mussolini Papers), microcopy T-586/415, frames 006439–43, National Archives, Washington, D.C. (hereafter cited as N.A.). Similar efforts were launched in Belgium and Germany, and extensive anti-British propaganda was pressed in the Middle East. Max Gallo used the T-586 series for his *Cinquième colonne, 1930–1940, et ce fut la défaite.* Gallo for some reason assigned pseudonyms to recipients of these funds. E. Polson Newman, author of *Ethiopian Realities* (London: George Allen & Unwin, 1936) and *Italy's Conquest of Abyssinia* (London: Butterworth, 1937), received an Italian subsidy.

43. Max Gallo, *L'affaire d'Ethiopie aux origines de la guerre mondiale,* pp. 188–89.

44. Ibid., chap. 1, prints these and similar manuscripts of the time.

45. Eugen Weber, *Action Française,* p. 362.

46. Simone de Beauvoir recalls how this notorious affair inclined her and her friends to the left (*The Prime of Life,* pp. 210–11).

47. Fabry, *J'ai connu . . . 1934–1945,* p. 87; *Le Temps,* 17 November 1935.

48. *Le Temps,* 18 November 1935.

49. *Times* (London), 5 October 1935.

50. Francesco Rossi, *Mussolini e lo stato maggiore,* pp. 24–26.

51. *Documents diplomatiques français, 1932–1939,* ser. 2, vol. 2, no. 24 (hereafter cited as *DDF*).

52. These criticisms were leveled cogently at two sittings of the foreign affairs committee on 29 January and 12 February 1936, recorded in *Procès-Verbaux du Seances de la commission des Affaires Étrangeres, 1935–1936,* 15th Legislature, box 2^2, file 56, Archives de la Chambre des Députés, Paris.

53. Peter J. Larmour, *The French Radical Party in the 1930's,* p. 188.

54. Michel Soulié, *La vie politique d'Édouard Herriot,* p. 467; A. Chamberlain to Hoare, 1 December 1935, F.O. 800/295, pp. 412–13.

55. Larmour, *French Radical Party,* p. 189; Charles Maurras in *L'Action Française,* 23 September and 4 October 1935 and 13 January 1936, marked Herriot (and other sanctionist deputies) for assassination (and went to jail in 1936 for incitement to murder), while Henri de Kerillis in the *Echo de Paris,* 6 November 1935, declared Herriot "public enemy number one."

56. Édouard Herriot, *Jadis,* 2:612. For a discussion of the economic effects in Britain, see F. Coghlan, "Armaments, Economic Policy, and Appeasement," *History* 57 (June 1972):205–16.

57. *Procès-Verbaux du Seances,* 15th Legislature, box 2^2, file 56.

58. *Le Temps,* 28 November 1935.

59. Fabry, *J'ai connu . . . 1934–1945,* p. 84–85.

60. *DDF,* ser. 2, vol. 1, no. 82.

61. Warner, *Pierre Laval,* p. 131.

62. Ibid., pp. 110–11; *Documents on German Foreign Policy, 1918–1945,* ser. C, vol. 4, nos. 412, 415, 425, 440 (hereafter cited as *DGFP*).

63. Reynaud, *Mémoires,* 1:434; F.O. 434/2, no. 76; *DGFP,* ser. C, vol. 4 no. 467.

64. Pierre Renouvin, *Les Crises du XXe siecle,* vol. 2, *De 1929 à 1945* (Paris: Hachette, 1958), p. 83.

65. Aloisi, *Journal,* p. 317, shows how the interceptions in October renewed Italian charges of bad faith on Britain's part.

66. Général [Maurice] Gamelin, *Servir,* 2:175.

67. F.O. 401/35, pt. 25, no. 57.

68. Luigi Villari, *Storia diplomatica del conflitto italo-etiopico,* p. 189.

69. F.O. 432/1, pt. 4, no. 49; Villari, *Storia diplomatica,* p. 189.

70. F.O. 371/19157, pp. 208–10.

71. F.O. 432/1, pt. 4, no. 47; Cab. 2/6(1), 14 October 1935, P.R.O.

4:   Getting Set

1. "Sanctions in the Italo-Ethiopian Conflict," *International Conciliation,* no. 315 (December 1935), p. 540.

2. This data for the Coordination Committee is found in Ser. 20311, carton R-3668, L.N.A.

3. League of Nations, *Official Journal*, Spec. Supp. no. 146, p. 32.

4. *Le Temps*, 20 November 1935.

5. League, *Official Journal*, Spec. Supp. no. 145, pp. 79–81.

6. Ibid., no. 146, pp. 37–38.

7. Earl of Avon, *The Eden Memoirs: Facing the Dictators*, p. 287.

8. League, *Official Journal*, Spec. Supp. no. 146, p. 61.

9. How Riddell came to make his proposal, and the ensuing furor in Canada, an affair that, in the words of James Eayrs, "cast a long shadow over the conduct of Canadian diplomacy in the years to come," are the subject of study in James Eayrs, *In Defence of Canada*, chap. 1, and in F. H. Soward et al., *Canada in World Affairs*, chap. 2.

10. League, *Official Journal*, Spec. Supp. no. 146, pp. 61–62.

11. Ibid., p. 46, no. 150, pp. 10, 15.

12. *Foreign Relations of the United States, Diplomatic Papers, 1935*, 1:664, 798 (hereafter cited as *FRUS*).

13. Cordell Hull, *Memoirs*, 1:429; Edgar B. Nixon, ed., *Franklin D. Roosevelt and Foreign Affairs*, 3:121.

14. *The Secret Diary of Harold L. Ickes*, p. 460; John P. Diggins, "Mussolini and America," *Historian* 28 (August 1966):569. Commented Alexander De Conde, "Regardless of Italian-American sentiment, the Ethiopian war marked a turning point in American relations with Italy" (*Half Bitter, Half Sweet*, pp. 223–24). Black Americans, seeing Ethiopia as a black man's country, became international-minded as never before (John Hope Franklin, *From Slavery to Freedom: A History of Negro Americans*, 3d ed. [New York: Alfred A. Knopf, 1967], p. 574; Red Ross, "Black Americans and Italo-Ethiopian Relief, 1935–1936," *Ethiopian Observer* 15 (1972):122–31; and William R. Scott, "Malaku E. Bayen," ibid., pp. 132–38).

15. Gilbert to Stanley Hornbeck, 1 March 1935, Hornbeck Papers, Hoover Institution, Stanford, Ca.

16. Gary B. Ostrower, "American Ambassador to the League of Nations—1933," *International Organization* 25 (Winter 1971):46–58; William E. Dodd, *Ambassador Dodd's Diary, 1933–1938*, pp. 208–11.

17. *FRUS, 1935*, 1:843.

18. F.O. 401/35, pt: 25, no. 39 P.R.O.; Mussolini's order to De Bono, 29 September 1935, *Opera omnia di Benito Mussolini*, 27:297.

19. Laval's proposal was made to Eden on 3 October 1935, F.O. 401/35, pt. 25, no. 25, encl.; League, *Official Journal*, Spec. Supp. no. 145, p. 31.

20. F.O. 371/19179, pp. 122–27. In October the president of the Ethiopian Red Cross (also minister of foreign affairs) requested permission to export to Ethiopia from America several ambulance airplanes. The U.S. government refused, as contrary to law (*FRUS, 1935*, 1:811).

21. Hull, *Memoirs*, 1:429–31.

22. Nixon, *Roosevelt and Foreign Affairs*, 3:17–18; *FRUS, 1935*, 1:794.

23. Nixon, *Roosevelt and Foreign Affairs*, 3:19–20; Herbert Feis, *Seen from E.A.*, p. 234.

24. Ickes, *Secret Diary*, pp. 44–45.

25. Brice Harris, Jr., *The United States and the Italo-Ethiopian Crisis*, p. 54; F.O. 401/35, pt. 25, no. 39.

26. Cab. Concl. 45(35)1, 9 October 1935, P.R.O.; FRUS, 1935, 1:801–2.

27. Nixon, *Roosevelt and Foreign Affairs*, 3:19–20; Harris, *United States and the Italo-Ethiopian Crisis*, pp. 77–78.

28. Nixon, *Roosevelt and Foreign Affairs*, 3:43; Feis, *Seen from E. A.*, pt. 3, chaps. 8, 9.

29. Stimson's radio address, 23 October 1935, in Henry L. Stimson and McGeorge Bundy, *On Active Service in Peace and War*, pp. 310–11.

30. *The Public Papers and Addresses of Franklin Delano Roosevelt*, 5:440.

31. *FRUS*, 1935, 1:819.

32. Nixon, *Roosevelt and Foreign Affairs*, 3:67–68.

33. Harris, *United States and the Italo-Ethiopian Crisis*, p. 92.

34. Cab. Concl. 50(35)2, 2 December 1935. Hugh Dalton used this fact to attack the government for profiting from dividends on these sales (5 December 1935, 307 H.C. Deb. 5th ser., cols. 324–25).

35. This thesis was developed by Massimo Magistrati, then first secretary in the Italian embassy in Berlin, in a letter to Ciano, 30 December 1935, P.N.F., Min. Cul. Pop., b. 113, f. 8, A.C.S. The letter is reprinted in Magistrati's *Il prologo del dramma*, pp. 204–8, with comments, pp. 68–69.

36. Albert Speer portrays Hitler pacing his garden in autumn 1935 saying: "I really don't know what I should do . . . I would far prefer to join the British. But how often in history the English have proved perfidious. If I go with them, then everything is over for good between Italy and us. Afterwards, the English will drop me, and we'll sit between two stools" (*Inside the Third Reich*, p. 71).

37. *DGFP*, ser. C, vol. 4, no. 166.

38. Klaus Hildebrand, *Von Reich zum Weltreich*, pp. 463–79. Neither Hildebrand nor W. W. Schmokel, *Dream of Empire: German Colonialism, 1919–1945* (New Haven: Yale University Press, 1964), draw a direct connection between Germany's reemerging colonial demands and the Ethiopian war, but the Italian campaign reawakened colonial concern throughout the world.

39. Massimo Magistrati, "La Germania e l'impresa italiana di Etiopia," *Rivista di studi politici internazionali* 17 (October–December 1950):593.

40. *DGFP*, ser. C, vol. 4, no. 360; on the connection Hitler drew between the Ethiopian war and communism, see his comments to Lord Lothian in 1937, in J. R. M. Butler, *Lord Lothian (Philip Kerr), 1882–1940*, p. 338.

41. Felix Gilbert, ed., *Hitler Directs His War*, p. 36.

42. "Germania: Situazione politica nel 1935," Ministero degli Affari Esteri, Mussolini Papers, microcopy T-586/1289, frames 107368–72, N.A.

43. Manfred Funke, *Sanktionen und Kanonen*, pp. 43–45; George W. Baer, *The Coming of the Italian-Ethiopian War*, pp. 160, 226–27.

44. The agents were David Hall, a counselor to the emperor and of German extraction, and Hans Steffan, Ethiopian counsel in Berlin. Their contact at the foreign ministry was Kurt Prufer, once minister in Addis Ababa and at the time deputy director of "department III," covering Britain, the Western Hemisphere, the Orient, and "colonial affairs." Steffan became something of an influential, and pessimistic, informant on Ethiopian matters. The requests were handled at high levels, as a matter of policy. There was also an observer on the war scene, Captain Roland E. Strunk, whose reports went directly to Hitler's personal military staff. They are found in Germany, Reichskanzlei, Adjuntatur des Fuhrers, Files 1933–38, Italo-Ethiopian War 1936, Strunk von Este Report, Hoover Institution, Stanford, Ca.

45. Mussolini, *Opera omnia*, 28:252; Magistrati, "La Germania e l'impresa italiana di Etiopia," pp. 594–95.

46. Ambassador Eric Phipps said on 7 November 1935 that Hitler's military advisers thought the conquest of Ethiopia would take a force equivalent to 500,000 German troops (F.O. 371/19159, p. 179). Here are some quotes attributed to Hitler in autumn 1935. "If Mussolini thinks he can chase away the English fleet from the Mediterranean with his own, he is very much mistaken." "Let the Italians have a hundred ships! We'll get them back, un-

damaged. They will go through the Suez canal but they will never go further." The British navy would turn them back. (Leonard Mosley, *On Borrowed Time*, p. 7.)

47. Manfred Funke, "Le relazioni italo-tedesche al momento del conflitto etiopico e delle sanzioni della Società delle Nazioni," *Storia contemporanea* 2 (September 1971):475–76.

48. Funke, *Sanktionen und Kanonen*, pp. 62–71.

49. Ibid., pp. 77–79; Felice Guarneri, *Battaglie economiche tra le due grandi guerre*, 1:391–92.

50. *DGFP*, ser. C, 4:930–31; Józef Lipski, *Diplomat in Berlin*, p. 242.

51. Report by Attolico, 26 September 1935, on the unsympathetic attitude of Goebbels and Göring, in P.N.F., Min. Cul. Pop., b. 113, f. 8; Filippo Anfuso, *Roma Berlino Salò, 1936–1945*, pp. 44–46, 72.

52. Speer, *Inside the Third Reich*, pp. 71–72.

53. *DGFP*, ser. C, vol. 4, nos. 334, 372, 398.

54. "Germania: Situazione politica nel 1935," Ministero degli Affari Esteri, Mussolini Papers, microcopy T-586/1289, frames 107368–72.

55. Funke, *Sanktionen und Kanonen*, pp. 113–17.

56. F.O. 371/19179, pp. 167–88.

57. Ser. 20692, carton R-3671, L.N.A.

58. F.O. 371/19180, pp. 9–20.

59. George L. Steer, *Caesar in Abyssinia*, pp. 125–27.

60. The story of Soley and the licenses is from F.O. 371/19184, pp. 186–229.

61. F.O. 371/19180, pp. 95–102.

62. Avon, *Facing the Dictators*, p. 290.

63. Mussolini, *Opera omnia*, 27:159; F.O. 371/20153, pp. 149–51.

64. F.O. 401/35, pt. 24, no. 36, 19 July 1935.

65. Raffaele Guariglia, *Ricordi, 1922–1946*, pp. 276–77.

66. Ministero della Marina, Gabinetto, b. 174, A.C.S. (hereafter cited as Min. Mar., Gab.).

67. Emilia Chiavarelli, *L'opera della marina italiana nella guerra italo-etiopica*, pp. 92–94.

68. Baron [Pompeo] Aloisi, *Journal*, p. 349.

69. Min. Mar., Gab., b. 175; Min. Mar., Gab., Archivio Segreto, b. 40; Francesco Rossi, *Mussolini e lo stato maggiore*, pp. 24–26.

70. F.O. 371/19157, pp. 201–4.

71. F.O. 371/19558, pp. 242–49; Jules-François Blondel, *Au fil de la carriere*, p. 335n. Ten years later an autopsy showed no signs of serious illness. For citations to autopsy information see Benito Mussolini, *Memoirs, 1942–1943*, p. 295.

72. Some $74,700 (1935 value) was spent on propaganda in England, subsidizing books and so on. These enterprises sponsored by the embassy were all marginal and uninfluential. Grandi's thirty-page report on these activities is found in Mussolini Papers, microcopy T-586/415, frames 006482–511. Italian propaganda in Egypt was not very successful during the war, when most Egyptian sympathies lay with Ethiopia. There was, however, a large and well-organized Italian community in Egypt, some 54,800 persons, many of them armed. Egyptian police had orders to round up the leaders in case of trouble. On 19 October the commanding officer in Egypt, George Weir, thought the possibility of "sabotage and disturbance" by these Italians was "very great" (C.O.S. 411, in Cab. 53/26). Nothing much developed during the war, but immediately afterward Italian propaganda started up again with renewed vigor, posing the argument that Britain, having let down Ethiopia, would let down Egypt. Subsidies to *al-Ahram*, the most widely read Arabic paper, could not, the Foreign Office feared, "but leave their mark in

time" (F.O. 371/20133, pp. 473–513). For Italian activity see Mussolini Papers, microcopy T-586/425, frames 012477–82.

73. Enrico Caviglia, *Diario,* p. 133. There was another value to sending troops to Libya —acclimation for east Africa. The official public explanation advanced by Mussolini was that the troops were to deal with agitation from Senussi exiles (*Opera omnia,* 27:128).

74. Mussolini Papers, microcopy T-586/415, frame 006476.

75. F.O. 371/19231, pp. 454–55.

76. David Kelly, *The Ruling Few,* p. 227; Arthur Marder, "The Royal Navy and the Ethiopian Crisis of 1935–36," *American Historical Review* 75 (June 1970):1344–45; C.O.S. 421 (J.P.), 19 December 1935, in Cab. 53/26.

77. C.O.S. 393, 12 August 1935, in Cab. 53/25; Marder, "Royal Navy and the Ethiopian Crisis," pp. 1331–32.

78. F.O. 401/35, pt. 25, no. 18; Cab. Concl. 45(35)1.

79. F.O. 401/35, pt. 25, no. 92; F.O. 371/19153, pp. 101–4.

80. Cab. Concl. 48(35)2, 23 October 1935. For Mediterranean concerns in general, see Lawrence R. Pratt, *East of Malta, West of Suez.*

81. F.O. 432/1, pt. 4, nos. 50, 54.

82. Aloisi, *Journal,* pp. 317–19.

83. F.O. 401/35, pt. 25, no. 133.

84. Aloisi, *Journal,* pp. 318–19.

85. F.O. 401/35, pt. 25, nos. 125, 133. A week before, the chief of the Imperial General Staff, Archibald Montgomery Massingberd, had argued a different conclusion to Vansittart. Italy could send large forces to Libya within about a week, but for Britain to send reinforcements to Egypt took about a month in peacetime and two months in war. There might be no warning of Italian reinforcements, and aircraft could be sent to Libya in a matter of hours. (F.O. 371/19231, pp. 496–500.)

86. Aloisi, *Journal,* pp. 319–20; F.O. 401/35, pt. 25, no. 86. 148, encl., no. 159; the collection is found in F.O. 371/19158, pp. 189–205.

87. F.O. 371/19160, pp. 167–73, 189–98.

88. F.O. 401/35, pt. 25, no. 184.

89. F.O. 432/1, pt. 4, no. 47, emphasis added.

90. F.O. 432/1, pt. 4, no. 56; F.O. 371/19155, pp. 97–99.

91. Paul Auphan and Jacques Mordal, *The French Navy in World War II,* pp. 10–18; report of meeting on 8 November 1935 between Admiral Ernle Chatfield and Rear Admiral Jean Decoux, F.O. 432/1, pt. 4, no. 58. The French, and the British too, letting propaganda and their own reservations add color to their fears, were ignorant of the weakness of the Italian forces: untrained men, old equipment, timid commanders. Correspondingly, the Italians estimated that the French fleet was superior to theirs ("Francia: Situazione politica nel 1935," Ministero degli Affari Esteri, Mussolini Papers, microcopy T-586/1291):

92. F.O. 432/1, pt. 4, no. 58.

93. C.I.D./D.P.R. meeting, 5 November 1935, in Cab. 16/236.

94. Pierre Masson, "Franco-British Staff Talks, 1935–1938," in *Les relations franco-britanniques, 1935–1939,* pp. 119 ff.

95. Marder, "Royal Navy and the Ethiopian Crisis," p. 1384.

96. Masson, "Franco-British Staff Talks," pp. 119 ff.

97. C.I.D./D.P.R. meeting, 26 November 1935, in Cab. 16/136.

98. F.O. 432/1, pt. 4, nos. 64, 66, 73.

99. Cab. Concl. 50(35)2, 2 December 1935; F.O. 432/1, pt. 4, no. 73.

100. D.P.R. 75, in Cab. 16/140, is the report on the conversations; C.O.S. 416, 4 December 1935, in Cab. 53/26, lists, provisionally, the assurances the chiefs of staff hoped could be obtained.

101. The British record of these talks is D.P.R. 77, in Cab. 16/140. The French record is cited in Jean Lecuir and Patrick Fridenson, "L'organisation de la coopération aérienne franco-britannique, 1935–mai 1940," *Revue d'histoire de la deuxième guerre mondiale,* no. 73 (January 1969), pp. 44–46.

102. Douhet died in 1930. His writings, including *Il domino dell aria* (1921, 1926), *Probabili aspetti delle guerra futura* (1928), *Riepilogando* (1929) and *La guerra del 19. . . .* (1930) were collected in *La guerra integrale,* ed. Emilio Canevari. "L'inghilterra e la difesa aerea" is chap. 10 of this book; the quotations are from pp. 299–300.

103. Anthony Verrier, *The Bomber Offensive,* pp. 10, 346.

104. Charles Webster and Noble Frankland, *The Strategic Air Offensive against Germany, (1939–1945),* 1:45.

105. 270 H. C. Deb., 5th ser., col. 632, 10 November 1932; Ronald W. Clark, *Tizard,* pp. 105–6.

106. At Bournemouth, 4 October 1935; reported in the *Times* (London), 5 October 1935; text in F.O. 401/35, pt. 25, no. 21.

107. C.I.D. meeting, 14 October 1935, in Cab. 2/6(1); F.O. 371/19167, pp. 166–67; Franco Bandini, *Gli italiani in Africa,* p. 525; Francesco Costantini, "Gli occhi del SIM nell'ambasciata inglese," *Candido,* 24 November 1957.

108. 307 H. C. Deb., 5th ser., col. 856; Thomas Jones, *A Diary with Letters, 1931–1950,* p. 160.

109. C.I.D./D.P.R. meeting, 20 December 1935; C.I.D. Paper 1217-B, in Cab. 4/24; D.P.R. Paper 73, in Cab. 16/140.

110. C.O.S. 406, in Cab. 53/25. At the outbreak of the Ethiopian war the number of such rounds on the island was less than 4,000.

111. Basil Collier, *The Defence of the United Kingdom,* pp. 20, 22, 61.

112. There was interesting discussion on what kinds of targets to establish. On 12 December the D.P.R. laid down responses in kind. Britain was never to be the first to strike at civilian targets, so as not to give "cause for stating we have broken humanitarian practice," to avoid provoking reprisals against British population centers. Against this view (held by the Foreign Office and the Admiralty) the air staff argued for wider reference. The old Hague rules, the sparing of civilian life, the air staff said, were almost impossible to follow if aerial bombardment were desired. Modern war made munitions factories and railroad junctions legitimate targets, or, at least, the siting of such places meant that bombs against them would entail civilian casualties.

113. C.I.D./D.P.R. meeting, 26 November 1935, in Cab. 16/136.

114. D.P.R. 77, in Cab. 16/140; Jean Fabry, *De la Place de la Concorde au course de l'Intendance,* pp. 72–73; Lecuir and Fridenson, "La coopération aérienne franco-britannique," pp. 44–46.

115. Cab. Concl. 53(35)1, 10 December 1935; C.I.D./D.P.R. meeting, 20 December 1935, in Cab. 16/136.

116. Paul Auphan and Jacques Mordal, *French Navy,* pp. 19–20.

117. C.I.D./D.P.R. meeting, 6 December 1935, in Cab. 16/136.

118. Marder, "Royal Navy and the Ethiopian Crisis," pp. 1332–41; idem, communication, *American Historical Review* 76, no. 2 (April 1971):580–81; Baer, *Italian-Ethiopian War,* pp. 259–61.

119. C.I.D. meetings, 22 November 1934 and 16 April 1935, in Cab. 2/6(1); Collier, *Defence of the United Kingdom*, p. 54.

120. John M. McCarthy, "Australia and Imperial Defence," *Australian Journal of Politics and History* 17 (April 1971):25–29. See also McCarthy's "Singapore and Australian Defence," *Australian Outlook* 25 (August 1971): 165–80.

121. Cab. Concl. 50(35)2, 2 December 1935.

122. C.O.S. 442, in Cab. 53/27.

123. Marder, "Royal Navy and the Ethiopian Crisis," pp. 1332, 1346; C.O.S. 421 (J.P.), in Cab. 53/26.

124. Cab. Concl. 54(35)1, 11 December 1935.

5: Search for Settlement

1. Mussolini, *Opera omnia di Benito Mussolini*, 27:183.

2. Ickes said later that his comment on 21 November was not a call on oil companies to stop shipments. Both his initial remark and his clarification, however, were vague, so his statement on the twenty-first was interpreted everywhere as implying a ban on oil. (*New York Times*, 22 November 1935; Ickes, *The Secret Diary of Harold L. Ickes*, pp. 472, 476–77; Herbert Feis, *Seen From E.A.*, pp. 257–58.)

3. The rumor was false (Edgar B. Nixon, ed., *Franklin D. Roosevelt and Foreign Affairs*, 3:90–9f). For another rumor about oil company pressure see William E. Dodd, *Ambassador Dodd's Diary, 1933–1938*, p. 289.

4. League of Nations, *Official Journal*, Spec. Supp. no. 150, pp. 246, 297.

5. *FRUS, 1935*, 1:862.

6. F.O. 371/19164, pp. 20–38, P.R.O.

7. An appreciation of the danger in the situation written by Neville Chamberlain on 29 November 1935 is found in Iain Macleod, *Neville Chamberlain*, pp. 187–88.

8. F.O. 401/35, pt. 25, no. 222.

9. *FRUS, 1935*, 1:866–70.

10. Cab. Concl. 50(35)2, P.R.O.

11. C.P. 236(35).

12. Feis, *Seen from E.A.*, pp. 307–8.

13. Roland N. Stromberg, "American Business and the Approach of War, 1935–1941," *Journal of Economic History* 13 (Winter 1953):65–66.

14. Hoare's cable of 4 December 1935, F.O. 401/35, pt. 25, no. 235.

15. Cordell Hull, *Memoirs*, 1:442.

16. F.O. 401/35, pt. 25, no. 245; *FRUS, 1935*, 1:873–74.

17. League, *Official Journal*, Spec. Supp. no. 148, pp. 69, 72, the first report of the committee of experts. See also the full record of the experts' petroleum study in Ser. 20311, carton R-3668, A.L.N.

18. Baron [Pompeo] Aloisi, *Journal*, 324–25.

19. So Sigamura told Jules Romains in 1937 (Romains, *Sept mystères du destin de l'Europe*, p. 319).

20. F.O. 371/19165, pp. 4–20.

21. Vittorio Cerruti, "Collaborazione internationale e ragioni dell'insuccesso della Società delle Nazioni," *Rivista di studi politici internazionali* 13 (January–June 1946):69.

22. Raffaele Guariglia, *Ricordi 1922–1946*, pp. 276–77.

23. W. P. Jolly, *Marconi*, pp. 269–70.

24. Daniele Varè, "British Foreign Policy through Italian Eyes," *International Affairs* 15 (January–February 1936):80–102, and *The Two Imposters* (London: Murray, 1949), pp. 115–16.

25. Hull, *Memoirs*, 1:438–40; Roosevelt, *FDR: His Personal Letters, 1928–1945*, 1:529; Hugh R. Wilson, Jr., *For Want of a Nail*, p. 59; *FRUS, 1935*, 1:826–33.

26. George W. Baer, *The Coming of the Italian-Ethiopian War*, pp. 310–17.

27. Mussolini, *Opera omnia*, 27:158.

28. Guariglia, *Ricordi*, pp. 284–86.

29. Ibid.; Alberto Berio, "L' 'affare' etiopico," *Rivista di studi politici internazionali* 25 (April–June, 1958):181–83, and *Dalle Ande all'Himalaya*, pp. 75–97; Renato Bova Scoppa, *La pace impossible*, pp. 123–27.

30. Cerruti, "Collaborazione internazionale e ragioni dell'insuccesso della Società delle Nazioni," p. 69.

31. Peter Howard, *Beaverbrook*, pp.114–15.

32. Luigi Villari, *Storia diplomatica dell conflitto italo-etiopico*, pp. 184, 190.

33. "Francia: Situazione politica nel 1935," Ministero degli Affari Esturi, Mussolini Papers, microcopy T-586/1291, N.A.

34. Edouard Herriot, *Jadis*, 2:612.

35. Berio, "L' 'affare' etiopico," p. 204.

36. F.O. 371/20173, pp. 13–19; F.O. 371/19168, pp. 5–7; F.O. 401/35, pt. 25, no. 219.

37. Emilio Canevari, *La guerra italiana*, 1:391.

38. Gianfranco Bianchi, *Rivelazioni sul conflitto italo-etiopico*, p. 239.

39. Renato Bova Scoppa, "L'Europea rischiò la guerra per l'impresa italiana in Etiopia" and "In segreto la diplomazia italiana si battè per fermare Mussolini," two articles in *Corriere della Sera*, 2 and 3 October 1965.

40. F.O. 371/19157, pp. 150–52; F.O. 371/19158, pp. 96–99.

41. F.O. 371/18155, pp. 17–21; F.O. 371/19154, pp. 110–12.

42. F.O. 401/35, pt. 25, nos. 141, 147.

43. Villari, *Storia diplomatica*, pp. 221–22.

44. League, *Official Journal*, Spec. Supp. no. 146, pp. 8–12.

45. Frank P. Walters, *A History of the League of Nations*, p. 664.

46. League, *Official Journal*, Spec. Supp. no. 146, pp. 8–12.

47. 305 H.C. Deb., 5th ser., cols. 345–47, 5 December 1935; Walters, *History of the League*, p. 664.

48. F.O. 371/19158, pp. 96–99.

49. F.O. 371/19160, pp. 189–98.

50. Ministero degli Affari Esteri, Mussolini Papers, microcopy T-586/1291. "Francia: Situazione politica nel 1935."

51. F.O. 401/35, pt. 25, nos. 184, 186.

52. Ibid., no. 204; Aloisi, *Journal,* pp. 324–25.

53. F.O. 401/35, pt. 25, nos. 205, 218, 219; F.O. 371/19163, pp. 273–81; F.O. 371/19170, pp. 110–12.

54. Drummond's dispatch in F.O. 371/19165, pp. 4–20; Vansittart's remarks in F.O. 371/19163, pp. 280–81.

55. F.O. 371/19163, pp. 279–81; Viscount Templewood, *Nine Troubled Years,* p. 172.

56. On Garibaldi's visit (to Vansittart on 25 November and then to Hoare on the twenty-eighth) see Guariglia, *Ricordi,* pp. 286–89; F.O. 401/35, pt. 25, nos. 218, 219; and F.O. 371/19164, pp. 68–77.

57. F.O. 371/19166, pp. 479–81.

58. Ibid.

59. Templewood, *Nine Troubled Years,* p. 178. Also see F.O. 371/19164, pp. 47–67; F.O. 371/19165, pp. 154–58.

60. Maurice Peterson, *Both Sides of the Curtain,* p. 119.

61. Cab. Concl. 50(35)2, 2 December 1935.

62. Bianchi, *Rivelazioni,* p. 239; Guariglia, *Ricordi,* pp. 289–90.

63. F.O. 371/19166, pp. 71–76.

64. Guariglia, *Ricordi,* p. 290.

65. F.O. 371/19166, pp. 154–64.

66. F.O. 401/35, pt. 25, no. 238.

67. Aloisi, *Journal,* p. 327; F.O. 401/35, pt. 25, no. 239.

68. Earl of Avon, *The Eden Memoirs: Facing the Dictators,* p. 298, Ian Colvin, *None So Blind,* pp. 74–75, 81. Colvin's book was first published in Britain under the title *Vansittart in Office.* Villari, telling this story, gives Hoare at the meeting and states that Hoare gave orders at once on 6 December that the press should start preparing a change in public opinion (*Storia diplomatica,* p. 224).

69. 307 H.C. Deb., 5th ser., cols. 345–47.

70. F.O. 401/35, pt. 25, no. 242.

71. Mussolini, *Opera omnia,* 27:196–99; F.O. 401/35, pt. 25, nos. 242, 244; F.O. 371/19167, pp. 203–5.

6:   The Hoare-Laval Proposals

1. C.I.D./D.P.R. 59, 6 December 1935, in Cab. 16/136, P.R.O.; F.O. 371/19167, pp. 1–4, 86, P.R.O., F.O. 371/19168, pp. 390–95.

2. The record of the 7 December 1935 meeting is in F.O. 432/1, pt. 4, no. 73. Hoare, Laval and Vansittart did the talking; Clerk, Peterson, Léger, Saint-Quentin, and Massigli sat in.

3. F.O. 432/1, pt. 4, no. 76.

4. F.O. 371/19168, p. 421; Michel Soulié, *La vie politique d'Édouard Herriot,* p. 468.

5. 307 H.C. Deb., 5th ser., col. 856; Peter Howard, *Beaverbrook,* pp. 114–15; Thomas Jones, *A Diary with Letters, 1931–1950,* pp. 159–60. See also Daniel Waley, "Mr. Baldwin's Sealed Lips," in *British Public Opinion and the Abyssinian War, 1935–6,* app.

6. Cab. 56(35), 18 December 1935 (Confidential Annexes 1923–1937).

7. Speech of 19 December 1935, 307 H.C. Deb., 5th ser., cols. 2007–16; Cab. Concl. 53(35), 10 December 1935.

8. 307 H.C. Deb., 5th ser., col. 2013.

9. Luigi Villari, *Storia diplomatica del conflitto italo-etiopico,* p. 222.

10. The Hoare-Laval proposals were published on 14 December 1935 in a British White Paper (Cmd. 5044) and in League of Nations, *Official Journal, January 1936,* pt. 1, pp. 40–41. Hoare's recommendation to the Cabinet of 8 December 1935, C. P. 235(35), is found in Cab. Concl. 52(35), 9 December 1935.

11. F.O. 371/19168, pp. 398–400; U.S. Department of State, Decimal file 765.84/3066, N.A.

12. *Times* (London), 9 December 1935; Viscount Templewood, *Nine Troubled Years,* pp. 180–82.

13. Earl of Avon, *The Eden Memoirs: Facing the Dictators,* p. 303.

14. 307 H.C. Deb., 5th ser., col. 2032, 19 December 1935.

15. Two well-known liberal French journalists broke the story: Geneviève Tabouis of *L'Oeuvre* (Paris) and André Géraud ("Pertinax") of the *Echo de Paris* and London's *Daily Telegraph.* Both were anti-Laval and pro-League. Tabouis tells plainly that she sought to ruin the chances of the plan by stirring up public opinion against it and confusing the issue in Geneva and Italy (*They Called Me Cassandra,* pp. 267–69). She says she pieced the terms together from hints and clues. Alfred Mallet asserts that, on the contrary, the diplomatic editor of Havas (Paris) gave the journalists a typescript of the proposals, reading it to Tabouis by phone to London, where she went, some said by direct arrangement with Léger, so the trail of the leak would not lead so blatantly to the Quai d'Orsay (*Pierre Laval,* 1:24). British officials always blamed the French foreign ministry. Laval thought the news came from the press attaché at the British embassy, Sir Charles Mendl, whom he held was in secret-service pay to discredit his ministry. (Geoffrey Warner, *Pierre Laval and the Eclipse of France,* p. 123). It is true that Tabouis got some clues, in a general way, from Mendl, but apparently without the sinister implications Laval attached. In Rome some Italians held that Eden leaked the terms to discredit Hoare (Baron [Pompeo] Aloisi, *Journal,* p. 333).

16. Avon, *Facing the Dictactors,* p 304.

17. Cab. Concl. 52(35), 9 December 1935.

18. France, Haute cour de justice, *Procès du Maréchal Pétain,* p. 184.

19. Édouard Herriot, *Jadis,* 2:621.

20. F.O. 401/35, pt. 25, no. 251; Jean Fabry, *De la Place de la Concorde au course de l'Intendance,* p. 73.

21. Cab. Concl. 53(35), 10 December 1935.

22. F.O. 401/35, pt. 25, no. 254.

23. 307 H.C. Deb., 5th ser., cols. 717, 855–60.

24. Cab. Concl. 54(35)3, 11 December 1935.

25. F.O. 371/19168, pp. 112–13; Avon, *Facing the Dictators,* pp. 301–2.

26. Frank P. Walters, *A History of the League of Nations,* p. 672.

27. Ibid., p. 669.

28. 307 H.C. Deb., 5th ser., cols. 343, 432.

29. *FRUS, 1935,* 1:874–75.

30. The minutes of the third Session of the Committee of Eighteen, 12, 13, and 19 December 1935, are in League, *Official Journal,* Spec. Supp. no. 147, pp. 7–17.

31. Herriot, *Jadis,* 2:623; Avon, *Facing the Dictators,* p. 307.

32. League, *Official Journal*, Spec. Supp. no. 147, p. 10; *ibid., January 1936*, pt. 1, pp. 41–42.

33. F.O. 371/19169, pp. 144–46; F.O. 371/19170, pp. 117–19.

34. Alfred Nemours, *Craignons d'être un jour l'Ethiopie de quelqu'un*, reprints his speech to the Assembly of 10 October 1935.

35. D.P.R. 68, 71, and 72, 12, 16, and 18 December 1935, in Cab. 16/136, record the mutual assistance questions asked and the responses and apprehensions of Yugoslavia, Czechoslovakia, Turkey, and Greece. The Romanian and Czechoslovakian ultimatum is recorded in William E. Dodd, *Ambassador Dodd's Diary, 1933–1938*, p. 287.

36. *FRUS, 1935*, 1:701–3.

37. Avon, *Facing the Dictators*, p. 307. Here is an echo to such a fear. In May 1936 the pro-German minister of defense of South Africa, Oswald Pirow, fearful that an Italian black army might one day unite with French African units and march against whites in southern Africa, argued that German resettlement in Tanganyika would act as counterbalance to more liberal British policy in the region (D. C. Watt "South African Attempts to Mediate between Britain and Germany, 1935–1938," in *Studies in International History*, ed. K. Bourne and D. C. Watt, p. 405).

38. Litvinov to the Soviet ambassador in Paris, 19 December 1935, "The Struggle of the U.S.S.R. for Collective Security in Europe during 1933–1935," *International Affairs*, no. 10 (Moscow: October 1963), p. 120.

39. F.O. 371/19170, pp. 182–86; F.O. 371/19171, pp. 9–12.

40. F.O. 371/19168, p. 7; Cordell Hull, *Memoirs*, 1:443.

41. Ickes, *The Secret Diary of Harold L. Ickes*, pp. 483–84; Dodd, *Ambassador Dodd's Diary*, p. 285.

42. Brice Harris, Jr., *The United States and the Italo-Ethiopian Crisis*, p. 111.

43. Edgar B. Nixon, ed., *Franklin D. Roosevelt and Foreign Affairs*, 3:111–12, 130.

44. Cmd. 5044 of 1935, p. 19, cited in Arnold J. Toynbee, *Survey of International Affairs, 1935*, 2:305.

45. League, *Official Journal,, January 1936*, pt. 1, pp. 41–42.

46. George L. Steer, *Caesar in Abyssinia*, pp. 207–16.

47. See ibid., pp. 214–45, for the complete statement. Stephen Heald, ed., *Documents on International Affairs, 1935*, 2:367, gives an incomplete and misleading text.

48. League, *Official Journal, January 1936*, pt. 1, p. 47.

49. Mussolini, *Opera omnia de Benito Mussolini*, 27:199–200.

50. P.N.F., Min. Cul. Pop., b. 185, f. 33, sf. 6, A.C.S.

51. Villari, *Storia diplomatica*, pp. 179, 227.

52. Fabry, *De la Place de la Concorde*, p. 73; *Documents on British Foreign Policy, 1919–1939*, ser. 3, vol. 3, no. 488; Charles de Chambrun, *Traditions et souvenirs*, p. 211.

53. Raffaele Guariglia, *Ricordi 1922–1946*, p. 292.

54. Mussolini to Laval, 25 December 1935, published in Hubert Lagardelle, *Mission a Rome*, pp. 282–83; Alessandro Lessona, *Memorie*, p. 243.

55. F.O. 401/35, pt. 25, no. 262; Templewood, *Nine Troubled Years*, p. 172; Mussolini to the Council of Ministers, 30 December 1935, *Opera omnia*, 27:207.

56. Emilio De Bono, *Anno XIIII*, p. 266.

57. *Opera omnia*, 27:304–5.

58. F.O. 371/19169, p. 6; Aloisi, *Journal*, pp. 328–29; F.O. 401/35, pt. 25, no. 263.

59. Herriot, *Jadis*, 2:621; Lagardelle, *Mission à Rome*, p. 193; Villari, *Storia diplomatica*, pp. 235–37.

60. Pius XI, *Discorsi di Pio XI*, 3:412–13.

61. For some comment by the Polish statesman Alexander Skrzynski on Fr. Ledochowski and the Vatican mood at this time, see Comte Jean Szembek, *Journal, 1933–1939*, p. 147.

62. For the calendar of Tacchi Venturi's visits see P.N.F., Seg. Part. Duce, C.R., b. 64, sf. 2, inserto D (1935), and Carteggio Ordinario, 500.693/1, A.C.S. Tacchi Venturi was at this time also consulting with Aloisi on a historical article concerning freemasonry (Aloisi, *Journal*, p. 326).

63. The Vatican scene is discussed by François Charles-Roux, *Huit ans au Vatican, 1932–1940*, pp. 147–48; by Lagardelle, *Mission à Rome*, p. 196; and in dispatches from Charles-Roux, *DDF*, Ser. 2, vol. 1, no. 107, and from Hugh Montgomery, first secretary of the British Holy See legation and acting chargé, F.O. 371/19227, pp. 167–69, and 371/19174, pp. 210–13.

64. Aloisi, *Journal*, pp. 329–30; Guariglia, *Ricordi*, pp. 292–94; Renzo De Felice, *Mussolini il duce*, pp. 920–23.

65. F.O. 371/19171, pp. 129–32.

66. Aloisi, diary entry of 14 December 1935, *Journal*, p. 330; Lessona, *Memorie*, p. 243; Jules-François Blondel, *Au fil de la carrière*, pp. 339–40.

67. *Opera omnia*, 27:202–3.

68. Cerruti's comments in trial testimony are found in Fulvio Suvich et al., *Il processo roatta*, pp. 44–45, 77. Villari regards the Pontina speech the critical factor that killed British support for the plan, arguing that the British government used the pretext of Mussolini's rejection there to renounce their own support (*Storia diplomatica*, pp. 234, 238–39). This overstates the case considerably, as I will show.

69. Guariglia, *Ricordi*, pp. 296–97.

70. Ibid. See also Lessona, *Memorie*, pp. 244–45.

71. De Felice, *Mussolini il duce*, pp. 718–24; De Bono's record of the meeting (diary of 19 December) is found in Gianfranco Bianchi, *Rivelazioni sul conflitto italo-etiopico*, p. 114. Mussolini talked about the session with Arnold Wilson in February 1936 (Arnold T. Wilson, *Thoughts and Talks*, pp. 112–13). Mussolini, *Opera omnia*, 27:204, gives the formal record. Some members of the council—Alberto De Stefani, Luigi Federzoni, and Giuseppe Volpi di Misurata—were against the war from the beginning.

72. Donald McLachlan, *In the Chair*, p. 163.

73. Ibid., p. 164.

74. *Times* (London), 14 December 1935.

75. [Stanley Morrison], *The History of the "Times,"* vol. 4, pt. 2, p. 897. For extracts from Dawson's diary preparing for the composition of the editorial see John Evelyn Wrench, *Geoffrey Dawson and Our "Times"* pp. 325–27.

76. Recorded in Harold Nicolson, *Diaries and Letters, 1930–1939*, p. 232. For the public reaction see Waley, "Hoare-Laval, the Outcry," in *British Public Opinion*, chap. 2.

77. Alexander Mackintosh, *Echoes of Big Ben: A Journalist's Parliamentary Diary, 1881–1940* (London: Jarrols, n.d.), p. 134; Keith Feiling, *The Life of Neville Chamberlain*, p. 274.

78. Jones, *Diary with Letters*, p. 161; Harold Macmillan, *Winds of Change, 1914–1919* (New York: Harper & Row, 1966), p. 407. Colin Coote, in *Editorial*, does not mention this, but there is sense enough of it in his dispatches.

79. Cab. 23/82; Avon, *Facing the Dictators*, p. 309; League, *Official Journal, January 1936*, pt. 1, pp. 10–11.

80. McLachlan, *In the Chair,* p. 165; Templewood, *Nine Troubled Years,* p. 185.

81. For Beaverbrook's constant support of Hoare and Vansittart in this period, his detestation of the League, and his conclusion that help from France was a futile hope, see A. J. P. Taylor, *Beaverbrook,* pp. 355–62.

82. Cab. 56(35), 18 December 1935. The sole record of this discussion was sealed by the Cabinet secretary, Maurice Hankey, immediately after Baldwin read it. No one else saw it. It was kept sealed for thirty-two years, save being opened once in 1946 by Lord Normanbrook. For an argument that Hoare should have stayed on and fought, see Howard, *Beaverbrook,* pp. 111–13.

83. 307 H.C. Deb., 5th ser., cols. 1007–16, 2030–39. Hoare hoped before his speech that the Italian government might accept the principle of negotiation, which would have given a fillip to his defense. He asked Grandi about this possibility (Guariglia, *Ricordi,* p. 300).

84. Charles A. Petrie, *The Life and Letters of the Right Hon. Sir Austen Chamberlain,* 2:404–6.

85. Ian Colvin, *None So Blind,* p. 83.

86. 307 H.C. Deb., 5th ser., cols. 2039–42. For some critical observations on Chamberlain's conduct see Roy Jenkins, *Mr. Attlee,* pp. 172–73.

87. Cited in Neville Thompson, *The Anti-Appeasers,* pp. 94–95.

88. Cab. 56(35).

89. Lord [Robert] Vansittart, *The Mist Procession,* p. 542.

90. Ibid.; see also Vansittart, *Lessons of My Life,* p. 52, and Keith Middlemas and John Barnes, *Baldwin,* p. 898n.

91. Colvin, *None So Blind,* p. 92.

92. Avon, *Facing the Dictators,* pp. 190, 309–11; League, *Official Journal, January 1936,* pt. 2, pp. 9–12, 14. The Committee of Thirteen had been established at the beginning of the war to report to the Council "a statement of facts of the dispute and the recommendations which are deemed just and proper thereto," as prescribed in paragraph 4, article 15 of the Covenant.

93. Carte Graziani, b. 8, f. 16, A.C.S.; Aloisi, *Journal,* p. 332; Alberto Berio, "L' 'affare' etiopico," *Rivista di studi politici internazionali* 25 (April–June 1958):207.

94. Walters, *History of the League,* p. 673.

95. Mussolini, *Opera omnia,* 27:204–5.

96. Aloisi, *Journal,* pp. 331–33.

97. Mussolini, *Opera omnia,* 27:205–7.

98. Blondel, *Au fil de la carrière,* p. 341.

99. Charles-Roux, *Huit ans au Vatican,* p. 148; F.O. 371/19174, pp. 210–13.

100. The exchange of letters is published in Lagardelle, *Mission à Rome,* pp. 275–84. See also Aloisi, *Journal,* p. 234, and Guariglia, *Ricordi,* pp. 299–300.

101. Mussolini, *Opera omnia,* 27:207–8; Lagardelle, *Mission à Rome,* p. 200.

102. U.S. Department of State, Decimal file 765.84/3006.

103. Chambre, *débats,* 1935, p. 2648.

104. This speech did his chances for future office no harm (John E. Dreifort, *Yvon Delbos at the Quai d'Orsay: French Foreign Policy during the Popular Front, 1936–1938* [Lawrence: University of Kansas Press, 1973], pp. 28–29). For the prompting of Georges Mandel behind this speech see John M. Sherwood, *Georges Mandel and the Third Republic* (Stanford: Stanford University Press, 1970), p. 176.

105. Reynaud's comments on his speech are found in *Mémoires,* 1:462–70; his impressions of the British scene, in *In the Thick of the Fight, 1930–1945,* pp. 70–76.

106. F.O. 432/1, pt. 4, no. 78.

107. Herriot, *Jadis,* 2:634; for the debate on 27 and 28 December 1935, Chambre, *débats,* 1935, pp. 2800–2866.

108. Alfred Sauvy, "La reprise paradoxale, 1935–1936," in *Histoire économique de la France entre les deux guerres,* vol. 2, chap. 11, gives a favorable appreciation of Laval's efforts and success.

109. F.O. 432/1, pt. 4, no. 17.

110. *Le Temps,* 31 December 1935, 1 January 1936.

111. Georges Bonnet, *Vingt ans de vie politique, 1918–1939,* p. 240; Peter Larmour, *The French Radical Party in the 1930's,* pp. 188–89.

112. Larmour, *French Radical Party,* p. 196. Herriot resigned the party leadership mainly because of fatigue and dislike of the heavy doses of abuse he was receiving and because he was tarred by implication (as a minister) in party attacks on Laval's horse-trading with Italy.

113. *Le Temps,* 20 and 21 January 1936.

114. Herriot was very sensitive to the attacks, not only from the Right over sanctions—that he had become "Herriot-la-guerre"—but also from his own party—that he was a horse-trader over Ethiopia. He complained to President Albert Lebrun about the way Laval bypassed the Council on foreign policy matters. Perhaps, also, Herriot did not want to see Laval presiding over the elections scheduled for the spring. On these matters see his memoirs, *Jadis,* 2:637–38; Soulié, *Vie politique d'Édouard Herriot,* pp. 475–77; and Larmour, *French Radical Party,* pp. 193–96.

115. Aloisi, *Journal,* p. 343; Avon, *Facing the Dictators,* p. 324.

116. Pierre Laval, *Laval parle,* pp. 23–24.

117. See Sherwood, *Georges Mandel,* pp. 176–78, for Mandel's work in forming the Sarraut government.

7: Italia contra Mundum

1. Alessandro Lessona, *Memorie,* pp. 269–70.

2. Ruggero Zangrandi, *Il lungo viaggio attraverso il fascismo,* pp. 66–67; Angelo Del Boca, *The Ethiopian War, 1935–1941,* pp. 57–58.

3. Mussolini, *Opera omnia di Benito Mussolini,* 27:192.

4. Gioacchino Volpe, ed., *La ragioni dell'Italia,* pp. 45–47.

5. Georges Wagnière, *Dix-huit ans à Rome,* p. 233.

6. Mussolini, *Opera omnia,* 27:159; Piero Melograni, ed., *Corriere della Sera, 1919–1943,* pp. 494–96; Mussolini, *Opera omnia,* 27:183–85.

7. Mussolini Papers, microcopy T-586/136, frame 036377, N.A.

8. Philip V. Cannistraro, "The Radio in Fascist Italy," *Journal of European Studies* 2 (June 1972), pp. 145–46.

9. P.N.F., Min. Cul. Pop., b. 185, f. 33, sf. 6, and p. 34, A.C.S.

10. Partito Nazionale Fascista, Situazione politica ed economica delle provincie, b. 7 (Milan), 3 January 1936, A.C.S.

11. Benito Mussolini, *Storia di un anno,* p. 78.

12. F.O. 401/35, pt. 25, no. 285, P.R.O.

13. Felice Guarneri, *Battaglie economiche tra la due grandi guerre,* 1:410–11; Luigi Salvatorelli and Giovanni Mira, *Storia d'Italia nel periodo fascista,* p. 869.

14. *Il lungo viaggio,* p. 69.

15. *Times* (London), 2 November 1935. Salvatorelli and Mira, *Storia d'Italia nel periodo fascista,* p. 866, stress the significance of this endorsement.

16. Nino d'Aroma, *Vent'anni insieme,* p. 238; Bianca Ceva, *Storia di una passione, 1919–1943,* pp. 24–31. See also Silvio Bertoldi, *Vittorio Emanuele III,* chap. 32.

17. Nino D'Aroma, *Mussolini segreto,* p. 98.

18. "Pio XI e la guerra etiopica," in *Opere di Gaetano Salvemini,* pt. 3, vol. 3, app. E, p. 754. A shortened revision of the appendix appears in English as "The Vatican and the Ethiopian War," in *Neither Liberty nor Bread,* ed. F. Keene, pp. 191–200.

19. The full texts of this and the following speeches in sympathy with the war are collected in Giulio de Rossi dell'Arno, *Pio XI e Mussolini,* pp. 69–139.

20. Edward R. Tannenbaum, *The Fascist Experience,* p. 198.

21. Mussolini, 9 January 1938, *Opera omnia,* 29:49.

22. Daniel A. Binchy, *Church and State in Fascist Italy,* pp. 675–78.

23. Ibid., p. 643. The argument that the pope's ambiguous position was contrived deliberately to avoid any criticism of the war is advanced by Salvemini in "Pio XI e la guerra etiopica."

24. Texts and analyses of papal announcements prior to October 1935 in George W. Baer, *The Coming of the Italian-Ethiopian War,* pp. 282–88.

25. Carlo Sforza, *Italy and Italians,* tr. E. Hutton (New York: Dutton, 1949), p. 77.

26. Comte Jean Szembek, *Journal, 1933–1939,* p. 131.

27. Pius XI, *Discorsi di Pio XI,* 3:413.

28. Charles Delzell, *Mussolini's Enemies,* pp. 131–43; Salvatorelli and Mira, *Storia d'Italia nel periodo fascista,* pp. 853–55, 876–78.

29. Zangrandi, *Il lungo viaggio,* p. 67; P.N.F., Seg. Part. Duce, C.R., b. 29 (Gran Consiglio), sf. 14, A.C.S.

30. *Opera omnia,* 27:242.

31. Roland Sarti, *Fascism and the Industrial Leadership in Italy, 1919–1940,* pp. 104–12.

32. Franco Catalano, "Les ambitions mussoliniennes et la réalité économique de l'Italie," *Revue d'histoire de la deuxième guerre mondiale,* no. 76 (October 1969) pp. 15–16.

33. Tannenbaum, *The Fascist Experience,* p. 100.

34. Ibid., pp. 101–2, and Franco Catalano, *L'economia italiana di guerra,* pp. 129–30.

35. For a full-scale study of the economic situation see Guarneri, *Battaglie economiche,* vol. 1, chaps. 10,11; Pierre Bartholin, *Aspects économiques des sanctions prises contre l'Italie;* H. V. Hodson, "The Economic Aspects of the Italo-Abyssinian Conflict," in Arnold J. Toynbee, *Survey of International Affairs, 1935,* 2:414–42; League of Nations economic reference works and four reports of the Coordination Committee (docs. #116, 119, 120, 125) covering financial and trade statistics. It should be noted here that publication of economic statistics was suspended in Italy, by decree, after November 1935.

36. *Battaglie economiche,* 1:493–94.

37. Starace's evaluation cited in Franco Catalano, *L'impresa etiopica e altri saggi,* p. 193.

38. For the criticism that Guarneri used his new position of state authority to reinforce the entrenched privileges of big business, see Ernesto Rossi, *Padroni del vapore e fascismo,* pp. 216–21. Guarneri and his office were advanced to ministerial rank in November 1937.

39. Howard J. Taubenfeld, *Economic Sanctions,* pp. 67–78.

40. Giorgio Rochat, *Militari e politici nella preparazione della campagna d'Etiopia*, p. 481.

41. Federico Baistrocchi, "L'attività dell'esercito per l'esigenza A.O.," in, *Le forze armate dell'Italia fascista*, ed. Tomaso Sillani, p. 112. By the end of the war, 174,900 tons of gas and lubricants were in reserve overseas.

42. P.N.F., Seg. Part. Duce, C.R., b. 29 (Gran Consiglio), sf. 14.

43. Guarneri, *Battaglie economiche*, 1:387–88, 390–91.

44. Ibid., p. 438; F.O. 401/36, pt. 26, no. 61.

45. Sarti, *Fascism and the Industrial Leadership*, p. 110.

46. Guarneri, *Battaglie economiche*, 1:394.

47. Edgar B. Nixon, ed., *Franklin D. Roosevelt and Foreign Affairs*, 3:154–55. Brice Harris, Jr., *The United States and the Italo-Ethiopian Crisis*, pp. 116–20, shows reaction abroad to Roosevelt's speech.

48. Baron [Pompeo] Aloisi, *Journal*, p. 339.

49. *DDF*, ser. 2, vol. 1, no. 33; F.O. 371/20153, pp. 36–37; Lessona, *Memorie*, pp. 237–42.

50. F.O. 371/20155, pp. 106–8; See also, Cab. Concl. 2(36) 4, 22 January 1936, P.R.O.

51. Mussolini, *Opera omnia*, 27:208, 307–9; Raffaele Guariglia, *Ricordi 1922–1946*, p. 301.

52. *DDF*, ser. 2, vol. 1, no. 1.

53. *DGFP*, ser. C, vol. 4, no. 532, encl.

54. Emilio De Bono, *Anno XIIII*, pp. 259–82; Gianfranco Bianchi, *Rivelazioni sul conflitto italo-etiopico*, pp. 192–96.

55. Lessona's report and comments on the inspection trip are found in his *Memorie*, pp. 188–201, and, more circumspectly, in *Verso l'impero*, pp. 180–90.

56. Badoglio's report and comments are printed in Lessona, *Memorie*, pp. 155–58, 189, 193, 201–19. Further notes, and a later memorandum to Mussolini, are printed in Rochat, *Militari e politici*, pp. 481–87.

57. Emilio Canevari, *La guerra italiana*, 1:400–402.

58. De Bono, *Anno XIIII*, pp. 161–81. Guido Battaglini was in charge of the construction work force. See his *Con S. E. De Bono*.

59. Mussolini, *Opera omnia*, 27:300–302.

60. Bianchi, *Rivelazioni*, pp. 110, 198–99.

61. For Badoglio's strategic thinking at this time see his memorandum of 5 November 1935 to Mussolini, in Rochat, *Militari e politici*, pp. 485–87; his observations in Quirino Armellini, *Con Badoglio in Etiopia*, pp. 80–85, 256–64; and Pietro Badoglio, *The War in Abyssinia*, pp. 19–34.

62. Vanna Vailati, *Badoglio risponde*, pp. 238–39.

63. Bianchi, *Rivelazioni*, p. 111; Enrico Caviglia, *Diario*, pp. 136–37.

64. Lessona, *Memorie*, p. 231.

65. Quotations from Del Boca, *Ethiopian War*, pp. 79, 108. Mussolini's orders for the use of gas are found in Mussolini, *Opera omnia*, 27:305–6. For good accounts of the December counteroffensive and the first battle of Tembien in January, see Del Boca, *Ethiopian War*, chaps. 6, 8; Franco Bandini, *Gli italiani in Africa*, chap. 20; George L. Steer, *Caesar in Abyssinia*, pp. 221–34; Theodore E. Konovaloff, *Con le armate del Negus*, pp. 71–85.

66. League of Nations, *Official Journal, February 1936*, pp. 240–41.

67. Bianchi, *Rivelazione*, pp. 114–15.

68. Giorgio Pini and Diulio Susmel, *Mussolini, l'uomo e l'opera*, 3:342.

69. Lessona, *Memorie*, pp. 237–42.

70. Reynolds and Eleanor Packard, *Balcony Empire*, pp. 24–25.

71. Rodolfo Graziani, *Ho difesa la patria*, p. 79.

72. Carte Graziani, b. 7, f. 14, and b. 70, f. 230, sf. 3, A.C.S.

73. Rochat, *Militari e politici*, p. 238. Afeworq's heroic defense is related in Steer, *Caesar in Abyssinia*, pp. 169–74. To discourage defeatism and prevent future abandonment of positions, Nasibu condemned to death for cowardice the officer who bore Afeworq away for treatment and who ordered a retreat from the garrison. The emperor commuted this sentence, but the officer suffered great punishment and disgrace. (Richard Greenfield, *Ethiopia*, p. 205; Steer, *Caesar in Abyssinia*, pp. 184–89.)

74. In his memoirs Graziani turns this defeat at Anale, in which Italian tanks were captured, into an Italian victory (*Il fronte sud*, pp. 190–92).

75. League, *Official Journal, January 1936*, pt. 1, p. 29.

76. Armellini, *Con Badoglio in Etiopia*, p. 243.

77. This correspondence is collected in Rochat, *Militari e politici*, pp. 238–47, 487–89.

78. Carte Graziani, b. 8, f. 16, and b. 67, f. 230, sf. 4.

79. Rochat, *Militari e politici*, p. 378.

80. League, *Official Journal, June 1936*, p. 630, records these figures, presented by Ethiopia.

81. F.O. 371/20165, p. 164. See also Alberto Sbacchi, "Legacy of Bitterness," *Genève-Afrique* 13 (1974):30–53.

82. Speech at Geneva, 30 June 1936, League, *Official Journal*, Spec. Supp. no. 151, p. 23.

83. *FRUS, 1936*, 3:39–40. For information on the bombing of Red Cross units and protests by Italy against misuse of the emblem, see *Rapport général du Comité international de la Croix-Rouge sur son activité d'août 1934 à mars 1938* (Geneva: Comité international de la Croix-Rouge, 1938), pp. 70–99, and Italian protest of 28 February 1936 to the League (C.104.M.45.136.VII).

84. Mussolini, *Opera omnia*, 27:307, 310.

85. Estimates are poor; figures are not clear. Junod, who was there, states Desta never had more than 15,000 men in Sidamo and that now there were only 4,000 to 5,000 (Marcel Junod, *Warrior without Weapons*, p. 48). Graziani put the figure around 15,000, but reported higher numbers to Rome (*Il fronte sud*, p. 225). British War Office estimates went as high as 90,000!

86. Junod, *Warrior without Weapons*, p. 48.

87. Graziani, *Il fronte sud*, pp. 227–30; Carte Graziani, b. 67, f. 230, sf. 4.

88. Aliosi, *Journal*, p. 343.

89. Carte Graziani, b. 8, f. 17; Graziani, *Il fronte sud*, p. 245.

90. F.O. 401/36, pt. 26, no. 123.

91. Graziani, *Il fronte sud*, p. 273.

8: Waiting Time

1. Baron [Pompeo] Aloisi, *Journal*, pp. 342–43, 348.

2. League of Nations, *Official Journal, February 1936*, pp. 240–41.

3. The best report of the secret meeting of the Committee of Thirteen is Gilbert's, in *FRUS, 1936,* 3:95–97.

4. Ser. 15227, carton R-3650, A.L.N.

5. F.O. 371/20179, pp. 100–109, P.R.O.

6. Meeting of Council, 23 January 1936, League, *Official Journal, February 1936,* pp. 106–7. Eden's position is stated in F.O. 401/36, pt. 26, no. 51.

7. *FRUS, 1936,* 3:98.

8. F.O. 401/36, pt. 26, no. 101. Titulescu also expressed these thoughts to Hugh Wilson, *For Want of a Nail,* pp. 80, 82–85.

9. *FRUS, 1936,* 3:34; F.O. 371/20165, p. 167.

10. U.S. Department of State, Decimal file 765.84/3708, N.A.; *DDF,* ser. 2, vol. 1, no. 100.

11. C.P. 9(36), in Cab. 24/259, P.R.O.; F.O. 371/20155, pp. 106–8; *DDF,* ser. 2, vol. 1, no. 67.

12. F.O. 371/20165, pp. 251–58; Cab. Concl. 3(36)2, 29 January 1936. Donovan saw Hugh Wilson, who thought his views of "overwhelming importance," in Geneva. Wilson tried to get Eden to meet with Donovan, but the unsettling circumstances upon the death of George V prevented a meeting. Wilson makes much of chance ("The death of a king may have been that fortuitous event which kept Europe on the steady path to disaster"), since Donovan's predictions, Wilson thought, might have changed Eden's mind, shifted British policy, and kept Italy from the Axis. (Wilson, *For Want of a Nail,* pp. 31–32, and *Diplomat between Wars* [New York: Longmans, Green & Co., 1941], p. 325.) This was wishful thinking. Donovan did see some officials at the Foreign Office, and left a report there, from which F.O. skepticism derived.

13. Cab. Concl. 2(36)4, 22 January 1936, and C.P. 10(36), "The Italian Situation in East Africa," a War Office appreciation, 17 January 1936, in Cab. 24/259; Vansittart's comment on a Board of Trade report on oil supply possibilities, F.O. 371/20180, pp. 186–206.

14. Cab. Concl. 1(36)4, 16 January 1936; Lord [Robert] Vansittart, *The Mist Procession,* p. 532.

15. Earl of Avon, *The Eden Memoirs: Facing the Dictators,* pp. 318–19.

16. Dennis Bardens, *Portrait of a Statesman,* p. 121.

17. *DGFP,* ser. C, vol. 4, no. 531.

18. Lord [Charles] Moran, *Churchill, Taken from the Diaries of Lord Moran,* pp. 755–56. Moran referred to a book by Eden's brother, Timothy Eden, *The Tribulations of a Baronet,* which showed the father as mentally ill, offering virtually no emotional support to his children.

19. Geoffrey McDermott, *The Eden Legacy and the Decline of British Diplomacy,* pp. 19, 30–31, 38; Thomas Jones, *A Diary with Letters, 1931–1950,* p. 176. To help out and eventually to replace Vansittart, Alexander Cadogan was brought in (in February 1936) as deputy undersecretary (Alexander Cadogan, *The Diaries of Sir Alexander Cadogan, O.M., 1938–1945,* pp. 12–13).

20. *Times* (London), 18 January 1936; *FRUS, 1936,* 3:92.

21. *Diplomat,* p. 79.

22. Ian Colvin, *None So Blind,* pp. 101–2.

23. Jones, *Diary with Letters,* p. 193.

24. Édouard Herriot, *Jadis,* 2:635.

25. Luigi Villari, *Storia diplomatica del conflitto italo-etiopico,* p. 237.

26. Aloisi, *Journal,* p. 342; F.O. 371/20153, pp. 124–27.

27. League, *Official Journal,* Spec. Supp. no. 148, pp. 6–9.

28. League, *Official Journal,* Spec. Supp. no. 150, pp. 332–37.

29. Cab. 16/136.

30. D.P.R. meeting, 14 January 1936, in Cab. 16/136; Arthur Marder, "The Royal Navy and the Ethiopian Crisis of 1935–36," pp. 1350–51; Pierre Masson, "Franco-British Staff Talks, 1935–1938," in *Les relations franco-britannique, 1935–1939,* pp. 119 ff.

31. *DDF,* ser. 2, vol. 1, nos. 29, 30.

32. *FRUS, 1936,* 3:87.

33. D.P.R. meeting, 14 January 1936, in Cab. 16/136.

34. Arthur J. Marder, communication, *American Historical Review* 76 (April 1971):581.

35. Comments on 4 and 25 November 1935, Sir Samuel Hoare, Private Papers, F.O. 800/295, pp. 340–44, 385–88, P.R.O.

36. Cab. Concl. 51(35)1, 4 December 1935.

37. D.P.R. meeting, 14 January 1936, in Cab. 16/136. The earlier desiderata and preliminary inquiries are found in C.O.S. 416, "Assurances to be Obtained from Other Powers to Safeguard the Situation in Event of an Aggression by Italy," 4 December 1935, and D.P.R. 74, "Military Conversations with Mediterranean Powers," 27 December 1935, both in Cab. 16/140.

38. F.O. 401/36, pt. 26, nos. 39–43.

39. Bernard Michel, "La Petite Entente et la crise des années 30," *Revue d'histoire de la deuxième guerre mondiale,* no. 77 (January 1970), pp. 15–24; *DGFP,* ser. C, vol. 4, no. 535.

40. League, *Official Journal,* Spec. Supp. no. 150, p. 336; *DGFP,* ser. C, vol. 4, no. 519.

41. Wilson, *For Want of a Nail,* pp. 69–70.

42. D.P.R. meeting, 14 January 1936, in Cab. 16/136; Cab. Concl. 1(36)4, 15 January.

43. Chambre, *débats* 1936, 1:185–92; Joseph Paul-Boncour, *Entre deux guerres,* 3:30–31.

44. Record of this talk is at F.O. 401/36, pt. 26, no. 106.

45. U.S. Department of State, Decimal file 765.84/3628.

46. *DGFP,* ser. C, vol. 4, no. 525.

47. *DDF,* ser. 2, vol. 1, nos. 82, 83; Fabry, *De la Place de la Concorde au course de l'Intendance,* p. 74; Fabry, *J'ai connu . . . 1934–1945,* pp. 233–38.

48. See Cab. Concl. 4(36)2, 5 February 1936.

9:   Stop and Go

1. Cordell Hull, *Memoirs,* 1:461.

2. Figures in post-gold-standard dollars. In January 1934, before war preparation, exports to Italian Africa came to $11,000 (Herbert Feis, *Seen from E.A.,* pp. 304–5).

3. Lowell R. Tillett, "The Soviet Role in League Sanctions against Italy," *American Slavic and East European Review* 15 (1956):11–16.

4. Feis, *Seen from E.A.,* pp. 306–7.

5. Chambre, *débats,* 1935, p. 2864, 28 December.

6. Cab. Concl. 3(36)3, 29 January 1936, P.R.O.

7. Robert A. Divine, *The Illusion of Neutrality,* p. 135.

8. Ibid., pp. 133–34.

9. Hull, *Memoirs*, 1:461.

10. Ibid., p. 463.

11. *DDF*, ser. 2, vol. 1, no. 13.

12. Ibid., no. 31.

13. Edgar B. Nixon, ed., *Franklin D. Roosevelt and Foreign Affairs*, 3:154. This speech drew inspiration from a letter Roosevelt received from Ambassador Dodd in Berlin, who wrote in mid-December that European diplomacy, in the wake of the Hoare-Laval debacle, was in disarray. Two-thirds of the German people "are now entirely in sympathy with the reported United States oil embargo of Italy." Dodd described the "crazy war activity" of Hitler. Roosevelt told his cabinet on 27 December that it was the most pessimistic letter he ever read. (Ickes, *The Secret Diary of Harold L. Ickes*, p. 494.)

14. F.O. 408/66, no. 14, P.R.O.; *DDF*, ser. 2, vol. 1, nos. 6, 7.

15. A range of foreign opinion interpreting the speech from many points of reference is found in Brice Harris, Jr., *The United States and the Italo-Ethiopian Crisis*, pp. 115–20.

16. Ickes's expression, *Secret Diary*, p. 533.

17. F.O. 371/20177, pp. 4–9.

18. The report is printed in League of Nations, *Official Journal*, Spec. Supp. no. 148, pp. 39–85.

19. Frank P. Walters, *A History of the League of Nations*, p. 676.

20. *FRUS, 1936*, 3:105–9.

21. *DGFP*, ser. C, vol. 4, nos. 535, 553; Baron [Pompeo] Aloisi, *Journal*, pp. 349–50.

22. F.O. 371/20180, pp. 235–44.

23. F.O. 371/20180, pp. 186–206, 290–93; F.O. 371/20162, p. 93.

24. F.O. 371/20172, pp. 174–79; F.O. 371/20177, pp. 336–37; F.O. 401/36, pt. 26, no. 144.

25. Cab. Concl. 8(36)3.

26. F.O. 401/36, pt. 26, nos. 153, 158; F.O. 371/20178, pp. 8–9.

27. F.O. 401/36, pt. 26, no. 160. Barton's appreciation of the military situation was based on information from the British military attaché, Holt, who was with the emperor at northern field headquarters at Dessye. In this connection it is interesting to read the evaluation of the French minister that Holt "more and more played the role of military adviser to the emperor," even trying to dismiss the Belgian officers serving as military advisers. Dispatch, 7 February 1936, *DDF*, ser. 2, vol. 1, no. 150.

28. F.O. 401/36, pt. 26, no. 154.

29. The dispatches are published in George W. Baer, "Haile Selassie's Protectorate Appeal to King Edward VIII," *Cahiers d'études africaines* 9 (1969):306–12. See also F.O. 371/20173, pp. 116–20, and Cab. Concl. 9(36)9, 24 February 1936.

30. 309 H.C. Deb., 5th ser., cols. 79, 81.

31. F.O. 401/36, pt. 26, no. 156; Earl of Avon, *The Eden Memoirs: Facing the Dictators*, p. 327.

32. F.O. 401/36, pt. 26, no. 166; *DDF*, ser. 2, vol. 1, no. 235.

33. Luigi Villari, *Storia diplomatica del conflitto italo-etiopico*, p. 242–44; *Journal*, pp. 352–54.

34. 310 H.C. Deb., 5th ser., col. 2508; F.O. 401/36, pt. 26, no. 181.

35. C.O.S. 445, 26 February 1936, in Cab. 53/27.

36. Thomas Jones, *A Diary with Letters, 1931–1950*, pp. 175–76.

37. Cab. Concl. 11(36)5, 26 February 1936; Aloisi, *Journal*, p. 353.

38. Mussolini, *Opera omnia di Benito Mussolini*, 27:224–27.

39. Joel Colton, *Léon Blum: Humanist in Politics* (New York: Alfred A. Knopf, 1966), pp. 115–17.

40. *DDF,* ser. 2, vol. 1, no. 216; Mussolini, *Opera omnia*, 27:107.

41. F.O. 401/36, pt. 26, no. 145; *DDF,* ser. 2, vol. 1, no. 216.

42. Aloisi, *Journal,* pp. 348–51. What operational planning the naval ministry in Rome did is found in Emilia Chiavarelli, *L'opera della marina italiana nella guerra italo-etiopica,* pp. 92–97; Min. Mar., Gab., b. 174–75; and Min. Mar., Gab., Archivio Segreto, b. 40, A.C.S.

43. *DDF,* ser. 2, vol. 1, nos. 224, 239.

44. F.O. 401/36, pt. 26, no. 167.

45. *DDF,* ser. 2, vol. 1, no. 224; Aloisi, *Journal,* p. 352.

46. *DDF,* ser. 2, vol. 1, no. 258.

47. Pierre-Étienne Flandin, *Politique française 1919–1940,* p. 188.

48. Angelo Del Boca, *The Ethiopian War 1935–1941,* p. 126.

49. Pietro Badoglio, *The War in Abyssinia,* p. 94. Franco Bandini, in an elaborate (and unconvincing) speculation on the secret history of the war, maintains that the attack on Amba Aradam was not the "strategic battle" Badoglio claimed, but rather a contrived tactical exercise meant to facilitate acceptance of a secret peace overture the Italians were presenting through an intermediary, Jacir Bey, a plan envisioning that the emperor would concede to terms following a prearranged defeat meant to justify his concessions (Bandini, "Una battaglia addomesticàto" [a rigged battle] in *Gli italiani in Africa,* chap. 22). Bandini based his work on the Salvemini collection, from which the master had himself hoped to write a history of the war. But here is Salvemini's own judgement: "As a matter of fact, there was no element of fake in either the battle of Tembien or the battle of Enderta. They were both real." (Gaetano Salvemini, *Prelude to World War II,* p. 418.)

50. Valle to Badoglio, 22 January 1935, Fondo Badoglio, b. 4, f. 6, A.C.S.

51. "L'inghilterra e la difesa aerea," published in 19 October 1928 in *Educazione fascista* and reprinted in Douhet, *La guerra integrale,* ed. Emilio Canevari, chap. 10.

52. Badoglio, *War in Abyssinia,* p. 78, 84–85.

53. Guido Mattioli, *L'aviazione fascista e la conquista dell'impero,* p. 31.

54. George L. Steer, *Caesar in Abyssinia,* pp. 268–69.

55. Badoglio, *War in Abyssinia,* pp. 98–99; Emilio Canevari, *La guerra italiana,* 1:364.

56. Theodore E. Konovaloff, *Con le armate del Negus,* pp. 110–16; Badoglio, *War in Abyssinia,* pp. 91, 139.

57. Steer, *Caesar in Abyssinia,* p. 267.

58. Cited in Del Boca, *Ethiopian War,* p. 141.

59. F.O. 401/36, pt. 26, no. 186. Badoglio gives these figures for the battle of Shire: 63 Italian officers and 894 Italian soldiers dead or wounded against Ethiopian casualties estimated at 7,000; for the second Tembien, 34 Italian officers, 359 Italian soldiers, 188 Eritreans, with Ethiopian losses at 8,000 men (*War in Abyssinia,* pp. 108, 119).

60. Steer, *Caesar in Abyssinia,* p. 275.

61. Badoglio, *War in Abyssinia,* p. 118; Quirino Armellini, *Con Badoglio in Ethiopia,* p. 185.

62. Del Boca, *Ethiopian War,* p. 156.

63. Badoglio, *War in Abyssinia,* p. 139.

64. Mussolini, *Opera omnia,* 27:313.

65. Del Boca, *Ethiopian War,* p. 145.

10: The World Looks On

1. *DDF,* ser. 2, vol. 1, no. 259.

2. 12 February 1936, *DGFP,* ser. C, vol. 4, nos. 553, 579.

3. Pierre-Étienne Flandin, *Politique française 1919–1940,* p. 188; F.O. 432/2, pt. 5, no. 25, P.R.O.

4. *DDF,* ser. 2, vol. 1, no. 241.

5. F.O. 401/36, pt. 26, no. 170.

6. Maurin to Flandin, 29 January 1936, *DDF,* ser. 2, vol. 1, no. 109.

7. *DDF,* ser. 2, vol. 1, nos. 235, 239; F.O. 401/36, pt. 26, nos. 156, 172.

8. *DDF,* ser. 2, vol. 1, no. 260.

9. F.O. 401/36, pt. 26, nos. 168, 170, 173.

10. League of Nations, *Official Journal,* Spec. Supp. no. 149, pp. 12–13.

11. Luigi Villari, *Storia diplomatica del conflitto italo-etiopico,* pp. 234–35; *DGFP,* ser. C, vol. 5, no. 1.

12. *DDF,* ser. 2, vol. 1, nos. 280, 313.

13. U.S. Department of State, Decimal file 765.84/3887, N.A.

14. Villari, *Storia diplomatica,* p. 243.

15. Ibid., pp. 246–47.

16. *DDF,* ser. 2, vol. 1, no. 295.

17. *DGFP,* ser. C. vol. 5, no. 30.

18. Cab. Concl. 11(36)5, 26 February 1936, P.R.O.

19. Cab. Concl. 15(36)1, 5 March 1936.

20. F.O. 401/36, pt. 26, no. 179, for the British-French meeting of 3 March 1936; for the appeal, League, *Official Journal, April 1936* (Minutes of the 91st Council), pt. 2, p. 395.

21. Frank P. Walters, *A History of the League of Nations,* p. 678.

22. Villari, *Storia diplomatica,* pp. 244–45.

23. League, *Official Journal,* Spec. Supp. no. 149, pp. 15–22.

24. F.O. 401/36, pt. 26, no. 179, annex.

25. F.O. 371/20413, pp. 182–92; the memorandum was drawn up by Owen O'Malley.

26. *DDF,* ser. 2, vol. 1, no. 295.

27. F.O. 401/36, pt. 26, no. 181.

28. Pietro Badoglio, *The War in Abyssinia,* p. 124.

29. By a note of 8 March the emperor put his minister in Paris "at the disposal of the Committee of Thirteen to furnish, whenever desired, any further information for which the Committee may ask" (League, *Official Journal, April 1936,* pt. 2, pp. 395–96).

30. F.O. 401/36, pt. 26, no. 189.

31. Baron [Pompeo] Aloisi, *Journal,* p. 354; the Italian charges are in "Ethiopian Atrocities and Misuses of the Red Cross Emblem in Ethiopia," League, *Official Journal, April 1936,* pt. 2, pp. 404–54.

32. *DDF,* ser. 2, vol. 1, no. 290.

33. F.O. 371/36, pt. 26, no. 193.

34. Aloisi, *Journal*, p. 335; *DGFP*, ser. C, vol. 5, no. 554.

35. League, *Official Journal, April 1936*, pt. 2, p. 395.

36. Harold Nicolson, *Diaries and Letters, 1930–1939*, p. 243.

37. *DDF*, ser. 2, vol. 1, no. 351.

38. *DGFP*, ser. C, vol. 4, no. 598.

39. Ibid., no. 603; Jens Petersen, *Hitler-Mussolini*, p. 473.

40. Esmonde M. Robertson, *Hitler's Pre-War and Military Plans, 1933–1939*, pp. 80–81.

41. Selections from this speech are found in Norman H. Baynes, ed., *The Speeches of Adolf Hitler, April 1922–August 1939*, 2 vols. (London: Oxford University Press, 1942), 2:1271–302.

42. *DDF*, ser. 2, vol. 1, no. 447; François Charles-Roux, *Huit ans au Vatican, 1932–1940*, p. 151.

43. Aloisi, *Journal*, p. 35.

44. Raffaele Guariglia, *Ricordi 1922–1946*, p. 306; *DGFP*, ser. C, vol. 5, no. 18.

45. *DGFP*, ser. C, vol. 5, no. 45.

46. Walters, *History of the League*, p. 698.

47. *DDF*, ser. 2, vol. 1, no. 407.

48. Ibid., nos. 492, 525; F.O. 432/2, pt. 5, no. 49; Jean Lecuir and Patrick Friedenson, "L'organisation de la coopération aérienne franco-britannique," *Revue d'histoire de la deuxième guerre mondiale*, no. 73 (January 1969), pp. 46–49; Nicolson, *Diaries and Letters*, p. 252.

49. C.O.S. 442, 16 March 1936, in Cab. 53/27.

50. France, Assemblée Nationale, *Rapport fait au nom de la commission chargée d'enquêter ser les évènetments survenus en France de 1933 à 1945*, C. Serre, recorder, 1947 session, 3:565; Villari, *Storia diplomatica*, p. 248; Cab. Concl. 18(36)1, 11 March 1936.

51. Alojsi, *Journal,* p. 360; Villari, *Storia diplomatica*, p. 248; F.O. 401/36, pt. 26, no. 208.

52. Cab. Concl. 18(36)1, 11 March 1936; Cab. Concl. 20(36)7, 16 March 1936.

53. Cited in Arthur Marder, "The Royal Navy and the Ethiopian Crisis of 1935–36," *American Historical Review* 75 (June 1970):1352.

54. Cab. Concl. 23(36)3, 19 March 1936.

55. Mussolini, *Opera omnia di Benito Mussolini*, 27:232.

56. Bandini argues this last purpose was the main point of Ruggero's mission (*Gli italiani in Africa*, pp. 384–85, 546–47).

57. Enrico Caviglia, *Diario*, p. 140; Aloisi, *Journal*, pp. 365–66.

58. *DDF*, ser. 2, vol. 1, no. 535; Aloisi, *Journal*, p. 365.

59. *DDF*, ser. 2, vol. 1, no. 535.

60. F.O. 401/36, pt. 27, nos. 21, 24, 29, 30.

61. Ibid., nos. 13, 24; F.O. 371/19186, pp. 221–24.

62. Badoglio, *War in Abyssinia*, pp. 142–43.

63. Mussolini, *Opera omnia*, 27:241–48.

64. Konovaloff, *Con le armate del Negus*, p. 146; Steer, *Caesar in Abyssinia*, p. 301; Badoglio, *War in Abyssinia*, p. 140.

65. League, *Official Journal, April 1936*, pt. 2, p. 455; F.O. 401/36, pt. 26, no. 214.

66. Great Britain, *Parliamentary Debates* (Lords), 5th ser., 100 (1936), cols. 354–58; F.O. 401/36, pt. 27, no. 26.

67. Memo of 7 April 1936, P.N.F., Min. Cul. Pop., b. 184, f. 25, A.C.S.

68. F.O. 401/36, pt. 26, no. 215.

69. Ibid., no. 40.

70. Cab. Concl. 27(36)2, 6 April 1936.

71. *DDF,* ser. 2, vol. 2, no. 23.

72. *Documents diplomatiques belges, 1920–1940,* 4:190; C.I.D. 1237-B, in Cab. 2/6(1).

73. Konovaloff, *Con le armate del Negus,* pp. 155, 162–63; Konovaloff, "History of Ethiopia," microfilmed typescript, p. 345, Hoover Institution, Stanford, Ca.

74. Mussolini, *Opera omnia,* 27:316.

75. Quirino Armellini, *Con Badoglio in Etiopia,* p. 224.

76. Konovaloff's memoirs are partially printed in George L. Steer, *Caesar in Abyssinia;* for this quote see pp. 325, 329.

77. Badoglio, *War in Abyssinia,* p. 148.

78. Ethiopian protest to the League, *Official Journal, April 1936,* pt. 2, p. 480; Haile Selassie to his American adviser, John Spencer, U.S. Department of State, Decimal file 765.84/4929; *John Melly of Ethiopia,* p. 240.

79. League, *Official Journal, April 1936,* pt. 2, pp. 404–87. The Ethiopian national chapter of the Red Cross was organized on 26 July 1935 and recognized by the International Committee on 26 September 1935. Its formation on the eve of the war was another effort to tie Ethiopia's cause as closely as possible to the international conventions of Europe. The president of the national chapter was the Ethiopian minister of foreign affairs; the vice-president was his son. Members of the national committee included the emperor's legal advisers Colson and Auberson and his personal physician and Greek consul-general Adrien Zervos.

80. Aloisi, *Journal,* p. 363, for Huber's visit, whereat Aloisi set the Italian conditions; Mussolini, *Opera omnia,* 27:315.

81. There were other volunteers. For example, a delegate from the International Save the Children Fund was in Ethiopia from 31 December 1935 to 26 March 1936, in the Fund's "first step in Africa," to see what could be done about the children's rights during the war and after (F. Small, "Mission en Ethiopie," *Revue internationale de la Croix-Rouge,* nos. 209 [May 1936], pp. 376–92, and 210 [June 1936], pp. 465–93).

82. Marcel Junod, *Warrior without Weapons,* p. 49; in the original Junod's book is entitled: *Le troisième combattant: De l'ypérite en Abyssinie à la bombe atomique d'Hiroshima.*

83. Brown, *Für das Rote Kruez in Aeithiopien,* p. 219.

84. Junod, *Warrior without Weapons,* pp. 60–61.

85. "Activities in Abyssinia," in *General Report of the International Committee of the Red Cross on its Activities from August 1934 to March 1938* (Geneva: ICRC, 1938), p. 89.

86. Junod, *Warrior without Weapons,* p. 83; Brown, *Rote Kruez in Aethiopien,* p. 168; F.O. 401/36, pt. 27, no. 26.

11: Conquest

1. For the conversation between Eden, Flandin, and Paul-Boncour, see F.O. 401/36, pt. 27, no. 46, P.R.O. Vansittart never rated Italians highly either; his comment is in F.O. 371/20167, p. 219.

2. *DDF,* ser. 2, vol. 2, no. 17.

3. *FRUS, 1936,* 3:116.

4. *DDF,* ser. 2, vol. 1, no. 533.

5. F.O. 401/36, pt. 27, no. 16.

6. Baron [Pompeo] Aloisi, *Journal*, pp. 361–62.

7. Cab. Concl. 27(36)1, 6 April 1936, P.R.O.; League of Nations, *Official Journal, April 1936*, pt. 2, p. 487.

8. Cab. Concl. 27(36)1, 6 April 1936.

9. F.O. 371/20401, p. 261.

10. League, *Official Journal*, Spec. Supp. no. 149, pp. 48–49.

11. Donald McLachlan, *In the Chair*, p. 120.

12. F.O. 371/20156.

13. Cab. Concl. 27(36)1, 6 April 1936.

14. Luigi Villari, *Storia diplomatica del conflitto italo-etiopico*, p. 251.

15. Aloisi, *Journal*, p. 377; *DDF*, ser. 2, vol. 2, no. 17.

16. Ibid.

17. Cab. Concl. 28(36)2, 8 April 1936.

18. League, *Official Journal, April 1936*, pt. 2, pp. 398–401; F.O. 401/36, pt. 27, no. 22; Villari, *Storia diplomatica*, pp. 249–51.

19. F.O. 401/36, pt. 27, no. 41.

20. *DDF*, ser. 2, vol. 2, nos. 46, 51, 55.

21. F.O. 401/36, pt. 27, nos. 36, 46; Villari, *Storia diplomatica*, p. 253; League, *Official Journal, April 1936*, pt. 2, p. 461; Aloisi, *Journal*, p. 369. The policy of the International Committee still holds. Requesting a look at the same material thirty-five years later, I got the same answer.

22. Eden-Flandin meeting on 10 April 1936, F.O. 401/36, pt. 27, no. 46.

23. Earl of Avon, *The Eden Memoirs: Facing the Dictators*, pp. 375–79. Pierre-Étienne Flandin, *Politique Française 1919–1940*, pp. 189–91; F.O. 432/2, pt. 5, no. 60; Aloisi, *Journal*, pp. 369–72.

24. F.O. 371/36, pt. 27, no. 46.

25. Mussolini, *Opera omnia di Benito Mussolini*, 27:250; Aloisi, *Journal*, p. 367.

26. Aloisi, *Journal*, p. 353.

27. Jacir Bey continued to drift around. It appears he contacted Colson in Alexandria in March 1936, when this adviser was there recuperating from a heart attack. In May he tried unsuccessfully to talk with Haile Selassie in Jerusalem. The main sources for the Jacir Bey story are Fulvio Suvich et al., *Il processo Roatta*, pp. 26, 57, 258–61; Clara Conti, *Servizio segreto*, pp. 63–73, 195–206; Franco Bandini, *Gli italiani in Africa*, pp. 351–402, 526–50.

28. Giuliano Cora, "Un diplomatico durante l'era fascista," *Storia e politica*, January–March 1966, p. 95; F.O. 371/20173, pp. 67, 150–52. As far as I can determine, this consul was Bivio Luigi Sbrana, not "Vezio Lucchini" who features in the Jacir Bey saga as cosigner of the Faldella contract and to whom Bandini constantly refers as the consul. Vezio Lucchini was a Fascist militiaman mysteriously on the scene. Mario Roatta, former secret service head, thought Lucchini might be an alias for a person to me unknown. It was to Sbrana as consul that Paolo Zappa dedicated his book *L'intelligence service el'Etiopia*. For Roatta's doubts, see Conti, *Servizio segreto*, p. 291.

29. See George W. Baer, "Haile Selassie's Protectorate Appeal to King Edward VIII," *Cahiers d'études africaines* 9 (1969): 310.

30. Raffaele Guariglia, *Ricordi 1922–1946*, pp. 304–5.

31. F.O. 401/36, pt. 27, no. 27; Bandini, *Gli italiani in Africa*, pp. 392–93; Carte Graziani, b. 67, f. 230, sf. 6, A.C.S.

32. F.O. 371/20173, pp. 233–35.

33. Aloisi, *Journal*, p. 366.

34. Ibid., p. 369.

35. Ibid., pp. 373–74.

36. Alessandro Lessona, *Memorie,* pp. 250–53; idem, *Verso l'impero,* pp. 213–15. For a warmer appreciation of Melchiade Gabba, his unusual culture and personal modesty, see Emilio Canevari, *La guerra italiana,* 1:391–92.

37. Lessona, *Verso l'impero,* pp. 212–17; F.O. 371/20175, p. 234.

38. Louise Weiss, *Mémoires d'une Européenne,* 3:80.

39. *DDF,* ser. 2, vol. 2, no. 72.

40. F.O. 401/36, pt. 27, no. 60.

41. League, *Official Journal, April 1936,* pt. 2, pp. 401–3.

42. *FRUS, 1936,* 3:129.

43. League, *Official Journal, April 1936,* pt. 2, p. 380.

44. *FRUS, 1936,* 3:120.

45. F.O. 401/36, pt. 27, no. 85; *DDF,* ser. 2, vol. 2, no. 133; *FRUS, 1936,* 3:126. This dispatch of Wilson's was picked up by the Italian intelligence service (Villari, *Storia diplomatica,* pp. 262–63). For these talks see also Hugh R. Wilson, *For Want of a Nail,* pp. 85, 92. Corbin told Vansittart not to count on much after the elections (*DDF,* ser. 2, vol. 2, no. 111.

46. League, *Official Journal,* Spec. Supp. no. 150, pp. 338–39; F.O. 401/36, pt. 27, no. 79.

47. League, *Official Journal,* Spec. Supp. no. 149, p. 41; Villari, *Storia diplomatica,* p. 262.

48. F.O. 401/36, pt. 27, no. 71; Avon, *Facing the Dictators,* p. 378.

49. *DDF,* ser. 2, vol. 2, no. 93.

50. U.S. Department of State, Decimal file 765.84/4175, N.A.

51. *DDF,* ser. 2, vol. 2, nos. 85, 90, 113.

52. Aloisi, *Journal,* pp. 377–78; F.O. 401/36, pt. 27, nos. 86, 93; *DDF,* ser. 2, vol. 2, no. 105; Charles de Chambrun, *Traditions et souvenirs,* pp. 148–49, 165–66.

53. *L'oeuvre de Léon Blum,* pp. 146–47.

54. *DDF,* ser. 2, vol. 2, no. 137.

55. The three memorandums are found in F.O. 371/20181, pp. 109–21, 171–79.

56. F.O. 371/20411, pp. 136–45; F.O. 371/20181, pp. 119–21.

57. Foreign Office comment here and immediately following is from F.O. 371/20174, pp. 9–19.

58. Cab. Concl. 31(36)4, 29 April 1936; Arthur Marder, "The Royal Navy and the Ethiopian Crisis of 1935–36," *American Historical Review* 75 (June 1970):1352–53.

59. Guariglia, *Ricordi,* pp. 309–10; *DGFP,* ser. C, vol. 4, no. 316.

60. F.O. 371/20181, pp. 4–9, minutes of 29 April 1936; Keith Feiling, *The Life of Neville Chamberlain,* p. 281.

61. Cab. Concl. 34(36)4, 6 May 1936.

62. Charles A. Petrie, *The Life and Letters of the Right Hon. Sir Austen Chamberlain,* 2:413. The speech itself is in 311 H.C. Deb., 5th ser., cols. 1767–73. See Arnold J. Toynbee, *Survey of International Affairs, 1935,* 2:454–58, for "least said soonest mended" arguments by Winston Churchill and others.

63. Eden's speech to his constituents in Leamington, *Times* (London), 4 May 1936; Aloisi, *Journal,* p. 380.

64. 311 H.C. Deb., 5th ser., cols. 1741–42; F.O. 432/2, pt. 5, no. 90.

65. Thomas Jones, *A Diary with Letters 1931–1950,* p. 193; *DDF,* ser. 2, vol. 2, no. 193.

66. Blum's views as expressed to Eden, F.O. 401/36, pt. 27, no. 141; F.O. 432/2, pt. 5, no. 69.

67. F.O. 432/2, nos. 60, 66; *DDF,* ser. 2, vol. 2, no. 111.

68. F.O. 401/36, pt. 27, nos. 108, 112; *DDF,* ser. 2, vol. 2, nos. 149, 150, 154.

69. Cab. Concl. 34(36)4, 6 May 1936; F.O. 401/36, pt. 27, no. 108; *DDF,* ser. 2, vol. 2, no. 161.

70. *DDF,* ser. 2, vol. 2, no. 148.

71. Ibid., no. 149.

72. F.O. 401/36, pt. 27, no. 73.

73. Ibid., no. 84.

74. Cab. Concls. 30(36)3, 22 April, and 31(36)4, 29 April 1936.

75. F.O. 371/20133, pp. 473–513.

76. Badoglio would have used bacteriological bombs against Ras Mulugeta at Amba Aradam if it had been necessary, but yperite did the job. His objections to bacteriological bombing were: civilian casualties in the north among populations favorably disposed toward Italy, destruction of livestock, and international outrage (Alberto Sbacchi, "Legacy of Bitterness," *Genève-Afrique* 13 [1974]:40).

77. Cited in Gaetano Salvemini, *Prelude to World War II,* p. 419.

78. Federico Baistrocchi, "L'attività dell'esercito per l'esigenza A.O.," in *Le forze armate dell'Italia fascista,* ed. Tomaso Sillani, pp. 109–10; Guido Mattioli, *L'aviazione fascista e la conquista dell'impero;* Pietro Badoglio, *The War in Abyssinia,* chap. 14.

79. For the navy's claims to credit see Emilia Chiavarelli, *L'opera della marina italiana nella guerra italo-etiopica,* pp. 129–34; Ministero degli Affari Esteri, *L'Italia in Africa: L'opera della marina, 1868–1943,* ed. G. Fioravanzo and G. Viti (Rome: Istituto poligrafico dello stato, 1959), 2:50–53.

80. Carte Graziani, b. 10, f. 19.

81. Cab. Concl. 31(36)4, 29 April 1936.

82. Quirino Armellini, *Con Badoglio in Etiopia,* pp. 221–26.

83. For the retreat to Addis Ababa see Theodore E. Konovaloff, *Con le armate del Negus,* chap. 8, and Richard Greenfield, *Ethiopia,* pp. 218–19.

84. Greenfield, *Ethiopia,* pp. 220–22.

85. George L. Steer, *Caesar in Abyssinia,* p. 366.

86. *FRUS, 1936,* 3:64; F.O. 401/36, pt. 27, nos. 103, 104.

87. Greenfield, *Ethiopia,* p. 222.

88. Ibid., p. 227.

89. Leonard Mosley, *Haile Selassie,* p. 232.

90. Greenfield, *Ethiopia,* p. 223.

91. The dispatch of the Punjabis to Addis Ababa was the work of Geoffrey Thompson in the Foreign Office. See his recollections in *Front-Line Diplomat,* pp. 110–12. On the protection of foreigners and relief and supply missions of the legations, see the war diary of the British commander of the Punjab Regiment, W.O. 191/58, P.R.O., and the dispatches of the American minister, Cornelius Engert, in *FRUS, 1936,* 3:254–64. Dramatic eyewitness reports of the rioting in the city are found in Marcel Junod, *Warrior without Weapons,* and Steer, *Caesar in Abyssinia,* pp. 370–400.

92. *FRUS, 1936,* 3:66–67; Flandin, *Politique française,* p. 191; Lessona, *Verso l'impero,* p. 220, for Mussolini's telegram.

93. F.O. 401/36, pt. 27, nos. 124, 175; F.O. 317/20176, pp. 174–81; F.O. 371/20177, pp. 87–89.

94. Aloisi, *Journal,* p. 383. For racial laws in Italian east Africa, and their influence on later racial and antisemitic laws in Italy, see Renzo De Felice, *Storia degli ebrei italiani sotto il fascismo,* 3d ed. (Turin: Einaudi, 1972), chaps. 4, 5; Richard Pankhurst, "Fascist Racist Policies in Ethiopia, 1922–1941," *Ethiopian Observer* 12 (1969):272–86; Luigi Preti, *Impero fascista, africani ed ebrei.*

95. Giuseppe Bottai, *Vent'anni e un giorno,* p. 113; Galeazzo Ciano, *Ciano's Diary, 1937–1938,* p. 74.

96. Rodolfo Graziani, *Il fronte sud,* p. 273.

97. Carte Graziani, b. 8, f. 16; F.O. 371/20165, pp. 212–20.

98. Graziani, *Il fronte sud,* p. 292; Angelo Del Boca, *The Ethiopian War, 1935–1941,* p. 187.

99. Graziani, *Il fronte sud,* pp. 297–99.

100. Ibid., pp. 302–3; Carte Graziani, b. 10, f. 19.

101. Carte Graziani, b. 10, f. 19.

102. Ibid.; see Graziani, *Il fronte sud,* pp. 310–11, for an edited version.

103. Greenfield, *Ethiopia,* pp. 225–26.

104. Graziani's account of these days is in *Processo Graziani,* 1:51–54.

12: Ethiopia Is Italian

1. Baron [Pompeo] Aloisi, *Journal,* p. 380; Charles A. Petrie, *The Life and Letters of the Right Hon. Sir Austen Chamberlain,* 2:414; Raffaele Guariglia, *Ricordi 1922–1946,* pp. 312–13.

2. Mussolini Papers, microcopy T-586/426, frames 012917–19, N.A. The published, highly edited version in the *Daily Mail* (London), 6 May 1936, is less conciliatory.

3. *Opera omnia di Benito Mussolini,* 27:265–66, 382–88.

4. F.O. 401/36, pt. 27, no. 137, P.R.O.

5. *Processo Graziani,* 1:51–66; Emilio Canevari, *Graziani me ha detto,* p. 23; Mussolini, *Opera omnia,* 28:264.

6. Mussolini, Opera omnia, 27:265; *Processo Graziani,* 1:60–61.

7. *DDF,* ser. 2, vol. 2, no. 173; F.O. 401/36, pt. 27, no. 117.

8. *DDF,* ser. 2, vol. 2, no. 189;

9. F.O. 401/36, pt. 27, no. 121.

10. Giorgio Pini and Duilio Susmel, *Mussolini, l'uomo e l'opera,* 3:350.

11. *Italia di ieri per la storia di domani,* pp. 233–34.

12. Charles de Chambrun, *Traditions et souvenirs,* p. 214; Rachele Mussolini, *La mia vita con Benito,* pp. 128–29.

13. Amedeo Tosti, *Pietro Badoglio* (Verona: Mondadori, 1956), pp. 191, 360; Benito Mussolini, *Storia di anno,* pp. 173, 193.

14. Gianfranco Bianchi, *Rivelazioni sul conflitto italo-etiopico,* pp. 120–22.

15. Quoted in Roy MacGregor-Hastie, *The Day of the Lion: The Life and Death of Fascist Italy, 1922–1945* (New York: Coward-McCann, 1964), p. 246.

16. Alessandro Lessona, *Memorie,* pp. 171–72.

17. Ibid., pp. 266–68.

18. *Opera omnia,* 34:210.

19. Mussolini, *Memoirs, 1942–1943,* p. 223–24, 238. Mussolini said 1,537 died. Reliable casualty figures for the Ethiopian campaign are 2,988 Italian nationals and 1,457 natives (Eritrean, Somalian, Libyan) dead, 7,845 nationals and 3,307 natives wounded (Emilio Canevari, *La guerra italiana,* 1:391).

20. Enrico Caviglia, *Diario,* p. 386.

21. *Discorsi di Pio XI,* 3:490.

22. Binchy, *Church and State in Fascist Italy,* pp. 648–51; François Charles-Roux, *Huit ans au Vatican, 1932–1940,* p. 154; Arnold J. Toynbee, *Survey of International Affairs, 1935,* 2:105–6.

23. Giuseppe Bottai, *Vent'anni e un giorno,* p. 125.

24. *DGFP,* ser. C, vol. 3, no. 318; F.O. 401/36, pt. 27, no. 127; *FRUS, 1936,* 3:227.

25. League of Nations, *Official Journal, June 1936,* pp. 660–61.

26. F.O. 371/20167, pp. 276–77.

27. Aloisi, *Journal,* p. 384.

28. F.O. 401/36, pt. 27, no. 127.

29. League, *Official Journal, June 1936,* pp. 535–36, 539–41.

30. Aloisi, *Journal,* pp. 384–85; *DDF,* ser. 2, vol. 2, no. 212.

31. Luigi Villari, *Storia diplomatica del conflitto italo-etiopico,* pp. 272–73.

32. Aloisi, *Journal,* p. 386.

33. Guariglia, *Ricordi,* pp. 316–24.

34. *DDF,* ser. 2, vol. 2, no. 203.

35. For the Belgian story see David Owen Kieft, *Belgium's Return to Neutrality,* chap. 6; Pierre Henri Laurent, "The Reversal of Belgian Foreign Policy, 1936–1937," *Review of Politics* 31 (July 1969):370–84; Paul-Henri Spaak, *Combats inachevés,* vol. 1.

36. F.O. 371/20175, pp. 98–102.

37. *DGFP,* ser. C, vol. 5, no. 332. In this connection, see Robert L. Rothstein, *Alliances and Small Powers* (New York: Columbia University Press, 1968), pp. 149–62, and the disquisition by Karl J. Newman, *European Democracy between the Wars,* tr. K. Morgan (London: George Allen & Unwin, 1970).

38. Lowell R. Tillett, "The Soviet Role in League Sanctions against Italy, 1935–1936," *American Slavic and East European Review* 15 (1956):11–16; Franco Catalano, *L'economia italiana di guerra,* p. 16.

39. Villari, *Storia diplomatica,* pp. 272–73; Aloisi, *Journal,* pp. 384, 386–87; *FRUS, 1936,* 3:136–37: James Barros, *Betrayal from Within,* pp. 116–17.

40. F.O. 432/2, pt. 5, no. 79.

41. Ibid., no. 80; Pierre-Étienne Flandin, *Politique francaise 1919–1940,* p. 191; *DDF,* ser. 2, vol. 2, nos. 220, 223.

42. For the Corbin-Eden talks see *DDF,* ser. 2, vol. 2, nos. 244, 245; F.O. 401/36, pt. 27, no. 167.

43. C.P. 154(36), 3 June 1936, in Cab. 24/262, P.R.O.; F.O. 371/20167, p. 299.

44. Cab. Concl. 39(36)8, 27 May 36.

45. Mussolini, *Opera omnia,* 28:5–8, translated in *Documents on International Affairs, 1935,* ed. Stephen Heald, 2:483–86.

46. Cab. Concl. 40(36)5, 29 May 1936.

47. Villari, *Storia diplomatica,* p. 279. Mussolini, *Opera omnia,* 28:14–17; Aloisi, *Journal,* pp. 386–87.

48. Rachele Mussolini, *La mia vita con Benito,* p. 134.

49. This was how Suvich outlined it to Drummond, F.O. 401/36, pt. 27, nos. 174, 176.

50. *DDF,* ser. 2, vol. 2, no. 264; F.O. 401/36, pt. 27, no. 178.

51. Guariglia, *Ricordi,* pp. 333–35.

52. For the hope of thereby getting some balance to American influence, see *FRUS, 1936,* 3:145–49, 155–59.

53. *DDF,* ser. 2, vol. 2, nos. 280, 291, 304.

54. F.O. 401/36, pt. 27, no. 186.

55. *DDF,* ser. 2, vol. 2, nos. 248, 254, 271, 272, 277, 284, 286, 287.

56. Villari, *Storia diplomatica,* pp. 286–87; F.O. 401/36, pt. 27, no. 180; Cab. Concl. 41(36)1, 10 June 1936.

57. Cab. Concl. 41(36)1; *DDF,* ser. 2, vol. 2, nos. 282, 289; F.O. 432/2, pt. 5, no. 95; F.O. 371/20175, pp. 137–38.

58. Cab. Concl. 41(36)2, 10 June 1936; Galeazzo Ciano, *Ciano's Diplomatic Papers,* ed. M. Muggeridge, tr. S. Hood (London: Odhams, 1948), p. 6.

59. Keith Feiling, *The Life of Neville Chamberlain,* p. 296–97; Heald, ed., *Documents on International Affairs, 1935,* 2:488.

60. Feiling, *Neville Chamberlain,* p. 296; R. A. C. Parker, "Great Britain, France, and the Ethiopian Crisis, 1935–1936," *English Historical Review* 89 (April 1974):331.

61. Cab. Concls. 42(36)1, 2, 17 June 1936.

62. Harold Nicolson, *Diaries and Letters, 1930–1939,* p. 265; 313 H.C. Deb., 5th ser., cols. 1197–207.

63. Robert Rhodes James, *Memoirs of a Conservative,* p. 411. For a record and comment of the "spiritual struggle" in Great Britain in the wake of Chamberlain's speech, see Toynbee, *Survey of International Affairs, 1935,* 2:466–69, 474–82.

64. *Le Temps,* 20 and 24 June 1936.

65. *FRUS, 1936,* 3: 197–98, 207, 211–12; *The Public Papers and Addresses of Franklin Delano Roosevelt,* 5:225.

66. Frank P. Walters, *A History of the League of Nations,* p. 684; Earl of Avon, *The Eden Memoirs: Facing the Dictators,* p. 388; Prentiss Gilbert, in *FRUS, 1936,* 3:182.

67. Genevieve Tabouis, *Vingt ans de "suspense" diplomatique,* pp. 288–89.

68. Emery Kelen, *Peace in Their Time: Men Who Led Us in and out of War, 1914–1945* (New York: Alfred A. Knopf, 1963), p. 324.

69. League, *Official Journal,* Spec. Supp. no. 151, pp. 19–21. Interesting appendices came with the letter, one listing the notables who submitted to the Italian government. These included Ethiopia's religious leaders, Ras Hailu of Gojam, and Medogras Afework, the former minister to Rome. Another appendix contained the law of 1 June that organized the annexed territories, showing the favor given to the Moslem population as against the long dominant Coptic-Amharic inhabitants. There was to be respect for local traditions, compulsory teaching of Arabic in Moslem territories, and permission for restoring mosques and religious schools. The purpose was to curry anti-Amharic sentiment, favoring the Italians as liberators.

70. *DDF,* ser. 2, vol. 2, no. 320; Villari, *Storia diplomatica,* pp. 297–301; F.O. 371/20176, pp. 326–34.

71. *DDF,* ser. 2, vol. 2, no. 339.

72. League, *Official Journal,* Spec. Supp. no. 151, p. 68–69.

73. Samuel S. Jones, *The Scandinavian States and the League of Nations*, p. 262.

74. *FRUS, 1936*, 3:182.

75. Villari, *Storia diplomatica*, p. 293; Walters, *History of the League*, pp. 684–85; Thomas Jones, *A Diary with Letters, 1931–1950*, p. 227.

76. Cab. Concl. 50(36)2, 6 July 1936.

77. League, *Official Journal*, Spec. Supp. no. 149, pp. 56–65.

78. *DDF*, ser. 2, vol. 2, no. 408; *FRUS, 1936*, 3:185.

79. 314 H.C. Deb., 5th ser., cols. 1397–98; Mussolini, *Opera omnia*, 28:24.

80. 314 H.C. Deb., 5th ser., col. 2025; Delbos, on 8 July, *DDF*, ser. 2, vol. 2, no. 408; F.O. 371/21183, p. 19.

81. Mussolini, *Opera omnia*, 28:23–26; 315 H.C. Deb., 5th ser., cols. 1121–23.

82. *Survey of International Affairs, 1935*, 2:514.

13: Conclusion

1. Francesco Coppola, "La vittoria bifronte," *Politica* 40 (August 1936):5–74; *DDF*, ser. 2, vol. 2, no. 417.

2. *DGFP*, ser. C, vol. 5, no. 457; ser. D, vol. 1, no. 115.

3. Alfred Duff Cooper, *Old Men Forget*, pp. 202–4; Cab. Concl. 63(36)3, 4 November 1936, P.R.O.

4. F.O. 371/21183, p. 19, P.R.O. For Avenol's trip to Rome, see F.O. 371/20490, pp. 96–121; Galeazzo Ciano, *Ciano's Diplomatic Papers*, ed. M. Muggeridge, tr. S. Hood (London: Odhams, 1948), pp. 33–34; James Barros, *Betrayal from Within*, pp. 126–35.

5. Arnold J. Toynbee, *Survey of International Affairs, 1935*, 2:474–75. Duke of Windsor, *A King's Story* (New York: Putnam, 1951), pp. 298–99; 313 H.C. Deb., 5th ser., col. 1629; Viscount [Robert] Cecil, *A Great Experiment*, p. 278; Daniel Waley, *British Public Opinion and the Abyssinian War, 1935–6*, chaps. 3, 4.

6. *Inside the Third Reich*, p. 72.

7. Earl of Avon, *The Eden Memoirs: Facing the Dictators*, p. 311.

BIBLIOGRAPHY

Public Documents and Archives Material

France. Assemblée Nationale. *Rapport fait au nom de la commission chargée d'enquêter sur les événetments survenus en France de 1933 à 1945.* C. Serre, recorder. 1947 session, vol. 3.
———Chambre des Députés. *Journal officiel, débats parlementaires,* 1935, 1936. Paris, 1935, 1936.
———Haute cour de justice. *Le procès Flandin devant la haute cour de justice, 23–26 juillet 1946.* Paris: Librairie de Medicis, 1946.
———Haute cour de justice. *Procès du Maréchal Pétain.* Paris: Imprimerie des journaux officiels, 1945.
———Senat. *Annales du Sénat, débats parlementaires,* 1935, 1936. Paris, 1935, 1936.
Geneva. Archives of the League of Nations. Series 15227, 20311, 20692.
Great Britain. House of Commons. *Parliamentary Debates.* 5th series. Vols. 270–315 (1932–36). London, 1932–36.
———House of Lords. *Parliamentary Debates.* 5th series. Vol. 100 (1936). London: 1936.
League of Nations. *Official Journal 1935, 1936.* Geneva: 1935, 1936.
———*Official Journal.* Special Supplement nos. 138, 145–51. Geneva: 1935–36.
London. Public Record Office. Foreign Office and Cabinet documents, 1934–38.
Paris. Archives de la Chambre des Députés. 15th Legislature, Box 2². *Procès-Verbaux du Seances de la commission des Affaires Étrangeres, 1935–1936.*
Rome. Archivio Centrale dello Stato. Carte Graziani.
———Fondo Badoglio.
———Ministero della Marina, Gabinetto.
———Ministero della Marina, Gabinetto, Archivio Segreto.
———Partito Nazionale Fascista, Ministero della Cultura Popolare.
———Partito Nazionale Fascista, Segretaria Particolare del Duce, Carteggio Riservato and Carteggio Ordinario.
———Partito Nazionale Fascista, Situazione politica ed economica delle provincie.
Stanford, Ca. Hoover Institution on War, Revolution, and Peace. Germany, Reichskanzlei. Adjuntatur des Fuhrers. Files 1933–38, Italo-Ethiopian War 1936. Strunk von Este Report.
———Hornbeck Papers.
Washington, D.C. National Archives. Microcopy T-586. Personal Papers of Benito Mussolini, together with Some Official Records of the Italian Foreign Office and the Ministry of Popular Culture, 1922–1944. (These documents include secret position papers from the Ministero degli Affari Esteri, "Situazione politica nel 1935," on various countries.)
———U.S. Department of State, Decimal file 765.84.

Published Diplomatic Documents

Documents diplomatiques belges, 1920–1940. Vol. 4, edited by Ch. de Vissher and F. Van-langenhove. Brussels: Palais des Acadèmies, 1965.

Documents diplomatiques français, 1932–1939. Ser. 2, vols. 1–3, edited by Maurice Baumont and Pierre Renouvin. Paris: Imprimerie Nationale, 1963–66. (Cited as *DDF.*)

Documents on British Foreign Policy, 1919–1939. Ser. 2, vols. 1–10, and ser. 3, vols. 3–6, edited by E. L. Woodward, R. Butler, et al. London: Her Majesty's Stationery Office, 1947–72.

Documents on Canadian Foreign Policy, 1917–1939. Edited by Walter A. Riddell. Toronto: Oxford University Press, 1962.

Documents on German Foreign Policy, 1918–1945. Ser. C, vols. 1–5, edited by Margaret Lambert, et al. London: Her Majesty's Stationery Office, 1957–66. (Cited as *DGFP.*)

Foreign Relations of the United States, Diplomatic Papers, 1935, 1936. Vols. 1–4 (1935). Vol. 1–5 (1936). Washington, D.C.: Government Printing Office, 1953–54. (Cited as *FRUS.*)

"The Struggle of the U.S.S.R. for Collective Security in Europe during 1933–1935." *International Affairs,* nos. 6, 7, 8, 10. Moscow, 1963.

General

Aldgate, Tony. "British Newsreels and the Spanish Civil War." *History* 58 (February 1973):60–63.

Aloisi, Baron [Pompeo]. *Journal: 25 juillet 1932–14 juin 1936.* Translated by M. Vaussard. Paris: Librairie Plon, 1957.

Andrews, Eric. "The 'Labor Daily's' volte face on the Abyssinian Crisis, 1935." *Australian Outlook* 19 (August 1965):207–12.

Anfuso, Filippo. *Roma Berlino Salò, 1936–1945.* Milan: Garzanti, 1950.

Angell, Norman. *After All, the Autobiography of Norman Angell.* London: Hamish Hamilton, 1951.

Aquarone, Alberto. *L'organizzazione dello stato totalitario.* Turin: Einaudi, 1965.

Araldi, Vinicio. *Generali dell'impero.* Naples: Rispoli, [1940?].

Armellini, Quirino. *Con Badoglio in Etiopia.* Milan: Mondadori, 1937.

Artieri, Giovanni. *Quattro momenti di storia fascisti.* Naples: Arturo Berisio Editore, 1968.

Asante, S. K. B. "The Catholic Missions, British West African Nationalists, and the Italian Invasion of Ethiopia, 1935–36." *African Affairs* 73 (April 1974): 204–16.

Atwater, Elton. *Administration of Exports and Import Embargoes by Member States of the League of Nations, 1935–36.* Geneva Special Studies, vol. 9, no. 6. Geneva: Geneva Research Center: 1938.

Auphan, Paul, and Mordal, Jacques. *The French Navy in World War II.* Translated by A. C. J. Sabalot. Annapolis: United States Naval Institute, 1959.

Avenol, Joseph. "The Future of the League of Nations." *International Affairs* 13 (March–April 1934):143–58.

Avon, Earl of [Anthony Eden]. *The Eden Memoirs: Facing the Dictators.* London: Cassell & Co., 1962.

Badoglio, Pietro. *La guerra d'Etiopia.* Milan: Mondadori, 1936.

———*The War in Abyssinia.* London: Methuen, 1937.

Baer, George W. *The Coming of the Italian-Ethiopian War.* Cambridge: Harvard University Press, 1967.

Baistrocchi, Federico. "L'attività dell'esercito per l'esigenza A.O." In *Le forze armate dell'Italia fascista,* edited by Tomaso Sillani. Rome: La Rassegna Italiana, 1939.

Baker, Nicolas. *Stanley Morrison.* London: Macmillan & Co., 1972.

Bandini, Franco. *Gli italiani in Africa; Storia delle guerre coloniali, 1882–1943.* Milan: Longanesi, 1971.

Bardens, Dennis. *Portrait of a Statesman.* New York: Philosophical Library, 1956.

Barman, Thomas. *Diplomatic Correspondent.* London: Hamish Hamilton, 1968.

Barros, James. *Betrayal from Within: Joseph Avenol, Secretary General of the League of Nations, 1933–1940.* New Haven: Yale University Press, 1969.

———*The Corfu Incident of 1923: Mussolini and the League of Nations.* Princeton: Princeton University Press, 1965.

Bartholin, Pierre. *Aspects économiques des sanctions prises contre l'Italie.* Paris: Vuibert, 1938.
Bastianini, Giuseppe. *Uomini, cose, fatti.* Milan: Vitagliano, 1959.
Bastin, Jean. *L'affaire d'Ethiopie et les diplomates, 1934–1937.* Brussels: Universelle, 1937.
Battaglini, Guido. *Con S. E. De Bono: Nel turbinìo di una preparazione.* Rome: A. Airoldi, 1938.
Beauvais, Armand Paul. *Attachés militaires, attachés navals, et attachés de l'air.* Paris: Editions A. Pedone, 1937.
Beauvoir, Simone de. *The Prime of Life.* Translated by P. Green. Cleveland: World, 1962.
Bechtel, Guy. *Laval vingt ans après.* Paris: Laffont, 1963.
Benelli, Sem. *Schiavitú.* Milan: Mondadori, 1945.
Beneš, Eduard. *Memoirs: From Munich to New War and New Victory.* Translated by Godfrey Lias. London: George Allen & Unwin, 1954.
Berg, Meredith William. "Admiral William H. Standley and the Second London Naval Treaty, 1934–1936." *Historian* 23 (February 1971):215–36.
Berio, Alberto. "L' 'affare' etiopico." *Rivista di studi politici internazionali* 25 (April–June 1958):181–219.
———.*Dalle Ande all'Himalaya: Ricordi di un diplomatico.* Naples: Edizioni Scientifiche Italiane, 1961.
Bertoldi, Silvio. *Vittorio Emanuele III.* Turin: Unione Tipografico-Editrice Torinese, 1970.
Bianchi, Gianfranco. *Rivelazioni sul conflitto italo-etiopico.* Milan: Centro Editoriale Insegnanti e Scrittori, 1967.
Biase, Carlo de. *L'impero di "Faccetta Nera."* Milan: Edizioni del Borghese, 1967.
Binchy, Daniel A. *Church and State in Fascist Italy.* London: Oxford University Press, 1941.
Birn, Donald S. "The League of Nations Union and Collective Security." *Journal of Contemporary History* 9, no. 3 (1974):131–59.
Bitteto, Prince Carlo Cito de. *Mediterranée-Mer Rouge: Routes imperiales.* Paris: Grasset, 1937.
Blondel, Jules-François. *Au fil de la carrière: Recit d'un diplomate, 1911–1938.* Paris: Hachette, 1960.
Blum, John M. *From the Morgenthau Diaries: Years of Crisis, 1928–1938.* Boston: Houghton Mifflin Co., 1959.
Blum, Léon, *L'histoire jugera.* 2d ed. Montreal: Arbre, 1943.
———.*L'oeuvre de Léon Blum, 1934–1937.* Paris: Editions Albin Michel, 1964.
Bolech, Donatella. "'L'accordo di due imperi,' l'accordo italo-inglese del 16 aprile 1938." *Il Politico* 39, (June 1974):299–333.
Bonis, Umberto de. *La lega delle nazioni.* Milan: Zucchi, 1937.
Bonnet, Georges. "La France et la Méditerranée." *Rivista di studi politici internazionali* 17 (July–September 1950):373–87.
———.*Vingt ans de vie politique, 1918–1939: De Clemenceau à Daladier.* Paris: Librairie Fayard, 1969.
Borra, Eduardo. *Prologo di un conflitto: Colloqui col segretario del Negus, dicembre 1934–ottobre 1935.* Milan: Edizione Paoline, 1965.
Bosca, Quirino. *Cronistoria dell campagna italo-etiopica dal 2 ottobre 1935 al 18 maggio 1936.* Rome: Guanella, 1937.
Bosworth, R. J. B. "The British Press, the Conservatives, and Mussolini, 1920–34." *Journal of Contemporary History* 5, no. 2 (1970):163–82.
Bottai, Giuseppe. *Vent'anni e un giorno.* 2d ed. Rome: Garzanti, 1949.
Bova Scoppa, Renato. "L'Europea rischiò la guerra per l'impresa italiana in Etiopia" and "In segreto la diplomazia italiana si battè per fermare Mussolini." *Corriere della Sera,* (Milan), 2 and 3 October 1965.
———.*La pace impossibile.* Turin: Rosenberg & Sellier, 1961.
Bramsted, Ernest. "Apostles of Collective Security: The League of Nations Union and Its Functions." *Australian Journal of Politics and History* 13 (December 1967):347–64.
Brown, Sidney H. *Für das Rote Kreuz in Aethiopien.* Zurich: Gutenberg, 1939.
Buccianti, Giovanni. "Hitler, Mussolini, e il conflitto italo-etiopico." *Il Politico* 37 (June 1972):415–28.

Butler, J. R. M. *Lord Lothian (Philip Kerr), 1882-1940.* New York: St. Martin's Press, 1960.
Cadogan, Alexander. *The Diaries of Sir Alexander Cadogan, O. M., 1938-1945.* Edited by D. Dilks. London: Cassel & Co., 1971.
Cairns, John C. "A Nation of Shopkeepers in Search of a Suitable France: 1919-1940." *American Historical Review* 79 (June 1974):710-43.
Cameron, Elizabeth R. "Alexis Saint-Léger Léger." In *The Diplomats, 1919-1939,* edited by Craig and Gilbert. Princeton: Princeton University Press, 1953.
Canevari, Emilio. *Graziani me ha detto.* Rome: Magi-Spinetti, 1947.
———*La guerra italiana: Retroscena della disfatta.* 2 vols. Rome: Tosi, 1948.
Cannistraro, Philip V. "The Radio in Fascist Italy." *Journal of European Studies* 2 (June 1972):127-54.
Carboni, Giacomo. *Memorie segrete, 1935-1948.* Florence: Parenti, 1955.
Il cardinale Ildefonso Schuster. Milan: Abbazia di Viboldone, 1958.
Cassels, Alan. *Mussolini's Early Diplomacy.* Princeton: Princeton University Press, 1970.
Castelli, Giulio. *La chiesa e il fascismo.* Rome: Arnia, 1951.
Catalano, Franco. "Les ambitions mussoliniennes et la réalité économique de l'Italie." *Revue d'histoire de la deuxième guerre mondiale,* no. 76 (October 1969), pp. 15-38.
———*L'economia italiana di guerra: La politica economico-finanziaria del fascismo dalla guerra d'Etiopia alla caduta del regime, 1935-1943.* Milan: Istituto Nazionale per la storia del Movimento di Liberazione, 1969.
———*L'impresa etiopica e altri saggi.* Milan: La Goliardica, 1965.
Caviglia, Enrico. *Diario: Aprile 1925-marzo 1945.* Rome: Casini, 1952.
Cecil of Chelwood, Viscount [Robert]. *All the Way.* London: Hodder & Stoughton, 1949.
———*A Great Experiment.* London: Cape, 1941.
Cerruti, Vittorio. "Collaborazione internazionale e ragioni dell'insuccesso della Società delle Nazioni." *Rivista di studi politici internazionali* 13 (January-June 1946):50-73.
Ceva, Bianca. *Storia di una passione, 1919-1943.* Cernusco sul Naviglio: Garzanti, 1948.
Chambrun, Charles de. *Traditions et souvenirs.* Paris: Flammarion, 1952.
Charles-Roux, François. *Huit ans au Vatican, 1932-1940.* Paris: Flammarion, 1947.
Chatfield, Lord [Ernle]. *The Navy and Defence.* Vol. 2, *It Might Happen Again.* London: Heinemann, 1947.
Chiavarelli, Emilia. *L'opera della marina italiana nella guerra italo-etiopica.* Milan: Giuffrè, 1969.
Churchill, Winston S. *The Second World War.* Vol. 1, *The Gathering Storm.* Boston: Houghton Mifflin Co., 1948.
Ciano, Galeazzo. *Ciano's Diary, 1937-1938.* Translated by Andreas Mayor. London: Methuen, 1952.
———*Diario, 1937-1938.* Bologna: Cappelli, 1948.
———*L'Europa verso la catastrophe.* Milan: Mondadori, 1948.
Clapham, Christopher. "Imperial Leadership in Ethiopia." *African Affairs* 68 (April 1969): 110-20.
Clark, Ronald W. *Tizard.* Cambridge: Massachusetts Institute of Technology Press, 1965.
Claude, Inis L., Jr. "The Collectivist Theme in International Relations." *International Journal* 24 (Autumn 1969):639-56.
Coghlan, F. "Armaments, Economic Policy, and Appeasement: Background to British Foreign Policy, 1931-1937." *History* 57 (June 1972):205-16.
Collier, Basil. *The Defence of the United Kingdom.* London: Her Majesty's Stationery Office, 1957.
Colvin, Ian. *None So Blind.* New York: Harcourt, Brace & World, 1965.
Conti, Clara. *Servizio segreto.* Rome: Donatello de Liugi, 1945.
Coote, Colin. *Editorial: The Memoirs of Colin Coote.* London: Eyre & Spottiswoode, 1965.
Coppola, Francesco. "La Società delle Nazioni e l'Italia." In *La ragioni dell'Italia,* edited by Gioacchino Volpe. Rome: Reale Accademia d'Italia, 1936.
———"La vittoria bifronte." *Politica* 40 (August 1936):5-74.
Cora, Giuliano. "Un diplomatico durante l'era fascista." *Storia e politica,* January-March 1966, pp. 97-98.

Costantini, Francesco. "Gli occhi del SIM nell'ambasciata inglese." *Candido,* 10, 17, 24 November and 1 December, 1957.

Cot, Pierre. *Le procès de la République.* 2 vols. New York: Editions de la maison française, 1944.

Craig, F. W. S., comp. and ed. *British General Election Manifestos, 1918–1966.* Chicester: Political Reference Publications, 1970.

Craig, Gordon A. "Totalitarian Approaches to Diplomatic Negotiation." In *Studies in Diplomatic History and Historiography in Honour of G. P. Gooch,* edited by A. O. Sarkissian. New York: Barnes & Noble, 1961.

Crozier, W. P. *Off the Record: Political Interviews, 1933–1943.* Edited by A. J. P. Taylor. London: Hutchinson, 1974.

Currey, Muriel I. *A Woman at the Abyssinian War.* London: Hutchinson, 1936.

Dalton, Hugh. *The Fateful Years: Memoirs, 1931–1945.* London: Muller, 1957.

Dampierre, Robert de. "Dix années de politique française à Rome." Pt. 2. *La Revue des Deux Mondes,* 15 November 1953, pp. 258–83.

D'Aroma, Nino. *Mussolini segreto.* Rome: Cappelli, 1958.

———*Vent'anni insieme: Vittorio Emanuele e Mussolini.* Rome: Cappelli, 1957.

De Begnac, Yvon. *Palazzo Venezia: Storia di un regime.* Rome: La Rocca, 1950.

De Bono, Emilio. *Anno XIIII: The Conquest of an Empire.* Translated by B. Miall. London: Cresset, 1937.

De Conde, Alexander. *Half Bitter, Half Sweet: An Excursion into Italian-American History.* New York: Charles Scribner's Sons, 1971.

De Felice, Renzo, *Mussolini il duce.* Pt. 1, *Gli anni del consenso, 1929–1936.* Turin: Einaudi, 1974.

Del Boca, Angelo. *The Ethiopian War, 1935–1941.* Translated by P. D. Cummins. Chicago: University of Chicago Press, 1969.

Dell, Robert. *The Geneva Racket, 1920–1939.* London: Robert Hale, [1940].

Delzell, Charles F. *Mussolini's Enemies: The Italian Anti-Fascist Resistance.* Princeton: Princeton University Press, 1961.

Diggins, John P. "Mussolini and America: Hero-Worship, Charisma, and the 'Vulgar Talent.'" *Historian* 28 (August 1966):559–85.

———*Mussolini and Fascism: The View from America.* Princeton: Princeton University Press, 1972.

Dinale, Ottavio. *Quarant'anni di colloqui con lui.* Milan: Edizioni Ciarrocca, 1953.

Divine, Robert A. *The Illusion of Neutrality: Franklin D. Roosevelt and the Struggle over the Arms Embargo.* Chicago: University of Chicago Press, 1962.

Dodd, William E. *Ambassador Dodd's Diary, 1933–1938.* Edited by W. E. Dodd, Jr., and Martha Dodd. New York: Harcourt, Brace & Co., 1941.

Douhet, Giulio. *La guerra integrale.* Edited by Emilio Canevari. Rome: Capitelli, 1936.

Du Bois, W. E. B. "Inter-Racial Implications: A Negro View." *Foreign Affairs* 14 (October 1935):82–92.

Duff Cooper, Alfred. *Old Men Forget.* London: Hart-Davis, 1953.

Dupuis, C. "Lake Tana and the Nile." *Journal of the (Royal) African Society* 35 (January 1936):18–25.

Eayrs, James. *In Defence of Canada: Appeasement and Rearmament.* Toronto: University of Toronto Press, 1965.

Eden, Anthony. See Avon, Earl of.

Eden, Timothy. *The Tribulations of a Baronet.* London: Macmillan & Co., 1933.

Edwards, Peter. "The Austen Chamberlain–Mussolini Meetings." *Historical Journal* 14 (March 1971):153–64.

———"The Foreign Office and Fascism, 1924–1929." *Journal of Contemporary History* 5, no. 2 (1970):153–61.

Egziabher, Salome G. "The Ethiopian Patriots, 1936–1941." *Ethiopian Observer* 12 (1969): 63–91.

Fabry, Jean. *De la Place de la Concorde au course de l'Intendance.* Paris: Editions de France, 1942.

———*J'ai connu . . . 1934–1945.* Paris: Deschamps, 1960.

Farnie, D. A., *East and West of the Suez: The Suez Canal in History, 1954–1956.* Oxford: Clarendon Press, 1969.

Federzoni, Luigi. "Hegemony in the Mediterranean." *Foreign Affairs* 14 (April 1936):387–98.

———*Italia di ieri per la storia di domani.* Verona: Mondadori, 1967.

Feiling, Keith. *The Life of Neville Chamberlain.* London: Macmillan & Co., 1946.

Feis, Herbert. *Seen from E.A.: Three International Episodes.* New York: Alfred A. Knopf, 1947.

Flandin, Pierre-Étienne. *Politique française 1919–1940.* Paris: Mouvelles, 1947.

Franco-British Colloquium. "Franco-British Relations in the Period 1935–1939." Proceedings held at the Imperial War Museum, London, 18–21 October 1971. Typescript.

François-Poncet, André. *Au palais Farnèse: Souvenirs d'une ambassade à Rome, 1938–1940.* Paris: Librairie Fayard, 1961.

Funke, Manfred. "Le relazioni italo-tedesche al momento del conflitto etiopico e delle sanzioni della Società delle Nazioni." *Storia contemporanea* 2 (September 1971):475–93.

———*Sanktionen und Kanonen: Hitler, Mussolini, und der internationale Abessinien konflikt, 1934–1936.* Düsseldorf: Droste Verlag, 1970.

Gallo, Max. *L'affaire d'Éthiopie aux origines de la guerre mondiale.* Paris: Editions du Centurion, 1967.

———*Cinquième colonne, 1930–1940, et ce fut la défaite.* Paris: Librairie Plon, 1970.

Gallup, George, and Robinson, Claude. "American Institute of Public Opinion—Surveys, 1935–1938." *Public Opinion Quarterly* 2 (July 1938):375–98.

Gambetti, Fidia. *Gli anni che scottano.* Milan: Mursia, 1967.

Gamelin, Général [Maurice], *Servir.* Vol. 2, *Le prologue du drame, 1930–août 1939.* Paris: Librairie Plon, 1946.

Garosci, Aldo. *La vita di Carlo Rosselli.* 2 vols. Florence: Edizioni U., [1945].

Gatti, Aldo. *Il XV, episodica guerriera di un battaglione eritreo.* Rome: Barulli, 1969.

Gayda, Virginio. *Italia e Francia: Problemi aperti.* 4th ed. Rome: Giornale d'Italia, 1939.

Gentizon, Paul. *Défense de l'Italie.* Lausanne: Editions de l'aiglon, 1948.

———*Difesa dell'Italia.* Rocca S. Casciano: Cappelli, 1949.

Géraud, André. "British Vacillations." *Foreign Affairs* 14 (July 1936):584–97.

———[Pertinax]. *Les Fossoyeurs.* 2 vols. New York: Editions de la maison française, 1943.

Gigli, Guido. "Sguardo ai rapporti fra Badoglio e Mussolini fino alla crisi etiopici del 1935–1936." In *Badoglio risponde,* by Vanna Vailati, app. Milan: Rizzoli, 1958.

Gilbert, Felix, ed. *Hitler Directs His War.* New York: Oxford University Press, 1950.

Giraud, Emile. *La nullité de la politique internationale des grandes démocraties, 1919–1939.* Paris: Sirey, 1948.

Gladwyn, Lord. *The Memoirs of Lord Gladwyn.* New York: Weybright & Talley, 1972.

Golant, W. "The Emergence of C. R. Attlee as leader of the Parliamentary Labour Party in 1935." *Historical Journal* 13 (June 1970):318–32.

Goldman, Aaron L. "Sir Robert Vansittart's Search for Italian Cooperation against Hitler, 1933–1936." *Journal of Contemporary History* 9, no. 3 (1974):93–130.

Goodrich, Leland M. "Peace Enforcement Perspective." *International Journal* 24 (Autumn 1969):657–72.

Graziani, Rodolfo. *Il fronte sud.* Milan: Mondadori, 1938.

———*Ho difesa la patria.* Rome: Garzanti, 1948.

———*Processo Graziani.* Vol. 1, *L'autodifesa dell'ex maresciallo nel resoconto stenografico.* Vol. 3, *Il testimoniale e gli incidenti procedurali.* Rome: Ruffolo Editore, 1948, 1950.

Greenfield, Richard. *Ethiopia: A New Political History.* New York: Praeger, 1965.

Griaule, Marcel. *La peau de l'ours.* Paris: Gallimard, 1936.

Guariglia, Raffaele. *Ricordi 1922–1946.* Naples: Edizioni Scientifiche Italiane, 1950.

Guarneri, Felice. *Battaglie economiche tra le due grandi guerre.* 2 vols. Milan: Garzanti, 1953.

Haas, Ernst B. *Collective Security and the Future International System.* Denver: University of Denver Press, 1968.

Hagglof, Gunnar. *Diplomat: Memoirs of a Swedish Envoy in London, Paris, Berlin, Moscow, Washington.* London: Bodley Head, 1972.

Harris, Brice, Jr. *The United States and the Italo-Ethiopian Crisis.* Stanford: Stanford University Press, 1964.
Harvey of Tasburgh, Lord. *The Diplomatic Diaries of Oliver Harvey, 1937–1940.* Edited by John Harvey. London: Collins, 1970.
Heald, Stephen, ed. *Documents on International Affairs, 1935.* Vol. 2. London: Oxford University Press, 1937.
Henderson, K. D. D. "The Sudan and the Abyssinian Campaign." *Journal of the (Royal) African Society* 42 (January 1943):12–20.
Herriot, Édouard. *Jadis.* Vol. 2, *D'une guerre à l'autre, 1914–1936.* Paris: Flammarion, 1952.
Hiett, Helen. *Public Opinion and the Italo-Ethiopian Dispute: The Activity of Private Organizations in the Crisis.* Geneva Special Studies, vol. 7, no. 1. Geneva: Geneva Research Center, 1936.
Highley, Albert E. *The Actions of the States Members of the League of Nations in Application of Sanctions against Italy, 1935–1936.* Geneva: Université de Genève, 1938.
———. *The First Sanctions Experiment: A study of League Procedures.* Geneva Special Studies, vol. 9, no. 4. Geneva: Geneva Research Center: 1938.
Hildebrand, Klaus. *Von Reich zum Weltreich: Hitler, NSDAP, und koloniale Frage 1919–1945.* Munich: Fink, 1969.
Hoare, Sir Samuel. See Templewood, Viscount.
Hodson, H. V. "The Economic Aspects of the Italo-Abyssinian Conflict." In *Survey of International Affairs, 1935,* by Arnold J. Toynbee, vol. 2. London: Oxford University Press, 1936.
Howard, Peter. *Beaverbrook: A Study of Max the Unknown.* London: Hutchinson, 1964.
Hull, Cordell. *Memoirs.* 2 vols. New York: Macmillan Co., 1948.
Ickes, Harold L. *The Secret Diary of Harold L. Ickes: The First Thousand Days, 1933–1936.* New York: Simon & Schuster, 1953.
Irving, David, ed. *Breach of Security: The German Secret Intelligence File on Events Leading to the Second World War.* London: Kimber, 1968.
Jablon, Howard. "The State Department and Collective Security, 1933–1934." *Historian* 23 (February 1971):248–63.
Jacobsen, Hans-Adolf. *Nationalsozialistische Aussenpolitik, 1933–1938.* Frankfurt am Main: Metzner, 1968.
James, Robert Rhodes. *Memoirs of a Conservative: J. C. C. Davidson's Memoirs and Papers, 1910–1937.* London: Weidenfeld & Nicolson, 1969.
Jankowski, James P. "The Egyptian Blue Shirts and the Egyptian World, 1935–1938." *Middle Eastern Studies* 6 (January 1970):77–95.
Jemolo, A. C. *Chiesa e stato in Italia dal risorgimento ad oggi.* Turin: Einaudi, 1955.
Jenkins, Roy. *Mr. Attlee: An Interim Biography.* London: Heinemann, 1948.
Jolly, W. P. *Marconi.* New York: Stein & Day, 1972.
Jones, Samuel S. *The Scandinavian States and the League of Nations.* Princeton: Princeton University Press, 1939.
Jones, Thomas. *A Diary with Letters, 1931–1950.* London: Oxford University Press, 1954.
Junod, Marcel. *Le troisième combattant: De l'ypérite en Abyssinie à la bombe atomique d'Hiroshima.* Paris: Payot, 1947.
———. *Warrior without Weapons.* Translated by Edward Fitzgerald. New York: Macmillan Co., 1951.
Keene, Frances, ed. *Neither Liberty nor Bread: The Meaning and Tragedy of Fascism.* New York: Harper & Bros., 1940.
Kelly, David. *The Ruling Few: Or, the Human Background to Diplomacy.* London: Hollis & Carter, 1952.
Kemp, Tom. *The French Economy, 1913–1939: The History of a Decline.* London: Longman, 1972.
Kieft, David Owen. *Belgium's Return to Neutrality: An Essay in the Frustrations of Small Power Diplomacy.* Oxford: Clarendon Press, 1972.
Killearn, Lord. *The Killearn Diaries, 1934–1946: The Diplomatic and Personal Record of Lord Killearn (Sir Miles Lampson).* Edited by T. E. Evans. London: Sidgwick & Jackson, 1972.

Kitsikis, Dimitri. "La Grece entre l'Angleterre et l'Allemagne de 1936 à 1941." *Revue historique* 237 (July–September, 1967):85–116.

Konovaloff, Theodore E. *Con le armate del Negus.* Translated by Stefano Micciche. Bologna: N. Zanichelli, 1937.

Kuhn, Axel. *Hitler's Aussenpolitisches Programm: Entstehung und Entwicklung, 1919–1939.* Stuttgart: Klett, 1970.

Lagardelle, Hubert de. *Mission à Rome: Mussolini.* Paris: Librarie Plon, 1955.

Langley, J. Ayo. "Pan-Africanism in Paris, 1924–1936." *Journal of Modern African Studies* 7 (1967): 69–94.

Larmour, Peter J. *The French Radical Party in the 1930's.* Stanford: Stanford University Press, 1964.

Laurens, Franklin D. *France and the Italo-Ethiopian Crisis, 1935–1936.* The Hague: Mouton, 1967.

Laurent, Pierre Henri. "The Reversal of Belgian Foreign Policy, 1936–1937." *Review of Politics* 31 (July 1969):370–84.

Laval, Pierre. *The Diary of Pierre Laval.* New York: Scribner's, 1948.

———*Laval parle . . . Notes et mémoires rédigés à Fresnes d'août à octobre 1945.* Paris: Bibliothèque du cheval ailé, 1948.

———*Le procès Laval: Compte rendu sténographique.* Paris: Editions Albin Michel, 1946.

Lecuir, Jean, and Fridenson, Patrick. "L'organisation de la coopération aérienne franco-britannique, 1935–mai 1940." *Revue d'histoire de la deuxième guerre mondiale,* no. 73, (January 1969), pp. 43–74.

Ledeen, Michael A. "Fascism and the Generation Gap." *European Studies Review* 1 (July 1971):275–83.

Lessona, Alessandro. *Memorie.* Florence: Sansoni, 1958.

———*Verso l'impero.* Florence: Sansoni, 1939.

Levontin, A. V. *The Myth of International Security: A Juridical and Critical Analysis.* Jerusalem: Hebrew University, 1957.

Lipski, Józef. *Diplomat in Berlin.* Edited by Wacław Jędrzejewicz. New York: Columbia University Press, 1968.

Long, Breckinridge. *The War Diary of Breckinridge Long: Selections from the Years 1939–1944.* Compiled and edited by Fred L. Isreal. Lincoln: University of Nebraska Press, 1966.

Luciolli, Mario [Mario Donosti]. *Mussolini e l'Europa: La politica estera facista.* Rome: Leonardo, 1945.

McCarthy, John M. "Australia and Imperial Defence: Co-operation and Conflict, 1918–1939." *Australian Journal of Politics and History* 17 (April 1971):19–32.

———"Singapore and Australian Defence, 1921–1942." *Australian Outlook* 25 (August 1971):165–80.

McDermott, Geoffrey. *The Eden Legacy and the Decline of British Diplomacy.* London: Leslie Frewin, 1969.

MacFie, J. W. S. *An Ethiopian Diary: A Record of the British Ambulance Service in Ethiopia.* Liverpool: University Press, 1936.

McLachlan, Donald. *In the Chair: Barrington-Ward of the "Times," 1927–1948.* London: Weidenfeld & Nicolson, 1971.

Macleod, Iain. *Neville Chamberlain.* London: Muller, 1961.

Madariaga, Salvador de. *Morning without Noon: Memoirs.* London: Saxon House, 1974.

Magistrati, Massimo. "La Germania e l'impresa italiana di Etiopia, Ricordi di Berlino." *Rivista di studi politici internazionali* 17 (October–December 1950):563–606.

———*L'Italia a Berlino, 1937–1939.* Verona: Mondadori, 1956.

———*Il prologo del dramma: Berlino, 1934–1937.* Milan: Mursia, 1971.

Mallet, Alfred. *Pierre Laval.* 2 vols. Paris: Dumont, 1955.

Marder, Arthur J. "The Royal Navy and the Ethiopian Crisis of 1935–36." *American Historical Review* 75 (June 1970):1327–56.

Marwick, Arthur. "Middle Opinion in the Thirties: Planning, Progress, and Political 'Agreement.'" *English Historical Review* 79 (April 1964):285–98.

Masson, Pierre. "Franco-British Staff Talks, 1935–1938." In *Les relations franco-britanniques, 1935–1939*. Paris: Centre Nationale de la Recherche Scientifique, 1975.
Matthews, Herbert L. *The Education of a Correspondent*. New York: Harcourt, Brace & Co., 1946.
————*The Fruits of Fascism*. New York: Harcourt, Brace & Co., 1943.
————*Two Wars and More to Come*. New York: Carrick & Evans, 1938.
————*A World In Revolution: A Newspaperman's Memoir*. New York: Charles Scribner's Sons, 1972.
Mattioli, Guido. *L'aviazione fascista e la conquista dell'impero*. Rome: L'Aviazione, 1939.
Melly, John. *John Melly of Ethiopia*. Edited by Kathleen Nelson and Alan Sullivan. London: Faber & Faber, 1937.
Melograni, Piero, ed. *Corriere della Sera, 1919–1943*. Milan: Cappelli, 1965.
Michel, Bernard. "La Petite Entente et la crise des années 30." *Revue d'histoire de la deuxième guerre mondiale*, no. 77 (January 1970), pp. 15–24.
Middlemas, Keith. *Diplomacy of Illusion: The British Government and Germany, 1937–1939*. London: Weidenfeld & Nicolson, 1972.
Middlemas, Keith, and Barnes, John. *Baldwin: A Biography*. New York: Macmillan Co., 1970.
Miller, Webb. *Notes from the Diary of a War Correspondent*. New York: United Press, 1936.
Moran, Lord [Charles]. *Churchill, Taken from the Diaries of Lord Moran: The Struggle for Survival, 1940–1965*. Boston: Houghton Mifflin Co., 1966.
Morrison, Stanley. *The History of the "Times."* Vol. 4, pt. 2, *The 150th Anniversary and Beyond, 1912–1948*. New York: Macmillan Co., 1952.
Mosley, Leonard. *Haile Selassie: The Conquering Lion*. London: Weidenfeld & Nicolson, 1964.
————*On Borrowed Time: How World War II Began*. New York: Random House, 1969.
Motta, Giuseppe. *Testimonia temporum: Series secunda, 1932–1936*. Bellinzona: Istituto Editoriale Ticinese, 1936.
Mussolini, Benito. *Corrispondenza inedita*. Edited by Duilio Susmel. Milan: Edizioni del Borghese, 1972.
————*Memoirs 1942–1943*. Edited by R. Klibansky, translated by F. Lobb. London: Weidenfeld & Nicolson, 1949.
————*Opera omnia di Benito Mussolini*. Edited by E. and D. Susmel. 36 vols. Florence: Casa Editrice La Fenice, 1951–63.
————*Storia di un anno: Il tempo del bastone e della carota*. Verona: Mondadori, 1944.
Mussolini, Rachele. *La mia vita con Benito*. Verona: Mondadori, 1948.
Mussolini, Vittorio. *Voli sulle ambe*. Florence: Sansoni, 1937.
Navarra, Quinto. *Memorie del cameriere di Mussolini*. Milan: Longanesi, 1946.
Nemours, Alfred. *Craignons d'être un jour l'Ethiopie de quelqu'un*. Port-au-Prince: Collège Vertières, 1945.
Nicolson, Harold. *Diaries and Letters, 1930–1939*. Edited by Nigel Nicolson. New York: Atheneum, 1966.
Nixon, Edgar B., ed. *Franklin D. Roosevelt and Foreign Affairs*. 3 vols. Cambridge: Harvard University Press, 1969.
Nizza, Enzo, ed. *Autobiografica del fascisimo*. Milan: Edizioni La Pietra, 1962.
Ormesson, Wladimir de, ed. *La sécurité collective à la lumière du conflict italo-éthiopien*. Geneva: Entr'aide universitaire internationale, 1936.
Ormos, Sz. "Apropos de la sécurité est—européenne dans les années 1930." *Acta Historica* 16: 307–21.
Ørvik, Nils. *The Decline of Neutrality, 1914–1941*. 2d ed. London: Frank Cass, 1971.
Ostrower, Gary B. "American Ambassador to the League of Nations—1933: A Proposal Postponed." *International Organization* 25 (Winter 1971):46–58.
Packard, Reynolds and Eleanor. *Balcony Empire: Fascist Italy at War*. New York: Oxford University Press, 1942.
Pankhurst, Richard. "The Ethiopian Patriots and the Collapse of Italian Rule in East Africa, 1940–1941." *Ethiopian Observer* 12 (1969):92–127.
————"Fascist Racist Policies in Ethiopia: 1922–1941." *Ethiopian Observer* 12 (1969):272–86.

————"The Italo-Ethiopian War and League of Nations Sanctions, 1935–1936." *Genève-Afrique* 13 (1974):5–29.

————"The Medical History of Ethiopia during the Italian Fascist Invasion and Occupation, 1935–1941." *Ethiopian Observer* 16 (1973):108–17.

Parker, R. A. C. "Great Britain, France, and the Ethiopian Crisis, 1935–1936." *English Historical Review* 89 (April 1974):293–332.

Paul-Boncour, Joseph. *Entre deux guerres.* 3 vols. Paris: Librairie Plon, 1945.

Perham, Margery. *The Government of Ethiopia.* London: Faber & Faber, 1948.

Petersen, Jens. "Die Aussenpolitik des faschistischen Italien als historiographisches Problem." *Vierteljahrschefte für Zeitgeschichte* 22 (October 1974):417–60.

————*Hitler-Mussolini: Die Entstehung der Achse Berlin-Rom, 1933–1936.* Tübingen: Niemeyer, 1973.

Peterson, Maurice. *Both Sides of the Curtain.* London: Constable, 1950.

Petrie, Charles A. *The Life and Letters of the Right Hon. Sir Austen Chamberlain.* 2 vols. London: Cassell & Co., 1939, 1940.

Pini, Giorgio. *Filo diretto con Palazzo Venezia.* Bologna: Cappelli, 1950.

Pini, Giorgio, and Susmel, Duilio. *Mussolini, l'uomo e l'opera.* vol. 3, *Dalla dittatura all'impero, 1925–1938.* 3d ed. Florence: Casa Editrice La Fenice, 1963.

Pius XI. *Discorsi di Pio XI.* Edited by Domenico Bertetto. 3 vols. Turin: Internazionale, 1960.

Pool, Ithiel de Sola. *The "Prestige Papers": A Survey of Their Editorials.* Hoover Institute Studies, ser. C: Symbols, no. 2. Stanford: Stanford University Press, 1951.

————*Symbols of Internationalism.* Hoover Institute Studies, ser. C: Symbols, no. 3. Stanford: Stanford University Press, 1951.

————*Symbols of Democracy.* Hoover Institute Studies, ser. C: Symbols, no. 4. Stanford: Stanford University Press, 1952.

Pratt, Lawrence R. *East of Malta, West of Suez: Britain's Mediterranean Crisis, 1936–1939.* London: Cambridge University Press, 1975.

Preti, Luigi. *Impero fascista, africani ed ebrei.* Milan: Mursia, 1968.

Pronay, Nicholas. "British Newsreels in the 1930's: Their Policies and Impact." *History* 57 (February 1972):63–72.

Quaroni, Pietro. "Le diplomate italien." In *Diplomatie unserer Zeit,* edited by K. Braunias and G. Stourzh. Graz: Styria, 1959.

————*Ricordi di un ambasciatore.* Milan: Garzanti, 1954.

————*Valise diplomatique.* Translated by Louis Bonalumi. Paris: Librairie Plon, 1958.

Reader, W. J. *Architect of Air Power: The Life of the First Viscount Weir of Eastwood, 1877–1959.* London: Collins, 1968.

Reale, Egidio. *La politique étrangère du fascisme des accords de Rome à la proclamation de l'empire.* Paris: Alcan, 1938.

Reynaud, Paul. *Au coeur de la melée, 1930–1945.* Paris: Flammarion, 1951.

————*La France a sauvé l'Europe.* Paris: Flammarion, 1947.

————*In the Thick of the Fight, 1930–1945.* Translated by J. D. Lambert. New York: Simon & Schuster, 1955.

————*Mémoires.* Vol. 1, *Venu de ma montagne.* Paris: Flammarion, 1960.

Rhodes, Anthony. *The Vatican in the Age of the Dictators, 1922–1945.* New York: Holt, Rinehart & Winston, 1973.

Robertson, Esmonde M. *Hitler's Pre-War Policy and Military Plans, 1933–1939.* London: Longmans, 1963.

————"Zur Wiederbesetzung des Rheinlandes 1936." *Vierteljahrshefte für Zeitgeschichte* 10 (April 1962):178–205.

Robertson, James C. "The British General Election of 1935." *Journal of Contemporary History* 9, no. 1 (1974):149–64.

————"The Origins of British Opposition to Mussolini over Ethiopia." *Journal of British Studies* 9 (November 1969):122–42.

Rochat, Giorgio. *Militari e politici nella preparazione della campagna d'Etiopia: Studio e documenti 1932–1936.* Milan: Franco Angeli, 1971.

———"Mussolini e le forze armate." *Il movimento di liberazione in Italia* 21 (April–June 1969):3–22. Published in French translation in Comité d'histoire de la deuxième guerre mondiale, *La guerre in Méditerranée, 1939–1945, Actes du colloque international tenu à Paris du 8–11 avril 1969.* Paris: Centre National de la Recherche Scientifique, 1971.

———"Il ruolo delle forze armate nel regime fascista: Conclusioni provvisorie e ipotesi di lavoro." *Rivista di storia contemporanea* 2 (April 1972):188–99.

Romains, Jules. *Céla depend de vous.* Paris: Flammarion, 1939.

———*Sept mystères du destin de l'Europe.* New York: Editions de la maison française, 1940.

Roosevelt, Franklin Delano. *FDR: His Personal Letters, 1928–1945.* Edited by Elliott Roosevelt. Vol. 1. New York: Duell, Sloan & Pearce, 1950.

———*The Public Papers and Addresses of Franklin Delano Roosevelt.* Edited by S. I. Rosenman. Vol. 5. New York: Random House, 1938.

Roskill, Stephen. *Hankey, Man of Secrets.* Vol. 3, *1931–1963.* London: Collins, 1974.

Ross, Red. "Black Americans and Italo-Ethiopian Relief, 1935–1936." *Ethiopian Observer* 15 (1972):122–31.

Rossi, Ernesto. *Padroni del vapore e fascismo.* Bari: Laterza, 1966.

Rossi, Francesco. *Mussolini e lo stato maggiore: Avvenimenti del 1940.* Rome: Regionale, 1951.

Rossi dell'Arno, Giulio de. *Pio XI e Mussolini.* Rome: Corso, 1954.

Rowse, A. L. *All Souls and Appeasement.* London: Macmillan & Co., 1961.

Rysky, Carlode. *Ali tricolori in Africa.* Osimo: Ismaele Barulli & Figlio, 1937.

Salvatorelli, Luigi, and Mira, Giovanni. *Storia d'Italia nel periodo fascista.* 3d ed. Rome: Einaudi, 1959.

Salvemini, Gaetano. "Can Italy Live at Home?" *Foreign Affairs* 14 (January 1936):243–58.

———*Opere di Gaetano Salvemini.* Pt. 4, *Scritti sul fascismo,* vol. 2. Edited by Nini Valeri and Alberto Merola. Milan: Giangiacomo Feltrinelli Editore, 1966.

———"Pio XI e la guerre etiopica." In *Opere di Gaetano Salvemini,* pt. 3, *Scritti di politica estera,* vol. 3, edited by Augusto Torre. Milan: Giangiacomo Feltrinelli Editore, 1967. *Prelude to World War II.* London: Victor Gollancz, 1953.

———"The Vatican and the Ethiopian War." In *Neither Liberty nor Bread,* edited by Frances Keene. New York: Harper & Bros., 1940.

"Sanctions in the Italo-Ethiopian Conflict." *International Conciliation,* no. 315 (December 1935), pp. 539–44.

Santarelli, Enzo. "Guerra d'Etiopia, imperialism e terzo mondo." *Il movimento di liberazione in Italia* 21 (October–December 1969):35–51.

Sarti, Roland. *Fascism and the Industrial Leadership in Italy, 1919–1940: A Study in the Expansion of Private Power under Fascism.* Berkeley and Los Angeles: University of California Press, 1971.

Sarubbi, Francesco A. "Il Trattato di pace con l'Italia e la sorte dei beni italiani in Etiopia." *Rivista di studi politici internazionali* 17 (January–March 1950):27–38.

Sauvy, Alfred. *Histoire économique de la France entre les deux guerres.* Vol. 2, *1931–1939: De Pierre Laval à Paul Reynaud.* Paris: Librairie Fayard, 1967.

Sbacchi, Alberto. "Legacy of Bitterness: Poison Gas and Atrocities in the Italo-Ethiopian War, 1935–1936." *Genève-Afrique* 13 (1974):30–53.

Scaroni, Silvio. *Con Vittorio Emanuele III.* Milan: Mondadori, 1954.

Schmidt, Carl T. *The Plough and the Sword: Labor, Land, and Property in Fascist Italy.* New York: Columbia University Press, 1938.

Schweitzer, Arthur. "Foreign Exchange Crisis of 1936." *Zeitschrift für die gesamte Staatswissenschaft* 118 (April 1962):243–77.

Scott, George. *The Rise and Fall of the League of Nations.* London: Hutchinson, 1973.

Scott, William R. "Malaku E. Bayen: Ethiopian Emissary to Black America, 1936–1941." *Ethiopian Observer* 15 (1972):132–38.

Selby, Walford. *Diplomatic Twilight, 1930–1940.* London: Murray, 1953.

Simon, Viscount [John]. *Retrospect.* London: Hutchinson, 1952.

Simon, Yves. *La campagne d'Ethiopie et la pensée politique française.* 2d ed. Lille: Société d'Impressions Litteraires, Industrielles et Commerciales, 1936.

354 TEST CASE

Slocombe, George. *A Mirror to Geneva: Its Growth, Grandeur, and Decay.* New York: Holt, 1938.

Somervell, D. C. *Stanley Baldwin: An examination of Some Features of Mr. G. M. Young's Biography.* London:.Faber & Faber, 1953.

Soulié, Michel. *La vie politique d'Édouard Herriot.* Paris: A. Colin, 1962.

Soward, F. H.; Parkinson, J. F.; MacKenzie, N. A. M.; and MacDermot, T. W. L. *Canada in World Affairs: The Pre-war Years.* Toronto: Oxford University Press, 1941.

Spaak, Paul-Henri. *Combats inachevés.* 2 vols. Paris: Librairie Fayard, 1969.

Speer, Albert. *Inside the Third Reich.* Translated by R. and C. Winston. New York: Macmillan Co., 1970.

Stannage, C. T. "The East Fulham By-Election, 25 October 1933." *Historical Journal* 14 (March 1971):165–200.

Starace, Achille. *La marcia su gondar della colonna celere A.O. e le successive operazioni nella Etiopia occidentale.* Milan: Mondadori, 1936.

Steer, George L. *Caesar in Abyssinia.* Boston: Little, Brown & Co., 1937.

Stimson, Henry L., and Bundy, McGeorge. *On Active Service in Peace and War.* New York: Harper & Bros., 1948.

Stromberg, Roland N. "American Business and the Approach of War, 1935–1941." *Journal of Economic History* 13 (Winter 1953):58–78.

Sturzo, Luigi. *Chiesa e stato: Studio sociologico-storico.* 2 vols. Bologna: N. Zanichelli, 1958.

Suarez, Georges. *Nos seigneurs et maîtres.* Paris: Editions de France, 1937.

Suarez, Georges, and Laborde, G. *Agonie de la paix, 1935–1939.* Paris: Librairie Plon, 1942.

Sulzberger, C. L. *A Long Row of Candles: Memoirs and Diaries, 1934–1954.* New York: Macmillan Co., 1969.

Suvich, Fulvio, et al. *Il processo Roatta.* Rome: Universale de Luigi, 1945.

Szembek, Comte Jean. *Journal, 1933–1939.* Translated by J. Rzewuska and T. Zaleski. Paris: Librairie Plon, 1952.

Tabouis, Geneviève. *They Called Me Cassandra.* New York: Scribner's, 1942.

——*Vingt ans de "suspense" diplomatique.* Paris: Editions Albin Michel, 1958.

Tannenbaum, Edward R. *The Fascist Experience: Italian Society and Culture, 1922–1945.* New York: Basic Books, 1972.

Taubenfeld, Howard J. *Economic Sanctions: An Appraisal and Case Study,* Ph.D. diss., Columbia University, 1958. Ann Arbor, Mich.: University Microfilms, 1958.

Taubenfeld, Rita F. and Howard J. "The Economic Weapon: The League and the United Nations." In *Proceedings of the American Society of International Law, April 23–25, 1964.* Washington, D.C., 1964.

Taylor, A. J. P. *Beaverbrook.* London: Hamish Hamilton, 1972.

Temperley, Arthur C. *The Whispering Gallery of Europe.* London: Collins, 1938.

Templewood, Viscount [Samuel Hoare]. *Nine Troubled Years.* London: Collins, 1954.

Terlinden, Vicomte Charles. *Le conflit italo-éthiopien et le Société des Nations.* Liège: Desoer, 1936.

Thompson, Geoffrey. *Front-Line Diplomat.* London: Hutchinson, 1959.

Thompson, J. N. "The Failure of Conservative Opposition to Appeasement in the 1930's." *Canadian Journal of History* 3 (September 1968):27–52.

Thompson, Neville. *The Anti-Appeasers: Conservative Opposition to Appeasement in the 1930's.* Oxford: Oxford University Press, 1971.

Thompson, Virginia, and Adloff, Richard. *Djibouti and the Horn of Africa.* Stanford: Stanford University Press, 1968.

Tillett, Lowell R. "The Soviet Role in League Sanctions against Italy, 1935–1936." *American Slavic and East European Review* 15 (1956):11–16.

Tomaselli, Cesco. *Con le colonie celeri dal Mareb allo Scioa.* Milan: Mondadori, 1936.

Toynbee, Arnold J. *Survey of International Affairs, 1935.* Vol. 2, *Abyssinia and Italy.* London: Oxford University Press, 1936.

Vailati, Vanna. *Badoglio racconta.* Turin: Industria libraria tipografica editrice, 1955.

——*Badoglio risponde.* Milan: Rizzoli, 1958.

Vansittart, Lord [Robert]. *Lessons of My Life.* New York: Alfred A. Knopf, 1943.
_____*The Mist Procession: The Autobiography of Lord Vansittart.* London: Hutchinson, 1958.
Varè, Daniele. "British Foreign Policy through Italian Eyes." *International Affairs* 15 (January–February 1936):80–102.
Vaucher, Paul, and Siriex, Paul-Henri. *L'opinion britannique, la Société des Nations, et la guerre italo-éthiopienne.* Paris: Centre d'Etudes de Politique Etrangère, 1936.
Verrier, Anthony. *The Bomber Offensive.* London: Batsford, 1968.
Villari, Luigi. *Storia diplomatica del conflitto italo-etiopico.* Bologna: N. Zanichelli, 1943.
Volpe, Gioacchino, ed. *La ragioni dell'Italia.* Rome: Reale Accademia d'Italia, 1936.
Wagnière, Georges. *Dix-huit ans à Rome: Guerre mondiale et fascisme, 1918–1936.* Geneva: A. Jullien, Editeur, 1944.
Waley, Daniel. *British Public Opinion and the Abyssinian War, 1935–6.* London: Maurice Temple Smith, 1975.
Walters, Frank P. *A History of the League of Nations.* 2 vols. 1952. Reprint (2 vols. in 1). London: Oxford University Press, 1960.
Warner, Geoffrey. *Pierre Laval and the Eclipse of France.* London: Eyre & Spottiswoode, 1968.
Watt, D. C. "South African Attempts to Mediate between Britain and Germany, 1935–1938." In *Studies in International History,* edited by K. Bourne and D. C. Watt. London: Longmans, Green, 1967.
Waugh, Alec. "History Textbooks as a Factor in International Relations." *International Affairs* 15 (November–December 1936):877–96.
Waugh, Evelyn. *Waugh in Abyssinia.* London: Longmans, 1936.
Weber, Eugen. *Action Française: Royalism and Reaction in Twentieth-Century France.* Stanford: Stanford University Press, 1962.
Webster, Charles, and Frankland, Noble. *The Strategic Air Offensive against Germany, 1939–1945.* Vol. 1. London: Her Majesty's Stationery Office, 1961.
Webster, Richard. *The Cross and the Fasces: Christian Democracy and Fascism in Italy.* Stanford: Stanford University Press, 1960.
Weiss, Louise. *Mémoires d'une Européenne.* Vol. 3, *1934–1939.* Paris: Payot, 1970.
Weiss, Stuart L. "American Foreign Policy and Presidential Power: The Neutrality Act of 1935." *Journal of Politics* 30 (August 1968):672–95.
Werth, Alexander. *The Destiny of France.* London: Hamish Hamilton, 1937.
Williams, John Fisher. "Sanctions Under the Covenant." In *British Year Book of International Law, 1936.* London, 1936.
Wilson, Arnold T. *Thoughts and Talks.* London: Longmans, Green, 1938.
Wilson, Hugh R., Jr. *For Want of a Nail: The Failure of the League of Nations in Ethiopia.* New York: Vantage, 1959.
Wrench, John Evelyn. *Geoffrey Dawson and Our "Times."* London: Hutchinson, 1955.
Young, G. M. *Stanley Baldwin.* London: Hart-Davis, 1952.
Young, Robert J. "Preparations for Defeat: French War Doctrine in the Inter-War Period." *Journal of European Studies* 2 (June 1972):155–72.
Zangrandi, Ruggero. *Il lungo viaggio attraverso il fascismo.* Milan: Giangiacomo Feltrinelli Editore, 1962.
Zappa, Paolo. *L'intelligence service el'Etiopia.* Milan: Corbaccio, 1936.

INDEX